THE SPOTTED HYENA

WILDLIFE BEHAVIOR AND ECOLOGY
George B. Schaller, Editor

THE SPOTTED HYENA

A Study of Predation and Social Behavior

Hans Kruuk

THE UNIVERSITY OF CHICAGO PRESS
Chicago and London

The University of Chicago Press, Chicago 60637
The University of Chicago Press, Ltd., London
© *1972 by The University of Chicago*
All rights reserved. Published 1972
Second Impression 1974
Printed in the United States of America
International Standard Book Number: 0–226–45507–6
Library of Congress Catalog Card Number: 70–175304

To Jane

There are few animals, whose history has passed under the consideration of naturalists, that have given occasion to so much confusion and equivocation as the Hyena has done. It began very early among the ancients, and the moderns have fully contributed their share.

James Bruce, 1790

Contents

Foreword

When John S. Owen, director of the Tanzania National Parks, following the initiative taken by Professor Bernhardt Grzimek and his late son Michael, founded the Serengeti Research Institute, one of the first young scientists to be recruited was Dr. Hans Kruuk, fresh from the university. It is of course for anyone a stroke of rare good fortune to be given such an opportunity at such an early stage, and Kruuk was naturally delighted to be called to East Africa, with its fascinating people and fauna. But he realized at once that it also meant a serious challenge. Unlike the visiting white hunters of the past and most of the tourists of today, professional biologists in Africa do a responsible and demanding job. On the one hand they have to make a worthwhile contribution to science; on the other, they have an obligation to their host country. Tanzania is faced with the difficult task of preserving, on behalf of all of us, its unique fauna; it can achieve this only if the National Parks can be maintained as sources of income of foreign currency, which is provided by the thousands of tourists attracted from all over the world. In this interesting and complex situation, the biologist has to resist the temptation of merely gazing in wonder and awe at the paradise in which he finds himself; he has to serve the interests of international science, of conservation, and of East Africa's economy—and he has to work against time.

It was for all these purposes that the Serengeti Research Institute was founded. Its small team of handpicked young men is trying to prove that, with careful planning, their work can provide the management of the National Parks with the scientific information it needs for the all-important task of maintaining the unique fauna of East Africa, and that in doing this "applied" research they can contribute substantially to "pure" science as well. They find that this serving of two masters (of which "pure" science is perhaps in less of a hurry than the managers, who need results quickly) is perfectly possible—and that while working for them one can enjoy oneself as thoroughly as the hunter or the sightseer and at the same time greatly enrich one's general outlook on life.

The program of the institute, carefully conceived with all this in mind, is comprehensive: the team is engaged in soil and vegetation studies (with observations on weather and on the effects of fire as integral parts), in research on the most important herbivores, and in work on "life at the top," that of the predators. The team is also closely integrated: all members are in continuous contact and exchange data, ideas, and criticism.

At first glance it might seem strange that Kruuk selected as his special object of study the spotted hyena. As a scavenger, it has long been thought that this much-maligned animal did little more than live on the spoils of the real predators, such as the lion, the leopard, and the wild dog—that they existed, so to speak, on the periphery of the eco- system and took little part in its self-regulatory processes. But Kruuk knew from the start that the popular images of animals are often amazingly wrong, and without discarding anything that experienced hunters told him, he quite rightly started by simply trusting the evi- dence of his own eyes. This book proves how right he was. By taking the trouble to study the hyena wherever and whenever he could create an opportunity (for instance by observing the hyenas throughout the night when they are most active), he made a surprising discovery: the spotted hyena is a truly formidable predator, no less formidable or less dreaded than the wolf, lion, or wild dog. Dr. Kruuk relates in detail how packs of hyenas hunt adult zebra and wildebeest at night, and he stresses that in this respect they resemble wolves hunting deer and moose. A full appreciation of the exceptionally detailed and disciplined re- search done by Dr. Kruuk will be gained from the substantial text; this monograph has drastically changed our conception of a fascinating species; we see the hyena for the first time in his true colors.

However, the main merit and relevance of Kruuk's study far exceeds that of a monograph on a little-known animal species. He shows to what an astonishing extent an animal's relations with its environment are controlled by its behavior, and his work is therefore an important con- tribution to the rather neglected science of behavioral ecology. It also shows the potential of systematically and critically conducted field- work, of patiently observing before collecting data, and of assessing the significance of the facts in the context of the natural environment. Only by such broadly conceived studies can the niche of a species, and the role it plays in the ecosystem, gradually be assessed. In all these respects, Kruuk's study can serve as a significant methodological contribution to behavioral ecology—indeed, in many respects, as a model for future work.

Finally, this monograph ought to make those people think again who believe that by tailoring one's research to potential practical applications one deviates from the purely intellectual pursuit of pure science. Without losing sight of the needs of the parks, Kruuk found himself from the start involved in an intellectually stimulating exercise, and his work will make ecologists of many types think anew about the nature of predator-prey interactions.

But, significantly, by satisfying his broad curiosity and comparing the hyena with other animals, Kruuk stumbled on to another, perhaps in the long run even more important, problem of an applied nature. One of Kruuk's important findings is that the hyena is one of those animals that combine carnivorous habits with group territoriality. In the combination of these traits, the hyena is obviously convergent not only with wolves and lions but, as many now begin to believe, with ancestral man as well. Many still doubt this, but it is worth stressing that the suspicion alone that man *may* well derive from ancestors with carnivorous and group-territorial habits justifies, and even demands, close studies of such convergent species. As everywhere in biology, evolutionary interpretations cannot be based only on comparison between closely allied species but must give equal weight to the study of convergence. It is therefore imperative for the healthy development of human biology that studies of primates be supplemented by work on animal species that have evolved adaptations to the same way of life as ancestral man. And so it is quite probable that the greatest value of Dr. Kruuk's studies will later be seen to lie in this sphere: as a contribution relevant to the biology of man himself, and so, ultimately, to the urgent task of "managing" Homo sapiens—of whom it can be truly said that he is "fiddling while Rome burns."

N. TINBERGEN

Acknowledgments

I have had a marvelous time in Africa while carrying out this hyena study, and I regret that it will be impossible to acknowledge everyone who helped me with it. I made many of the observations with my wife Jane, and she helped with everything, including the evaluation and writing up; she loves hyenas as much as I do. The book owes a great deal to Professor N. Tinbergen, F.R.S., with whom I first drew up the plans to study this problem, and who discussed it with me many times afterward in the field. His enthusiasm has spurred me on many times. The director of Tanzania National Parks, Mr. John S. Owen, first suggested that I should come to the Serengeti, then successfully approached grant-giving organizations and subsequently assisted me in several different ways. Also, the facilities I enjoyed in the Serengeti Research Institute are there thanks to his initiative, and in all areas I am deeply indebted to him.

The project was generously sponsored by the Netherlands Foundation for the Advancement of Tropical Research (W.O.T.R.O.), with an additional equipment grant from the East African Wildlife Society. The director of the Serengeti Research Institute, Dr. H. F. Lamprey, allowed me to neglect other duties while writing this book in the employ of the institute, and I want to thank him very much. Also, it would have been impossible to do this research without the permission of the trustees of the Tanzania National Parks to work in the Serengeti, and the permission of the conservator of the Ngorongoro Conservation Area, Mr. S. Ole Saibull, to work in the Ngorongoro Crater and use the very convenient log cabin by the Mungi stream.

Many people told me about their observations of hyenas—too many to mention them all. I am most indebted to Dr. G. B. Schaller in this respect; he gave me many of his data on hyenas and showed a constant interest in this project. I often discussed it with him, and he also provided many helpful criticisms of the manuscript. Dr. P. J.

Jarman and Dr. M. Norton-Griffiths, too, suggested many improvements of the manuscript, and I thank them both for their valuable help.

I am grateful to Dr. J. M. Cullen for help with numerical problems, to Messrs. W. Holz and H. Baldwin for assisting with the radio-location observations, to Mr. R. Carcasson for identifying dung beetles, to Dr. C. Craik for chemical analysis of fecal samples, and to Messrs. H. Braun and D. Herlocker for providing vegetation data. Dr. L. Lemieux and Mr. P. Desmeules, Mr. A. J. Sinclair and Dr. R. O. Skoog also allowed me to use unpublished material, for which I would like to express my appreciation.

The chief park warden of the Serengeti National Park, Mr. P. A. G. Field, has assisted me in many different ways, and I am very much indebted to him. Mr. M. Turner, park warden of the Serengeti, states that he hates hyenas; nevertheless, he helped me whenever he could. His assistance and keen interest in anything that moves on four legs is gratefully acknowledged. Miss Jennifer Owen typed the final draft of the manuscript. For the drawings, I wish to thank my sister, Mrs. I. Leupen-Kruuk; for the skillfully prepared graphs and histograms, Mrs. A. Norton-Griffiths. The National Geographic Society kindly allowed me to use two maps and plate 18, and Blackwell Scientific Publications granted permission to use figures 8, 9, and 24.

Finally, I want to salute our tame hyena, Solomon, who gave us so much fun under the guise of scientific information.

THE SPOTTED HYENA

1 Introduction

BACKGROUND

Serengeti, Ngorongoro. The driving force for the present study is the desire to contribute to the conservation and management of these wonderful areas, the desire to understand their ecology so that man may be able to coexist with this wilderness for a long time to come.

I have studied spotted hyenas (*Crocuta crocuta* Erxleben 1777) there, not just because I happened to like them, but because they are very numerous, clearly often predators in their own right and not merely the proverbial ghastly scavengers. Among relationships between the animals in the regions I will be writing about, the ecology of large predators is of immediate importance for management. The relationships between predators and other animals are also important from a more theoretical point of view—for the understanding of natural selection and of the mechanisms which maintain the natural harmony. Finally, while looking at my hyenas as an ethologist I found that an insight into the social organization and its evolution among large carnivores could be of fundamental importance for our understanding of the origins of human behavior.

The first priority for the study was to provide knowledge for the purpose of managing the Serengeti National Park. One could formulate the purpose of this national park as the perpetuation of the area's fauna and vegetation in their present harmony, so that man may enjoy them now and in the future. At first sight it seems that no active management would be necessary to attain this end, if only human influence could be eliminated altogether. But the Serengeti National Park is not a self-contained ecological system; increasing settlement along the boundaries forces herbivores out of their habitat and into the national park, man-made fires sweep the country, and poaching is rife. As an example of things which may happen in the near future with the present trends of settlement around the national park, in a few years the vast migrating herds will no longer be able to roam far beyond the

3

park's boundary as they do now, and a drought may cause serious over-grazing problems which at present the animals can still avoid. For these reasons or through political pressure, those in charge may some day be forced to control animal numbers in the national park; then it will be essential to know what role the numerous predators play in the natural control of the herbivore population. Of course, an appreciation of the natural role of predators is only a small aspect of the knowledge required for effective management. My study is only one of many carried out under the auspices of the Serengeti Research Institute, all aimed at understanding the factors that govern animal populations and their habitats in the Serengeti. The research institute has been built up since 1962, and at this time (1971) comprises sixteen scientists. This development is almost entirely due to the efforts of one man, the director of National Parks, John S. Owen.

Until 1956 the Ngorongoro Crater was part of the Serengeti National Park. It is an area of tremendous beauty and of enormous scientific interest, and contains most of the same mammal species as the Serengeti. It is almost a self-contained ecosystem—an island of plains country in a sea of mountains and forest. Many of the relationships between species, and between species and their habitat, which apply to the Serengeti can be studied in the Ngorongoro Crater on a smaller and simpler scale—almost in vitro. The animals are tamer there than in the Serengeti, and do not move over such vast distances; for all of these reasons, I decided to study predation in the Ngorongoro Crater as well as in the Serengeti National Park. It was an important decision; the comparison of data between the two areas is of major significance throughout the study.

Apart from the management significance of this work ("What is the effect of hyenas on the other Serengeti animals?"), its involvement with predator-prey relationships brings it into contact with the whole complex of problems related to the natural regulation of animal numbers, which is of considerable theoretical interest. Many theories about the importance of predation in population regulation have been advanced, and predators have variously been assessed as being major population suppressants, as having no effect at all on the prey numbers, or as being beneficial to the latter. Hypotheses often vary, probably because studies have been made on different predators and prey species and in different situations. Obviously the impact of predation varies, and what are needed now are more case histories of predation. The present studies provide some, and in fact show how predator-prey relations between the same species may vary with the environment.

This finding means that, from the predator's point of view, the relations with its food supply can vary according to environment. I have made use of this variation to see to what extent other aspects of the predators' behavior are adapted to differences in food supply. Social behavior is especially interesting in this context, because the spotted hyena is a gregarious species with a very flexible social organization. Once I started looking into this relation between social organization and predation, I had to take things a step further and compare my findings with what is known from other carnivores. After that, I could not help speculating about man's social behavior in this connection.

THE PROBLEMS

The spotted hyena is the most common carnivore in the Serengeti as well as in Ngorongoro, and for that reason I have chosen it as the focal point of my interest.

Within the framework of the study, questions could be grouped under an ethological heading and an ecological heading. The ecological problems are concerned with interactions between hyenas and herbivores; ethological questions deal with the adaptations of the hyena's behavior to its ecology and vice versa.

The ecological theme can be split into a number of major questions: How many hyenas are there? How are they distributed and organized? What affects their numbers? What do they eat and how? How do prey species cope with hyena predation? What is the effect of hyenas on the herbivore populations?

The behavioral questions I asked were:

a. How is the species organized socially, and how does this compare with other carnivores?

b. What are its foraging habits, and how do these compare with the feeding habits of its carnivorous relatives?

c. How are the answers to (a) and (b) related?

For various reasons, I have been unable to stick to this sequence of questions. In the introductory chapters I have described the background of the study and presented an outline of the problems discussed and a brief description of the stage on which the scene is set. I have added to this introduction a short description of some important features of hyena natural history, features which will be elaborated upon in much more detail in the following chapters.

In the next two chapters, I have discussed the more ecological problems. Chapter 3 deals with numbers, density, distribution, and movement of hyenas, and in chapter 4, prey selection and consumption and the effect of hyena predation on herbivores are considered, as well as the way hyena populations are affected by their food supply. Various feeding habits and the predator/prey interactions (with hyenas as the predators) are presented in behavioral detail in chapter 5, and chapter 6 deals with my observations on social behavior and organization.

The data presented in chapters 3 to 6 are further considered in the three final sections, in which they are compared with information from other carnivores and predator-prey situations. The first of these discussions deals with how the social organization of hyenas and other carnivores is related to predation; after that the antipredator behavior of ungulates is discussed, and in the last chapter I have elaborated on the implications of my ecological observations for the management of national parks. I felt when writing these discussions that the significance of the relationships between social organization and feeding habits in carnivores is such that I had to make a special plea to those interested in the evolution of human behavior to extend their field of research from nonhuman primates to carnivore realms.

Hyena Natural History
When I talk about the hyena, I mean the spotted species. There are two others, both occurring in Africa: the brown hyena and the striped hyena. The former occurs in southern Africa, and the range of the latter extends from East Africa throughout the north far into Asia. These two species both belong to the genus *Hyaena* and look rather different from the spotted one. The family Hyaenidae is related to the Viverridae (mongooses and civet cats); so in fact hyenas are more closely related to felids than to canids, although superficially they look rather dog- or bearlike.

Hyenas inspire horror in people. Often this human reaction is covered up by laughter (especially in Africa); in people's minds, hyenas are inexorably linked with garbage cans, corpses, feces, bad smells, and hideous cackles. Indeed, in places hyenas subsist on the refuse of human society, and that side of their behavior is, of course, most often noticed. But there is much more to their behavior and ecology, and it is with the "natural" hyena that I will be concerned here. The reasons for some popular misconceptions will become clear later on.

Little has been written about hyenas and their ecology or behavior, apart from occasional scathing remarks. Some observations have been made on animals in captivity (Grimpe 1916; Schneider 1923, 1926, 1952; Pournelle 1965). The first reliable field observations come from Matthews (1939*b*), who collected some data on the hyena's natural history in the Serengeti while capturing the animals to study their reproduction and subspecific variation (Matthews 1939*a, c*). Later, an informative paper by Deane (1962) appeared, and aspects of the hyena's behavior have been noted by Bigalke (1953) and Eloff (1964).

I will come back to these papers at various places where they are relevant. But here it may be helpful to outline a few prominent features of the hyena's natural history. These features will all be discussed at length in the following chapters, but since some knowledge of the species' natural history is required to understand the various sections of the book without too much cross-reference, I will very briefly summarize a few characteristics.

Hyenas are predators, as are lions or wild dogs, and their food in nature consists mostly of prey which they kill themselves. They often take large animals like wildebeest and zebra, not all of which are old or sick. If hyenas get a chance to scavenge they will take it—as will almost all other carnivores—but hyenas are probably better equipped to make use of such chances. On the whole, the amount of scavenging they do seems to depend on the availability of carrion.

Hyenas live in large communities, "clans," of up to eighty animals. However, in some areas like the Serengeti, there are such large temporary fluctuations in food supply (caused by the migration of prey animals) that the clan system is disrupted, though still recognizable. These clans defend territories and put scent marks along their boundaries. During this territorial defense, one may observe complete warfare between groups from neighboring clans, and hyenas actually kill each other. Within the clans, females dominate males, and a whole set of behavioral mechanisms has evolved which probably function to prevent fighting within the clan. The sexes have an equal role within the social and feeding activities. They look very much alike and females have even evolved external genitalia much like those of males. Each clan has one central denning site in which all females with cubs (usually two per litter) leave their offspring. Each female suckles only her own cubs. They do not regurgitate or carry food back for their young—a trait that seems curiously maladaptive.

METHODS

Almost all the data reported here were collected between June 1964 and January 1968 while my wife and I were living in Seronera, the headquarters of the Serengeti National Park. From there, I went out on daily (or nightly) trips; other more remote areas of the Serengeti were usually visited while camping. We regularly stayed in a small log cabin in the Ngorongoro Crater for periods of several weeks.

All together I spent about thirty months with the hyenas in the Serengeti and ten months with those in Ngorongoro, usually out in the field every day and during many nights. But it is difficult to state exactly the amount of time spent with them; during some whole nights' observations I saw virtually nothing, whereas on other occasions I might spend an hour watching fifty hyenas simultaneously.

The most important tool for this study was the Land Rover which enabled me to follow hyenas closely through most of their habitat, at any time of the day or night, without frightening them. Also vital were a pair of field glasses ("night glasses" 7 × 50) and a dictaphone or notebook. The distance from which hyenas could be observed depended on circumstances. I always tried to stay far enough away not to cause any disturbance; Ngorongoro hyenas could be approached more closely than those of the Serengeti, at night they would allow me nearer than during the day, and on open grassland they were shyer than when near cover. Usually hyena behavior was observed from 30–50 m away, but there were occasions when hyenas came and chewed at the car in which I was watching, whereas at other times they were alarmed when I came within 200 m.

Whereas in Ngorongoro observations were made everywhere in the crater, I had to be selective in the Serengeti because of the size of the area. Most of my work was done on the open Serengeti grassland plains and along their edges, and only few additional observations came from the sparsely populated woodlands in the north of the park. The plains and woodlands in the west of the park (the "corridor") took an inter-mediate position in my interest; I spent many weeks of observation there, but most of the effort was always directed at the central portion of the Serengeti.

I adapted my method of observation to the kind of information I wanted to collect and to circumstances; I followed one hyena or a group, or I scanned the country from vantage points, looking for kills and other hyena activities. This way of collecting data introduced biases, and I have discussed these in the relevant sections. Many of my observations had to be made by night because of the hyenas' nocturnal activities. But most information was collected when hyenas were active under reasonable light conditions, that is, during the short dawn and dusk. Night watching is perhaps easier than it sounds, if use is made of moonlit nights; the moonlight is so clear and the country so open that often I could even drive cross-country without using headlights. During a full moon and with good field glasses, one can recognize a hyena as such when more than 1 km away. I have tried several infrared observation devices, but none of them met the requirements set by the fast-moving hyenas; the field of vision was very narrow and the range was short. I therefore stuck to moonlight.

For specific purposes, I used various pieces of equipment which are described in different sections of this report. They included a light aircraft (Piper Super-cub), radio transmitters and receiver, tape recorder and loudspeaker, tools for capturing and marking, and equipment for fecal analysis. Finally, special mention ought to be made of some observations I made on our tame hyena, who was completely unrestricted and used our house as his den.

2 Serengeti and Ngorongoro: Country and Inhabitants

THE SERENGETI ECOSYSTEM

When I am away from the Serengeti, I picture it as consisting of flat, vast grasslands, in places studded with flat-topped acacia trees. But although this may be the most striking landscape of the Serengeti, there are many others as well. About one-quarter of the Serengeti ecosystem (fig. 1) and of the national park consists of treeless grass steppe (plate. 1); the rest, around the rivers and hills, is fairly flat and grassy, but with many different types of woodland. This is not the place to present a detailed description of the vegetation (see Pearsall 1957; Grzimek and Grzimek 1959, 1960b), but a few characteristics and features of the landscape that are important for this study should be mentioned.

Most important for my purpose were the open Serengeti plains, whose vegetation has been classified by Anderson and Talbot (1965) and in much greater detail by Braun (in preparation). Large areas in the east of the Serengeti plains are covered with very short grass, often less than 10 cm high. The most important grass species which grow there are *Microchloa kunthii, Digitaria macroblephara, Harpachne schimperi*, and a sedge, *Kyllinga nervosa*. Along the western edge of the plains, especially in a large area in the northwest, the grass gets much longer, up to 1 m high. There, *Themeda triandra, Pennisetum mezianum, Digitaria macroblephara*, and *Aristida adoensis* are the most important species, although in large areas, especially in the northwest, *Cymbopogon excurvatus* dominates the vegetation. There is a transitionary zone of grasses of intermediate height between the long-grass and short-grass areas in which, especially, *Andropogon greenwayi* and *Sporobolus fimbriatus* grow together with some of the short-grass species already mentioned. Here many herbs may also be found, especially *Indigophora, Solanum*, and *Heliotropium* species. Large areas of the long grass are usually burned in the dry season, although they grow up again during the wet time of the year. Thus, short-grass conditions prevail over almost the whole Serengeti plains during most of the year. The rest of the park, the west

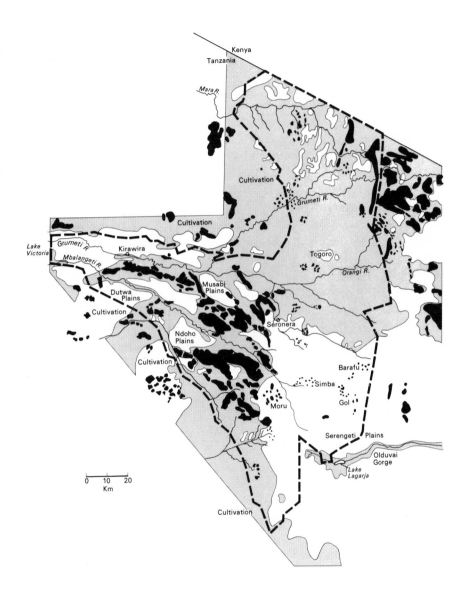

Fig. 1. The Serengeti ecosystem. Hills are indicated in black, woodlands are dotted, open grasslands are white. National Parks Headquarters and the Serengeti Research Institute are in Seronera.

and north, consists of woodland interspersed with open grasslands of varying size—here, too, the grass species are largely the same as those of the long-grass areas of the plains. Several tree communities can be distinguished, in most of which acacia species are dominant. These communities vary from the tall gallery forests along the main rivers, which contain a great many species, to the "typical" Serengeti woodlands which are dominated by *Acacia tortilis–Commiphora trothae*, by *A. tortilis–A. clavigera*, or by *A. senegal–A. hockii*. Large areas are covered by just one thin, unimpressive-looking tree species, the whistling thorn, *A. drepanolobium*.

Almost the whole ecosystem is situated between 1,200 m and 1,800 m above sea level, and monthly averages of maximum daily temperatures fluctuate between 25° C and 32° C, minimum daily temperatures between 11° C and 18° C.

The driest areas in the ecosystem are undoubtedly the eastern plains, where the average rainfall is below 50 cm per annum. As you go west, the area gets progressively more rain, reaching a maximum at Kirawira (about 40 km from the shore of Lake Victoria) of 107 cm per annum during my study. The far north also had more rain than the plains proper (about 100 cm per year). Not only is there more rainfall toward the west and north, but also the temporal distribution of the rain is more favorable to plant growth. The Serengeti plains have a very pronounced dry season, generally lasting from the end of May until early November, when virtually no rain falls, although in the west and the north the impact of the drought is lessened by showers which often occur throughout the dry season. On the open plain no green grass or surface water is available during the dry time.

About one million large animals reside in this Serengeti ecosystem (Swynnerton 1958), of which more than twenty species of ungulate and over twenty species of carnivore are at least fairly common. The most numerous species have been listed in table 19 (chap. 4). Most of these animal inhabitants are migratory, especially the wildebeest, zebra, Thomson's gazelle, and eland, and part of the populations of some other species. Most migrants spend the wet season out on the open plains, and then move westward when these begin to dry out. This usually happens at the end of May. Many stay there in the "midwest" for the whole dry season, but later in the dry time the large majority of wildebeest move to the north of the Serengeti National Park and sometimes even well into Kenya. In November and December they once again converge on the Serengeti plains. The zebra migrations are more erratic, and during the dry season this species is to be found anywhere in the woodlands. The same can be said of Thomson's gazelle (tommies), which concentrate on the green "flushes" caused by occasional showers, wherever these occur in the ecosystem. Generally, wildebeest, zebra, and Thomson's gazelle are almost continually on the move. The woodland species (impala, buffalo, etc.) do not migrate as extensively as this, nor do the Grant's gazelle, which even during the dry season are mostly out on the open grass plains.

Reproduction of the migratory species is also tied into this pattern of movements. The more than 300,000 wildebeest which occupy the Serengeti congregate in huge herds in January and February, usually in the central, eastern, and southern areas. There, almost all cows over three years old produce a calf in the short space of four to six weeks. This fantastic abundance of easily available young animals has a profound effect on predation. More than 200,000 zebra also drop foals on the plains during that time, though over a longer term (less synchronized) than the wildebeest. Even many Thomson's gazelle (of which current estimates run between one-quarter and three-quarter million) fawn then, but they also reproduce at other times of the year (wildebeest and zebra have offspring every year, Thomson's gazelle probably twice per year).

The area I refer to as the Serengeti ecosystem is in fact larger than depicted in figure 1. The term "ecosystem" may be used to designate various things, depending on one's aims of research. For instance, it may be defined in terms of energy flow or of distribution of certain communities. Here I have used "Serengeti ecosystem" to indicate the area covered habitually by the annual migration of Serengeti wildebeest (Watson 1967). This species has the largest biomass of all, whereas its annual range coincides almost entirely with that of zebra and completely encompasses that of tommies. According to Watson (1967), the Serengeti wildebeest move over almost 25,000 km², an area including part of Kenya and a large proportion of the Ngorongoro Conservation Area. Approximately half of the ecosystem is the Serengeti National Park (12,500 km²). It extends somewhat farther southeast (up to the Ngorongoro highlands) and north (into the Kenya Mara) than is indicated on figure 1; no accurate cartography of those areas is available.

The Serengeti animals live in peaceful coexistence with man (the pastoral Masai) when outside the national park in the areas to the north and east. This cannot be said for the areas northwest and southwest of the park, where a number of tribes (Wasukuma, Wanata,

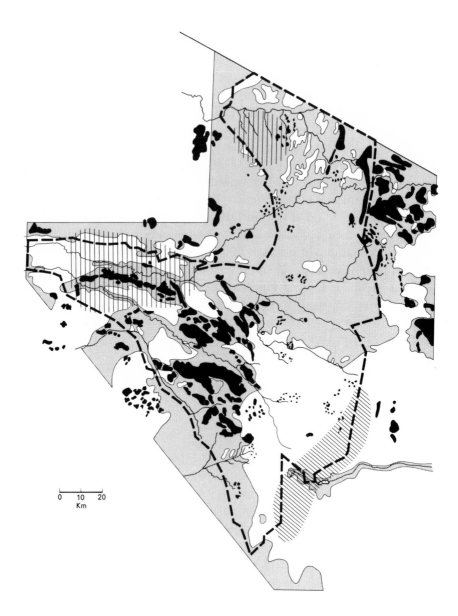

Fig. 2. Wildebeest concentrations (areas of highest occupance) in the Serengeti (from data of Watson 1967). Total area of distribution is considerably larger. Vertical hatching = dry-season concentrations; diagonal hatching = wet-season concentrations. Rest of legend as in figure 1.

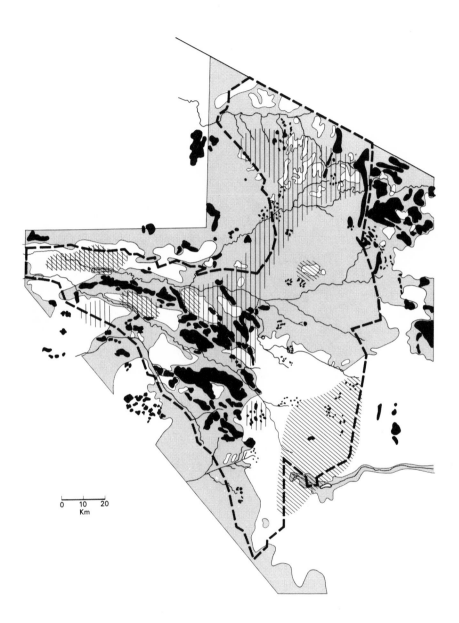

Fig. 3. Zebra concentrations in the Serengeti; legend as in figure 2.

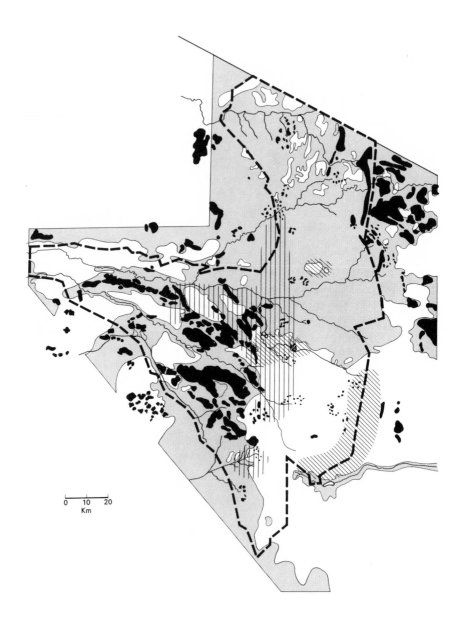

Fig. 4. Thomson's gazelle concentrations in the Serengeti: legend as in figure 2.

Waikoma, Wakuria, Waikesa, and others) have moved their agricultural settlements right up to its boundaries. In some places this has almost excluded wildlife; these tribes hunt whenever opportunity arises, both inside and outside the park. The ecosystem is thus bordered by cultivation, especially in the northwest (but also in the southwest), and by natural boundaries, mostly mountains, in the east.

Figures 2, 3, and 4 are an approximation of the distribution of the wildebeest, zebra, and Thomson's gazelle during the period of Watson's study, 1962–65 (Watson 1967). These data are not accurate but give a reasonable idea of the distribution of the herbivore concentrations in the ecosystem.

NGORONGORO CRATER

Ngorongoro Crater has also been the subject of several detailed descriptions (Pearsall 1957; Grzimek 1960*b*; Dirschl 1966; Estes 1969). It is a vast caldera with walls 400–500 m high, which are mostly covered with dense forest. The floor of the crater, where I carried out this study, is an open grass plain; these grasslands and the wildlife they carry form a virtually self-contained "ecological unit" (fig. 5). The 250-km² crater floor is essentially flat, with some hills in the north and east. The grasslands themselves are treeless, but there are two small patches of fever-tree forest (*Acacia xanthophloea*), a lake, some marshes, a spring, and three permanent streams with trees scattered along them. The grasslands are short (dominated by *Sporobolus marginatus* and *Digitaria scalarum*), medium short (especially *S. marginatus* and *Cynodon dactylon*), or of medium height up to 70 cm (especially *Andropogon greenwayi* and *D. scalarum*). The swamps carry very thick stands of *Eschynomene schimperi* and *Cyperus immensus*, which grow up to 4 m high.

The crater floor is approximately 1,800 m above sea level, somewhat higher than most of the country in the Serengeti. It is therefore slightly colder, especially at night. Rainfall averaged about 75 cm per year over 1964–67, a figure comparable to that of the central Serengeti National Park. On the rim of the crater, rainfall is considerably higher.

There are amazing numbers of animals inside this caldera. Although there are fewer species than in the Serengeti (for instance no topi, warthog, impala, giraffe, and others), the common ungulates and carnivores occur in both areas. Wildebeest are the most numerous, followed by zebra, then gazelle; there are relatively more Grant's gazelle in Ngorongoro than in the Serengeti. All together, the crater carries a density on the order of 95 large wild mammals per km²

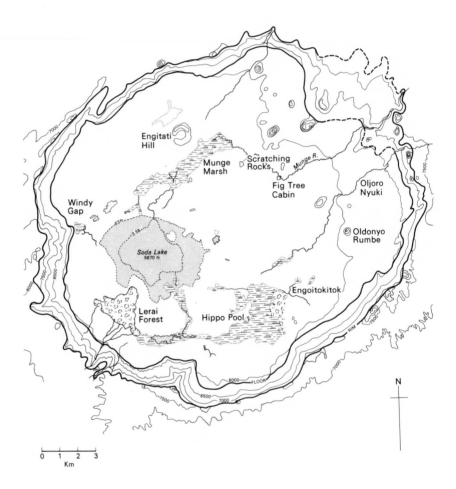

Fig. 5. Ngorongoro Crater.

(table 20), to which have to be added some cattle, sheep, and goats. Two Masai villages (*manyattas*) were usually occupied during my study period, and up to 2,000 head of livestock could be seen, but this number was rather variable.

One major difference between Ngorongoro and Serengeti is that the game inside the Ngorongoro Crater is resident, that is, nonmigratory. There are, of course, movements within the crater, especially daily movements between the sleeping and grazing areas, to and from drinking places, and sometimes to areas where the grazing happens to be favorable; but there is nothing comparable to the large-scale migrations of the Serengeti. The way bull wildebeest may occupy the same very small area for years has been documented by Estes (1969); zebra appear to move through very much larger areas of the crater (Klingel 1969). However, some game movements can also be observed into and out of the caldera, especially during the wet season. Formerly, it was thought that almost all wildebeest left to calve on the Serengeti plains (Pearsall 1957), but the study of the Grzimeks (1959, 1960b) showed that this was not so. The more detailed work of Estes (1969) on wildebeest, and Klingel (1967) on zebra indicated that only a small proportion of the Ngorongoro ungulate population spends a short time of the year outside the caldera, exiting along a few narrow game trails leading up its steep walls.

3 Habitat and Population Ecology

The spotted hyena occurs everywhere in Africa south of the Sahara except in the Congo Basin; however, in recent times it has disappeared from large areas in South Africa (Lydekker 1926; Ellermann, Morrison-Scott, and Hayman 1953). It overlaps its nearest relatives, the striped hyena (*Hyaena vulgaris*) in the east, and the brown hyena (*Hyaena brunnaea*) in the southern parts of its range, although there is no geographical overlap at all between the striped and the brown hyenas. Within its vast range the spotted hyena occurs in many different landscapes, from extremely hot and arid low-lying areas in the north and south to the cold heights of dense mist forests on mountains in East Africa and Ethiopia up to 4,000 m (my own observations and Brown 1969). The species seems extremely adaptable and is able to coexist with human habitation—for many people's taste, it is too adaptable.

However, there are large variations in hyena density within this range of habitats. Whereas only an occasional individual occurs in the dense forest of the Aberdares and on Mount Kenya (M. Coe, personal communication), large numbers of the species have always been known to exist in Ethiopia and British Somaliland, where they often congregate around human habitation. I have also observed large numbers of hyenas near Harar in the east of Ethiopia (Kruuk 1968). In East Africa hyenas occur almost everywhere, but in substantial numbers only near concentrations of plains game or near human settlement. Many villages, especially those of pastoral tribes, have their attendant hyenas, which, by the very nature of their modus vivendi, make themselves conspicuous. In densely settled areas they have usually been exterminated. Apart from this distribution near human habitation, the species is commonest in the savannah type of plains game "paradises" like the Serengeti and the floor of the Ngorongoro Crater, and is most infrequent in the heavy forests. The long-grass plains of Mikumi National Park in southern Tanzania carry a fair number of small- and

20

medium-sized ungulates and hyenas; the same may be said of part of the Selous Game Reserve north of the Rufiji River. But it is extremely difficult to arrive at an estimate of the hyena population in these areas because of their shy and nocturnal habits; the hyenas in East Africa have a long history of being shot at by man.

The Nairobi National Park in Kenya has very few hyenas, as they were almost wiped out by the park's management and by neighboring farmers several years ago; considerable numbers occur on the open plains with the ungulates of the Amboseli Game Reserve.

In Southern Africa, the number of spotted hyenas appears to be related to densities of medium-sized ungulates. For instance, the Kruger National Park and the north of Wankie National Park carry high numbers of resident ungulates and many hyenas (Pienaar 1969), whereas in the Zambezi Valley, the Kafue National Park, and the south of Wankie, the few ungulates support a low population of hyenas (P. Jarman, personal communication).

At least in the part of Africa I worked in, hyenas reach their greatest densities in fairly flat, open country with few or no trees and short grass, with as many ungulates as possible. Of the places mentioned in East Africa, the highest densities occur in the Ngorongoro Crater and the Serengeti National Park, which I will therefore consider as optimal habitat for the species.

One of the major difficulties in attempting to assess hyena densities in different habitats is the relative inaccessibility of the bush areas. With a pair of field glasses, a hyena walking on the open plains can be seen several km away, but in the more wooded areas, visibility is sometimes reduced to less than 100 m. Therefore, merely comparing numbers of hyenas observed per unit of observation time does not really have any value, and the overall impression one immediately gets that far fewer hyenas inhabit bush country than open plains could well be due to this kind of error in observation.

However, there are a number of additional observations which strongly suggest that in the Serengeti National Park, as well as in Ngorongoro, hyenas prefer open plains to wooded areas. First, hyena dens are usually located in the plains. Even when following hyenas in the bush country, it often soon becomes clear that they are based in plains dens, though these plains may be very small. This is especially clear during the dry season when the large herds of wildebeest and zebra are in the bush country, and a sizable proportion of the hyena population still has its dens along the edge of the Serengeti plains and has to move over vast distances through bush country to get at its food supply (see p. 57).

Another interesting point in this context is the hyena's dislike for tsetse flies, three species of which abound in many woodland areas of the Serengeti National Park. Although hyenas may sometimes ignore the tsetse flies buzzing around them, more often one sees them snapping wildly. Our tame hyena was harassed by these biting flies when camping with us in tsetse areas and even used to leave his favorite sleeping place, the tent, for more open plains country if he could find some relief from tsetse that way. Since tsetse are usually inactive at night (Glover 1964), this dislike of flies may well contribute to the readiness of hyenas to move about in the bush country only at night and their reluctance to have dens in these places.

Hyenas have a strong tendency to follow roads or paths, especially in bush country, and the paucity of hyena spoor on such tracks in these areas indicates a low density. Hyena droppings are large and conspicuously white; it is indicative that few are found in the woodlands. Furthermore, as any traveler in Africa knows, wherever hyenas are abundant, their calls can be heard over large distances at night. Merely by listening to hyena voices on the plains and in the bush country, one gains the impression that relatively few hyenas are inhabiting the large tracts of woodland country of the Serengeti. However, this difference in density does not apply to the bush country immediately along the northwestern and northern edges of the Serengeti plains.

On the undulating Serengeti plains, hyena dens are generally located at the higher points, on ridges rather than in valleys. They have this in common with burrows of most other burrowing animals like warthogs, jackals, springhares, and so on; one has the impression that the function of this particular habitat choice is the prevention of flooding and possibly easier digging rather than selection of vantage points.

Although water is an obvious attraction to hyenas, they can live in areas far from fresh water; even in the dry season they are still to be found on the open Serengeti plains when their water supply may be 30 or more km away. Presumably these animals drink during their travels to the food supply.

SERENGETI AND NGORONGORO: HYENA NUMBERS AND DENSITIES

It is now feasible to get a good estimate of numbers and densities of most of the large ungulates in the Serengeti and Ngorongoro by direct census, especially with aircraft and aerial photography (Grzimek and

Grzimek 1959; Turner and Watson 1964; Watson 1967). Hyenas prove too elusive for this approach. They spend their day sleeping in holes, under a tree, or out on the open plain, but even in the last case they are so well camouflaged that aerial observation is difficult. The same objections hold true for counts from the ground; with observations of this kind one might be able to compare relative densities, but they would give little idea of absolute numbers.

I have therefore tried to get an idea of the numbers of hyenas with an indirect method, using the "Lincoln-index." One of the first to use this method was Jackson (1933) for estimating populations of tsetse flies here in East Africa, and it has since been considerably refined, as summarized in Southwood (1966). A number of individuals from a population are marked, and from subsequent observations it is established what proportion of the population these marked animals constitute; from this the total population can be calculated. There are several possible sources of error; the animals should not be affected by their marks, the population should be sampled randomly with respect to its marked part, immigration/emigration and births and deaths must be known. But these difficulties could be overcome for the hyena populations.

Hyenas were captured after immobilizing them with a succinyl-choline chloride injection which was administered by a dart gun (pl. 2; for details, see appendix A). Triangles were then clipped out of their ears to make them individually distinctive; by distinguishing between cuts in the upper, middle, and lower ear (coded 1, 2, and 3, respectively), sixty-three individually distinct combinations are possible (see pl. 3). The hyena's ears are large and, as they usually cock their ears toward a car when it comes within a certain range, the marks are very readily distinguishable in the field. With field glasses, a marked hyena may be identified under favorable light conditions up to one km away. There was no indication that the hyenas were physically affected by their ear clippings after the initial discomfort had passed. They were more shy of cars for about a year after marking, but this difference with other hyenas did not affect the chance of recovery, for it operated well within the range at which marks could be distinguished.

The method was first tried on the hyenas in the Ngorongoro Crater; fifty-one hyenas were individually marked there in February and March 1965 and their place of marking and all following resightings were plotted on maps. During every visit to various areas of the Ngorongoro Crater, the number of marked and unmarked hyenas sighted in these areas was noted, and these figures form the basis for appendix D. 1. I tried initially to establish the ratio of marked to unmarked in a number of different ways; it was possible that the marked hyenas formed a sample which was somehow selected from the population and, if my resighting procedure were to entail the same selectivity, this might bias the results. I therefore collected observations on marked hyenas in three different ways; by driving around and observing hyenas (*a*) encountered incidentally (which could be selective in the same way as the marking procedure); (*b*) at kills at dawn, at dusk, and at night; or (*c*) attracted to my Land Rover by the tape-recorded sounds of hyenas on a kill.

For this last method, I stationed my Land Rover at a vantage point and played from a large loudspeaker on the hood some hyena calls which I had recorded near a kill at Seronera. Hyenas would come running up to my Land Rover from as far as 3 km away, especially from downwind, and as many as thirty-nine might gather at a time. In several instances, they ran at great speed upwind toward and past the car without paying attention to it, just running on and disappearing into the distance. Sometimes other interested parties also gathered around the car; for instance, tawny eagles, hooded vultures (Kruuk 1967), lions, and jackals.

It soon became clear when comparing the returns from the different methods of observation that the percentages of marked hyenas obtained were very similar. For instance, in June 1965 I found the percentage of marked hyenas in the incidentally encountered animals in three clan areas to be 11.7, and 14.5% of those attracted to the playback were marked; during August and September in the same areas, 15.2% were found marked in the incidentally encountered animals and 14.7% among hyenas attracted by sounds. It was more difficult to get enough comparable data for the percentage of marked animals on kills, but nevertheless it was obvious that no significant differences would arise from using any of the three methods. All the results have therefore been put together. The percentage of marked hyenas in later years was assessed almost entirely from incidentally encountered animals and kills.

In appendix B I have explained in greater detail how I calculated the total number of hyenas in the Ngorongoro Crater by adding up the populations of the various ranges within the crater which were estimated by the Lincoln index. In this way I arrived at a total of 385 adult hyenas. If the number of hyenas is to be used in calculating food consumption, some immatures must still be included, for young hyenas start eating from kills long before they are fully grown. I have assumed that about half, the mature half, of the young animals partake in kills (see p. 248); this adds another 42 animals (appendix D. 2) making the total about 430. For the 250 km² of the Ngorongoro Crater, this means an average density of 1.5 adults, or of 1.7 meat-eating hyenas per km².

Although the methods employed in the Serengeti were essentially the same as in Ngorongoro, a number of modifications had to be introduced. A much larger number of hyenas were marked in the Serengeti, making it impossible to give each one a different ear cut. Although 21 hyenas had unique cuts, all the other 179 hyenas caught had their ears cut in a way that differed according to area. Thus 12 hyenas marked just east of the Masai Kopjes all had $L_{13}R_{13}$ cut in their ears and 28 hyenas from the Musabi Plains had L_2R_2. But also the evaluation of the resightings was done differently in the Serengeti, to take the entirely different movement pattern into account. Hyenas in the Serengeti move over vast distances and have different home ranges at different times of year. There is a great deal of mixing throughout the whole population, but there are also clear tendencies to go back to the same area (see p. 52). We are therefore not a priori entitled to assume that marked and unmarked animals of the whole population mix randomly, which is necessary for use of the Lincoln index method for estimating the population. Also, the Ngorongoro method of splitting up the whole population into a number of randomly mixed subpopulations is not allowed in the Serengeti. One might ask whether the Lincoln index method of estimating Serengeti hyenas is valid at all, since there may be a number of immigrants and emigrants, a difficulty absent in Ngorongoro.

Dealing with the last difficulty first, table 1 shows that the observed percentage of marked hyenas over the same period in subsequent years

TABLE 1 *Resighting of marked hyenas in the Serengeti at comparable times of the year, plains only*

Date	No. of marked hyenas resighted	Total no. of hyenas observed	% marked hyenas in sample
Nov. 1966–Jan. 1967	77	817	9.42
			−5.3%
Nov. 1967–Jan. 1968	104	1,165	8.92
			−5.0%
Nov. 1968–Jan. 1969	41	485	8.47

is not subject to any great change; this confirms our belief that the Serengeti population, although moving a great deal within the area, is clearly distinct from neighboring hyena populations. If we arrange the dry-season and wet-season estimates of hyena populations for various areas, as in table 2, the results suggest a slightly higher percentage of

TABLE 2 *All resightings of marked hyenas in the Serengeti, in different seasons*

Date	No. of marked hyenas resighted	Total no. of hyenas observed	% marked hyenas in sample
1966 Dry	43	396	10.9
1966/67 Wet	207	2,056	10.1
1967 Dry	37	323	11.4
1967/68 Wet	104	1,165	8.9
1968 Dry	—	—	—
1968/69 Wet	67	779	8.6

unmarked hyenas during the wet season (on the plains), although the differences are not statistically significant. So there may be a small amount of exchange with surrounding areas, which, however, does not cause any long-term changes, merely seasonal fluctuations in marked percentages. The small differences between subsequent seasons, moreover, suggest a very low recruitment rate, as is discussed on p. 30.

I have explained the calculation of numbers of hyenas in the Serengeti in appendix C. The estimate of 3,000 hyenas (adults plus meat-eating juveniles) is, admittedly, a crude one; it appeared that estimating numbers in areas covered by the marked hyenas is not too difficult, but in the woodland areas outside the marked hyenas' range I could only make a rough guess. Most likely, the 3,000 constitutes an overestimate; it means that in the approximately 25,000 km² covered by the herbivore migrations, there are fewer than 0.12 hyenas per km², about one-fourteenth of the density in Ngorongoro.

It is also interesting to note that the only other important large carnivore, the lion, occurs in the Serengeti in lower densities than in Ngorongoro. Schaller (personal communication) estimates 2,000–2,400 lions in the Serengeti ecological unit, or less than 0.1 per km²; in the Ngorongoro, the estimated population of 40–60 constitutes a density of 0.16–0.24 per km² during my study period. In later years, the latter number has probably increased slightly.

Aspects of Population Ecology

Sex Ratio

The numbers of hyenas in both Ngorongoro and the Serengeti seem evenly distributed over the sexes. Since one cannot be certain of the sex of some adult hyenas one sees walking about, counts from mere field observations may not be valid; the only reliable evidence on sex ratio comes from captured animals. Even there, immatures give no clue to their sex and one can use only adults. Thus restricted, I found among animals darted in Ngorongoro 20 males and 21 females, and in the Serengeti 98 males and 95 females. I feel justified in assuming that these samples were random in distribution of sexes; for all purposes, they indicate an equal sex ratio (101.7 males per 100 females). It is interesting to note that Matthews (1939a), who collected hyenas mostly when they were scavenging around his camp, obtained 63 males and 40 females in 1937 in the eastern Serengeti. Most likely, the difference can be explained by the different sampling methods (females might be less likely to scavenge than males), but it is of course possible that a change has occurred since 1937. No fetal sex ratios are known.

Birth and Recruitment

It is very difficult to obtain an idea of the number of cubs present in a hyena population; and, similarly, data on lactation and gestation are almost impossible to obtain from mere field observations, because external signs of this are often impossible to discern. My information on these points is therefore scanty.

Hyena cubs may be born at any time of the year, for a group of cubs on a den often has all ages represented. This is corroborated by evidence from the size of fetuses from Matthews (1939a), who collected hyenas in the eastern Serengeti and made anatomical observations on their reproductive systems.

However, there may be a birth peak in the wet season. I estimated the age of cubs I saw on dens in the Serengeti and Ngorongoro and, from those of less than ten months old (the age up to which I could estimate with any accuracy), deduced when they were probably born (appendix D. 4). The data do not show a statistically significant difference in breeding season between the two areas,[1] but nevertheless they are worth considering separately. In figure 6, I have plotted the results of appendix D. 4 after smoothing; the graphs indicate a clear birth

1. Breeding season, Serengeti/Ngorongoro: $\chi^2 = 4.77$; $df = 4$; $p < 0.50$.

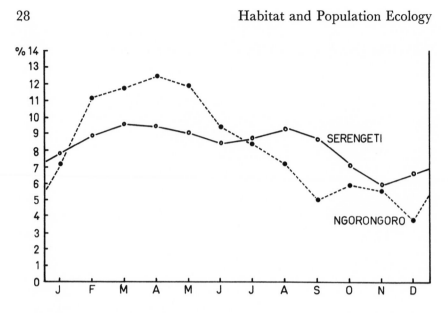

Fig. 6. Breeding season of hyenas in the Serengeti and Ngorongoro. Monthly cub production from estimated ages of cubs, smoothed by $b_s = (a + 2b + c)/4$.

peak around April in Ngorongoro, but a more even distribution of births in the Serengeti. Of course, this may not actually indicate a high in the number of births; it may also be caused by a difference in survival up to the age of ten months at different times of the year. I have no means of checking this, although it seems most likely that we are, indeed, dealing with a birth peak. If this were confirmed, it would be interesting to compare this with seasonality of food supply (p. 71). The Ngorongoro peak comes about a gestation period after an abundance in food supply; in the Serengeti adult hyenas probably always have food in plenty.

Evidence on seasonal breeding from South Africa is conflicting; Shortridge (1934) and Stevenson-Hamilton (1947) indicate a clear preference for the winter season, but Pienaar (1963) comments on the absence of a preference.

In captivity, the gestation period seems to be rather variable; it has been stated as 98–99 days (Grimpe 1916) and 109–11 days (Schneider 1926). Schneider also mentions data from Düsseldorf Zoological Gardens in which the gestation period varied from 97 to 132 days and describes the birth of a cub whose mother died six days later with another cub in her uterus. Matthews (1939a) takes Schneider's average of 110 days as an approximation and I will also use it here.

Indications of the length of the lactation period also vary. Matthews

(1939a) estimates that lactation lasts for approximately six months. Grimpe (1916) took cubs away from their mothers in captivity after six months, before they were naturally weaned. Our tame hyena was given meat at three months of age but, although becoming increasingly carnivorous, was still an enthusiastic milk-bottle feeder when twelve months old. In the field it is usual to see hyenas twelve to fourteen months old suckling from their mothers, but at a later age, this is exceptional (though I do have one observation of an approximately eighteen-month-old cub suckling). I have rarely seen young hyenas less than six months old eating meat from a kill (two observations of three-month-old cubs), but from six months onward the proportion of meat in their diet must be increasing steadily, although obviously milk feeding plays a very important role until they are at least one year old. I assume, therefore, that the lactation period covers twelve to fourteen months.

The female hyena is polyestrous, with an estrous cycle of about fourteen days (Grimpe 1916; Schneider 1926; Matthews 1939a). Both sexes reach sexual maturity just after they are fully grown, the female somewhat later than the male (Matthews 1939a); this is probably around the age of three years (three years also for a female in captivity; Schneider 1926).

The typical litter size is two; I have only occasionally seen three cubs who obviously belonged together and sometimes I saw just one cub on its own. But in these last cases, it is very difficult to be sure that there is no sibling somewhere down a hole. The litter size of two is confirmed by Matthews (1939a) and Deane (1962). In zoo hyenas, Schneider (1926) found thirty-three cubs in seventeen litters, Pournelle (1965) eleven cubs in five litters, and Crandall (1964) fourteen cubs in seven litters, so in captivity the average litter size is also two.

I calculated that, in the Ngorongoro Crater during my study period, there had been an average annual recruitment of young hyenas (one and one-half to two years old) to the numbers of adults of 13.5% (p. 32). This means about $0.135 \times 385 = 57$ young animals. I had previously estimated that there were some 84 cubs in the crater (p. 303); with the low cub mortality (p. 36) and a high mortality during the first months of independence (of marked "yearlings," 30% had died within three months), these 84 would approximately provide the required recruitment.

It is probably a fair estimate that the 84 cubs will belong to about 45 litters. Since all fully grown females (age-class III and over) are capable of reproducing (Matthews 1939a), there are about 140 sexually mature females in the Ngorongoro population (p. 307). If these would all reproduce with a shortest possible birth interval with little cub mortality (sixteen months, of which twelve months is lactation), 75% would be lactating and there should be some 105 litters of cubs about. However, only 32% of these females has cubs; the discrepancy means that the average birth interval is, in fact, much longer than sixteen months, or that a very high percentage of cubs die shortly after birth. Matthews (1939a) found 10 of 23 parous females in anestrus (4 were pregnant, 6 lactating, and 13 in anestrus or proestrus) which suggests that in the Serengeti in 1937, hyenas were not reproducing as fast as they could, owing to a very long anestrus period. The same thing may be happening now in Ngorongoro.

I could estimate a total of seven birth intervals from five females in the crater by assessing the ages of cubs seen suckling. I could be reasonably certain that these females did not have cubs between recorded births. The recorded intervals were approximately 26, 26, 17, 16, 15, 13, and 9 months (average 17.4)—in the case of the 9-month interval, the cubs may have died before independence. Probably the sample is not representative, for the females were selected for the very fact that they were seen to reproduce at least twice. It does show, however, that at least some females reproduced with the shortest birth interval; this is strengthened by the observation that of five females seen mating in the crater, three had cubs at foot of approximately one year old. There must be considerable variation between females, some having longer birth intervals than others. Further study of behavioral differences between females may well give important clues about factors inhibiting reproduction.

In the Serengeti, resightings of the marked population (table 1) showed an annual recruitment plus immigration of 5.3% and 5.0% (average 5.2%), with immigration probably insignificant. Of the adult females caught for the marking program, 26/70 = 37% were lactating on capture (a figure rather similar to the 32% of females with cubs in Ngorongoro). If the litter size is two, the sex ratio equal, the lactation period twelve months and there is no mortality among cubs, these females would produce an annual recruitment of 37%, which is vastly in excess of the 5.2% observed. We can be fairly confident about my first two assumptions, the litter size of two and equal sex ratio; if the cubs do not die, lactation might last slightly longer than a year, but not much. It is therefore most likely that the discrepancy is caused by a high mortality among the cubs. Cub mortality in the Serengeti is as difficult to check as in the Ngorongoro, but I have some observations of cubs dying, which I will refer to on p. 35.

The low percentage of lactating females in the Serengeti may indicate that long anestrous intervals occur there also, as in 1937 when Matthews (1939a) made his collection.

Mortality

Of the two marked populations, only in Ngorongoro was it possible to obtain an idea of the number of hyenas disappearing from the population during the study, for in the Serengeti the number of resightings of individuals was far too small and too irregular. In Ngorongoro, the disappearance of a marked hyena from a range meant with a fair degree of certainty that this animal had died or had moved to another range inside the crater. There is, of course, a possibility that hyenas which had disappeared had moved outside the crater, but there is no evidence for this. It seems especially unlikely for hyenas which disappeared from clans which are surrounded on all sides by other clans in the center of the crater. Moreover, since female hyenas disappear at a slightly faster rate than male hyenas, and male hyenas are more likely to change clans, this also suggests that the phenomenon of "disappearing" is different from changing clan or moving away.

During every visit to Ngorongoro I made notes of the sightings of

TABLE 3 *"Absence periods"* of live marked hyenas in Ngorongoro Crater

No. of negative observations between resightings	Times observed	Proportion of visits where such intervals could have been observed	Correction factor	Corrected distribution of absence periods	Cumulative %
0	235	12/12	12/12	235.0	99.9
1	45	12/12	12/12	45.0	26.5
2	16	11/12	12/11	17.5	12.4
3	7	10/12	12/10	8.4	7.0
4	5	9/12	12/9	6.7	4.4
5	2	8/12	12/8	3.0	2.3
6	1	7/12	12/7	1.6	1.4
7	0	6/12	12/6	—	0.9
8	0	5/12	12/5	—	0.9
9	1	4/12	12/4	3.0	0.9
				320.2	

marked hyenas, and if a marked hyena was not seen during five consecutive visits the chance that it would ever turn up again was smaller
than 2.3%. Hence all hyenas which were not seen for at least five
consecutive visits were considered dead (table 3).

TABLE 4 *Mortality among marked hyenas in Ngorongoro Crater*

	♂♂	♀♀	♂ + ♀	Yearling when marked	Total
No. marked	18	21	39	10	49
Died 1st year	2	3	5	3	8
Percentage	11.1	14.3	12.8	30.0	16.3
Died 2d year	2	4	6	1	7
Percentage	12.5	22.2	17.6	14.3	17.1
Average percentage	11.8	18.2	15.2	22.2	16.7

In table 4, I have accounted for the losses of marked hyenas in the
crater during two years of the study—the above definition of "death"
necessitated a long period of observation after the end of the year during
which mortality was supposed to have taken place. The mortalities of
various categories were not statistically different from each other during
the two years;[2] in fact, although the figures are small, they are all
surprisingly similar, with the exception of mortality within the one-to-
two-year category. This may, indeed, mean a higher mortality of the
yearling age-group, especially as all three cases mentioned occurred in
the first three months after marking. But at present the figures are too
small to draw any definite conclusions, and it may be prudent to use
merely the overall average of 16.7% as an indication of annual mortality
of hyenas of one year old and over in the crater.

It is interesting to note here that the percentage of marked animals
among the Ngorongoro hyenas over the three years decreased from
13.95% in 1965 to 11.90% in 1966 and 10.45% in 1967, an annual
decrease in marked percentage of 14.7% and 12.2%. This decrease, of
course, represents the annual recruitment and immigration (if we assume that mortality and emigration are the same for marked and
unmarked hyenas), of which immigration is probably insignificant.

2. Mortality, male/female: $\chi^2 = 0.17$; $df = 1$; $p < 0.90$. Mortality, male/yearling:
Fischer e.p. test, $p < 0.30$.

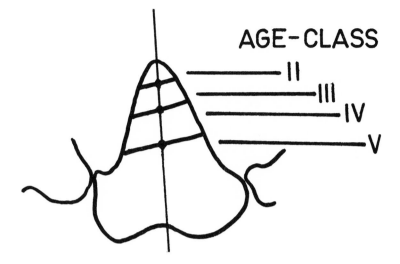

Fig. 7. Third premolar in the lower jaw of a hyena. The amount of wear characteristic for the age-classes is indicated.

Bearing in mind the crude methods involved, my figure of an average
annual recruitment of 13.5% compares well with the mortality rate of
16.7% and supports the impression of a stable population.

In order to see whether there are differences in mortality of age-
classes, I first divided the population into a number of tooth-wear
classes, then compared the mortality for those. Tooth wear in hyenas is
conspicuous, especially on the second upper premolar and the first
lower premolar, both of which are used for bone crushing. These
teeth are conical and pointed in early life but are worn down to the
gums at old age, and it is not difficult to assess the part of the tooth that
has been worn off (fig. 7). In figure 8 (and appendix D. 5), I have divided the marked population of Ngorongoro into four age-classes this
way, and compared the mortality rates. It is very difficult to find in the
crater any skulls of hyenas that died—this would have given a good
check on the mortality rate of marked animals. Probably all the skulls
of hyenas there are eaten by their fellows; this happens much less in the
Serengeti (see p. 116). From figure 9 there appears to be little difference
in mortality between age-groups in Ngorongoro; the youngest animals
seem to disappear just a little faster, but not significantly so.[3] Assuming
therefore a flat annual mortality rate of 16.7% for all age-groups of one
year and over, we can now construct a life table for hyenas starting at

3. Mortality in different age groups, Ngorongoro: $\chi^2 = 0.24$; $df = 2$; $p < 0.90$.

the age of one. From this, a one-year old would have a 48% chance of reaching five years old, and only 3% of these yearlings would survive to the age of twenty. Assuming a constant population size and comparing this life table with the distribution of age-classes based on tooth wear, it is actually possible to put an absolute age to each tooth-wear class; class II of appendix D. 5 would be some one to three years old, class III three to six years, class IV six to sixteen years, and class V sixteen years and older. It is unlikely that all assumptions are met, but these figures may still give a rough indication of age. Flower (1931) found that the average life of hyenas in zoos is twelve years (fifty-four individuals); the maximum life span was twenty-three to twenty-five years. Crandall (1964) mentions eighteen, twenty-three, and twenty-five years as longevity records.

In the Serengeti, I had to rely on another source of information for mortality data, for there were too few individually known animals and I saw them much less frequently than in the crater. But luckily a hyena carcass (especially the skull) in the Serengeti does not disappear nearly as fast as in the crater, and there at least I was able to collect skulls and compare the tooth wear of animals that died with that of

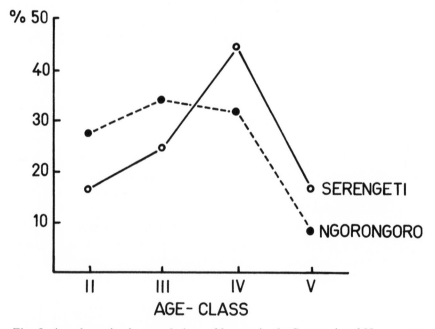

Fig. 8. Age-classes in the populations of hyenas in the Serengeti and Ngorongoro, adults only (from Kruuk 1970).

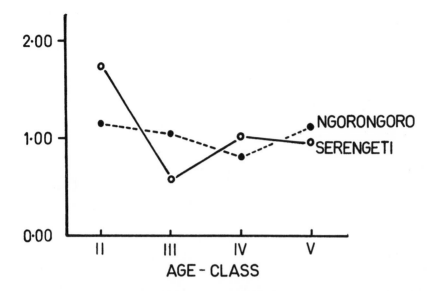

Fig. 9. Hyena mortality in the Serengeti and Ngorongoro. For each age-class, the ratio (% of hyenas found dead)/(% in the population) is given (from Kruuk 1970).

200 immobilized animals (appendix D. 5). I assumed that the latter constituted a good cross-section of the adult sex and age groups.

From appendix D. 5, it is clear that in the Serengeti relatively few skulls ere collected in age-class II, "young middle age," but there is no statistically significant difference in age distributions of the two sets of observations.[4]

I noticed a striking difference when comparing the age-classes of the live adult hyenas in Serengeti and Ngorongoro (fig. 8): the Serengeti hyenas are, on the whole, older.[5] This can only be caused by a difference in mortality, and although my figures are not sufficient to show this conclusively, they tentatively suggest that the Serengeti hyenas have a relatively low mortality during "young middle age" (fig. 9).

The mortality of cubs (less than one year old) is even more difficult to assess than that of adults, for almost certainly most cubs that die do so inside the den. I have found the remains of juvenile hyenas in the entrances of dens at Ngorongoro, Serengeti, and Amboseli; Sutcliffe (1969) excavated a hyena den in the Queen Elizabeth National Park in Uganda and found a skeleton of a cub. Thus, disappearance of known

4. Mortality in different age-groups, Serengeti: $\chi^2 = 7.44$; $df = 5$; $p < 0.20$.
5. Age of live hyenas, Serengeti/Ngorongoro: $\chi^2 = 8.69$; $df = 3$; $p < 0.05$.

cubs may mean that they died down a hole or that they have moved to another den.

In Ngorongoro, I had the general impression that cubs I knew disappeared rarely, although I did not collect systematic data on this. In the Serengeti, disappearance was frequent—but there I knew, too, that cubs often moved to other holes. There is some circumstantial evidence indicating a difference in mortality between the areas. In the Serengeti cubs are often seen in bad condition, especially when the herbivores are far from the den; this happens only rarely in Ngorongoro. But I also found this difficult to quantify. This superficial impression is confirmed, however, when we compare data on recruitment. In the Serengeti, the annual recruitment to the adult population is of the order of 5%, and 37% of the adult females were found lactating. In Ngorongoro I estimated that 32% of the adult females had cubs, an insignificant difference from the Serengeti—but there annual recruitment was about 13%. This difference must have been caused by a difference in mortality among cubs, which is apparently higher in the Serengeti.

TABLE 5 *Causes of mortality among hyenas*

Cause	Victim		Total	%
	Adult	Subadult		
Lion	8	5	13	55
Hyena	4	—	4	17
Man	1	1	2	8
Starvation/ disease	1	4	5	21
			24	101
Unknown	—	4	4	
	14	14	28	

Table 5 lists those occasions on which I found hyenas that had recently died, to give some idea about the causes of hyena mortality. Only five of the twenty-eight deaths were in Ngorongoro, and therefore I did not have enough evidence to compare the two areas. On four occasions the carcass had been damaged by scavengers to such an extent that I could not determine the cause of death, but of the remaining twenty-four, I could establish that the majority died a violent death (79%). This included four of the five Ngorongoro kills (I could not establish the cause of death of the fifth). Cullen (1969) mentions lions as killers of hyenas, and also one leopard (in Amboseli) which had turned into a hyena killer. At least seven of my thirteen lion victims were killed near a carcass, as was at least one of the four intraspecific kills. Some of my notes:

One early morning in February 1967, I found two male lions on the Serengeti plains, near the carcasses of two wildebeest; the evidence pointed to the lions as the killers. One of the wildebeest was already almost entirely eaten; a group of two bloated lionesses and five cubs which were lying $\frac{1}{2}$ km farther on probably had their share from that one. One of the lions was standing over a dead hyena approximately 50 m away from the nearest dead wildebeest. The lion proceeded to pull out some intestines and liver through a hole in the middle of the dead hyena's back without eating them. He then ate a few small pieces of dorsal muscle, joined the other male lion, and began to eat the wildebeest. This was the only occasion on which I had any evidence of lions eating anything from a dead hyena.[6] On closer inspection the hyena appeared to be still very warm, and it must have been killed just before my arrival. It was a young animal about twelve months old, and its major injury was a broken back, with the two parts completely separated from each other. Hemorrhages around the neck indicated that the lion had grabbed it in that part of its body as well.

In June 1966 some Masai living in the Ngorongoro Crater had illegally struck up a "manyatta" (group of huts in a circle, with a thorn fence around it and cattle kept inside at night) along the Mungi River, in the range of the Scratching Rocks clan. One afternoon I found an adult male hyena lying dead some 300 m away from this manyatta, and I estimated that it had died several hours earlier. It appeared in good health without any injuries apart from a large wound that was probably caused by the thrust of a spear. The spear had entered the body on the right side in the thorax, narrowly missing the heart but passing through both the lungs and coming out on the other side. The lung cavity was filled with blood.

In July 1968 a male hyena in obviously very bad condition was seen around Banagi in the Serengeti (A. Young, personal communication). It could stagger only a few paces at a time and was very emaciated, and it died between the houses in the compound nine days after it was first seen. The post mortem carried out by Young showed that the animal was suffering from anemia and, among many other characteristic

---

6. Schaller (personal communication) saw one completely eaten at a time when little other food was available to the lion.

symptoms, a blood count produced only 1.4 million corpuscles per mm³ instead of the more usual 5 million. The anemia was caused by a massive erythrophagocytosis of uninfected blood corpuscles, but the cause of this could not be ascertained.

[See also field notes on p. 132 and p. 256 for causes of mortality].

Little is yet known about the diseases and parasites from which hyenas may suffer. Tests have shown the presence of antibodies against brucellosis, rinderpest, and anaplasmosis in hyena blood (Sachs and Staak 1966), which means that they must have contracted the diseases and recovered. *Trypanosoma congolense*, the cause of the notorious "nagana" in cattle, was found in all three Serengeti hyenas examined by Baker (1968). Baker suggests that these trypanosomes are transmitted from herbivores to hyenas especially by the latter's eating infected ungulates, rather than by the normal way of bites from the tsetse fly. Hyenas also act as hosts to parasites which have another part of their life cycle in various herbivores; for instance, *Taenia hyaenae* Baer occurs in hyenas as adult tapeworm and has larval stages as cysts (measles) in the muscles of various antelopes (Sachs 1966), and *Taenia olngojinei* Dinnik and Sachs, another adult intestinal tapeworm in hyenas, occurs in the larval stage within the sacrum of large antelopes, a place accessible almost only to a bone crusher like the hyena (Dinnik and Sachs 1969). Then there is *Trichinella spiralis*, found as cysts in hyena muscles (Sachs and Taylor 1966). However, none of these seems to affect the condition of the animal, for they were all collected from "healthy" hyenas.

Conclusions about Hyena Numbers, Mortality, and Recruitment

The methods employed for assessing some of the basic facts about the hyena population were crude, and the results are somewhat vague. However, some fairly clear-cut conclusions can be drawn. First, there is the higher hyena density in Ngorongoro as compared with the Serengeti. Second, I found a difference in the age structure of the two populations, the adult Serengeti hyenas being on the average older than those in Ngorongoro. It seems likely that this difference is caused by a lower death rate among Serengeti hyenas of "young middle age." Annual adult mortality in Ngorongoro amounts to about 17%, recruitment to about 14%; the difference between the two may well be due to my crude census methods. In the Serengeti I have been unable to estimate the adult mortality except to note that it is lower than in Ngorongoro; also, it appeared that the annual recruitment to the numbers of adults is less than approximately 5% and, since the Serengeti population gives the impression of stability, the annual adult mortality may also be of that order. The higher adult mortality in the Ngorongoro is matched by a lower mortality among cubs there. Finally, an important point is that most of the adult mortality occurs in connection with competition over food, most hyenas being killed either by the teeth of their conspecifics in struggles over a kill, or by the teeth and claws of their major ecological competitor, the lion (also often over a kill). The fact that adult mortality is higher in Ngorongoro should be seen in conjunction with the difference in competition over food in the two areas; I will try to put these population data in perspective with the hyenas' food ecology on p. 102.

MOVEMENTS

In Ngorongoro

For every marked hyena in the crater, I kept a map with notes of when and where it was seen, and it soon became clear that hyena movements throughout Ngorongoro were far from random. I had caught the hyenas in as many different places as possible and, after I had resighted these individuals a few times, I noticed that each had only a relatively small home range. Also, many hyenas had exactly the same range, whereas others might occupy different areas, these being mutually exclusive. I found in this way that the whole Ngorongoro Crater could be divided into eight areas (fig. 10), seven of which had a permanent group of hyenas living in them and one of which had temporary occupants. These groups I called "clans," and they are further discussed in chapter 6.

In 93% of the 654 occasions on which I sighted marked hyenas, they were in the same range where they had been seen previously. I always gave the benefit of the doubt to hyenas that I met in the boundary areas between, and scored them as if they had occurred within their own range. Although it was clear that hyenas stuck to certain home ranges, a number of them were sighted well outside these ranges; some 47% of the marked individuals were at one time or another outside their previous range. Some individuals were more likely to cross their "boundary" than others, and males especially seemed prone to wander (table 6).[7]

An observation of an animal outside its previous range might mean a

7. Wandering outside clan-range, male/female: normal test $p < 0.02$.

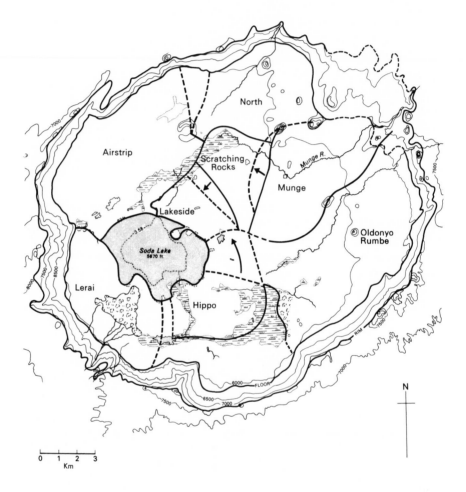

Fig. 10. Clan ranges in Ngorongoro: *Dotted lines*, exact location of boundary uncertain, either because of lack of information or because boundary itself is vague.
Arrows indicate long-term shifts of boundaries.

TABLE 6 *Movements of hyenas between clan ranges*

	No. marked	No. of resightings	No. of resightings outside range where seen previously	% moved
♂♂	18	241	31	13
♀♀	21	340	10	3
yearlings	10	73	6	8
	49	654	47	7

permanent shift from one range to another, but it might also mean just a short visit to the neighbor's garden. The first is most likely for males, the second almost equally for males and females (table 7).[8]

TABLE 7 *Hyenas seen outside their previous ranges*

	"Permanent" shift	Short visit	Doubtful	Total
♂♂ (excluding L_1R_{23})	11	6	4	21
♀♀	1	7	2	10
yearlings	3	1	2	6
	15	14	8	37

One of the males, L_1R_{23}, appeared to belong to two ranges for the first half year of its time under observation, and was accepted by individuals from both clans; one day it was even seen to feed in the morning with one group and in the evening with another. This unusual behavior stopped in June 1966, however, and from then on it was seen only in the area in which it had been marked originally. Later, it played such an important part in the food acquisition in the range that I nicknamed it "the butcher."

The short visits by individual hyenas to neighboring clans might last from a few hours to a few days. This "trespassing" could well have been related to the presence and absence of ungulates in the ranges. Once in December 1967, for instance, the wildebeest and zebra had been very scarce on the Scratching Rocks grounds for several weeks; during that time, I saw several of my marked animals from Scratching

8. Permanent shift versus short visit away from clan range, male/female: Fischer e.p. with Tocher's modification, $p < 0.05$.

Rocks right inside the Airstrip range, where there were large numbers of wildebeest. During the times I observed them, they went unnoticed by the Airstrip clan. But intrusions by hyenas into other ranges were not always related to game movements, and sometimes it was impossible to guess why a hyena should go so far from his home grounds, just for a short visit, when there were many animals in his own range and when he ran the risk of encountering the rightful owners of the territory.

The boundaries between the clan ranges were sometimes very clearly defined, but some were much more vague (fig. 10). The clear or vague delineation of a boundary did not seem to have anything to do with the presence of natural obstacles like rivers or bushes; the natural obstacles had to be very large indeed to play an important role in boundary formation—as, for instance, the Mungi Marsh between the Airstrip range and the Scratching Rocks, the large lake, and so on. In some areas, my definition of the boundary of a range is vague because I did not have enough observations there; in others, however, it was clear that there was no clear-cut boundary line but rather a no-man's-land between hyena groups. To some extent this seemed to depend on hyena density, and in those areas where many hyenas occurred (for instance, along the boundary between the Scratching Rocks and the Mungi, and between Scratching Rocks and the Lakeside) the boundary area was extremely narrow and almost a line.

So far, the boundary has been considered as a line or area surrounding the various ranges in which marked hyenas had been consistently observed; however, it was also clearly marked by the occurrence of aggressive behavior of hyenas toward nongroup members (territorialism) and various related behavior patterns which will be discussed on p. 251.

Although after the first year of the study these hyena clan ranges seemed permanent to me (Kruuk 1966a, b), I noticed later that changes did occur. Of the groups on the eight ranges described, one proved to be very impermanent (the North clan), whereas one other considerably expanded its range at the cost of others (the Hippo clan). The other six areas proved to be much more stable units, but even there small changes in the exact position of the boundaries did occur over the period of three years. As this phenomenon may be important, especially when comparing the much more "fluid" hyena population in the Serengeti, I will go into these observations in more detail.

Until approximately May 1966, only occasionally was a hyena seen in the area now called the North range; but since before then this area had been covered with long grass, only very few wildebeest and zebra occurred there. However, this pattern changed after a grass fire in June 1966. Large herds of wildebeest and zebra moved into the area and suddenly hyena groups could be seen hunting there. Several marked hyena were observed among them which were obviously drawn not just from neighboring clans but from the whole of the crater (Mungi, Lakeside, Oldonyo Rumbe). It was clear that a completely new group of hyenas had emerged, consisting of hyenas from various other clans. This situation remained until the middle of January 1967, when the newly formed group dispersed again and most marked hyenas returned to their old groups, although one joined the Hippo clan, which at that time began to expand considerably. In the case of the Hippo clan, too, it was clear that hyenas were drawn to it from various other clans, though not necessarily from neighboring ones (North clan, Lerai, Scratching Rocks). The Hippo clan, which in early 1965 consisted of only some fifteen animals, had expanded by the end of 1967 to approximately thirty-five. The expansion of the Hippo range was almost entirely at the cost of the range of the Lakeside group. A large area south of the Hippo range up to the wall of the crater did not appear to be occupied by any of the clans, and hyenas were rarely seen there, although occasionally there were many ungulates.

The shifting of sharply delineated boundaries which occurs in places of high hyena density appeared to be a much slower process than the fairly sudden changes described above. The shift which I was able to observe most closely was the one occurring during the second half of 1967 in the boundary between the Mungi clan and the Scratching Rocks. The Mungi clan moved their den to a place only a few hundred meters from the boundary and, after that, they "pushed" their range gradually farther and farther into Scratching Rocks territory until, at the end of 1967, they had enlarged their range some 500 m beyond the original limit. The Scratching Rocks den at the same time moved farther in the direction of the boundary between Scratching Rocks and the Lakeside and, correspondingly, this boundary also shifted, probably by just under 1 km in the direction of the center of the Lakeside range. Therefore, the Lakeside hyenas were encroached upon simultaneously by the Scratching Rocks and the expanding Hippo clan but did not themselves expand their range in another direction. These relatively small changes in the boundaries between clans were accompanied by conspicuous territorial behavior, as described on page 253.

There were some differences in size of the ranges. The Lerai range was probably the smallest, since it had a forest which was little used by the hyenas (except occasionally for sleeping during the day), whereas both the Airstrip and Oldonyo Rumbe ranges were very large. However, the latter range was not as large as it looks on the map; a considerable part of it was long grass and was infrequently used by either ungulates or hyenas. Comparing the size of the area with the numbers of hyenas in each clan, one can see a likely relationship between the two—the larger the clan, the larger the range. But the relation is necessarily vague, since it is difficult to estimate the proportion of suitable habitat within each range.

Movements in and out of the crater.   Although the crater wall forms a formidable barrier 300–400 m high, and although most of the animal inhabitants probably never leave the area, there are a number of game trails leading in and out of the caldera. There are several routes on the northeast side up and through the Ngorongoro highlands; zebra especially seem to use them and, at some times of the year, spend several weeks in the open and less densely wooded areas of the Ngorongoro highlands. On the northwest side of the crater, one or two game trails zigzag up the crater wall and come down to the Malanja depression and Olbalbal, the plains which are virtually the beginning of the Serengeti plains. In these areas, some Ngorongoro wildebeest and zebra can be seen, especially during the rains, and in Olbalbal they even mix with the Serengeti herds. It is not known what numbers of animals are involved but, at least during the years I was there, it was clear that the great majority of all the ungulates stayed on the Ngorongoro Crater floor throughout the year. Some hyenas may follow these ungulate movements in and out of the crater; in fact, in April 1965, Mr. Goddard observed a marked yearling hyena (L_2R_3, a male) some 20 km from the crater in Olduvai Gorge, feeding on the remains of a Masai cow. This animal had been marked in the Airstrip range which is on the Olduvai side of the crater and from which game trails lead over the northwest rim; I saw it again in August of that year back in its original range where it has been observed many times since.

I was unable to locate one den, that of the Oldonyo Rumbe clan, during several months in 1966. Game tracks led from the range out of the crater in a northeast direction. Few hyenas were observed in that range and only very few wildebeest and zebra were present; it could well be that they moved temporarily out of the crater and later returned. On the whole, however, even for those clans like this one at the "outlets" of the crater, movements outside the caldera are of relatively minor importance; for the other clans in the center, it is unlikely that this kind of migration plays any role at all.

The focal point of hyena activity within the clan range is the communal den site, of which there is usually only one. If two or more sets of holes are occupied by the clan at the same time, they are usually close together and there is a regular traffic of adults and cubs between them. A den site is occupied for several months; then, for no reason that I can see, a whole set may move, in some cases over 1 km away, but always within the clan range. It appears that at least sometimes the initiative for a move from one denning site to another comes from the cubs, who wander around after being fed by their mothers and may spend the night in another hole. When their mother fails to find the cubs in the usual place on her return from the hunt, she looks for them until she finds them and then lies down and suckles the cubs in front of the new site, where other adults and cubs may join her.

The denning sites are by no means always central in the clan range; both the Mungi and the Hippo clans, during their expansions, moved their dens right up to the new border. But most clans usually had their dens far away from any boundary.

Movements in the Serengeti

Seasonal distribution. I had found after tracking the movements of hyenas in the Ngorongoro Crater that they rarely left an area averaging 30 km², and thus it came as a surprise to see the large open Serengeti plains with very few hyenas during the dry season and yet considerable numbers during the rains. This became clear, for instance, from the results of some aerial counts at different times of the year; table 8

TABLE 8 *Aerial counts of hyenas in the Serengeti*

Area	No. of hyenas in	
	Wet season (March 1966)	Dry season (July 1966)
Central plains, northeast of Lake Lagarja, approximately 80 km²	66	0
Eastern plains, east of Barafu kopjes, approximately 30 km²	27	0
Northwestern plains, southwest of Seronera River, approximately 80 km²	11	14

shows the large differences in numbers in areas of the eastern and central Serengeti plains (Barafu and Lake Lagaja). These counts were carried out from a low-flying Piper Super-cub aircraft as "total counts," along parallel strips covering an area of specified size. They were flown during the first hours of daylight, when almost certainly some hyenas had already retired into holes for the day. However, the figures will give a good indication of the differences in hyena density in these general areas. The table also shows that there was no obvious difference in hyena numbers between wet and dry seasons in the third area, the northwestern part of the plains.

These aerial observations are supported by the general impression one has on the ground; it appears that during the wet season the great majority of hyenas are out on the open Serengeti plains, whereas during the dry time of the year they are to be found along the northern and western edges of the plains and in the adjoining woodlands. To obtain more detailed observations on this, I studied the movements of marked hyenas.

The 200 hyenas I marked with ear cuts in the Serengeti were not all caught simultaneously; 18 animals were captured in March 1965 on the central Serengeti plains, 28 in June and July 1965 on the Musabi plains (an area in the woodlands to the northwest of the Serengeti plains), and the remaining 154 were caught in March 1966, again on the open Serengeti plains. Only 21 of them were marked individually; the others had cuts in their ears of a pattern which was identical for animals marked in one particular area. As in Ngorongoro, I attempted to split the hyena marking as much as possible over the whole area covered, but this was by no means successful and there were clear agglomerations of marked individuals. For reference, I divided the Serengeti plains into a number of areas (fig. 11). The boundaries of these areas were arbitrary, known to me in the field and to some extent dependent on landscape features which I could recognize. Areas farther away from my home base tended to be slightly larger than areas nearby.

An interesting set of resightings came from the hyenas marked during the dry season on the Musabi plain, which often holds large numbers of ungulates at that time. During the subsequent wet season, these hyenas were seen on the Serengeti plains, and their distribution is shown in figure 12. A few of them were resident on the Musabi plain during the rains, but most of the hyenas with their ears marked L_2R_2 spent the rains in a belt across the main Serengeti plains.

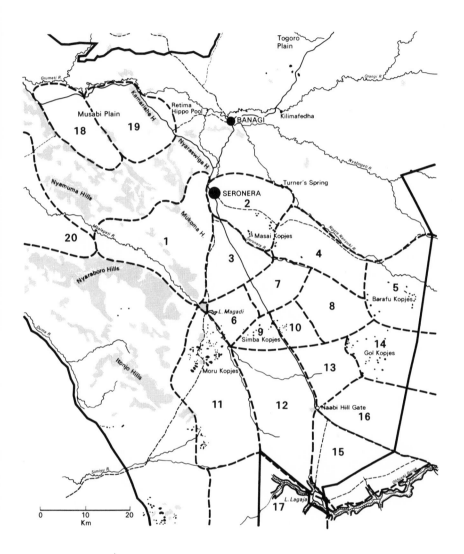

Fig. 11. Areas designated for evaluating resightings of marked hyenas in the Serengeti.

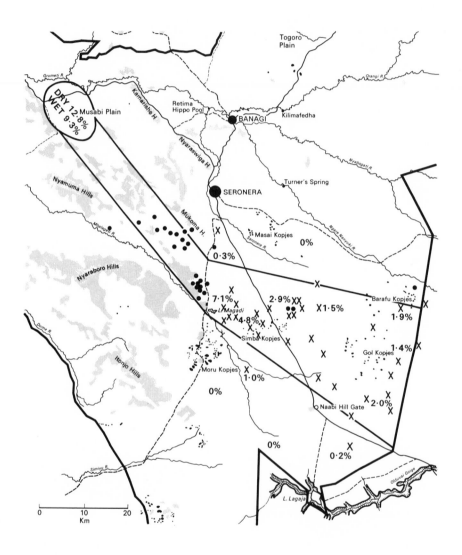

Fig. 12. Resightings of twenty-eight hyenas marked on the Musabi plains during the
dry season of 1965: × = resightings during subsequent dry seasons; ● = resightings
during subsequent wet seasons; % = percentage Musabi-marked hyenas in the total
number of hyenas observed in that area during wet seasons.

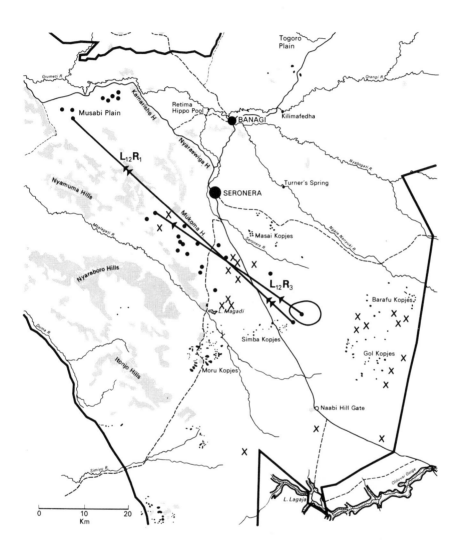

Fig. 13. Resightings of hyenas marked during the wet season near Simba kopjes (*circle*): × = resightings during subsequent wet seasons; ● = resightings during subsequent dry seasons. Lines indicate distance traveled by hyenas in five days (♂ $L_{12}R_1$, October 1965) and two days (♀ $L_{12}R_3$, November 1966). In marking area, hyenas were resighted sixteen times in the dry season and thirteen times in the wet season.

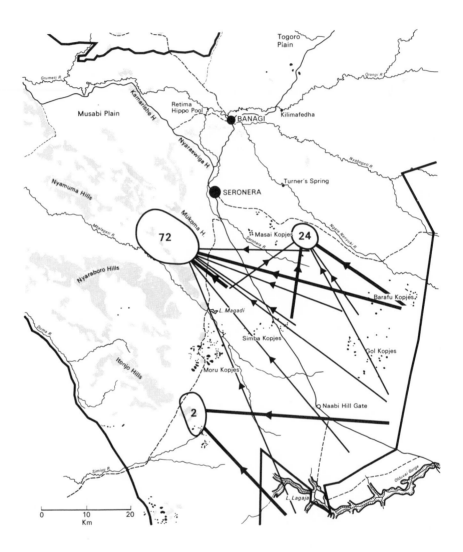

Fig. 14. Areas along the edge of the Serengeti plains, with the "wet-season origin" of marked hyenas observed there between wet and dry seasons. Thick lines connect with the areas where most marked hyenas originate—"major trends." Number of marked hyenas observed is indicated.

A similar picture is obtained if we plot the movements of hyenas marked on the central Serengeti plains during the wet season (fig. 13) and also the "origin" of marked hyenas observed between dry and wet seasons on the Mukoma plains. This is a small region at the north-western edge of the Serengeti plains which is obviously a very important area of passage for ungulates and hyenas between their wet- and dry-season ranges (fig. 14). Several individuals seen at Mukoma later turned up at Musabi. Plotting the origin of hyenas seen between wet and dry seasons at other places along the north and western edge of the plains, it seemed that hyenas there arrived from slightly different wet-season ranges (fig. 14). In general, therefore, after spending the wet season on the open Serengeti plains, hyenas moved northwest of the plains during the dry season.

Dry-season movements. I have little information about how far the plains hyenas move in this northwest direction and to what extent they move on into the northern extension of the national park. The absence of resightings west of Musabi-Nyamuma ("midwest") indicates that they go little beyond that area, although the plains in the "far west" may have fair numbers of hyenas in the dry time. These are probably mostly "resident" hyenas remaining in the west of the park the whole year round, concentrating on any area that has a fair population of game. One rarely sees many hyenas at any one time in the northern extension of the national park, with the occasional exception of the nearby Togoro plains. This dearth of hyenas is especially striking in the most northern area (around the Mara River), even when the large concentrations of wildebeest are there; corpses of ungulates lie unattended by any car-nivore, and there are few hyena tracks and droppings about. In 3.8 flying hours during the early morning hours of the dry season (Septem-ber) of 1969, I saw six hyenas there (1.6 per hour) amid the wildebeest, whereas in the same period in similar habitat between Musabi and the Serengeti plains, I saw twenty-one in 1.5 hours (14 per hour). It is most likely that during the whole of the dry season, the area north of the Mbalangeti River and southwest of the Seronera River, east of Kirawira and south of the park's boundary, hold the majority of the Serengeti hyenas.

At this point is is useful to look again at the distribution of ungulates in the dry season (figs. 2, 3, 4). From their wet-season ranges on the central plains, the main concentrations of all three important herbivore species moved northwest, the bulk of the wildebeest more west (Musabi-

Kirawira area), the zebra more to the northern half of the park, and the gazelle in between, staying in the woodlands immediately west and northwest of the plains. These populations were not stationary during the dry season, however, and the maps indicate only the total time spent. For some of the time during every dry season, the wildebeest moved from the west to the north of the park (on the Mara River), but there were also always some migratory herds left in the west. The same held true for the other species—the concentrations might be temporarily elsewhere but there were always some of their numbers remaining in the west of the park. The hyena population therefore moved during the dry season to the area which is central in the distribution of the ungulates. There is some tendency to stay in close proximity to the wildebeest herds, but this is far less pronounced than during the wet season.

In this dry-season range, hyenas find themselves together with individuals from many different wet-season areas. For instance, one early morning in November 1966 I found a group of hyenas with a wildebeest kill, just after they had pulled the victim down. There were twenty-one hyenas in all, of which four were marked; one had a Musabi cut and the others had been marked in three different areas of the central Serengeti plains (about 60 km east, 20 km east-southeast, 70 km southeast respectively). There was no animosity between any of these individuals, save of course for the usual scuffling over a kill. In figure 15, three such cases have been illustrated.

These groups in which hyenas are included who originated from very different areas often establish themselves in an area for a period of weeks, apparently behaving very much like the resident clans of Ngorongoro. They also defend their range against other clans (chapter 6). This happens especially in those places where there is a temporary high concentration of ungulates, for instance at the edge of the Serengeti plains at the end of the dry season when wildebeest are amassing there to spill out onto the plains as soon as the grass greens. Then, when the ungulates spread out and away from such an area, the hyena groups also dissolve. Places which have a resident hyena population may suddenly see their numbers of hyena swell when the migrating ungulates move through (for example, the Musabi plains and Seronera); the new arrivals associate with the residents for the time being, disappearing again when food grows short.

Wet-season movements.   Of the hyenas marked during the wet season, 37% were seen in the same area of the Serengeti plains where they had

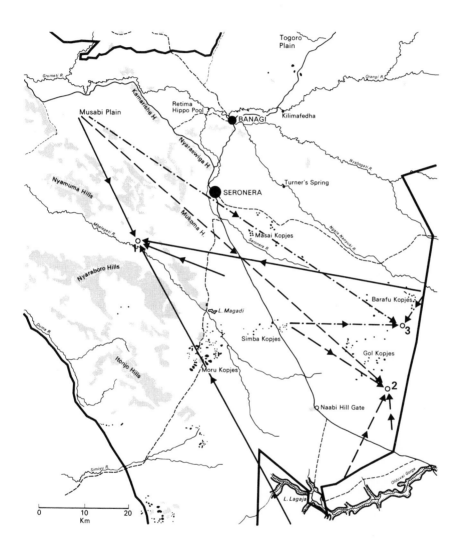

Fig. 15. Three instances of hyenas marked in different places observed feeding together on a kill (1, 2), or lying together in a waterhole (3).

been marked, when they were resighted in subsequent wet seasons. This means that there is a clear tendency to return to the area of marking in following seasons, and this is probably even stronger than expressed in the 37%; this percentage merely indicates the amount of time spent in the area where the animals were first encountered. Presumably, most hyenas are based in one particular spot during every wet season and from there go on foraging expeditions. Hyenas marked in areas which, during the wet season, almost always have some ungulates, for instance around Lake Lagarja, stick more to that area than those which were marked in areas that even in the wet season are temporarily devoid of game. Of wet-season resightings of hyenas marked just northeast of Lagarja, 90% (forty-eight observations) were in that same area, whereas this holds good in only 5% (nineteen observations) of resightings of hyenas marked northeast of the Simba kopjes. Quite likely, these last hyenas were only passing through the area when they were caught there.

Apart from the return to a certain "home area," no particular pattern can be discerned in the distribution of wet-season resightings—away from the home area, hyenas seem to move randomly on the Serengeti plains as far as the geography is concerned. The few hyenas that live in the woodlands during the rainy season probably reside there the whole year round, centered in areas where there are resident herds of topi, zebra, and so on. Some hyenas marked on the Musabi plains during the dry season also lived there during the rains and were seen during all seasons; each of the larger plains farther west in the park has its own resident population of hyenas, especially around Kirawira and the Dutwa plains.

Although, during the rains, the hyenas on the Serengeti plains appear to move around randomly, it is not at all unlikely that their movements are associated with those of the herbivores. The follow-up of the large Serengeti migrations by hyenas and other predators is well known among hunters and tourists (e.g., Huxley 1964). I have tried to establish whether one can, indeed, observe such an association between hyenas and any of the common ungulates when they are all out on the Serengeti short-grass plains.

During the wet season in short-grass areas, it is possible to get an idea of the hyena population by scanning the area with field glasses between six and eight o'clock in the morning. Undoubtedly, some are overlooked, but for comparative purposes this counting method is useful (provided that, in comparisons, the habitat is exactly the same—in this case very short grass). Using straight tracks and the park boundary, I stopped the Land Rover at 1.6-km intervals, counted the hyenas (if any) that I saw within an estimated 0.8 km from the car and the wildebeest, zebra, Thomson's gazelle, and other antelopes within 1.6 km. For the ungulates, I noted if there were fewer than 100, fewer than 1,000, or more than 1,000. For the main calculation, I only used the criterion presence or absence of any of a particular species, and tried to assess whether the presence of hyenas was related to that of any of the herbivores.

TABLE 9 *Coefficients of association[a] between hyenas and ungulates on the short-grass Serengeti plains, wet season, presence/absence only*

	Wildebeest	Zebra	Gazelle
Hyena	0.60 ± 0.09	0.08 ± 0.11	−0.27 ± 0.28
Wildebeest		0.38 ± 0.10	−0.20 ± 0.30
Zebra			0.49 ± 0.65

NOTE: Based on appendix D. 6.
[a] Cole 1947.

The results of these observations are given in table 9 and appendix D. 6 and can be summarized as follows:

There was a highly significant association between hyenas and wildebeest, virtually no association between hyenas and zebra, and a nonsignificant (negative) association between hyenas and Thomson's gazelle. Also, there was a significant association between wildebeest and zebra, and a nonsignificant negative association between wildebeest and Thomson's gazelle. These observations were made over a number of days in different periods when the ungulate distribution was often completely changed, and there was little doubt that the association between hyenas and wildebeest was caused by simultaneous fluctuations in numbers in various areas. Most likely, of course, hyenas follow the wildebeest herds rather than vice versa.

It may be that the tendency of hyenas to stick to wildebeest herds rather than to herds of any of the other ungulates is merely an attraction to large numbers; wildebeest aggregate in much larger groups than the others. However, there is little evidence for this; there is no obvious relation between the numbers of zebra and the presence or absence of hyenas (table 10), and the figures are not very conclusive for wildebeest either.[9]

TABLE 10 *Associations between different densities of hyenas and zebra and wildebeest*

	Zebra		
Hyenas	0	less than 100	100–1,000
0	18	21	10
1–8	22 } 59%	28 } 58%	7 } 43%
9–20	4	1	1
	44	50	18

	Wildebeest		
Hyenas	0	less than 1,000	1,000–10,000
0	33	13	3
1–8	9 } 25%	28 } 71%	20 } 89%
9–20	2	0	4
	44	41	27

The degrees of association were calculated for one type of habitat only, the short-grass plains during the wet season. They may not be applicable to other habitats and conditions, but at least they partly explain the hyenas' movements in the wet season.

During the rainy season, from about November until May, the wildebeest herds are on the open plains, moving into the woodlands only when the rains stop and few or no rainwater pools are left. When they are on the open Serengeti plains, they are concentrated and at any particular time occupy only part of the vast expanses of grassland, moving across it in dense herds. This is true, too, of the zebra and Thomson's gazelle, though these are usually more scattered. The gazelle, moreover, are habitually on shorter grass areas than the others and there is little overlap between their concentrations and those of wildebeest—hence the negative association indicated above. Zebra are often found near wildebeest herds.

The movements of wildebeest across the wet-season Serengeti plains are apparently followed by the hyenas—I have shown before that in the dry season, the picture is rather different. During the rains, the hyenas'

9. Hyenas present versus absent at ungulate density high versus low: zebra, $\chi^2 = 0.51$; $df = 1$; $p < 0.50$; and wildebeest, $\chi^2 = 2.78$; $df = 1$; $p < 0.30$.

movements in the Serengeti appear to be determined largely by the tendency to stay in a certain area and by the pull of the wildebeest herds; during the dry season, hyenas are less inclined to follow the wildebeest migrations (but see p. 72).

Movements and dens. One interesting aspect of the hyena movements in the Serengeti is the change in denning sites. First there is a change in location, as might be expected; the majority of dens move to the edges of the plains with the dry season, whereas they are found spread out over the plains during rains (fig. 16). During the rains, 13% of the dens I knew were within 5 km of the woodland edge of the plains, and during the dry season this was true of 72%.[10] There are only a few exceptions, dens which are permanent or semipermanent. With the move, dens also change in size; the average number of cubs per den is only 4.4 in the wet season on the plains, but is 7.2 during the dry time of the year (fig. 17).[11] This is probably because a greater number of females den together during the dry season. Plotting the distribution of cubs over various den sizes (fig. 17), it is most likely that females in the wet season are about equally inclined to attach themselves to a small or a large den (or have their cubs completely separate from other hyenas) but are much more likely to bring their litters together in large groups in the dry time.

From these large dry-season dens, regular hyena paths can be seen radiating out. These do not lead in all directions, however; from almost all the dens that I have looked at, there was one favored direction in which the main trail disappeared, somewhere between west and north —the direction in which the large herds were to be found. I could follow some of these trails over long distances, up to 15 km, but then they faded out or disappeared, often into thick bushland. In figure 16, I have indicated the direction in which the main trail left some of the large dens.

During the dry season, there is often no game around these hyena dens, but the hyena trails suggest from which direction the den inhabitants get their food supply. This was confirmed in another way as well: when analyzing fresh droppings of hyenas, I often found large quantities of wildebeest and zebra hair (p. 72), prey which must have been eaten at least 30 km away from the dens and often farther. In those

10. Dens near/away from woodland edge of plains in dry/wet season: $\chi^2 = 12.93$; $df = 1$; $p < 0.001$.

11. Number of cubs per den, dry/wet season: Mann-Whitney U test: $U = 300$; $z = -3.03$; $p = 0.0012$.

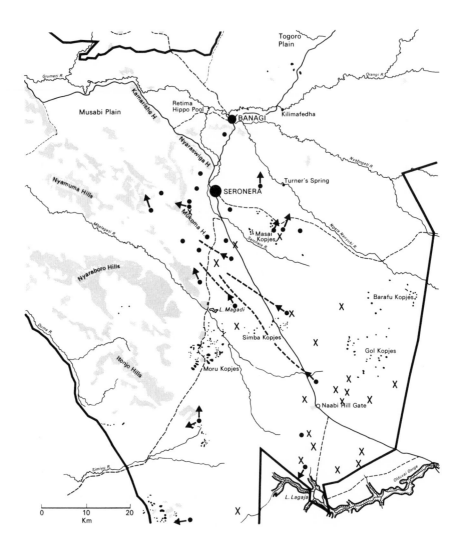

Fig. 16. Locations of some hyena dens on the Serengeti plains. × = wet-season observations; ● = dry-season observations; dotted line with arrows = main path leading from den.

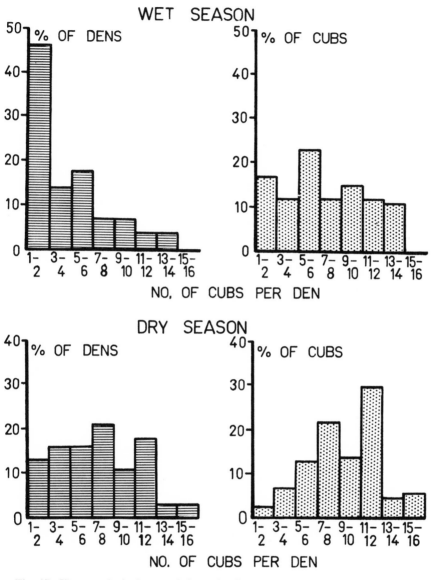

Fig. 17. Hyena cubs in Serengeti dens of different sizes, in wet and dry seasons.

areas along the northwestern edge of the Serengeti plains, one regularly sees hyenas in the evening walking steadily northwest in the direction of the large herds and disappearing into the woodlands; in the morning there is a general trend of hyenas moving the other way toward the dens, often at a slow gallop, with mouths frothing after the long journey.

On three occasions I saw individually marked animals one day on the Serengeti plains and a few days later near the wildebeest herds. A particular male was seen on a den at the plains edge and one and one-half days later amid the nearest wildebeest herds at Musabi, 47 km away. Six days after that I saw him back again on the plains edge, slowly galloping from the direction of the Musabi plains. A month later he was out with the wildebeest migration on the open Serengeti plains, about 100 km from Musabi. Another hyena, also a male, came in less than five days from a den near Simba kopjes on the central Serengeti plains to the nearest wildebeest herds in Musabi, a distance of 70 km. On yet another occasion, I saw a marked female suckling her cubs on the den at the plains edge and one and one-half days later I found her 40 km away, walking fast toward Musabi. Eloff (1964) found that hyenas in the Kalahari may walk in one night to a feeding place 40 km away from their den and back—a total of 80 km.

These incidental observations add up to the following general picture. When the migratory herds of ungulates are withdrawn from the Serengeti plains far into the woodlands, the hyena population concentrates along the edges of the plains and in the adjoining woodlands, following the wildebeest some distance but not all the way. Hyenas concentrate their dens from many small ones into fewer larger ones and from there make foraging trips to wherever the herds of ungulates happen to be nearest. Some hyenas remain with the wildebeest herds almost permanently, but at least some others travel up and down from dens on the edge of the plains.

An important aspect of the commuting way of life of many hyenas, especially during the dry season, is that mothers with suckling cubs have to leave their young behind, often for several days. Five of the fourteen females caught near the wildebeest herds at Musabi had very large udders, in two of them so large that they chafed against their hind legs, causing skin abrasion. One female on a den near Mukoma stayed away from the den at least three days; on her return she fed her six-month cubs and stayed with them for at least two days. I was reasonably certain that one other female in the same area did not see her cubs for at least three days before she returned; her cubs were between seven and nine months old. But probably the mothers often have to stay away for much longer than the three days that I observed when the herds are such huge distances away from the hyena dens. Cubs in such commuter dens often appear to be in bad condition, thin and lethargic, and I am fairly sure that during these times many cubs die.

This point is very difficult to assess quantitatively because at times cubs remain in their holes for a whole day, and if one does not see a particular cub near the hole where it was last seen, it may also mean that it has moved rather than died. I did find three that died, however, almost certainly of starvation (two of one month and one of five months old).

Hyena Movements in Ngorongoro and Serengeti: A Comparison

One immediate conclusion of the previous pages is that although the hyenas in the crater are residential, the ones in the Serengeti are mostly on the move—the residential versus the migratory system. However, it is not only differences that are important here, and it must be stressed that in each system there are clear elements of the other. For instance, the hyenas in Ngorongoro sometimes change clans, they go on foraging expeditions into their neighbor's range if prey conditions are more favorable there, and they even set up new groups in previously unoccupied ranges if these have filled up with game.

In the Serengeti, there is a clear tendency to return to the same ground in subsequent seasons, and territories are set up whenever a larger density of hyenas is staying in any one area over a length of time. Hyenas do move around with the ungulates, but they do not go the whole way of the wildebeest migration; usually the hyena concentrations are lagging behind those of the wildebeest, staying rather more in the center of the map, whereas the ungulates move from one edge to another. Except in a few areas with resident game, the clan system is very unstable in the Serengeti; groups exist for short periods only, then break up when individuals move in different directions, establishing new bonds elsewhere.

Thus, the Serengeti system is generally more variable than the one in the Ngorongoro Crater, and also less successful, if success is expressed as number of hyenas per unit prey or per km^2. There are many aspects in the hyena's biology which are difficult to reconcile with a migratory way of life, for instance the long period of dependence on the mother and the relative immobility of cubs. This could be overcome if cubs were born only at the most favorable time of the year, but they are not (fig. 6). It would also be an advantage if hyenas would care for each other's cubs. On the other hand, there are several behavior patterns which are clearly connected with the defense of a territory (chap. 6)— the "border patrols," the various ways of scent marking, direct aggression to intruders—all of which are shown by Serengeti hyenas and which often seem rather out of context.

It is tempting, therefore, to describe the Serengeti system of hyena movements and residence and the conditions there as suboptimal. Hyenas seem much better adapted to conditions in the Ngorongoro Crater and many of their behavior patterns fit in very well with their existence in resident clans.

4 Food Ecology

In this chapter I would like to evaluate my food-habit data in order to arrive at a conclusion about the "impact" of the whole hyena population in the Serengeti and Ngorongoro on the ungulates in these areas. This was, in fact, the major question at the outset of this project, and it is here that the hyena work links up with other studies in these areas, especially those on population dynamics of the wildebeest (Watson 1967; Sinclair, 1970).

I will first present evidence about the diet of hyenas, and discuss various problems to be overcome. From the annual diet compared with the availability, conclusions may be drawn about the hyenas' selectivity. With this knowledge of diet, the data on the total consumption of the individual animals and on the total populations of hyenas and prey species, I have tried to evaluate the mortality caused by hyenas per year.

DIET

Direct Observations

By following hyenas in the two areas and by scanning the landscape for kills, I gradually collected evidence for the range of food items eaten by hyenas; several persons also told me about their observations and kindly allowed me to use these, especially Dr. George Schaller.

Tables 11 and 12 list all observations over the study period of hyenas eating carcasses, killed or scavenged, and the number of hyenas involved in those observations. I have presented separately those observations which were concerned with hyena-killed victims and the number of hyenas involved in eating from hyena-killed prey. The tables list food species of any size between a termite and a buffalo, a list of names which could probably be considerably increased with more observation.

Hyenas have been found to catch fish (Stevenson-Hamilton 1947), tortoise (Pienaar 1969), man (Balestra 1962), black rhino (Deane 1962),

Table 11 *Food of hyenas in Serengeti, direct observations*

Prey species	No. of carcasses from kills + scavenging		No. of hyenas eating from kills + scavenging		Kills only, number of carcasses		Kills only, no. of hyenas eating	
Wildebeest, adult	199	(38.8%)	1,824	(55.8%)	85	(38.4%)	1,073	(59.8%)
Wildebeest, calf	64	(12.5%)	305	(9.3%)	33	(14.9%)	191	(10.6%)
Zebra, adult	55	(10.7%)	478	(14.6%)	19	(8.6%)	242	(13.5%)
Zebra, foal	13	(2.5%)	62	(1.9%)	4	(1.8%)	17	(0.9%)
Tommy, adult	101	(19.7%)	323	(9.9%)	32	(14.5%)	103	(5.7%)
Tommy, fawn	49	(9.6%)	89	(2.7%)	30	(13.6%)	50	(2.8%)
Grant, adult	4	(0.8%)	11	(0.3%)	1	(0.5%)	4	(0.2%)
Grant, fawn	3	(0.6%)	3	(0.1%)	3	(1.4%)	3	(0.2%)
Topi, adult	2	(0.4%)	23	(0.7%)	1	(0.5%)	1	(0.1%)
Topi, juvenile	3	(0.6%)	13	(0.4%)	3	(1.4%)	13	(0.7%)
Kongoni, adult	1	(0.2%)	16	(0.5%)	1	(0.5%)	16	(0.9%)
Waterbuck, adult	1	(0.2%)	37	(1.1%)	1	(0.5%)	37	(2.1%)
Eland, adult	2	(0.4%)	30	(0.9%)	1	(0.5%)	25	(1.4%)
Buffalo, adult	3	(0.6%)	28	(0.9%)	—	—	—	—
Impala, adult	1	(0.2%)	10	(0.3%)	1	(0.5%)	10	(0.6%)
Warthog	4	(0.8%)	7	(0.2%)	1	(0.5%)	3	(0.2%)
Hare	1	(0.2%)	1	(0.03%)	1	(0.5%)	1	(0.1%)
Springhare	1	(0.2%)	4	(0.1%)	1	(0.5%)	4	(0.2%)
Ostrich eggs	1	(0.2%)	1	(0.03%)	1	(0.5%)	1	(0.1%)
Bat-eared fox	1	(0.2%)	—	—	1	(0.5%)	—	—
Golden jackal	2	(0.4%)	5	(0.2%)	1	(0.5%)	1	(0.1%)
Afterbirth	2	(0.4%)	2	(0.1%)	—	—	—	—
	513	(100.2%)	3,272	(100.06%)	221	(100.6%)	1,795	(100.2%)
Total wildebeest + zebra + tommy/ grant		(95.2%)		(94.6%)		(93.7%)		(93.7%)

hippo calves (Cullen 1969), young elephant (Bere 1966), pangolin (Pienaar 1969), python (J. Goddard, personal communication), and a vast number of different species of ungulates (e.g. Matthews 1939*b*; Deane 1962; Eloff 1964; Hirst 1967; Pienaar 1969). Lions are readily eaten by them, as are jackals and domestic dogs (Pienaar 1969). The literature is flooded with references to the hyenas' habit of scavenging around human habitation and, as Matthews (1939*b*) says, "no carrion is too foul for its taste." In the Kruger National Park, they even have acquired the habit of begging along roadsides (Pienaar 1963, 1969).

Despite the variety of food indicated, the great majority of my observations deal with medium-sized ungulates, and in both Ngorongoro

TABLE 12 *Food of hyenas in Ngorongoro, direct observations*

Prey species	No. of carcasses from kills + scavenging		No. of hyenas eating from kills + scavenging		Kills only, number of carcasses		Kills only, no. of hyenas eating	
Wildebeest, adult	131	(44.1%)	2,758	(62.6%)	109	(44.6%)	2,571	(64.5%)
Wildebeest, calf	74	(24.9%)	394	(8.9%)	69	(28.3%)	374	(9.4%)
Zebra, adult	36	(12.2%)	701	(15.9%)	29	(11.1%)	595	(14.9%)
Zebra, foal	18	(6.1%)	318	(7.2%)	18	(7.4%)	318	(8.0%)
Tommy, adult	5	(1.7%)	28	(0.6%)	—	—	—	—
Tommy, fawn	10	(3.4%)	13	(0.3%)	7	(2.9%)	10	(0.3%)
Grant, adult	5	(1.7%)	47	(1.1%)	1	(0.4%)	8	(0.2%)
Grant, fawn	1	(0.3%)	1	(0.02%)	1	(0.4%)	1	(0.03%)
Waterbuck, adult	1	(0.3%)	7	(0.2%)	1	(0.4%)	7	(0.2%)
Buffalo, adult	1	(0.3%)	69	(1.6%)	1	(0.4%)	69	(1.7%)
Hare	1	(0.3%)	1	(0.02%)	1	(0.4%)	1	(0.03%)
Porcupine	1	(0.3%)	8	(0.2%)	1	(0.4%)	8	(0.2%)
Puff adder	1	(0.3%)	1	(0.02%)	1	(0.4%)	1	(0.03%)
Domestic stock	1	(0.3%)	19	(0.4%)	—	—	—	—
Bat-eared fox	1	(0.3%)	4	(0.1%)	1	(0.4%)	4	(0.1%)
Lion	1	(0.3%)	4	(0.1%)	—	—	—	—
Hyena	5	(1.7%)	21	(0.5%)	1	(0.4%)	12	(0.3%)
Termites	3	(1.0%)	9	(0.2%)	3	(1.2%)	9	(0.2%)
Afterbirth	1	(0.3%)	1	(0.02%)	—	—	—	—
	297	(99.8%)	4,404	(100.18%)	244	(99.9%)	3,988	(100.09%)
Total wildebeest + zebra + tommy/ grant		(94.4%)		(96.6%)		(95.9%)		(97.3%)

and the Serengeti, observations of hyenas feeding on wildebeest were more frequent than observations of eating any of the other species. In the Ngorongoro Crater, zebra take a clear second place and Thomson's gazelle third, whereas in the Serengeti the positions of these last two species are reversed. However, before further considering these figures as representative of the hyenas' diet in the two areas, we will have to deal with a number of possible sources of bias which might cause my data to differ from the actual hyena diet.

When one hyena is eating a small Thomson's gazelle fawn, it may take less than two minutes for the victim to disappear completely, eaten in utter silence. Clearly, this is a relatively inconspicuous affair compared with, say, twenty-five hyenas noisily eating an adult wildebeest, which often takes more than an hour. This difference in detection probability must have influenced my figures in a way that would be virtually impossible to correct. If all the tabulated figures had been collected merely by following individual hyenas on their foraging expeditions, there would not have been such bias, but it is likely to arise when an observer is scanning an area for eating hyenas. A further source of error might be that hyenas kill different species of prey at different times of the day; I had the impression, for instance, that Thomson's gazelle were more likely to be killed during the day than wildebeest or zebra. Since my observations were not equally distributed over day and night and since when observing during the day a much larger area can be covered than at night, this possibility of mistake may also have been affecting my results. Then, the different habitat preferences of prey species lead to these species' being killed in areas with different changes of detection, a bias which is most obvious when, for instance, comparing the chance of seeing a gazelle or an impala being killed. All together, the number of possible biases in this kind of observation are many, and I did not feel justified in accepting any conclusions from these direct field observations without information obtained in an entirely different manner, in this case by fecal analysis.

Fecal Analysis

Hyena feces are large, almost always bright white, and usually conspicuous in the field. I collected especially in the areas around hyena dens, but sometimes also from other places within the area sampled. Hyenas frequently deposit their droppings in special "latrines" (p. 258), which could make the collecting of samples very easy. However, since these latrines are often situated on the boundary between two clan ranges and are then used by members of both clans, I could not use them in areas where I was interested in the difference in food of two neighboring groups. Usually only feces less than a few days old were collected. In general there was no difficulty in obtaining enough samples, although it was not easy to collect them during the rainy season. This was so not only because feces were less easy to find in the tall grass but also because at that time two species of dung beetle, *Trox tuberosus* and *T. luridus* (ident. R. H. Carcasson, National Museum, Nairobi), disposed of them in a short time. Each set of droppings was collected at any one time from any one area. A total of 810 samples were taken to the laboratory in polythene bags and dried in the sun until they were lumps of dry bone powder with a little hair of the prey. To extract the hair, I ground the droppings in an electric coffee grinder or a mortar, retaining the hair after sieving off the powder.

The hair was then collected in glass tubes and all samples were stored in the Serengeti Research Institute.

Hairs were identified under a binocular microscope with reflected light, usually with magnifications of less than 32 ×. For identification, I made a reference collection of hair from all species of larger mammals from the Serengeti and Ngorongoro, from several species kept in the area as domestic stock, and from a number of small rodents. These hairs either were collected from animals found dead in the field or were kindly given to me by the curators of the National Museum in Nairobi and the Museum of the Mweka School of African Wildlife Management. For recognition of hair, characters such as shape, overall length, overall width, and pigmentation were used. Although it could be difficult to identify a single hair, it turned out that almost invariably only one or two different species of prey were represented in any one set of droppings of the hyena. This enormously facilitated identification of the prey.

For the quantitative evaluation of the analysis of carnivore feces, several methods have been proposed (for a review see, among others, Lockie 1959). I had several reasons to suspect that there would not be a useful relation between the quantity of hair found in a set of droppings and the amount of that particular prey species ingested, as Lockie showed for foxes. Although the hyena eats its prey with the skin, a large proportion of it is regurgitated; moreover, since at a kill some hyenas eat very little skin, whereas others eat a great deal of it, one could expect a relation between food and hair in the feces to be blurred by considerable variation. I decided, therefore, that only a presence/ absence way of scoring would be practical, and the results are presented in tables 13 and 14. It should be remembered, of course, that the totals of tables 13 and 14 are not comparable with those of tables 11 and 12, as the former are made up of collections that were purposely nonrandom.

Several sources of bias could act on this evaluation. For instance, the amount of hair per pound of flesh varies between prey species, and it might be that, for instance, an average hyena meal of zebra leaves its traces over a longer series of droppings than an average hyena meal of wildebeest. To some extent, this effect will be counteracted by the hyena's passing more hair per dropping of the relatively hirsute species, an effect which would go undetected in my scoring method. If a hyena eats a really large quantity of hair in one session, he will regurgitate this afterward and this could affect the results from different species differently. All these variables, and there may be more, may have acted on

TABLE 13 *Serengeti, hair of prey in hyena feces*

Samples containing hair of:	Plains Dry season	%	Plains Wet season	%	Woodlands Dry season	%	Woodlands Wet season	%	Overall total No.	%
Wildebeest	49	19.4	138	50.0	46	43.8			233	35.4
Zebra	49	19.4	61	22.1	21	20.0			131	19.9
Gazelle	123	48.6	68	24.6	23	21.9			214	32.5
Topi/kongoni	26	10.3	2	0.6	6	5.7	7	29	41	6.2
Impala	4	1.6	1	0.4	5	4.8	11	46	21	3.2
Buffalo							4	17	4	0.6
Ostrich	1	0.4							1	0.2
Mongoose	1	0.4							1	0.2
Small bird			1	0.4					1	0.2
Domestic stock			4	1.4	4	3.8	2	8	10	1.5
Unidentified			1	0.4					1	0.2
Total	253	100.1	276	99.9	105	100.0	24	100	658	100.1
No. of samples	147		172		65		17		401	

TABLE 14 *Ngorongoro, hair of prey in hyena feces*

Samples containing hair of:	Clan range													Total		Total without airstrip	
	Airstrip		Mungi		Scratching Rocks		Oldonyo Rumbe		Lakeside								
	No.	%	No.	%	No.	%	No.	%	No.	%				No.	%	No.	%
Wildebeest	46	39	42	49	74	60	105	58	75	54				342	52.8	296	55.8
Zebra	16	14	38	44	36	29	56	31	36	26				182	28.2	166	31.3
Gazelle	11	9	5	6	8	6	20	11	25	18				69	10.7	58	10.9
Kongoni			1	1	1	1								1	0.2	1	0.2
Eland					3	2								4	0.6	4	0.8
Domestic stock	43	37							1	1				44	6.8	1	0.2
Unidentified	1	1			2	2			2	1				5	0.8	4	0.8
Total	117	100	86	100	124	100	181	100	139	100				647	100.1	530	100.00
No. of samples	78		50		84		128		86					426		348	

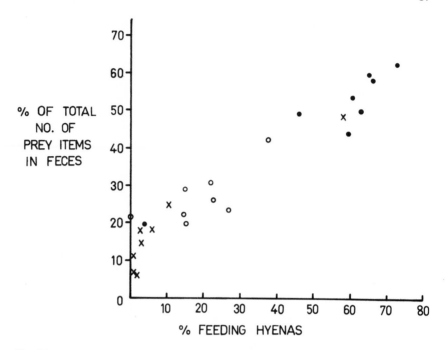

Fig. 18. Prey remains in feces versus number of hyenas feeding on those prey species. Presented are the percentages of wildebeest (●), zebra (○), and gazelle (×) in feces plotted against percentages of numbers of hyenas seen feeding on these prey species, in eight areas of the Serengeti and Ngorongoro.

my results, and I have found no way to estimate how. But almost certainly the direction of the possible biases in fecal analysis is different from that in direct observations; for instance, the relatively hairy species are the smaller ones, and therefore might be overrepresented in feces, but underrepresented in direct observations.

However, in figure 18 I have plotted the percentages of total occurrence of wildebeest, zebra, and Thomson's gazelle in feces from different ranges in Ngorongoro and from areas in the Serengeti at different times of the year against percentages of actual observations of individual hyenas feeding in those areas at the same time. There appears to be a close correlation between the two sets of observations. Thomson's gazelle may be either relatively underrepresented in direct kill observations or overrepresented in fecal analyses, and vice versa for the wildebeest. These differences are relatively small, however, and I have decided that the corroboration of field observations by the results from hyena droppings is sufficient evidence to rely on these direct field observations as a reasonably accurate representation of the hyenas' diet in the various areas. It means that even if my observation methods are suffering from some biases, those biases tend to cancel each other out. This is probably not true for observations on wildebeest calves (which have been left out of the above comparison of fecal data and direct observations); this will be discussed below.

Seasonal Fluctuations

It was not always possible to collect the same number of observations each month, partly because of variations in terrain accessibility, visibility in different habitats, and so on. For an evaluation of the overall annual diet, it was necessary to assess seasonal fluctuations in the hyena food, and in figure 19 I have plotted the hyena diet at various periods of the year, presented as the percentage that each prey species constituted of the total number of direct observations during the period over the three years of study. Data from several months have been drawn together to avoid making the total number of observations per period too small. In this way, the year was divided up into five periods, approximately corresponding with the short dry season, the long rains, first and second half of the dry season, and the short rains.

In the following pages, I have ignored one observation 16 November 1966 when hyenas killed many gazelle without eating them. This appears to be a very rare occurrence and has been discussed separately on p. 89.

It is clear that there are considerable fluctuations in the hyena diet. The most striking seasonal phenomenon occurs in the consumption of wildebeest calves, especially in the Ngorongoro Crater; it seems likely that in that area the sudden availability of large quantities of very vulnerable wildebeest calves determines these annual fluctuations to a

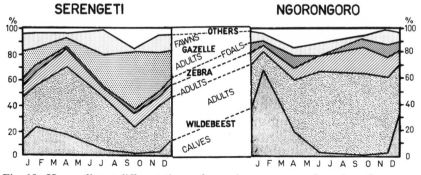

Fig. 19. Hyena diet at different times of year, in percentage of number of carcasses consumed.

large extent. This is less so in the Serengeti, although there wildebeest calves are available in very much the same fashion as in Ngorongoro; it may well be that there the other kinds of prey are relatively more vulnerable (p. 102), and therefore the availability of wildebeest calves does less to change the overall availability of food. In the Serengeti there is also a large change in the hyenas' diet at the time when the wildebeest herds leave the open Serengeti plains and disappear in the bush country; more hyenas are then seen eating gazelle, which stay on the plains longer than the wildebeest. But there is a catch here; when the wildebeest disappear in the bush country, hyena predation on their numbers is much more difficult to observe, whereas the hunting of gazelle can still be easily seen. It may well be that this part of figure 19 is not entirely accurate in indicating the change in hyena diet, but I think, nevertheless, that the observed general trend is a true one. When the wildebeest move off the plains, most hyenas are reluctant to follow them into the wooded areas, and stay at the plains' edges. From there some go on "expeditions" into the bushlands, where they prey on the large herds and return to the plains several days later. During the dry times when hyenas are on the plains at least 50 km from the nearest wildebeest, they may be seen to produce droppings full of wildebeest hair. But the extent to which this happens is very difficult to assess, as is the number of hyenas actually staying in the vicinity of the herds. What is certain is that a considerable number of hyenas are to be seen on the plains (especially on the edge of the woodlands) who, from fecal analysis, appear to be feeding mostly on gazelle (in contrast with their feeding when the wildebeest are on the plains). Thus an increase in the importance of gazelle in the hyena diet when the wildebeest move away is clearly indicated.

There is little evidence that the annual fluctuations in the hyena diet are caused by anything other than availability of the various food species. The actual mechanism of selecting prey may be complicated, but nevertheless it seems possible to explain the major seasonal fluctuations in diet on the basis of kinds of prey present.

Another point where the data presented in figure 19 are probably biased is the importance of wildebeest calves. Certainly in Ngorongoro and probably also in the Serengeti, it must have happened many times that I overlooked the killing of a wildebeest calf, whereas I was fairly certain to observe all the adult wildebeest killed at that time in the same area. Moreover, there are several indications that at the time when wildebeest calves are available the hyenas eat considerably more than at other times of the year. In Ngorongoro especially it was striking that at that time even the yearling hyenas (which so often look thin and scruffy) walked around with extended stomachs, and often abandoned a large part of the carcass to the vultures. The wildebeest calving time is the only period when, in Ngorongoro, one can see an almost complete wildebeest or zebra carcass (killed by hyenas) with most of the bones left uneaten, the head hardly touched except by vultures. At other times of the year, such a carcass would disappear within an hour (except the head, which would be eaten in a few hours save the horns and teeth), and in fact even these carcasses of animals killed in January and February are completely eaten a few weeks later. In short, at wildebeest calving time, the hyenas are probably eating so much that they are completely satiated, often eating only the choicest bits. So they are doubtless also killing more meat than at other times of the year, and therefore if we want to read figure 19 as an indication of the time when various species are eaten by hyenas, the peak for wildebeest calves in the hyena diet should be considerably higher than as drawn at present. The other kinds of prey are probably little affected.

Overall Annual Diet

Taking into account the seasonal fluctuations in the diet in figure 19, we can now estimate the percentage which each of the species mentioned makes up in the annual toll taken by the hyenas, with the

TABLE 15 *The annual diet of hyenas, corrected for seasonal fluctuations*

Prey species	Percentage of kills and scavenged carcasses	
	Serengeti	Ngorongoro
Wildebeest, adult	17.3– 39.1	48.9
Wildebeest, calf	2.1– 4.7	16.7
Zebra, adult	17.5– 18.0	12.4
Zebra, foal	1.9– 2.0	5.7
Gazelle, adult	36.2– 16.3 ⎫	7.3
Gazelle, fawn	12.4– 5.6 ⎭	
Others	12.7– 14.3	9.0
	100.0–100.0	100.0

NOTE: For the Serengeti two estimates are presented for the whole hyena population, because of the difference in dry-season observations on the plains and in the woodlands.

exception of wildebeest calves. These percentages are presented in table 15, and they are substantially the same as the "uncorrected" figures of tables 11 and 12. In calculating these annual percentages for the Serengeti, I have used not only the direct observations of hyenas feeding, but for the months June through October also results from fecal analysis of droppings collected in the wooded areas and on the plains, assuming that the actual consumption of the whole population will be somewhere between the estimates from the woodlands and the plains (the reason for this is explained on p. 72). This produced the two different estimates for the Serengeti in table 15. The fecal analysis estimates differ somewhat from those based on direct observations only in the case of wildebeest calves, adult zebra, and "other prey." Since wildebeest calves are difficult to assess as hyena food for other reasons also, I will consider them separately on p. 77, and for zebra estimates I have used figures based partly on direct, partly on fecal observations.

From table 15, we can calculate that in Ngorongoro, the adults of the main prey species occur in the hyenas diet in ratios:

$$\text{wildebeest/zebra} = 3.9/1;$$
$$\text{wildebeest/gazelle} = 14.0/1;$$
$$\text{zebra/gazelle} = 3.5/1.$$

From table 20, we can see that in the Ngorongoro herbivore population, these species occur in approximate ratios:

$$\text{wildebeest/zebra} = 3.0/1;$$
$$\text{wildebeest/gazelle} = 2.7/1;$$
$$\text{zebra/gazelle} = 0.9/1.$$

Comparing these figures, it would seem that wildebeest and zebra occur in the diet in the same ratio as in the populations, but both occur in the diet more often than would be expected if animals were eaten randomly from the present population, and gazelle occur less often. (Also, gazelle are more often scavenged from other carnivores than are wildebeest or zebra, which makes the point even stronger, p. 74.) From these figures, one cannot decide whether there is a difference in percentage of individuals which are "available" for hyena predation or whether this is a matter of active prey selection between species. Behavioral mechanisms of prey selection are discussed on p. 201, where the suggestion is made that both mechanisms are important; it is likely that at least in some cases hyenas select between prey species on the basis of previous experience with their "availability."

In the Serengeti the picture is considerably more blurred, but at least some differences from the Ngorongoro Crater are apparent. There the adults of the three prey species occur in the hyena diet:

$$\text{wildebeest/zebra} = 1.0\text{--}2.2/1;$$
$$\text{wildebeest/gazelle} = 0.5\text{--}2.3/1;$$
$$\text{zebra/gazelle} = 0.5\text{--}1.1/1;$$

whereas in the herbivore population

$$\text{wildebeest/zebra} = 1.3/1;$$
$$\text{wildebeest/gazelle} = 1.5/1;$$
$$\text{zebra/gazelle} = 1.2/1 \qquad \text{(from table 19)}.$$

In the Serengeti, the hyena's diet appears to be much more similar to the population of medium-sized ungulates present, and there is no obvious preference. This is a clear contrast to Ngorongoro and may well be related to the fact that in the Serengeti, because of the vast movements of prey species from area to area, the hyenas are inclined to take what comes.

CONSUMPTION

Consumption per Individual

In order to calculate the total annual toll taken by the whole hyena population from the herbivores, we need to know something more about the quantities each individual kills and uses. There are some captivity records about this; for instance, in zoos in Frankfurt and Basel, hyenas are kept on an average of $1\text{--}1\frac{1}{2}$ kg of meat and bones per day (Dr. R. Faust, Dr. H. Wackernagel, personal communication). I had four adult hyenas myself which were caught as adults, kept in cages of 3×6 m for seventeen days, and then released. These hyenas were fed an average of 3.5 kg per day each (meat including bone and hair) which they always eagerly finished completely. I was able to weigh only three of them before and after the experiment; Frances slimmed from 58.5 kg to 56.0 kg and Grahame from 50.8 kg to 50.3 kg, and Hugh gained weight from 45.4 kg to 48.2 kg, all three on virtually the same amount of food (Frances was very nervous and walked a great deal up and down the fence, whereas Hugh was the quietest of the four and lay down most of the time). These few data show that there may be a great deal of difference between records from captivity and also that individual differences play an important role. For these and other reasons,

I am reluctant to extrapolate data on food consumption from captivity to the natural situation, and I have tried to get direct information from the field.

One immediately encounters difficulty when trying to collect this sort of data, because hyenas are very irregular feeders. They can go without food for days—for instance, the hyena with the radio collar in Ngorongoro ate with intervals of at least 2, 2, 1, 5, and 2 days.

When they do eat, they consume large quantities in one session. Once I presented the remains of two female Thomson's gazelle (all except intestines, stomach, liver, lungs, etc.) to a male hyena I met wandering on the plain, which I estimated to weigh between 45 and 50 kg. This animal looked healthy and did not have a full stomach, but I did not know how long ago it had had its last meal. When presented with the meat, the hyena took it off and within 45 min, ate 14.5 kg of it; he was still going strong when another hyena ran up and took the last remains of the meal away from him. I then gave chase to the other hyena to recover the stolen food and managed to retrieve it before anything had been eaten, in order to weigh it again. It showed that even though the hyena had not quite finished and may not have been completely empty before he started, he had eaten almost one-third of his own body weight at one time, an exceptionally high figure for mammals. Another female hyena, obviously well fed before she began, ate 9.3 kg of a dead gazelle before leaving with the remains.

Because of the irregular way individuals feed, I decided that it would be best to try to estimate the killing rate of all the hyenas in one area, a clan territory. I used the Scratching Rocks clan in Ngorongoro for this, because its range could be overlooked from one vantage point, was very accessible by day and night, and was next to our cabin on the crater floor. During a time of the year (August to October) when I could be reasonably certain of detecting all the kills in that area at any time of the day, I watched the Scratching Rocks clan for three periods of seven, seventeen, and fourteen days. Using the estimated number of hyenas in this clan (appendix D. 1) and the estimated weight of the kinds of prey involved, I could then calculate the killing rate per hyena per day. I obtained another series of observations in the same clan range by following, with the help of radio location, one particular hyena (a female) over twelve days. Her daily food consumption was estimated by observing the feeding frequency and the share she got from any carcass, dividing the estimated weight of the kind of prey involved by the number of hyenas feeding on it. The food consumption of this female was

Table 16 *Quantities killed by hyenas in Ngorongoro*

Estimated number of hyenas	Number of days observed	Number of prey killed	Total weight killed	Per hyena per day
76	7	6	1,095 kg	2.06 kg
76	17	13	2,303 kg	1.78 kg
76	14	12	1,863 kg	1.75 kg
Average number of hyenas eating from carcass with radio-collared hyena				
36	12	5	1,069 kg	2.47 kg

Average per hyena per day: 1.98 kg

close to that of hyenas in the other estimates (table 16), and from these figures I have assessed the average daily killing rate in the dry season in the Ngorongoro at 2.0 kg per day. This includes meat scavenged by lions, jackals, and vultures, but only the amount of meat scavenged by lions is substantial in this wastage, probably 10%–20% of the kill (lions stole 31% and 26% respectively of wildebeest and zebra kills in the crater; they got substantially less than half of each kill). Actual food consumption at that time in the crater must have been 1.5–1.8 kg per hyena per day.

During the wildebeest calving season in January and February, it was obvious that hyenas were eating more than at other times. But it proved to be very difficult to estimate the number of calves killed in an area from direct observations, and I have been unable to make the same kind of observations on killing rate at that time of the year as I did during the dry season. What I actually observed killed during a twelve-day period of observation in February in the Scratching Rocks range amounted to 1.08 kg adult wildebeest per hyena per day and 0.51 kg calves, a total of 1.6 kg per hyena per day. But as was discussed before, although I could be reasonably certain to spot all adult wildebeest kills during that period, this was not so for calves. During the period in which I could account for the disappearance of 389 calves, some 3,300 must have died (killed by hyenas who ate more and left more to scavengers than usual). Applying this discrepancy as a correction factor, the hyenas of the Scratching Rocks clan must have killed $(3,300/389)0.51 = 4.3$ kg calves per hyena per day during my observation period, making a total of 5.4 kg of animals per hyena per day. Wastage is much greater during this time; of adult wildebeest killed only the meat and most of the skin is eaten, but the rest of the carcass is left (and eaten weeks or months later). Hyenas frequently kill and eat a wildebeest calf on their own, sometimes merely eating part of the soft meat and leaving the remains of it to the vultures and jackals. It is not possible to evaluate this wastage here; probably actual food consumption of hyenas at this time in the crater is in the order of 3–4 kg per day. This increase in food consumption is also indicated by the appearance of the hyenas; they look bloated at that time, even the often skeleton-thin yearlings. There is much less competition over carcasses—the number of animals feeding from an adult wildebeest is considerably lower at this time than later in the year (fig. 20).[1]

Although there is a clear increase in the killing rate during the wildebeest calving season, it is apparent that this increase is entirely at the cost of the wildebeest calves. For the purpose of evaluating the annual hyena diet from figure 19, therefore, I have assumed a constant

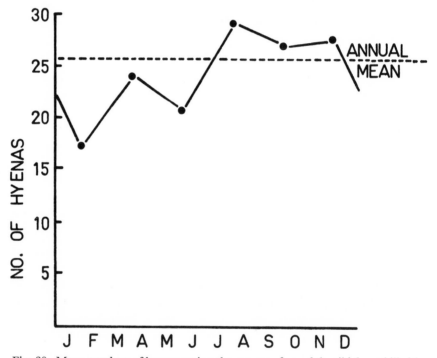

Fig. 20. Mean numbers of hyenas eating the carcass of an adult wildebeest killed by hyenas in Ngorongoro, at different times of year.

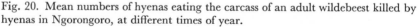

1. Number of hyenas feeding from an adult wildebeest at different times of year: $\chi^2 = 10.4$; $df = 4$; $p < 0.05$.

killing rate of 2.0 kg per hyena per day for calculating the role of adult wildebeest, zebra, and so on, in the hyena's diet. Wildebeest calves I will have to consider separately.

In the Serengeti, I have not been able to collect the same data on killing rates; it was not possible to keep one clan under observation as I did in Ngorongoro, and I did not have equipment there for radio location. There is circumstantial evidence, however, that the consumption per hyena in the Serengeti is higher than in the crater; the number

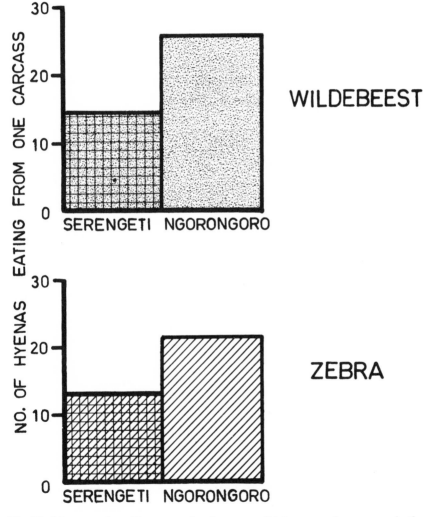

Fig. 21. Mean number of hyenas eating from one wildebeest or zebra carcass, in the Serengeti and Ngorongoro.

of hyenas per carcass is considerably smaller than in the Ngorongoro (fig. 21) and more is left when hyenas are full and finished with a carcass.[2] In other words, in Ngorongoro a carcass is completely finished in a very short time, whereas in the Serengeti hyenas cannot even eat it all, leaving especially the bones. Vultures get much more from Serengeti hyenas than from those in Ngorongoro. In view of this and keeping in mind the estimated daily killing rate of hyenas in Ngorongoro during the time of food abundance, I estimate the daily killing rate in the Serengeti to be approximately 3 kg. I use the words "killing rate" here in the sense of kilograms of meat appropriated, either killed or scavenged; the 3 kg per day also includes waste.

Total Killing Rate of the Two Hyena Populations

The estimates of hyena numbers, diet, and consumption are considerably less accurate in the Serengeti than in the Ngorongoro Crater.

TABLE 17 *Consumption by the Serengeti hyena population*

Prey species	Percentage in diet		Average weight (for sex and age ratio as consumed by hyenas)	Weight in sample of 100 prey in kg		No. of animals killed/scavenged per year by whole hyena population	
	a	a^1	b	c	c^1	d	d^1
Wildebeest adult	17.3–	39.1	172 kg	2,975.6–	6,725.2	5,592–	9,226
Wildebeest calf*	2.1–	4.7	16 kg	33.6–	75.2	679–	1,109*
Zebra adult	17.5–	18.0	232 kg	4,060.0–	4,176.0	5,657–	4,247
Zebra foal	1.9–	2.0	22 kg	41.8–	44.0	614–	472
Gazelle adult	36.2–	16.3	21 kg	760.2–	342.3	11.701–	3,846
Gazelle fawn	12.4–	5.6	2.5 kg	31.0–	14.0	4,008–	1,321
Others	12.7–	14.3	178 kg	2,260.6–	2,545.4	4,105–	3,374
	100.1	100.0		10,162.8	13,922.1	32,356	23,595

NOTE: In a, c, and d, dry-season fecal estimates from the plains are used, but in a^1, c^1, and d^1, dry-season fecal estimates from the woodlands are used.

*Underestimated; see p. 77.

$a \times b = c$ $a^1 \times b = c^1$
$d = a \times f$ $d^1 = a^1 \times f$
$f = 3,285,000/10,162.8 = 323.238$ $f = 3,285,000/13,922.1 = 235,956$
(f = weight total hyena kill/Σc)   (f = weight total hyena kill/Σc^1)

2. Number of hyenas feeding from a carcass, Ngorongoro/Serengeti, Mann-Whitney U-test: wildebeest carcass, $U = 4,684.5$; $z = 5.6$; $p < 0.00003$; and zebra carcass, $U = 153.5$; $z = 2.09$; $p = 0.0183$.

TABLE 18 *Consumption by the Ngorongoro hyena population*

Prey species	Percentage in diet	Average weight (for sex and age ratio as consumed by hyenas)	Weight in sample of 100 prey in kg	No. of animals killed/scavenged per year by whole hyena population
	a	*b*	*c*	*d*
Wildebeest adult	48.9	181 kg	8,850.9	1,140
Wildebeest calf*	16.7	16 kg	267.2	389*
Zebra adult	12.4	250 kg	3,100.0	289
Zebra foal	5.7	22 kg	125.4	133
Gazelle adult and fawn	7.3	20 kg	146.0	170
Others	9.0	108 kg	972.0	210
	100.0		13,461.5	2,331

NOTE: $a \times b = c$
$d = a \times f$
f = weight total hyena kill/Σc = 313,900/13,461.5 = 23.318
*Underestimated; see p. 77.

In comparing the figures from the two areas, I will use the highest estimate from the Serengeti, so that any bias will work against my main conclusions.

In Ngorongoro, some 430 hyenas kill or scavenge 2 kg per day each; the total population disposes of 430 × 2 × 365 = 313,900 kg per year. Similarly, in the Serengeti, 3,000 hyenas disposing of 3 kg per day each would account for 3,000 × 3 × 365 = 3,285,000 kg per year. In tables 17 and 18, I have summarized the procedure for calculating the total number of animals of each prey category taken annually by hyenas. Knowing the composition of each sample of 100 prey animals (column *a*), we can calculate the weight of that sample by using known live weights as found by Lamprey [1964], Sachs [1967], Watson [1967], and my own observations, and taking into account the sex and age composition of that kind of prey as taken by hyenas in that area; see table 23, p. 91 (column *b*). Dividing the total weight of prey taken by the hyena population per year by this weight of a sample of 100 prey animals (column *c*), we find a factor *f*, by which we multiply the number of each kind of prey in the sample of 100 in order to obtain the real number of that kind of prey taken annually by the whole hyena population (column *d*).

Before I further discuss these total numbers taken, I will consider the number of the various species concerned in the two areas.

NUMBERS OF HERBIVORES IN NGORONGORO AND THE SERENGETI

In tables 19 and 20, various estimates of the animal numbers in Ngorongoro and the Serengeti have been compiled; from these figures, I have deduced "working estimates" for the purpose of this study. The wildebeest in Ngorongoro show considerable constancy in numbers over a long period (Jaeger 1911, Swynnerton 1958), and especially during the period of study. There may have been a decline in numbers of zebra, but gazelle also appear fairly constant. In the Serengeti, the wildebeest counts suggest an increase up to 1963 (Pearsall 1957; Swynnerton 1958; Grzimek and Grzimek 1960a; Stewart and Talbot 1962), then relative constancy in numbers; this is confirmed by a recent evaluation of Watson's (1967) data on fluctuations in mortality and recruitment by Sinclair (1970). Little is known about zebra and especially about gazelle numbers in the Serengeti. Watson's (1967) gazelle figures collected with sampling methods are far out of range of Hendrichs's sample results, and several observers feel that Watson may have underestimated the numbers of gazelle. I have maintained his estimate, however, because (a) Watson's methods are the best ones used so far (aerial sampling counts in stratified areas) and (b) for many conclusions of this study, a low estimate is a conservative one. Brooks's (1961) estimate of gazelle on the Serengeti plains come close to Watson's (approximately 200,000).

Comparing the two tables, it appears that in Ngorongoro the wildebeest are relatively more numerous. The Serengeti has a larger number of other fairly abundant herbivores. But differences between the two areas are apparent especially when comparing the densities; Ngorongoro carries far higher numbers per km^2 during the whole year than the Serengeti (noted before by Talbot and Talbot 1963). At any particular moment, there are areas in the Serengeti of the size of Ngorongoro Crater that may carry a higher biomass than the crater—but the total area covered by the migrating masses of the Serengeti carries a smaller number than the Ngorongoro.

THE EFFECT OF THE HYENA POPULATION

If we express the annual takings by the whole hyena population (tables 17 and 18) as a percentage of the populations of prey species (tables 19 and 20), as I have done in table 21, the Ngorongoro hyenas

TABLE 19 *Estimates of numbers of ungulates in the Serengeti*

Prey species	May 1963 [a]	May 1965 [a]	May 1966 [a]	1967–68 [b]	1968 [c]	Estimates made for this study	Range for which estimate is valid (in km²)	Density per km²	Available per hyena (0.12 per km²)
Wildebeest	322,000 (22% calves)	381,875 (13% calves)	334,425 (9% calves)		370,000	360,000 (300,000 adults only)	25,000	14.3 (11.9 adults only)	120.0 (100.0 adults only)
Zebra			270,501		193,000	280,000	29,500	9.5	89.4
Thomson's gazelle					980,000				
Grant's gazelle			243,000		3,100	243,000	19,600	12.4	77.5
Eland					7,200	7,000	12,500	0.6	4.7
Topi			16,308	25,000	26,000	25,000	20,700	1.2	10.1
Kongoni					20,000	20,000	20,700	1.2	8.1
Buffalo				48,000	38,000	48,000	12,500	3.8	32.0
Impala				20,000	75,000	70,000	12,500	5.6	46.7
Waterbuck					3,200	3,000			1.0
Reedbuck					1,700	2,000			0.7
Warthog					17,000	17,000	12,500	1.4	11.3
Giraffe		39,000			8,000	8,000	12,500	0.6	5.3
								50.8	406.8

SOURCES: [a] Watson 1967; [b] R. Bell and A. Sinclair, personal communication; [c] H. Hendrichs, personal communication.

TABLE 20 *Estimates of numbers of ungulates in the Ngorongoro Crater*

Prey species	Dec. 1959 [a]	Sept. 1961 [b]	Feb. 1964 [c]	1964–65 [d]	March 1966 [e]	March 1968 [f]	Sept. 1968 [g]	Estimate for purpose of this study	Density per km²	Available per hyena
Wildebeest	9,721 ± 1,450	7,800	14,222 (28% calves)		11,944 (inc. calves)	14,417 (inc. calves)		13,528 (inc. calves) 10,100 (adults only)	54.1 (40.6 adults only)	30.8 (23.6 adults only)
Zebra			5,038	5,500	3,935	3,058	4,269	4,500	18.0	10.5
Thomson's gazelle			4,500	3,500				3,500	14.0	8.1
Grant's gazelle				1,500	2,377		1,376	1,500	6.0	3.5
Eland			342	350	488	355	213	400	1.6	0.9
Waterbuck			>35	150	47	26	62	60	0.2	0.1
Kongoni			>49	100	52	19	139	100	0.4	0.2
Buffalo						25	1	60	0.2	0.1
Reedbuck			11	100	67		5	60	0.2	0.1
									94.7	54.3

SOURCES: a Talbot and Talbot 1963; b Moore-Gilbert (in Dirschl 1966); c Turner and Watson 1964; d Estes 1967; e Turner and Bell (in Dirschl 1966); f Lemieux and Desmoules, personal communication; g Mweka College, personal communication.

TABLE 21 *Annual percentages of prey populations killed and scavenged by hyenas in the Serengeti and Ngorongoro*

Prey species	Serengeti		Ngorongoro	
	Killed and scavenged	Killed only	Killed and scavenged	Killed only
Wildebeest adult	1.9–3.1	1.6–2.6	11.2	11.0
Zebra adult and foal	2.2–1.7	1.0–0.8	9.4	9.0
Gazelle adult and fawn	6.5–2.1	3.5–1.1	3.4	1.8

appear to take a strikingly higher proportion of the wildebeest and zebra than their confreres in the Serengeti. This is not clear for gazelle, where hyena predation may show no difference between the two areas; it is as well to remember, however, that the total gazelle population estimates from the Serengeti may be underestimates, therefore the percentages taken by hyenas would be overestimates.

For the wildebeest in the Serengeti and Mara region, Talbot and Talbot (1963) calculated an annual adult mortality of 8% in the years 1959–61. Watson (1967) calculates an adult mortality rate of 4.2% in 1962–63 (June to June), 4.6% in 1963–64, 5.9% in 1964–65, and 15.7% in 1965–66. There are no accurate observations on the mortality in the last year of my study (1966–67), but probably it is not much lower than in 1965–66. It is clear that the 1.6%–2.6% which is annually removed by the hyenas is only a small proportion of the wildebeest's mortality; in 1965–66, hyenas killed or scavenged between 10% and 17% of the wildebeest that died during that period. However, it may well be that in 1962–65 hyenas accounted for a much larger proportion of the mortality. During the years of my study, wildebeest often died from other causes, not only predation, but also disease or starvation. Every year, especially during the height of the dry season, when the herds are up to 150 km away from the Serengeti plains on the Mara River in the north of the park, scores of wildebeest are found dead without any predators having come near them.

Watson (1967) states that the Ngorongoro wildebeest reach puberty earlier than those in the Serengeti. Bulls participate in the rut in their fourth year, and 75% of the cows mate successfully in their second year; in the Serengeti, bulls do not mate until their fifth year, and only about 35% of the cows reproduce in their second year and 80% in their third. Sinclair (1970) found in 1968 an even lower proportion of two-year-old wildebeest cows that were pregnant in the Serengeti, only one in a sample of twenty-seven. Almost all the older females in both populations reproduce at a rate of a calf every year; this means that virtually all the variation in the calf production per wildebeest cow is caused by variations in the fecundity of the youngest age classes.

Thus, the Ngorongoro wildebeest have a higher fecundity than the Serengeti ones and, as Watson points out, this means that the crater wildebeest population is either increasing faster or turning over at a faster rate. As there is no evidence of an increase after 1964, it remains that there is a higher turnover in the population of the crater or, in other words, that the wildebeest there die younger. This conclusion is confirmed by my data on the ages of hyena-killed wildebeest (p. 94).

Very little mortality is caused by agents other than hyenas in Ngorongoro; I have never found a wildebeest that died of disease in the crater, lions kill them only infrequently, and the rare wild dogs kill year-old wildebeest very occasionally, adults hardly at all (Estes and Goddard 1967). I calculated above that hyenas ate 11.1% annually of the adult wildebeest population in the crater; as this is the only important source of mortality, and the wildebeest numbers are fairly stable, one might expect this figure to be approximately matched with recruitment. The adult wildebeest population in June 1967 contained 13.6% yearlings, and 9.4% of the total population consisted of calves born earlier that year (a sample of 5,135 animals); the latter percentage will increase a little until the calves enter the adult population as yearling recruits (because most of the hyena predation is centered on the adult wildebeest after the calves are a few weeks old). Thus, recruitment is of the same magnitude as mortality from hyenas.

The fate of wildebeest calves is much more difficult to account for because of the observational bias mentioned on p. 77. For Ngorongoro, for instance, I calculated in table 18 that if hyenas ate the same quantity of food per hyena per day during the wildebeest calving season, they would account for only 390 calves. However, in 1967, there must have been some 4,300 calves born (calculated on a basis of 5,000 females, of which 14% were yearlings who did not bear calves), and a sample count in June showed that about 940 calves survived the calving season. This leaves a total of about 3,000 calves unaccounted for. Field observations leave little doubt that most calves dying are killed by hyenas, and it is also apparent that hyenas are actually eating and wasting considerably more at the time the calves are dropped. The 430 hyenas would have to kill an extra 7 calves each per calving season to explain the total losses, and this is, of course, easily possible. A similar increase in the Serengeti hyena kills would increase the estimate of total numbers of calves killed to about 22,000, a much smaller proportion than in Ngorongoro of the estimated number of calves that died in the first six months of life (61,000 in 1965, 80,000 in 1966 calculated from Watson [1967]). Although these figures are rough, they indicate the same phenomenon that is operating among the adult wildebeest; that is, that hyenas are responsible for a much smaller part of the mortality in the Serengeti than they are in the crater.

Little is known of zebra population dynamics. Klingel (1967, 1969a, b), when studying social behavior of some groups of zebra in Ngorongoro, found an annual mortality among adults of about 3%, and found that 50% of the mares had a one-year old foal. If representative of the whole population, this would have caused a large increase in the numbers of zebra, whereas in fact these were rather stable. It is likely, therefore, that Klingel's sample was not typical for the rest of the population. R. O. Skoog (personal communication) finds in the Serengeti that almost all fully adult mares are pregnant; as the mares come into estrus only a few days after giving birth and the gestation period is approximately one year, this probably means that the birth interval, and hence recruitment of foals, of the zebra is fairly similar to that of the wildebeest. If this is so, the effect of hyena predation on the zebra populations may be comparable to the effect on the wildebeest, as the percentages taken from the two species do not appear to differ greatly. But we will have to await results from studies of zebra population dynamics which are going on at present for further evaluation of the importance of hyena predation.

Information on Thomson's gazelle ecology is even scantier. Birth intervals are shorter than in the other two species, and a more rapid turnover may be expected. This means that the effect of hyena predation on mortality is relatively smaller than indicated by the percentage taken from the population, if compared with wildebeest and zebra. Here, also, other sources of mortality are clearly very important, not only in the Serengeti but also in the Ngorongoro Crater. Bourlière (1963) pointed out that tommies probably have more enemies than any of the other ungulates, and their importance to other carnivores has been confirmed by Estes and Goddard (1967), Kruuk and Turner (1967), and Schaller (1968 and personal communication). In the Serengeti, gazelle are often found with diseases or killed by disease (see p. 100); in the Ngorongoro, predation by other carnivores (especially golden and black-backed jackals and wild dogs) is likely to outstrip all other mortality sources.

In these last sections, I have treated all carcasses on which hyenas were seen feeding as "kills." This assumption is, of course, not accurate: hyenas scavenge considerably and to different extents in the two areas. This has been expressed in table 22. This may be a good time to return to this assumption and see how it affects some of the main conclusions.

TABLE 22 *Scavenging and killing of different kinds of prey by hyenas*

Prey species	Serengeti			Ngorongoro		
	% killed by hyenas	% scavenged	Total no. of carcasses	% killed by hyenas	% scavenged	Total no. of carcasses
Wildebeest adult	62.5	37.5	136	98.2	1.8	111
Wildebeest calf	68.8	31.2	48	98.6	1.4	70
Zebra adult	50.0	50.0	38	93.6	6.4	31
Zebra foal	33.0	67.0	12	100.0	0	18
Gazelle adult	41.6	58.4	77	0	100.0	4
Gazelle fawn	81.0	19.0	37	77.8	22.2	9

NOTE: Doubtful observations have been discarded.

Table 22 makes it clear that in Ngorongoro, hyenas scavenge very few wildebeest and zebra carcasses, but they usually eat gazelle after these have been killed by another predator (often wild dog or jackal). In the Serengeti, scavenging plays an important role in the acquisition of all kinds of prey. If we combine these data with the figures from tables 17 and 18 the differences between the two areas in numbers of wildebeest and zebra killed by hyenas are even more obvious than in the total numbers appropriated (table 21). It is difficult, however, to decide what importance to attach to the scavenging habit when considering the impact of hyena predation on the ungulate populations. On the one hand, it may be argued that scavenging itself does not affect population size of the prey; on the other hand, however, scavenging detracts from the food supply of other carnivores, who may then have to kill more, and it is likely that if hyenas had nothing to scavenge they would, in any case, kill for themselves. However, with the present supply of carcasses of animals dead from disease, old age, and so on, in the Serengeti, the conclusion seems warranted that scavenging there seems to detract more from the impact of the hyena population on the herbivores than in the Ngorongoro Crater; this would increase the difference between the two areas in this respect even further.

SURPLUS KILLING

In previous pages, the amount of wastage from a carcass by hyenas has usually been considered fairly low. In exceptional circumstances, however, the wastage may be colossal. Once in November 1966, a group of hyenas killed, in one night, more than 110 Thomson's gazelle and maimed many others, eating small parts of only a few victims (13 in a sample of 59). The carnage had taken place on a very dark night with heavy rain, and the hyenas had been able to kill at leisure (see also p. 204 and Kruuk 1972). Here, two points are important in discussing the effect of predators on their prey populations: first, a slaughter like this is a very rare occurrence and, second, because the hyenas ate little of what they had killed, there is probably little or no relation between numbers killed and numbers of predators present.

It would seem obvious that if this kind of event were not very rare the habit of mass killing would change the numerical predator-prey relations—there would be danger of exhaustion of food supply by the hyenas themselves. As it is, mass killing seems to be of little importance because of its rarity; I have not, therefore, considered it together with the normal foraging of hyenas. Thus, the figures of tables 11, 15, 17, 21, 22, and 23 do not include the results of this interesting "accident."

CHARACTERISTICS OF ANIMALS KILLED BY HYENAS

In evaluating the hyena's role in the population dynamics of the various prey species, it is important to know whether hyenas kill animals of either sex, of any particular age-class, unhealthy ones, and so on. Direct observations of the hyena's hunting behavior (p. 148) indicated that some clear selective processes may be at work. For instance, in wildebeest hunting I regularly saw the hunters dash into a large herd, causing the wildebeest to run; then the running hyenas would stop and look at the running animals, and so would any hyena that might be looking on along the side. Suddenly one of the onlookers might single out a wildebeest from the herd and start a chase which ended with the wildebeest's either being pulled down or escaping. I myself was rarely able to detect any difference in the animals that were chosen, at least in Ngorongoro they usually seemed to be in perfect condition. But this does not mean, of course, that the hyenas saw no difference; while some people can make a sound judgment about a horse's performance by looking briefly at its gait, I would not be able to do so, and we should not be surprised if a hyena can do even better than a horse dealer. In the following section, I want to discuss some ecological aspects of hyena prey selection, especially among wildebeest.

Selection of Sex

In figure 22, I have presented the percentage of males among the adult wildebeest killed by hyenas for various times of the year, and also the percentage of calves among all the wildebeest seen killed. In both

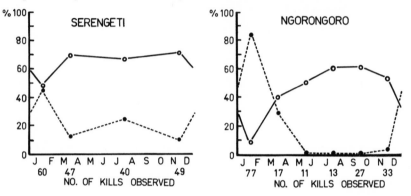

Fig. 22. Percentage of males among adult wildebeest (● ———— ●), compared with the percentage of calves among all wildebeest (● – – – ●) which were killed by hyenas in different months in the Serengeti and Ngorongoro.

areas, the female wildebeest run the highest risk (and males the lowest) during calving time, January and February;[3] this can be explained by the fact that in the last weeks before and during birth, females are less mobile than at other times.

The overall sex ratios of killed adult wildebeest in the crater is almost 1:1 (0.94 males to 1 female) (table 28); and in a sample of 933 live animals I found no significant deviation from the 1:1 ratios (1.12 males to 1 female).[4] In the Serengeti the sex ratio of hyena kills is different—1.84 males to 1 female—and it deviates from the 1:1 ratio we would expect after the work of Talbot and Talbot (1963) and of

3. Ratio male/female wildebeest during Jan.–Feb./other months: $\chi^2 = 9.87$; $df = 2$; $p < 0.01$.

4. Ratio male/female among adult wildebeest killed by hyena in Ngorongoro: binomial test, $N = 97$; $x = 47$; $P = Q = \frac{1}{2} \rightarrow z = -0.64$; $p = 0.261$. Ratio male/female among adult wildebeest alive in Ngorongoro: binomial test, $N = 933$; $x = 440$; $P = Q = \frac{1}{2} \rightarrow z = -1.58$; $p = 0.057$.

TABLE 23 *Sex of adult hyena-killed prey animals*

Prey species	Place	Male	Female	Total	No. of males per female
Wildebeest	Serengeti	68 (65%)	37 (35%)	105	1.8/1
	Ngorongoro	47 (48%)	50 (52%)	97	0.9/1
Zebra	Serengeti	8 (33%)	16 (67%)	24	0.5/1
	Ngorongoro	9 (29%)	22 (71%)	31	0.4/1
Thomson's gazelle	Serengeti	41 (76%)	13 (24%)	54	3.1/1

Watson (1967) if hyenas were killing indiscriminately; these authors suggested that the two sexes are equally abundant in the Serengeti.

I cannot make any suggestions about the cause of the difference in mortality between males and females in the Serengeti. It may be that neither Talbot and Talbot's nor Watson's figures on the sex ratio of the live population are correct, and that there is a preponderance of adult males which would explain my results. Sinclair (personal communication) finds a predominance of males among animals dead from disease or starvation during the dry season, a cause of mortality which is probably more important than all the others; Schaller (personal communication) mentions the same for mortality caused by lions. Watson (1967) mentions that of 369 wildebeest skulls found and sexed in the Serengeti, 77.5% were males; he explains this by a larger rate of destruction of female skulls but, although this may be true to a small extent, it is unlikely to bias his results as much as he suggests. Watson based his assessment of the sex ratio largely on counts from aerial photographs of herds; this method might not be valid, since the difficulty of distinguishing the sexes on an aerial photograph is considerable; furthermore, the spatial distribution of the two sexes in the live population is so different that an observational bias may easily arise. An incorrect assessment by the earlier workers is therefore not unlikely, but until a proper count of the sexes has been done again, this matter will have to be left undecided. If there is indeed such a predominance of males in the Serengeti wildebeest population, it would be interesting from the population dynamics point of view, but this is not the place to consider this further.

The sex ratio of animals killed by hyenas from the zebra populations is quite different. In both areas, females predominate in the kills (table 23); the sex ratios are 0.50 males to 1 female in the Serengeti and 0.41 males to 1 female in Ngorongoro. The difference between the two areas is insignificant, but the overall sex ratio differs significantly from parity.[5]

Again, there are difficulties in interpreting these results, since proper sex ratio counts in the live populations have yet to be made. These counts are more difficult than in the wildebeest, since the sexes are harder to identify; also, the heterogenous distribution of the zebra population in family groups and herds of males (Klingel 1967) creates a need for large samples. The first impression is of equal representation of both sexes, but this may be deceptive. Schaller (personal communication) finds, in the older age-classes, a slightly higher number of male than female zebra being killed by lions in the Serengeti (1.22 males to 1 female), without indications from direct observations that either sex is more vulnerable to lion predation. If my present assumption is correct, and male and female zebra are equally abundant in the two areas, the sex ratio as found in hyena kills would fit in well with behavioral observations of hyena hunting (p. 184); from these one would predict a greater vulnerability of the female zebra.

Hyenas have only rarely been observed hunting Thomson's gazelle in the crater; if tommies are eaten by hyenas there, it is most often a scavenged meal. But in the Serengeti they are a frequent item on the hyena's food list, and, although it is not possible to draw comparisons between tommy data of the two areas, there are some interesting aspects in the Serengeti material which are worth considering in themselves. Of the adult gazelle killed by hyenas, the great majority are males;[6] the sex ratio is 3.15 males to 1 female, even though the adult sex ratio in the live population shows, if anything, a slight predominance of females (Walther, personal communication; Schaller 1968). De Vos and Hvidberg-Hansen (1967) found, in two samples of 4,800 and 3,633 tommies, 49% males and 54% males (overall 51% males); their samples included roadside counts which tend to include relatively more males.

It seems then that males of the tommy population are eaten by hyenas more often than would be expected if both sexes were equally vulnerable. This is also indicated in the gazelle killed by wild dogs in

5. Adult zebra killed by hyena, ♂/♀ in Serengeti/Ngorongoro: $\chi^2 = 0.0029$; $df = 1; p > 0.95$.

Ratio ♂/♀ among adult zebra killed by hyena in Serengeti and Ngorongoro: Binomial test, $N = 55; x = 17; P = Q = \frac{1}{2} \rightarrow z = -2.70; p = 0.0035$.

6. Ratio ♂/♀ among adult Thomson's gazelle killed by hyena in Serengeti: Binomial test, $N = 54; x = 13; P = Q = \frac{1}{2} \rightarrow z = -3.68; \quad < 0.0002$.

the Serengeti (1.48 males to 1 female in a sample of 67)[7] and Ngorongoro (3 males to 1 female; Estes and Goddard 1967). More male tommy are killed by leopards than females, but this is not so for cheetah; lions kill slightly more males (Schaller 1968 and personal communication). The cause of these differences is still obscure; the suggestion by Estes and Goddard (1967) that wild dogs tend to kill territorial male tommies has not been substantiated, and there are other possible mechanisms. B. Schiemann (personal communication) collected 37 diseased gazelle in the Serengeti, in which he found 1.47 male to 1 female[8]—it may be that the sex difference in vulnerability to disease explains some of the kill data. Alternatively, sick male gazelle may be extra conspicuous both to predators and to a human collector.

The consequences for the prey population of differential pressure on the sexes may be considerable, but until we know more about the other mortality factors and their impact on males and females, these consequences are difficult to evaluate. Only for zebra in Ngorongoro is the case fairly clear-cut, since other causes of mortality appear to be of little importance and there is evidence for a substantial difference in predation on the two sexes. Predation pressure on zebras appears greater on the females than on the males, and because virtually all the females take part in the reproductive process, whereas many males stay together in stallion groups which are inactive in reproduction, the effect of hyena predation on the population is greater than if it were largely directed at the males. It might well be that hyenas could exploit the zebra population more "economically" if they were to concentrate on males rather than females—that is, they would be able to take a higher annual percentage of the zebra population on a sustained-yield basis.

Selection of Age

The timing of tooth eruption and wear has long been established as a means of assessing relative age of mammals. Recently a more accurate method has come into use which is based on increment rings in the teeth, first used by Laws (1952) in his study on elephant seals and later by various other workers. Watson (1967) based his aging of the Serengeti wildebeest on this last method, and appeared to be able to establish

7. Ratio ♂/♀ among adult Thomson's gazelle killed by wild dog in Serengeti: Binomial test, $N = 67$; $x = 27$; $P = Q = \frac{1}{2} \rightarrow z = -1.46$; $p = 0.072$.

8. Ratio ♂/♀ among adult Thomson's gazelle found diseased or dead of disease in Serengeti: binomial test, $N = 37$; $x = 15$; $P = Q = \frac{1}{2} \rightarrow z = -1.46$; $p = 0.197$.

the absolute age of individuals this way. Unfortunately, preparing a tooth for the assessment of the number of rings is an elaborate process which also demands a fair amount of equipment; because of this, I had to be satisfied with dividing the kills into a number of relative age-classes based on tooth wear, which at least allows one to make a number of comparisons. It is assumed, therefore, that an animal whose teeth have worn down farther is usually older. The description of tooth-wear classes is presented in appendix D. 7; the separation in classes is, of course, arbitrary, hence the number of years of age encompassed by different tooth-wear classes will not be the same. In other words, the number of animals in one age (tooth-wear) class cannot be compared with that in another; only whole age-class distributions can be related. The foregoing does not apply to zebra; for that species Klingel's (1966) method is used, with which absolute ages can be obtained for various stages of eruption and wear of the incisors.

Wildebeest. In figure 23, I have presented the age-class distribution of hyena victims in the crater and in the Serengeti. In Ngorongoro, a larger proportion of the wildebeest were found killed as young calves (see also table 24); also, once adult, the animals in the Serengeti are

TABLE 24 *Young animals among wildebeest killed by hyenas*

Age	Serengeti	Ngorongoro
0–12 months old	47 (36%)	77 (60%)
13–24 months old	18 (14%)	3 (2%)
over 24 months old	66 (50%)	48 (38%)
	131	128

killed at a significantly greater age than in Ngorongoro.[9] Yearlings are relatively more represented in kills in the Serengeti than in the crater (table 24);[10] this will be discussed further below. No significant difference was found in the age distribution of the two sexes killed by hyenas.[10]

9. Wildebeest calves/adults killed by hyenas in Serengeti/Ngorongoro: $\chi^2 = 14.33$; $df = 1$; $p < 0.001$.
    Adult wildebeest killed at different ages by hyenas in Serengeti/Ngorongoro: $\chi^2 = 16.97$; $df = 6$; $p < 0.01$.
    10. Wildebeest yearlings/adults killed by hyenas in Serengeti/Ngorongoro: $\chi^2 = 9.80$; $df = 1$; $p < 0.01$.
    Age of ♂/♀ adult wildebeest killed by hyenas in both areas, median test: (Ngorongoro $\chi^2 = 1.70$; Serengeti $\chi^2 = 0.17$); combined $\chi^2 = 1.87$; $df = 2$; $p < 0.50$.

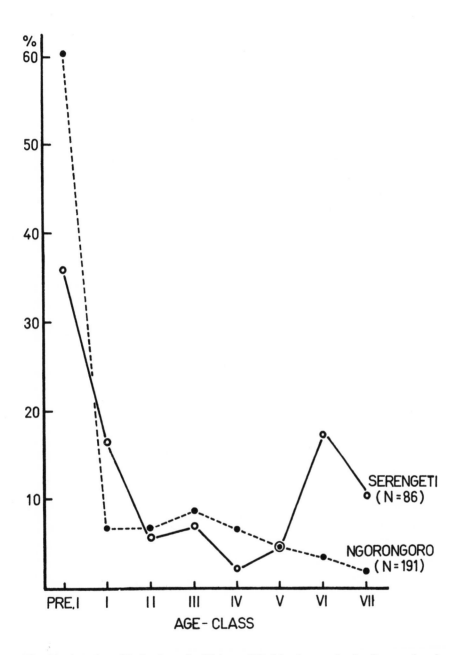

Fig. 23. Age-class distribution of wildebeest killed by hyenas in the Serengeti and Ngorongoro.

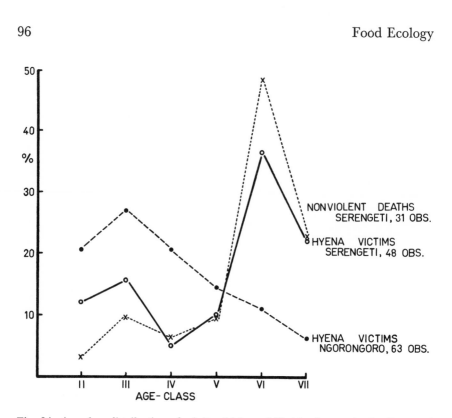

Fig. 24. Age-class distribution of adult wildebeest killed by hyenas in the Serengeti and Ngorongoro, and of adult wildebeest which died a nonviolent death in the Serengeti.

Unfortunately, little is known about the age-class distribution of the live wildebeest population, but a number of interesting observations can be made. In figure 24, I have compared the age-class distribution of adult wildebeest killed in the Serengeti by hyenas with that of wildebeest that died there through nonviolent causes (disease, old age, starvation); the latter category was collected by Sinclair in 1967. Because no yearlings were collected, I have, for comparison with my hyena data, used only the age-classes II–VII, and I have presented the Ngorongoro hyena kills in the same way. From figure 24, a great similarity is apparent between the graphs for hyena kills and for nonviolent deaths; indeed, there is a high degree of correlation between the two.[11]

The age-class distribution of adult wildebeest killed in the Serengeti by lions, collected by Schaller, is also significantly different from the

11. Correlation between age-class distribution of wildebeest that died of disease, etc., and that were killed by hyenas, Serengeti: $r_s = 0.87$; $p < 0.05$.

hyena prey age-class distribution; lion kills are on the whole younger.[12] These Serengeti lion kills are older on the average, however, than the wildebeest killed by hyenas in Ngorongoro.[13] Unfortunately, lions in Ngorongoro scavenged most of their food, so they did not provide me with comparable data.

The explanation that first comes to mind to cover these relations is the following. Because of their hunting methods, hyenas are most likely to select the physically least able animals from a herd; lions, killing wildebeest after stalking or ambushing, are more likely to obtain a random sample (although they also will take an obviously sick animal). This explains the difference between the Serengeti hyena- and lion-kill samples, and the correlation between age distribution of Serengeti hyena kills and wildebeest which died of disease, and so on. The selection mechanism is probably the same in Ngorongoro hyenas; but in the crater there simply are not many old wildebeest (hence the difference between Serengeti lion kills and Ngorongoro hyena kills). In other words, the difference in age of wildebeest killed by hyenas in Ngorongoro and the Serengeti partly reflects a difference in the age structure of the two wildebeest populations. The greater percentage of calves in the Ngorongoro kills indicates the large hyena pressure on the very young animals in that area during the short times that these are available; in the Serengeti, this pressure is also high, but less so because there are more old wildebeest which are relatively easy to obtain.

All this does not explain the relatively large percentage of wildebeest of one to two years old in the Serengeti hyena sample; one would expect this age-class to be very resilient against hyena predation. However, these animals in the Serengeti seem particularly prone to disease, and especially the one-year-olds are frequently found ill (Schiemann, personal communication). In the crater, predation on the calves is much higher, and this may remove part of the age-class which would later die of disease.

Zebra. After aging the skulls of hyena victims with Klingel's method, we can split up the sample into age-groups which are comparable to each other (table 25). Although the samples are small, it is clear that

---

12. Serengeti wildebeest age class distribution, lion kills/hyena kills: $\chi^2 = 9.92$; $df = 4$; $p < 0.05$.

13. Wildebeest age class distributions, lion kills Serengeti/hyena kills Ngorongoro: $\chi^2 = 24.30$; $df = 5$; $p < 0.001$.

TABLE 25 *Age of zebra killed by hyenas*

Age	Serengeti	Ngorongoro	Total
Up to 4 years old	8	14	22 (48%)
Over 4, up to 8 years	2	5	7 (15%)
Over 8, up to 12 years	5	4	9 (20%)
Over 12, up to 16 years	2	6	8 (17%)
	17	29	46 (100%)

more zebra are killed in their first four years of life than in any following four-year period. The adult zebra that are killed by hyenas are fairly evenly spread over the remaining age-classes; there is no statistically significant difference between the age-class distribution of the Serengeti and Ngorongoro victims.[14] Comparison with data on age-class distributions collected by Skoog shows that hyenas may prefer old animals, but the data are inconclusive.[15]

Thomson's gazelle.   In appendix D. 7 I have listed tooth-wear criteria for distinguishing age-classes, and the age-class distribution of gazelle kills has been presented in figure 25. Forty-two of ninety-eight tommies (43%) killed by hyenas in the Serengeti were fawns, probably all less than three weeks old. This suggests a very strong selection of young gazelle by hyenas, which can be confirmed after considering their hunting methods (p. 187). The hyenas kill relatively more young tommies than do wild dogs (who took only 17% fawns out of sixty gazelle killed).[16] My data on the age distribution of adult tommies are insufficient to draw any conclusions about differences between various sources of mortality. I have explained above that there are reasons to believe that the "massacre" in which, during one night, over one hundred gazelle were killed by hyenas was not selective for age; the age distribution of the sample taken from that occasion may well be

14. Zebra killed by hyenas, age-class distribution Serengeti/Ngorongoro: $\chi^2 = 0.008$; $df = 1$; $p > 0.90$.

15. Zebra age distribution of individuals killed by hyenas versus zebra collected by Skoog, Serengeti: $\chi^2 = 4.56$; $df = 2$; $p < 0.20$.

16. Thomson's gazelle, adult/juvenile killed by hyenas/wild dogs: $\chi^2 = 10.1$; $df = 1$; $p < 0.01$.

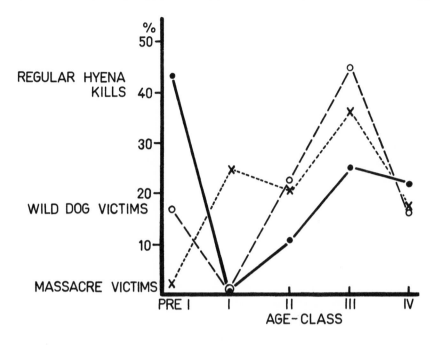

Fig. 25. Age-class distribution of Thomson's gazelle killed in the Serengeti by hyenas and wild dogs, and of gazelle killed by hyenas in the "massacre."

representative for the live tommy population at that time. There is a slight indication that hyenas (and wild dogs) kill relatively more older animals in the adult population, but this is not at all significant.[17]

The Condition of the Prey Animals

I found it difficult to obtain information about the condition of animals caught by hyenas; carcasses are often consumed entirely and the vital organs disappear very rapidly after the prey has been killed. It is clear that hyenas will select a physically inferior animal from a group if they happen to see it, and they probably even search for such prey (p. 201). But most likely the hyenas' criteria are far more sensitive than mine, because I can rarely see anything different in the behavior of an animal that has been selected by hyenas. In a number of such instances, there was indeed something wrong with such selected quarry. Orr and Moore-Gilbert (1964) released a tagged adult wildebeest

17. Thomson's gazelle, adults of age I + II/III + IV, killed by hyenas regularly/ during massacre: $\chi^2 = 2.78$; $df = 1$; $p < 0.10$.
  Thomson's gazelle, adults of age I + II/III + IV, killed by wild dog/killed by hyenas during massacre: $\chi^2 = 1.10$; $df = 1$; $p < 0.30$.

male in the Ngorongoro Crater when they thought it had fully recovered; three hours later a hyena noticed it and killed it after a chase
of three miles. The authors assumed that the hyena was attracted to the
animal because of the aftereffects of the drug (succinylcholine chloride)
rather than because of the marking (other wildebeest, a day or longer
after tagging, did not attract hyenas' attention); they themselves could
not see anything different in it. When immobilizing yearling wildebeest in the crater, also using darts with succinylcholine chloride, I was
at cross-purposes with hyenas on several occasions. Two of thirty-two
tagged wildebeest were attacked within minutes after their release,
although to me they looked normal and were able to run at what I
thought was full speed; I had to keep the hyenas away from the wildebeest with the car. On two occasions, a wildebeest was attacked soon
after being hit with the dart, and at least one was an animal in which
the dart had failed so it was not under the effect of the drug. Both were
discovered by a single hyena while they were running in a panic, and
other hyenas then joined the chase; although I tried hard to keep the
hyenas away with the car, there was little I could do. The chase went
fast over rough terrain, and the hyenas grabbed the wildebeest and
killed one of them. The dart had not discharged the drug at all. The
other wildebeest escaped his assailants by running across a clan boundary; I never knew why the dart did not take effect.

I have already pointed out that there seemed to be more sick animals
in the Serengeti than in Ngorongoro. Only once in Ngorongoro did I
find an ungulate (a zebra) that clearly had died of disease, whereas this
happened frequently in the Serengeti. Among the ungulates found
diseased in the Serengeti, Schiemann (personal communication)
diagnosed anthrax, sarcoptic mange, hoof gangrene (wildebeest);
anthrax (zebra); and anthrax, sarcoptic mange, haemonchus, lung-
worm, pleuritis, nephritis, and orchitis (Thomson's gazelle). Broken
limbs also occur rather frequently. In the Ngorongoro, on the whole, it
is rare to see any sick or disabled animals. Klingel (1967) mentions old
zebra in bad condition in the Ngorongoro, and I also very occasionally
saw zebra there which were limping badly or which looked obviously
diseased. Sometimes one saw zebra with large flaps of skin torn off or
with large scratch or bite marks, presumably after an escape from
predators. It is interesting that, in the crater, these diseased or wounded
animals occurred among zebra and not at all, or hardly ever, among
other species—this is probably because the male zebra defends his
family against the attacks of the main source of mortality, the hyena,

whereas the other species can almost only save themselves by running very fast. Klingel (1967) shows that in some instances a sick animal in a zebra family is not abandoned, as other members of the family wait for it to catch up when they are moving around.

The role of starvation in the pattern of diseases is still very uncertain. In the Serengeti, during the height of the dry season when starvation might be expected, large numbers of animals (especially wildebeest) have been found dead or dying in the Serengeti, but they have not been studied enough to enable me to state that starvation was the certain cause of their death.

Characteristics of Animals Caught by Hyenas: Conclusions

From all three main prey species, hyenas select certain categories. Very young animals are obviously extremely vulnerable, as are the very old wildebeest and probably gazelle, though in this last species, the evidence was insufficient. In zebra, age is probably less important once an animal is fully grown, because of the different antipredator mechanism in this species. The evidence on differential selection of one sex is mostly inconclusive; there is a preference for male gazelle, and maybe for male wildebeest in the Serengeti (though not in the crater), but the mechanism of this is not at all clear. Hyenas kill more female zebra in both areas, which may be explained by the species' antipredator behavior. The role of disease is virtually unknown; from direct observations, hyenas appear to select sick animals if they are present, but no systematic data could be collected. In the Serengeti, disease is a more frequent cause of death than in Ngorongoro.

The hyenas' selection and hunting methods cause them to select the least physically fit from the populations, at least in wildebeest and gazelle; in zebra, the interaction is complicated by the active defense of the family group by the stallion. This by no means signifies that hyenas eat only very young, old, or diseased animals, but if these are available, they will be selected. In the Ngorongoro the latter categories are hardly present at all, and the hyenas have to be content there with what are probably perfectly healthy prey in the prime of life. As one general conclusion about the difference in predation effect in the Serengeti and Ngorongoro, it is clear that the hyenas' selection within the prey species increased this difference between the two areas even more. In the Serengeti, the animals that are selected may well be the ones that would soon die in any case.

Thus, an important feature of predation by hyenas (and several other species of carnivore) is indicated: it is not merely supplementary to other sources of mortality but interacts closely with them. If other mortality is numerically important (e.g., in the Serengeti), predation merges with it and hyenas take what has died already or what would otherwise have died of another cause. If other causes of mortality are absent, hyenas act as an independent mortality agent (e.g., in Ngorongoro). This buffer mechanism is of obvious ecological importance.

THE NUMBERS OF PREDATORS AND PREY: DISCUSSION AND CONCLUSIONS
Before I discuss the implications of my results further, it may be useful to summarize briefly the main points of the previous pages.

In the range of available prey sizes, hyenas appear to take the medium-sized ungulates (wildebeest, zebra) rather than the larger (buffalo) or smaller ones (Thomson's gazelle) (p. 74). Hyenas have not shown any obvious preference between wildebeest and zebra, and the presence of these species in the annual diet corresponds closely with their relative abundance.

When comparing the two areas I studied, I noted first of all the large difference in density of animals that would be the main source of food for hyenas—wildebeest, zebra, and gazelle. They occur in larger numbers per km^2 in Ngorongoro (tables 19 and 20) and also in that area they are permanent residents. In the Serengeti, they move over large distances, leaving vast tracts of country with virtually no ungulates for several months per year—thus causing a relatively low density over the whole Serengeti ecosystem. In the Ngorongoro Crater, there are also more hyenas per km^2 (p. 26) and per unit of prey (p. 84) than in the Serengeti; other predators (lions) occur in equal numbers per unit of prey in the two areas. In the crater, hyenas outnumber lions overwhelmingly and they represent the greatest carnivore biomass, but in the Serengeti, the number of lion is relatively higher, though still exceeded by the hyenas. Generally, there are more carnivores per herbivore in Ngorongoro, and hyenas make up a higher proportion of these carnivore numbers there.

Hyenas kill most of their prey themselves, but they also scavenge a considerable amount—in the Serengeti more than in the crater (fig. 26), because they take what is easiest and in the Serengeti more animals die of disease or are killed by lions and other predators (p. 85). When hyenas do kill (mostly wildebeest), they are more likely to get very young or old animals in the Serengeti than in Ngorongoro (fig. 23), where they often kill healthy middle-aged wildebeest. This difference is not true for zebra, and this can probably be explained by the particular manner in which hyenas catch them (p. 180). Both adult wildebeest and adult gazelle are hunted in such a way that the physically least able are most likely to get caught; because there are so many more prey animals per predator in the Serengeti, there will be more old and decrepit ones available per hyena. The wildebeest in the Ngorongoro Crater die younger and reach puberty at an earlier age than those in the Serengeti (p. 85); the population in the crater seems fairly constant and mortality is caused largely by hyenas.

Predation pressure by the hyenas is therefore very high in Ngorongoro (table 21), and it seems likely that the higher turnover in the wildebeest population is caused by this. For zebra also, it could be shown that the hyena predation pressure in the crater is far higher than in the Serengeti, but we do not have the evidence to show that this has any effect on the population composition; it is likely that it has. Hyenas in Ngorongoro killed few gazelle, and a comparison between the areas for this species is not possible. In Ngorongoro, gazelle are hard pressed by other predators as well as hyenas, whereas in the Serengeti not only predation but also disease plays a role (p. 87).

For wildebeest and zebra in Ngorongoro, there is another side to the picture: there is evidence that hyenas themselves are to some extent controlled by their food supply. There is more competition between hyenas over food in the crater than in the Serengeti (fig. 21, p. 79), and mortality among hyenas is to a large measure related to this competition over food (table 5; p. 39). In the Serengeti, it seems that food (or rather the lack of it) has an important effect on the survival of young cubs when the adults go off on their day-long foraging expeditions (p. 60). This difference in survival of the young cubs is likely to hold the key to the difference in population density between Ngorongoro and Serengeti. The larger amount of competition between adults in the Ngorongoro is probably expressed in the fact that adult hyenas there die younger (figs. 8 and 9).

From the present evidence, it seems likely that both the hyena populations are to some extent controlled by food supply, the hyenas in the crater by food for the adults and the hyenas in the Serengeti by food for the cubs. This in turn means that in Ngorongoro, the number of adult hyenas could increase up to the limits of its food supply, whereas in the Serengeti this is prevented. And this implies that in Ngorongoro, hyenas would be able to exert a limiting effect on the prey populations, whereas in the Serengeti they cannot.

Here we arrive at a crucial point in the argument. If, in Ngorongoro, hyenas are controlled by the numbers of their prey, it would be theoretically impossible that they should limit the size of that food supply themselves. One might say they are in balance with each other—the level of the balance must be determined by something else. Hyenas may affect the turnover within the prey populations, and they may play an important role by damping small fluctuations in population size (switching to another prey, eating more or less). But, logically, the level around which that sort of fluctuation would take place must be determined by something else. The most likely possibility here would be the food supply of the prey population; in fact, Nicholson (1947) has already suggested that if a predator is most likely to take the weaklings from the population, it would be the food supply for the prey that checks the predator's numbers. Hyenas would indeed be eminently suitable for a role in which they would adjust the ungulates' numbers to the range conditions without large fluctuations in numbers. Any animal that, because of slight undernourishment, was in worse condition than its neighbor would be cropped immediately, and a rise in numbers of undernourished animals could be dealt with without delay.

Similarly, a sudden improvement of the grasslands might cause hyenas to catch fewer prey of one kind, so they would have to switch to another; if both the important prey species were affected, hyenas would have to eat less, and allow the prey to increase up to the new food level, and so on. It is not at all unlikely that the Ngorongoro ungulates are close to the limits of their food supply. There are no data available about the productivity of the Ngorongoro grasslands, but they do appear to be comparatively heavily used. Certainly, the crater floor carries a higher ungulate biomass the whole year round than most others areas in East Africa (on present counts some $16,200 \text{ kg/km}^2$, without taking Masai cattle into account); for similar faunas, only references from the Albert National Park in the Congo exceed the figures from Ngorongoro (Bourlière and Verschuren 1960; Lamprey 1964; Foster and Coe 1968).

If it is true that, in the crater, the relation between the ungulates and their food supply is modified by hyenas, we would like to know how this relation is maintained in the Serengeti, where apparently predators have little effect on the ungulate populations. Maybe there the migration, the very phenomenon that prevents predation from playing an important role, enables the herbivore populations to adjust themselves to food supply without major short-term population fluctuations. But this is no more than a guess, and the mechanisms of this still remain obscure.

It is interesting to compare the main hypotheses of this chapter, regarding predation as a population-regulating factor, with some findings about predation in other animals. One of the best-known studies in this field is that of Errington (1943), who found that mink predation on muskrats removed almost only those animals which were social outcasts, the "surplus" of the population; he suggested (1946) that this is a widely distributed characteristic of predation. Essentially the same phenomenon was found by Jenkins, Watson, and Miller (1964, 1967) and by Watson (1967) for predation on the Scottish Red Grouse— territorial birds were hardly affected at all, but those that could not establish themselves on a territory were killed by predation (or by disease). What actually determines the density of territorial birds is still unknown—it is probably a factor in the birds' food supply. The parallels of these studies with my results from Ngorongoro are obvious; here, probably, it is not the wildebeest's or zebra's territorial behavior that is involved in determining how many animals will be safe from hyena predation, but some other aspect of their relation to habitat and food supply. It has been suggested for the relation between wolves, moose, and browse conditions on Isle Royale that there also food supply for the moose determines its vulnerability to wolf predation (Mech 1966).

With the different distribution of the prey population, the Serengeti shows an entirely different pattern of predation—the carnivore populations have not been able to increase to a level where they could exercise a regulatory function. To some extent, this is comparable to the relation between most of the well-studied bird populations and their enemies; predation usually accounts for only a negligible portion of the mortality (for review see Lack 1966). In many areas of Europe and America, raptors have been almost exterminated by man, and this may partly account for the lack of predation on birds in these areas. But some bird populations in Africa also have relatively few predators, death of potential prey species usually being caused probably by starvation (e.g., Ward 1963, 1965). It may well be that the low level of predation on these populations of birds is caused by their relatively high mobility.

5 Hyenas' Feeding Habits and Relations with Other Carnivores

Scavenging versus Hunting

Literature

A hyena is scavenging when it is eating from the carcass of an animal which neither it nor other hyenas have killed. It is commonly supposed that the hyena scavenges most or all of its diet—hence the public distaste for hyenas and the use of their name as an insult. We find references to the hyena's liking for offal in many earlier writers on Africa's fauna, and it would be pointless to mention details. But several authors do also mention the hyena's ability to kill for itself. Schweinfurth (undated, quoted in Brehm 1877), for instance, found that hyenas, like wolves, hunted fully grown antelopes at night, and Johnston (1884) stated that "the spotted hyena is a much more predatory animal than one generally imagines. Not only does it steal sheep and calves from the herds, but it even carries off children and will often attack a wounded or weakly man." Brehm (1877) discusses several cases in which hyenas terrorized native villages by killing children and livestock, especially in South Africa and the Sudan. Stevenson-Hamilton (1947) believed that the spotted hyena was a "beast that cannot, unless under exceptional circumstances, hope to secure as prey an able-bodied larger animal," but even he states later that "instances, in fact, have been reported in the Kruger National Park of several spotted hyenas having combined to attack and kill even full-grown larger antelopes, which they have in some manner succeeded in cornering." Matthews (1939*b*) mentions that hyenas will pull down game as large as zebras, but obviously considers this a rare event. So does Deane (1962), who earlier (1960) described the kill of an apparently healthy wildebeest by one hyena, as observed from tracks in the sand. According to Pienaar (1963), the hyena diet in the Kruger National Park is mainly carrion, but hyenas may on occasion kill their own prey—usually disabled or sick animals no larger than a kudu. Later the same author (Pienaar

106

1969) elaborates on the hyenas' hunting habits. In the Serengeti and Ngorongoro, the role of hyenas has always been assumed to be that of a scavenger and killer of the very young or feeble (Wright 1960; Estes 1967b).

The first writer to describe a situation where hyenas were predominantly hunting predators, chasing their quarry in packs, was Eloff (1964), who was able to deduce his information from tracks in the sand of the Kalahari Desert in South Africa. There, packs of hyenas chased and killed, their prey being mostly gemsbok, but also blue wildebeest, eland, and springbok.

Thus the sum of previous knowledge pointed to the hyena as first and foremost a scavenger, a view which influenced the results and conclusions of workers in such related fields as paleontology (von Koenigswald 1965), archaeology (Hughes 1954a, b, 1958), and students of behavior and ecology of African plains game (Talbot and Talbot 1963, Estes 1967b, Watson 1967).

Importance of Scavenging

The hyena shows some morphological and physiological features which make it the supreme utilizer of every bone or scrap of animal remains. For this it is better equipped than any of the other common large carnivores, its main advantage being special bone-crushing teeth such as the third premolars in the upper and lower jaws (thickset conical teeth which rapidly blunt with age), which are particularly used for cracking large bones (pl. 4). Farther back in the hyena's mouth one finds the carnassial shear, where the long blades of the upper fourth premolar and the lower first molar cooperate in cutting thick pieces of hide or tendon. Ewer (1954) found that the spotted hyena has gone further in the specialization of both crushing and shearing mechanisms than the other two hyenas, whose teeth are slightly more "all purpose." In the field, one can see hyenas using their different teeth for different purposes: soft meat is pulled out of the carcass with the front incisors and canines, bones are crunched farther back in the mouth (for this, they often hold single bones with their forelegs, or stick the head of the male gazelle upright in the ground by the horns); pieces of skin and so on are cut far back in the mouth with the carnassials. The Felidae and Canidae also have this carnassial shear, though relatively smaller than in the hyenas, but they do not have the conical bone crushers.

Not only are hyenas able to splinter and eat even the largest bones of wildebeest and zebra, but they are also able to digest them completely. Their droppings consist almost entirely of very fine white powder with a few hairs in it. Chemical analysis shows that this white powder consists of $Ca_3(PO_4)_2 \cdot 1.5\ Ca(OH)_2$ (Dr. C. A. Craik, personal communication), which is also the formula of the inorganic matter in bone. Thus bone is digested and only the inorganic part is excreted with the feces; it is clear that hyenas are able to utilize all the organic components present, not just the marrow. Bone meal may contain up to 40% organic matter (Craik, personal communication) mostly collagen, and this portion is absorbed. Other carnivores are also able to digest occasional small pieces of bone, but no species can manage such large quantities as do hyenas. Thus, because of these morphological and physiological adaptations, hyenas can use parts of a carcass which other carnivores cannot.

Several behavioral adaptations for obtaining carrion are also evident. Hyenas roam over vast distances, often alone, and in this way they are more likely to come across carrion than, for instance, the more stationary cats or the exclusively pack-hunting wild dogs. They react to alighting vultures more promptly than many other carnivores, and they are more likely to stay around a lion kill or human settlement than any other predator (except maybe the jackals).

But although hyenas are particularly adapted to scavenging, all carnivores are scavengers to some extent (except maybe the cheetah), and I will mention a few examples of this. The scavenging habits of lions were most forcefully brought home to us when once, in the middle of a hot Serengeti afternoon, a large male lion came running up from over 1 km away to take a piece of meat from the birds' feeding place near the porch of our house which had been put out to attract vultures; then also, the lion's habit of stealing hyena kills, as will be described later, provides ample evidence, and frequently I noticed that lions were attracted to alighting vultures (from a position where they could not see or smell the carcass on which the vultures were descending). I twice saw lions steal the kill of wild dogs, but I have never seen cheetahs eat meat which they had not killed themselves, and neither had Schaller (1968). But since the species seems to keep very well in zoos if fed on dead meat, it is likely that in nature a cheetah would appropriate a carcass if it came across one. On the whole, though, a cheetah's much shyer nature will make it less likely to scavenge than any of the others. Leopards will eat carrion whenever they can, and this habit is made use of by hunters, who lure a leopard to a tree by putting bait up in it.

Mr. S. Downey (personal communication) once saw a leopard in the Serengeti steal a tommy carcass from a hyena (who had just stolen it from a cheetah). Wild dogs will readily eat an animal killed by somebody else (contrary to Kühme 1965); four times I saw packs of wild dogs steal tommy carcasses from hyenas and once they stole a zebra carcass. On two occasions a pack of wild dogs found a carcass on the plains, once a wildebeest which the alighting vultures showed them and the other a dead tommy lying in a hole. Although in the Serengeti the diet of the two common species of jackal, the black-backed and the golden, consists largely of small mammals they have caught themselves, young gazelle, insects, and even fruits, these two little Canidae come and scavenge at many of the big game kills. In Ngorongoro Crater, scavenging is the mainstay of the jackals' diet (Wyman, personal communication).

The main point of this survey of other predators is that to some extent all of them scavenge; but the hyena seems better equipped for it behaviorally, morphologically, and physiologically. Nevertheless, early in the study I began to suspect that, although hyenas were so obviously adapted to a scavenging way of life, it was very unlikely that the large populations of hyenas in both the Serengeti and Ngorongoro Crater were entirely supported by carrion. There were many obviously well-fed hyenas walking around, there was little activity during the day, and I did not find that many dead animals (and if there were carcasses, it often took some time before hyenas found them, if they did at all). Also, other carnivores often left very little of their kills for somebody else to eat.

That hyenas were scavengers only to a minor extent in the area studied is shown in figure 26, in which carcasses that hyenas were seen eating are classified as hyena kills or otherwise. Before elaborating on the conclusions from this, I will discuss details of how I arrived at these figures. When hyenas were found eating, I used all the evidence I could find to decide whether the victim had been killed by hyenas. Often this evidence came from observing the hyenas directly before they started eating, but such direct information was not always available. When I came on a "kill" only after the hyenas had already arrived, I had to use indirect evidence about how they acquired the food. This indirect evidence could be, for instance, nearby tracks from which the recent saga could be reconstructed, or might be based on extrapolation from my direct observations. If other carnivores were present at the kill, it was often possible to decide whether they had been there before the

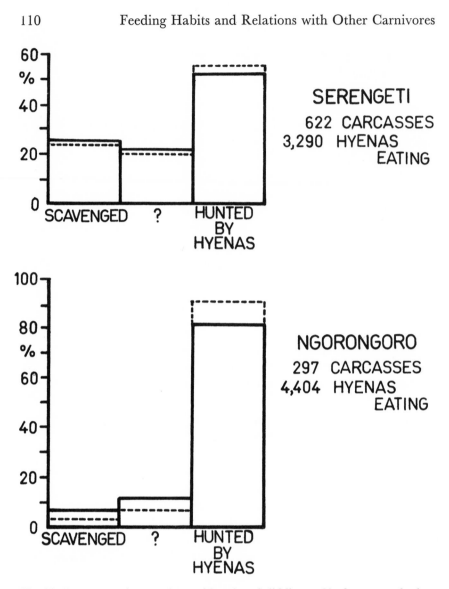

Fig. 26. Frequency of scavenging and hunting: Solid line = % of carcasses; broken line = % of participating hyenas.

hyenas or the other way round. If lions and hyenas were found together, the lions were almost always at the kill itself and the hyenas some distance away. This might mean that the hyenas were waiting for the spoils of a lion kill (and this is, indeed, the most commonly drawn conclusion). But I knew from direct observations that lions often appropriate hyena kills, which results in the same placing of predators around the carcass. Therefore I tried to judge the amount that had been eaten from a kill and, looking at this in conjunction with the size of the stomachs of the lions, I realized that often much more was gone from the carcass than the lions could possibly have eaten. Another recurring clue was the hyenas' bloody mouths and heads, which indicated that they had been there before the lions, and frequently I also found that, say, a whole leg was missing from a dead wildebeest or zebra although a lion was lying next to it. Since lions seldom carry away anything from the kill, I could be fairly sure that hyenas had been there before the lion, for they carry off large parts of a carcass as soon as they can. Often the wounds inflicted on the victim would give clues; the throat bite of a lion leaves its marks, as do the scratches along the flanks of a victim they make when killing. Hyenas kill their larger prey by bites in the abdomen and often in the hind legs. If hyenas were the only carnivores present on a kill, I estimated the time that had elapsed between the death of the animal and the time of the observation by feeling its body temperature; hyenas are such rapid eaters that if they are eating from a cold carcass it is fairly certain that they have found it dead. When an animal is killed by a predator, its rumen contents are often brought up into the mouth and the tongue hangs out, but when an animal has died quietly of disease or old age this rarely happens.

The data used for figure 26 show that if we exclude the "uncertain" cases in Ngorongoro, 96% of the hyenas observed feeding there were eating from hyena killed game (or 93% of the victims were hyena-killed); in the Serengeti, 70% of the observed hyenas ate hyena-killed meat (or 68% of the victims involved were killed by hyenas). Thus, although hyenas in both areas killed more than they scavenged,[1] the percentage of carcasses scavenged is greater in Serengeti than in Ngorongoro[2] for all prey species except gazelle.

There is a discrepancy between the percentages for the numbers of hyenas involved and the number of victims (fig. 26) because the average number of hyenas eating from a hyena kill is slightly higher than the number of hyenas scavenging on any occasion. My observational uncertainty is greater in the Serengeti than in the Ngorongoro Crater because in the Serengeti hyenas are more difficult to follow at night and

1. Ratio number of hyenas on kills/number of scavenging hyenas for every month: this ratio was > 1 in 23 months, < 1 in 2 months in Ngorongoro (p < 0.001, binomial test), and > 1 in 23 months, < 1 in 8 months in Serengeti (p < 0.01).

2. Difference between above ratios for Serengeti and Ngorongoro: Mann-Whitney test $U = 207$; $p = 0.0016$.

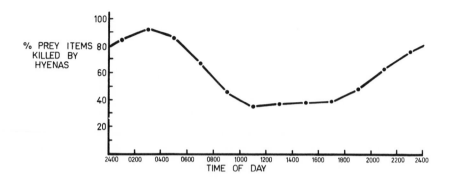

Fig. 27. Killing versus scavenging at different times of day in the Serengeti.

this meant that more often I had to use indirect evidence in establishing the origin of any "kill."

We have to be careful in interpreting this kind of figure. Observations may be biased by misjudgment of indirect evidence, by the time of the day when they were carried out, and possibly by the consistent following of hyenas which at the outset were more likely to behave one way or another. I do not think that a wrong interpretation of indirect evidence has influenced my data very much, for when only direct evidence is taken into account, the kill percentages of hyenas in the two areas are similar to those of figure 26. But the time of day when observations were carried out is important, as is illustrated in figure 27; hyenas on a kill in the daylight were more likely to have scavenged it than at night.[3] It is, of course, this particular factor that has greatly influenced previous knowledge about hyenas, and it certainly has also influenced my figures to some extent. The time-of-day factor seems easy to explain, since during daylight hours hyenas could spot carrion more easily than at night when the vultures were not flying.

Although I can point out this daytime factor, it is not really feasible to allow for it in my observations. One might want to correct for differences between day and night by taking into account the observation time during daylight and at night but, since the field of observation during the day is so much greater than at night (and this factor would be impossible to quantify), one would not really be justified in doing so. On the whole I spent more hours on daytime observations than on nighttime observations, and covered a much larger area. Because of this, figure

3. Number of kills versus number of scavenged carcasses, at different times of day: $\chi^2 = 34.8$; $df = 9$; $p < 0.001$.

26 tends to overestimate the proportion of food scavenged by hyenas and underestimate the proportion killed by the hyenas themselves.

In summary, although hyenas are better adapted to a scavenging existence than any of the other large carnivores in the area, they largely kill their own food, at least in the Serengeti and the Ngorongoro Crater. Why has this not been generally recognized previously? The answer to this is found, first, in the hyenas' inclination to scavenge by daylight; second, in the fact that when hyenas do come into contact with man around settlement, it is in their capacity as scavengers (see below); third, in the hyenas' tendency to demolish a nocturnal kill completely, often not leaving a single bone; and, last, in their remarkable relations with lions (see below).

The observations represented in figure 26 have mostly been made some distance from any human settlement. Proximity of settlement undoubtedly influences hyenas' feeding habits; this showed up, for instance, in the fecal analyses of various groups of hyenas in the Ngorongoro Crater. Details of the method used have been discussed in chapter 4. The Airfield hyenas are much more involved in scavenging than any of the other clans in the Ngorongoro Crater; of 78 fecal samples from the Airfield clan, 46 (59%) contained domestic stock remains. Of 348 samples from all other Ngorongoro clans, only 1 (0.3%) contained such remains. In the Airfield clan range there is a Masai village (manyatta), which was just within the boundaries of the Airfield clan; the hyenas on the other side of that boundary (the Lerai clan) did not get scraps from the manyatta, although their den was very close to it. They showed that sheer proximity to settlement is not the only criterion which decides whether hyenas will or will not scavenge. It is doubtful that hyenas could derive a substantial amount of food from scraps found around a Masai manyatta, for these findings are mostly bones, bits of hair, leather, and skin, cloth, and so on. In the Serengeti, also, hyenas prowl around human settlement and obtain what food they can in this way. Right in the center of the national park, a group of hyenas lives around the park headquarters, aptly christened the "Dustbin Brigade" by Park Warden Myles Turner.

At the end of the dry seasons in 1964 and 1965, when no other game was to be seen out on the plains, a group of some ten hyenas lived inside the national park 10 km away from a Masai manyatta near Lake Lagarja; every evening they could be seen slowly walking in the direction of the manyatta and, in the twenty-seven droppings of this group which I analyzed, I found hair of domestic stock in twenty-six. And once, at night, I followed a hyena from inside the park for some 15 km until he finally, outside the park in dense bush, found a dead zebra strangled by a poacher's snare. Thus, human presence also exerts an influence on the diet of hyenas inside the national park; but, generally, it is obvious that the total amount of food that hyenas get this way is very small.

This is not so in more densely settled areas of East Africa, especially where domestic stock is kept in abundance. In any of the farming areas, hyenas are considered a major pest and are able to inflict serious damage on cattle or sheep. They have been destroyed by the thousand by game control officers through strychnine poisoning, shooting, and trapping. In the Ethiopian town of Harar, I saw hyenas both in and outside the town and learned from the inhabitants that hyenas feed almost exclusively on refuse; only occasionally do periods occur in which the hyenas take livestock. These scavengers are tolerated in Harar, and are even encouraged by the local population (Kruuk 1968).

On the whole, a picture emerges of individual hyenas or groups of hyenas taking to scavenging, especially near human settlement—but even there this is not invariably true. At least in Ngorongoro and the Serengeti, scavenging from human settlement is only of minor importance, and I think it likely that this is also true in other wilderness areas.

In table 26, observations are tabulated in which hyenas were scavenging from various sources. Again we have to be fairly careful with the interpretation of these results; for instance, we must bear in mind that some predators kill mostly at night (lions and leopards) and others during daylight (wild dogs and cheetah), so there will be a tendency for overrepresentation of scavenging by hyenas from daylight hunters. When a lion leaves his kill at night and a few hyenas move in to take away the last bones and skull of the prey, this may go unnoticed, whereas the very conspicuous spectacle of a pack of wild dogs hunting in daylight will attract the attention of an observer from a long distance, and if hyenas take away the remains of their kill, this will go on record. The hyena removing the last bit of a leopard kill from a very dense patch of bush is more likely to be overlooked than the hyena stealing bones of a cheetah kill in broad daylight in the middle of the plain. Thus it will be safe to consider the figures of table 26 as only a qualitative indication of the sources of hyena-scavenged food; one should remember that a considerable proportion of the hyenas' scavenged food originates from animals dead from disease or old age.

It is noticeable that hyenas are able to eat almost everything of any

TABLE 26 *Hyenas scavenging in the Serengeti: cause of death of the carcass*

Carcass	Cause of Death								Total
	Disease, etc.	Lion	Wild dog	Cheetah	Leopard	Jackal	Man	Unknown	
Wildebeest adult	7	130	49	—	—	—	—	41	227
Wildebeest calf	—	5	20	—	—	—	—	7	32
Zebra adult	21	50	—	—	—	—	2	24	97
Zebra foal	20	2	2	—	—	—	—	8	32
Thomson's gazelle adult	13	—	31	6	3	1	—	22	76
Thomson's gazelle fawn	—	—	—	—	—	3	—	1	4
Grant's gazelle	—	—	—	—	—	—	—	1	1
Eland	—	5	—	—	—	—	—	—	5
Buffalo	20	3	—	—	—	—	—	5	28
Topi	—	22	—	—	—	—	—	—	22
Hyena	—	4	—	—	—	—	2	2	8
Cattle	—	—	—	—	—	—	19	—	19
	81	221	102	6	3	4	23	111	551

Note: Figures indicate number of hyenas seen eating.

kill except for horns and rumen contents (though not from carcasses of very large animals like elephants), and the number of bones lying about in the field is therefore an indication of hyena density in relation to food supply. If there is an abundance of ungulates but there are few hyenas in an area, for instance, in the north of the Serengeti National Park, one finds numerous bones and often whole skeletons of zebra, buffalo, and wildebeest left to bleach in the sun; but if there are many hyenas, such bones will be demolished completely. In areas where dense populations of hyenas are present (for instance, Ngorongoro Crater), one rarely finds a single bone, and even the skulls of zebra and wildebeest are eaten almost entirely—except in the season when the wildebeest calve. Then the hyenas have such a vast and easy food supply that the larger skeletons lie around for as long as three or four weeks after the calving season has ended. This occurs only in January and February, however, and at other times of the year even the skeleton of an adult rhinoceros will usually disappear in a few days—the largest bones being scattered over a wide area.

Eating Habits and Differences in Feeding between Hyenas

Foraging Differences between Individuals

Within the large hyena communities, differences between individuals were most striking where the ratio of scavenging to hunting was concerned. Some of the distinctions correspond with age-groupings; for instance, cubs join in on a kill from about six months old onward but will never kill for themselves until they are at least one and one-half years old. Several of the older members of the clan, especially the very fat and baggy females, simply cannot run at any speed, and they also leave the hunting to others. But certain individuals hunt very regularly (for instance, one particular marked male I called "the butcher" was often among the hunters of the Scratching Rocks clan), whereas others invariably come in after the victim is killed; these differences may be related to social status of individuals, but I have no good data to substantiate this.

One wonders what the advantage is to an individual of expending so much energy in hunting if it could just as well run up to somebody else's kill. The hunters have the chance to start eating from a kill before the others arrive, and with so many competitors about this may be quite an incentive. It is likely that the later arrivals fare less well from a carcass, except perhaps for the large dominant females.

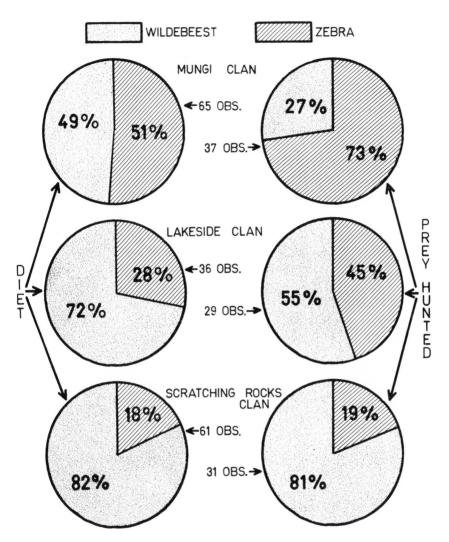

Fig. 28. Clan differences in diet and hunting, in Ngorongoro.

Foraging Differences between Clans

There were striking variations between Ngorongoro clans in feeding habits; one clan scavenged more than others, and there were differences too in the relative numbers of wildebeest and zebra taken (fig. 28).[4] This disparity was also found in the numbers of wildebeest and zebra

4. $\chi^2 = 15.72$; $df = 2$; $p < 0.001$.

chased by these clans,[5] and so the contrast cannot be explained just by a difference in hunting success.

We may, of course, be dealing with mere differences in food availability in the clan ranges, as is doubtless the case where hyenas scavenged on a Masai manyatta. This point is very difficult to assess for the three clan ranges with respect to wildebeest and zebra, since these ungulates move in large herds and may pass in and out of the ranges within a matter of hours. Both wildebeest and zebra may graze for long periods during the day in one clan range and spend the night in another. It may well be that the two clans eating the most zebra live in ranges which on the average have more zebra on them, but such differences can only be small. Moreover, even when for considerable periods hardly any zebra

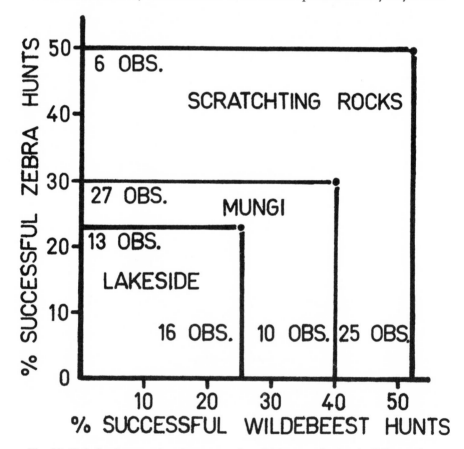

Fig. 29. Relation between hunting success for wildebeest and zebra in different clans.

5. $\chi^2 = 19.67$; $df = 2$; $p < 0.001$.

but masses of wildebeest inhabit the range of, for instance, the Mungi clan (staunch zebra hunters), these hyenas still hunt zebra. There are strong indications, therefore, that various clans have different prey preferences.

Some clans also seem more successful in catching prey than others, whether the prey is wildebeest or zebra (fig. 29)—if they are proficient in catching one, the same is true for the other. However, this is not statistically significant.[6]

Storage of Food

Hyenas leaving a kill often carry a large chunk of meat or bone away with them, which is usually eaten quietly some distance off. Occasionally, however, they cache it by dropping it into 30–50 cm of standing water and collect it again later. In Ngorongoro, I have seen them do this three times, always in the central lake, and in the Serengeti both Schaller and I once saw a hyena leave part of a carcass in a small waterhole. On several occasions I found fresh pieces of carcass partly or wholly submerged in Serengeti waterholes, without hyenas nearby; but from the way the food was partly eaten, it was all but certain that hyenas had put them there. In the crater lake, hyenas had to wade up to 10 m from the shore to reach the proper depth. They usually returned to a cache within a day, but the many bones that were exposed when part of the Ngorongoro lake dried up probably meant that several caches had been left unused. A cache can most likely be recovered only by visual relocation, and this is not always effective enough. I twice saw a hyena wade into the lake and repeatedly plunge his head deep under water in a small area, obviously searching but eventually leaving without finding anything. But I also twice saw a hyena successfully recover a cache in this way, once the head of a wildebeest and the second time the remains of a dead lion; neither of these was in any way visible from above the surface of the extremely muddy water.

The function of this storage in water is evident; there are many interested parties trying to steal meat that is left exposed, all spotting their food by sight and smell. Underwater it is perfectly safe (except from crocodiles, but there were none of these in places I saw hyenas use for meat storage); fish may be the only "illegal" benefiters. In the climate of East Africa, of course, meat cannot be preserved very long, so storing is unlikely to have any long-term use, as it sometimes has for foxes (Kruuk 1964; Tinbergen 1965).

6. Success of three different Ngorongoro clans in hunting wildebeest or zebra: $\chi^2 = 5.28$; $df = 2$; $p < 0.10$.

Eating: Number of Hyenas per Carcass

In table 27 I have presented the mean number of hyenas eating from carcasses they killed themselves, and also the carcass weight divided by the number of hyenas eating, to obtain the size of the average meal obtained from various victims. Sometimes other carnivores interfered, but this did not change the picture appreciably. The percentage of offal from a carcass might also have differed between prey species, but as hyenas eat bones as well as flesh, this difference can only be small.

On p. 79, I commented on the contrast between the Serengeti and Ngorongoro in the number of hyenas per kill; therefore I will concentrate here on the difference between prey species. This variation is very similar in the two areas. Adult zebra are clearly the most rewarding per eating hyena, and wildebeest are next with buffalo and eland following (although I have only very sparse observations of these last two). Almost all other prey are "low-reward" species.

The figures of table 27 can be expressed more generally by calculating the corresponding correlation factors and regression lines. In both areas, the number of hyenas per carcass increased with the weight of the prey species (figs. 30, 31);[7] however, hyenas can also obtain significantly more food per eating individual when the carcass is larger (figs. 32, 33).[8]

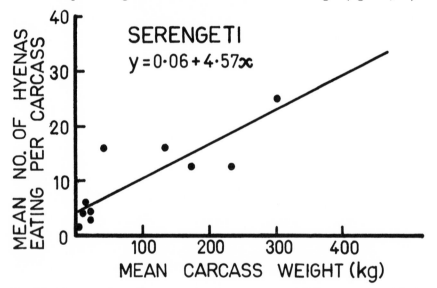

Fig. 30. Mean number of hyenas eating from carcasses of different mean weight in the Serengeti.

7. Serengeti: $r = 0.83$; $p < 0.01$. Ngorongoro: $r = 0.98$; $p < 0.001$.
8. Serengeti: $r = 0.87$; $p < 0.01$. Ngorongoro: $r = 0.76$; $p < 0.05$.

TABLE 27 *Number of hyenas eating from a carcass (hyena-kills only) and mean carcass weight per eating hyena*

Carcass	Serengeti				Ngorongoro			
	No. of observations	Mean weight per carcass (in kg)	Mean no. of hyenas eating	Weight available per hyena (in kg)	No. of observations	Mean weight per carcass (in kg)	Mean no. of hyenas eating	Weight available per hyena (in kg)
Wildebeest adult	85	172	12.6	13.6	109	181	23.6	7.7
Wildebeest calf	33	16	5.8	2.8	69	16	5.4	3.0
Zebra adult	19	232	17.7	18.3	29	250	20.5	12.2
Zebra foal	4	22	4.2	5.2	18	22	15.7	1.4
Thomson's gazelle adult	32	20	3.2	6.3	—	—	—	—
Thomson's gazelle fawn	30	2.5	1.7	1.5	7	2.5	1.4	1.8
Buffalo adult male	—	—	—	—	1	750	69	10.9
Topi calf	3	13	4.3	3.0	—	—	—	—
Kongoni adult male	1	134	16	8.4	—	—	—	—
Eland adult female	1	300	25	12.0	—	—	—	—
Impala adult female	1	42	16	2.6	—	—	—	—

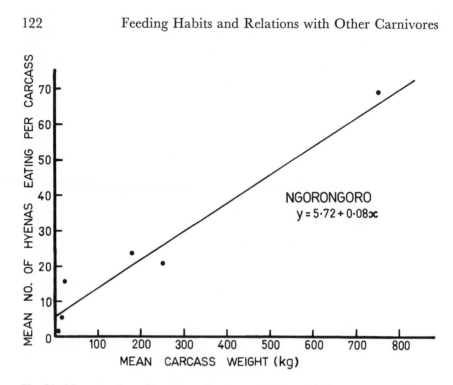

Fig. 31. Mean number of hyenas eating from carcasses of different mean weight in Ngorongoro.

At this stage, it would be interesting to compare the energy exerted per hunting hyena in the pursuit of these species. The distance covered by the chase is approximately the same for adult wildebeest, zebra, and Thomson's gazelle, although speeds differ (gazelle are chased fastest, then wildebeest), and the success rate is similar. This, together with table 27 and figures 32 and 33, enables us to appreciate why gazelle is a less popular prey than wildebeest or zebra. Zebra is obviously the best value for energy but needs a special social effort. Wildebeest calves are a low-reward prey, but the distance they are chased is much shorter and the speed is not very fast. With two hyenas cooperating, the success rate of hunting this particular prey is very high, and all together less energy is expended. Zebra foals are caught in the same way as adults, but seem to be a "bad draw" compared with the reward gained from killing an adult. The very large kinds of prey such as buffalo and eland are probably very difficult for hyenas to catch (because of their size, and for other reasons, p. 206); otherwise they would certainly give a good reward. Although these conclusions must all be very tentative, they may go at least some way toward explaining the hyena's food preferences.

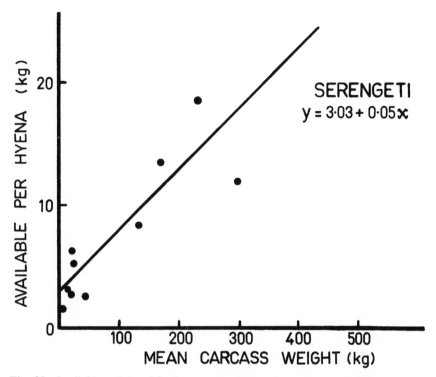

Fig. 32. Available weight of food per eating hyena, for carcasses of different mean weight in the Serengeti.

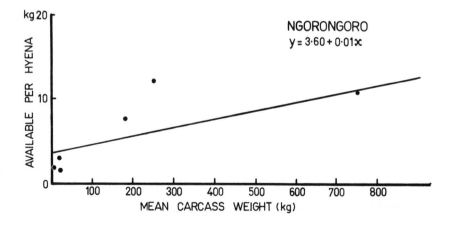

Fig. 33. Available weight of food per eating hyena, for carcasses of different mean weight in Ngorongoro.

Relations between Eating Hyenas

One hyena can eat at least 14.5 kg at a meal (p. 76). Most kinds of prey, therefore, provide less food than the hyenas present can eat. Some parts of the kill are preferred by the hyenas (see below) and others are less palatable. All this means that around a carcass we can expect competition for food. With thirty or more hyenas frequently eating side by side (I have seen up to fifty-two eating together), considering their powerful jaws, such communal feeding could lead to some very nasty fighting, but in practice this does not happen. On large kills (where there is relatively more meat per hyena), the participants eat quite peacefully together, though each hyena eats as fast as possible. They push in shoulder to shoulder, sometimes climbing over and on top of each other until the carcass is completely buried beneath a writhing mass of hyena bodies (pl. 5). Once hyenas are able to bear pieces away from the carcass (which they do as soon as possible), one may see more aggression over these smaller bits, and the same is true for smaller kills.

When aggression does occur over food, this rarely results in actual bites. If our tame hyena, even when really hungry, had acquired a piece of meat, I could always take this away from him without running the risk of being bitten; he would struggle frantically to keep his piece of meat, pulling and holding on to it and trying to run away with it, but he would never bite me. In the wild, hyenas pull meat away from one another and chase the ones that have run off with a chunk (trying to grab them by the hind leg). Sometimes, when hyenas are eating close together, one may snap at another and give an obviously very superficial bite, but I have never seen this develop into a real fight. A hyena with a piece of meat will protect it against others by turning his back or by running away with it.

During these interactions, hyenas use a large vocabulary of calls which I have described in appendix D. 8. These usually make a hyena kill a very noisy gathering. Postures of hyenas often reveal an aggressive motivation among the eaters, and manes and tails are frequently raised (p. 216).

Certain dominance rules are observed at a kill, though these are rather inconspicuous; there is no sign of them at larger kills when all hyenas are eating together; but if a male and a female are contesting the same piece of bone next to a kill, or the same small prey, the female is usually victorious. It is also quite common to see one or two females eating from a small kill with several males standing around, not allowed to come near and obliged to wait for any spoils. Cubs come last, but females often protect their own offspring against other hyenas, even when the young ones are already adult size; a cub may be quietly eating from a piece of carcass with the mother standing next to it, not eating herself but keeping other hyenas away. I have several times seen a hyena who had killed a small prey (especially with gazelle fawns) keep other hyenas away by snapping at them and even chasing them; the others usually gave in. The one who had done the killing asserted dominance over the others—I was never sure whether this was because it had done the killing or whether dominant hyenas were more likely to kill than others.

Around a large kill, especially, there is a great deal of chasing, the pursued hyenas carrying away bones and uttering various calls like the laugh and the yell, indicating fear. But often there are indications that it is not merely competition for food that causes all this. A hyena intending to eat his piece of meat or bone will walk a good distance away from the main kill (pl. 6), especially if the other hyenas are showing interest. On some occasions, however, a hyena will walk around a kill with a bone in its mouth (often with tail up, indicating excitement), and if another hyena chases it, the two hyenas run around in large circles, keeping near the others all the time. One gets the strong impression that the pursued hyena does not try to get away and even that it invites pursuit. If the pursuer gets hold of the bone, the roles may be reversed or there may be a short struggle. Adults and young hyenas indulge in this behavior, which looks more like play than serious food competition.

Sequence of Eating a Carcass

If hyenas find a corpse which has already been opened up by other carnivores, they will merely continue eating where the others left off. If the carcass is intact, however, or if the victim is still alive after being hunted down, they tear open the belly and loins; the first parts to go are usually the testicles or udder. If there are many hyenas trying to feed at the same time, there is not room for everyone to bite in the loins, and so some will attack the anal region or, if that is already occupied, any part of the corpse they can get at. Once the abdomen is opened, the entrails are pulled out and the soft parts eaten; if the victim is a pregnant female, the fetus is one of the first things to be consumed. The stomach is pulled out, the stomach wall eaten, and the contents spilled out over the ground. At this stage, hyenas begin eating the abdominal and leg muscles and the skin; if there is plenty, the lungs are torn out and left aside to be eaten afterward by the hyenas or by the vultures. Once a large part of the muscles has been consumed, the hyenas are able to start tearing off legs, and one sees the first animals running off with their loot. The ribs are eaten on the spot if there are enough hyenas around, but the pelvis and vertebral column are carried off. The head is always the last part of a kill to remain, often with part of the vertebral column and back skin still attached to it, but in the end this is also borne off to a quiet place.

If any part of a corpse is left by the hyenas in both Ngorongoro or Serengeti, the skull is the most likely to remain uneaten, followed by the vertebrae, ribs, pelvis, and the ends of the large leg bones.

Competition between feeding hyenas expresses itself in speed of eating rather than in actual fighting, and the time in which a prey animal can vanish is truly amazing. To mention some examples: in Ngorongoro, a yearling wildebeest (estimated weight approximately 100 kg) was chased for 5 min by a hyena and died 2 min after being caught by two hyenas; 7 min after its death, one of the twenty-one hyenas eating from it ran off with a leg; another 3 min later only the head and spine were left; and 3 min more from the time of death there was only a dark spot on the grass to show what had happened. On another occasion in the crater, hyenas killed, simultaneously, a female zebra and her two-year-old foal (estimated weights approximately 220 and 150 kg). All together, thirty-five hyenas ate from the two carcasses, clearing the spot of all remains of the two-year-old zebra in 24 min, and of the adult female in 36 min after their deaths. In the Serengeti, I have seen a gazelle fawn (approximate weight 2.5 kg) swallowed up by a single hyena in just under 2 min, and the largest measured amount of food I ever gave a wild hyena (two disemboweled gazelle carcasses, of which the hyena ate 14.5 kg) disappeared in 45 min.

Hyenas can swallow large pieces of meat or bone in one gulp, which must help them in consuming their food quickly. Of course, they may take hours over the larger bones and skull, but these more time-consuming jobs are usually executed well out of the range of possible competition.

Other Eating Habits

When hyenas are scavenging around human habitation, they pick up all sorts of different materials and eat them; but elsewhere they also chew and eat all manner of things. Some obviously liked crunching up the tail lights of my car when I was watching them, and cubs often chew on pieces of wood. Adults occasionally eat grass and sometimes fresh wildebeest droppings. Another unexpected foraging habit is termite eating. At times, especially at the beginning of the rainy season, masses of termites leave their nests in the evening and the termite hills look as if they are smoking. I have seen hyenas stand next to termite holes and snap up the termites as they flew off.

Hyenas are surprisingly adept at eating in water. Stevenson-Hamilton (1947) describes how a hyena standing "in shallow water with forelegs well straddled out, in this position snaps up any incautious fishes, large or small, as well, no doubt, as any other water-living creatures." I have never seen this, but I have several times seen them feed off a wildebeest that they had chased into water (p. 7). Once in Ngorongoro, for instance, a male wildebeest drowned in the central lake after being chased in by the hyenas, about 200 m from the shore at a place where the lake was 1.20–1.50 m deep. No hyenas swam out to the carcass until the next day, when thirty-two of them gathered on the shore—by then the carcass was floating and one horn and the flank were just visible above the surface of the water. First one, then several hyenas swam out to it, and soon three were feeding on it. They dived under the surface and bit pieces out of the corpse, completely disappearing from view and coming up to swallow whatever they had managed to get. I timed seventy-five periods when the hyenas were submerged; they disappeared for up to 12 sec, but the average was 4.8 sec. Nobody made any attempt to drag the corpse to the shore, but after I had had a look at the carcass and brought it farther toward the shore (to about 15 m from the shore in 0.7 m of water), the hyenas first fed from it standing with their hind legs on the lake bottom and then pulled it to the shore, where they finished it in half an hour.

Drinking

Although hyenas are at ease in or near water, they often live in very dry country where they have to do without water for days. The female hyena who carried a radio collar in Ngorongoro, and whom we followed for twelve days, drank nine times in that period; any hyena coming across fresh water in the Serengeti will stop and drink. It is obvious, however, that they can do without for long periods, maybe several weeks; I have watched females who stayed with their cubs on the dry plains for over a week, during which time they almost certainly did not drink. When hyenas do drink they do not consume much at a time; they almost never spend more than 30 sec at a drink, and hyenas coming to our birdbath near the house never drank more than $\frac{1}{2}$ to 1 liter at a time.

RELATIONS BETWEEN HYENAS AND OTHER CARNIVOROUS ANIMALS

Hyenas and Lions

Food competition.

From field notes:

> One night in November 1965, I followed a pack of eight hyenas, which left the "club" (p. 180) of the Mungi clan at 2040 hr, in my Land Rover; there was a bright moon and it was easy to follow the hyenas at some distance while they walked in the direction of hills along the crater rim. At 2055 and 2115, two of the hyenas chased some wildebeest over a short distance, but they did not seem very serious about it, and the other hyenas did not follow the chase. Gradually, they came closer together, often stopping and changing direction, but clearly all going in the direction of the hills, away from the large wildebeest concentrations on the floor of the crater. They were heading for a small distant herd of zebra about halfway up the slopes along the Mungi River. The eight hyenas began to walk closer together and gradually stepped up their pace; at 2140, they reached the zebra, which did not notice them until they were about 50 m away. The zebra slowly moved out of the way and then began to run, splitting up into two groups of about ten animals each. The hyenas followed one group, a family whose stallion vigorously defended the group and chased the hyenas. The zebra ran fairly slowly (about 20 km per hour) in a tight bunch, and the hyenas followed behind trying to bite different animals. Suddenly one of the zebra dropped slightly behind the bunch with two hyenas biting at it and hanging on to it; immediately all the other hyenas converged on this particular zebra while the other zebra continued running. One young male zebra of one to one and one-half years old turned from the group to the mare which was being held by the hyenas, but he was bitten by a hyena and immediately ran back to the group of zebra. The captured zebra fell down approximately 5 mins after being caught, and died after another 6 min, at 2155. Two more hyenas joined the pack and ten hyenas were eating when suddenly another pack of six hyenas turned up from the direction of the den of the neighboring clan, and chased off the original ten. The six newly arrived hyenas began to eat almost immediately, but only 4 min after their arrival, they all stopped and stared with a heads-up attitude toward a large black-maned lion who came running up to the kill. When the lion was still some 100 m away the hyenas ran off

uttering their alarm grunt. The lion galloped toward the kill with his tail up, but pursued the hyenas in several directions before settling down to it. When he was eating, the hyenas returned to some 60 m from the kill, but 5 min later the lion got up and chased two hyenas for over 200 m before running back to the kill. Several times he had to chase away an odd jackal, but the hyenas left him to it and walked back to their den, about 3 km away, and when I left at 2430, the lion was still quietly eating the dead zebra.

This is a typical occurrence in Ngorongoro Crater. It shows the lion as a scavenger of hyena kills, and I found that this habit of the lion is very common. Hyenas may scavenge from lions and lions scavenge from hyenas; it is worth considering the relation between these two common East African carnivores in more detail. One wonders about the effect they have on each other, and to what extent they compete ecologically or benefit from each other. Moreover, the relations between lions and hyenas have a bearing on predation of ungulates.

In figure 34 I have compiled observations in which lions and hyenas fed from the same carcass—either both carnivores were present simultaneously or they followed each other very shortly to the kill. This figure shows that, especially in Ngorongoro but also in the Serengeti, hyenas killed the victim in the majority of the cases.[9] Sometimes it was not possible to decide who made the kill; if we consider only the cases in which the killer was clearly indicated, hyenas had done the killing in 93% of the observations of lion and hyena sharing a kill in Ngorongoro and in 61% of the observations in the Serengeti.[10] Here also there is a possibility of bias in the figures tabulated. The causes of bias would be the same as in figure 26, but the most important one, the bias caused by my following hyenas rather than lions, could be checked on by comparing my observations with those of other observers who were more interested in the lions than the hyenas. In my own observations, 53% of corpses on which both lions and hyenas had fed in the Serengeti had been killed by hyenas and 33% were lion kills, the remaining being uncertain cases. In observations reported to me by others, Schaller in particular, over the same period in the same area, 54% had been killed by hyenas and 34% by lions. The agreement between the two sets of observations is close.

It is clear that in Ngorongoro there is direct and active competition between lions and hyenas for food and that lions more often make use of

9. Serengeti: $p = 0.24$ (binomial). Ngorongoro: $p < 0.00003$ (binomial).
10. Difference Serengeti/Ngorongoro: $\chi^2 = 16.41$; $df = 1$; $p < 0.001$.

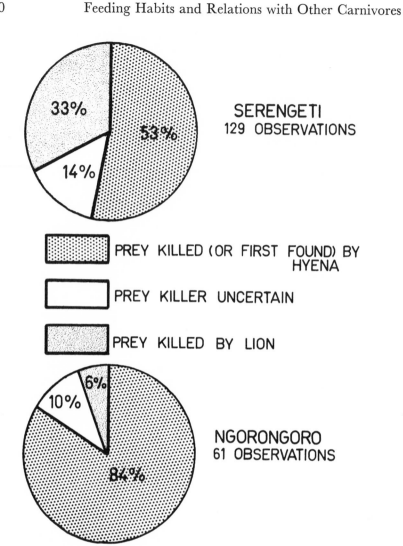

SERENGETI
129 OBSERVATIONS

PREY KILLED (OR FIRST FOUND) BY HYENA

PREY KILLER UNCERTAIN

PREY KILLED BY LION

NGORONGORO
61 OBSERVATIONS

Fig. 34. Observations where lions and hyenas fed from the same carcass, with either of the two species scavenging from the other.

food killed by hyenas than the other way round. The role this competition plays in the feeding of either of the two is largely dependent on their relative numbers and probably also on their absolute density—in other words, the amount of contact between individuals of the two species. In the Ngorongoro Crater the number of lions, after reaching a minimum during a stomoxys plague in 1962 (Fosbrooke 1963), increased during the study period from an estimated 30 (Estes 1967b) to an estimated 50–60 by the end (0.12 to 0.23 per km²), and I estimated 1.7 hyenas per km²; there is a great deal of contact between the two, and lions are far in the minority. Consequently, of 63 kills on which lions were seen feeding, 51 had been killed by hyenas (81%). Hyenas scavenge very little in the Ngorongoro, and of the kills that hyenas themselves made there, lions turned up in 51 (21%) of the 244 observations. Whenever lions did turn up at a hyena kill, they ate a substantial amount in 63% of the observations, a little in 27%, nothing in 8% and an unknown quantity in 2%. Lions turned up especially for the larger prey species killed by hyenas; at hyena kills of adult wildebeest, lions were present in 31% of the observations and at 26% of the kills of adult zebra. Of course, my figures on the number of hyena kills at which lions turned up must suffer somewhat from observational bias, for it takes lions longer than hyenas to finish a carcass and thus one is more likely to come across them. This may have slightly influenced the percentages of hyena kills that we observed to have been taken over by lions, but it should have had no effect on the observations on the origins of lion food; hence these data show the lion population in Ngorongoro as leading a predominantly scavenging existence, profiting from what the hyenas kill. Also, they obviously take a substantial amount from the total hyena bag.

The immediate effect of this on predator-prey relations is, of course, that the hyenas will have to kill more often; this means that, although two different predator species are using the same food supply, prey selection takes place almost only according to the whim of the hyenas. The increase in lion numbers in the crater, which began during my study there, may well lead to a change in relations between lions and hyenas. An increased amount of lion scavenging could seriously affect the hyenas' food supply; and conversely, lions might be forced to kill more for themselves. The development of this relation is worth further study.

The situation is different in the Serengeti ecosystem. Here the lion population is estimated at some 2,000–2,400 (Schaller, personal communication), which means a density of 0.16–0.20 per km². I found 0.24 hyena per km², and it is clear when comparing the Serengeti figures with those of Ngorongoro that the amount of contact between lions and hyenas (if randomly distributed through the habitat) is small, and that the differences in relative abundance are smaller in the Serengeti than in the crater. Consequently, we find that on the plains only approximately 18% of lion meals are stolen from hyenas (Schaller, personal communication), and 7% of hyena meals (22% of carcasses scavenged) have been obtained from lions. In the Serengeti woodlands, the amount of overlap is even smaller. In this situation, a lion has to kill for himself, since scavenging from hyenas is more difficult, and therefore hyenas have more chance to scavenge from lion kills. After lions have finished with a large carcass, hyenas will very often eat the bones—sometimes several days later. This may make a considerable contribution to the hyena diet, but is difficult to account for and has not been included in the above figures.

Thus the prey population in the Serengeti falls victim to lions as well as hyenas, which both exert their particular prey selection pressure, in contrast to the situation in Ngorongoro.

Behavior of hyenas toward lions, and vice versa.   Lions usually ignore hyenas, (pl. 8), except on kills or when harassed by them. However, hyenas often show clear reactions to the presence of lions, whether on a kill or not. A solitary hyena walking about will go far out of his way to have a look at a lion walking or lying down. He approaches the lion, or group of lions, and circles around until he comes downwind. He then stands with tail hanging down and head fairly low, ears cocked forward. In this kind of situation a hyena does not usually approach a lion closer than 20 m. Sometimes hyenas will spend a long time walking around the lion, obviously attracted by it but at the same time keeping a distance from it. If hyenas are walking in a group, however, they are much more audacious and keep close together behind a walking lion at a distance of 4–5 m (pl. 9), often showing some signs of aggression with their tails up, manes slightly raised, ears cocked forward, and head held fairly high; their calls include lowing, grunt-laughing, and fast whoops (appendix D. 8).

Lions often respond clearly to this treatment and may walk away or lash out at the hyenas and chase them. On one occasion in November 1966, I saw a group of two male and two female lions walking over one of the plains in the western Serengeti (Musabi). They met a group of twelve hyenas, who followed them at some 40 m distance, several times calling excitedly (fast whoop). When the hyenas got closer, one lioness turned round and ran at full speed after an old fat female hyena. After a run of about 100 m, with the hyena laughing loudly, the lioness overtook the hyena, slapped her forepaws against the hyena's hind legs (pl. 10), which bowled her over, and then grabbed her in the belly. The other lions immediately joined in and lay down around the hyena, biting and pawing at their quarry. After about 20 sec the hyena lay motionless, but 10 sec later, when I thought she must be dead, she jumped up and slowly ran off, bleeding profusely from the sides and head. The lions did not follow her. Four minutes later, however, one of the lionesses got up and started slowly trotting after the old hyena who was walking away. Again a short, slow run followed, and the lioness caught up and slapped twice at the hyena's hind legs, bowling her over. Then the lioness lost interest and once more walked away. The hyena slowly limped off and lay down some 300 m farther on and she was still lying there several hours later, obviously seriously injured. She probably died of her injuries, as I knew her well and never saw her again.

Sometimes, though, the shoe is on the other foot. One night, in August 1968, I was awakened in Seronera at 0400 hr by very loud lion growls and the calling of my hyenas about 1 km from our house. When I arrived in the car I found two lionesses, one high up in an acacia tree, and another about 20 m farther on, surrounded by eighteen hyenas. All were silent until the lioness on the ground walked a few steps; this precipitated a chorus of grunt-laughs, laughs, and growls from the hyenas, who ran toward the lioness. The hyenas all took up very aggressive postures and many bit, or tried to bite, the lioness, especially from behind. The lioness crouched down, growling and snapping and swatting at the hyenas, but they were in a dense pack around and on top of her. After about 10 sec of this, the lioness suddenly managed to break loose and ran off for 40 m chased by the whole horde of hyenas, who went on biting at her while she ran. Then she reached a large acacia tree and climbed into a fork about 2 m above the ground. She was bleeding from some slight wounds in the hind legs and rump, but still growled and hissed at the hyenas dancing around on their hind legs trying to reach her. Then all noise died down, and after 5 min the hyenas slowly drifted away, leaving the two lionesses up the trees. Twelve min after the last hyena had disappeared, first one and then the other lioness came down and ran off in the opposite direction from that taken by the hyenas. The lionesses both seemed very healthy and normal, the hyenas looked well fed, and there was no indication of a kill anywhere near (nor did either lions or hyenas have bloody mouths). This clearly then was not a clash over a kill; it may have been mobbing, hunting, or both.

Although I have rarely seen hyenas actually attempting to bite lions when they are not on a kill, when I have seen it the hyenas' postures indicated an element of aggression, not only fear, and an attraction which might be called curiosity. Thus the reactions of hyenas toward lions are very reminiscent of the reactions of many species of birds toward small carnivores, owls, and birds of prey. This behavior has been called "mobbing"; its causation has been studied by, among others, Hartley (1950), Miller 1952), Nice and ter Pelkwyk (1941), Andrew (1961), and Curio (1961, 1963). Very little is known about the function of this behavior in birds, but since sometimes (as in the case of the hyenas and lions observed at Musabi) mobbing birds are actually killed by the predator (reference in Hartley 1950; and Smith 1969), there must be strong compensatory advantages in this behavior. It may well be that by mobbing predators are induced to leave the area, and since it is to the hyenas' advantage to have the competitive and dangerous lions out of the way, there may be similarities in function and motivation between the hyenas' behavior and that of the mobbing birds.

Relations between lions and hyenas are even more strained when they are actively competing for food. If the hyenas have a kill it may attract lions from distances of over three km; in fact, once in Ngorongoro I saw a lioness running after a pack of hyenas who were chasing a wildebeest, even before the hyenas had caught it. And on two occasions, I witnessed lions turning up at the scene when hyenas had brought a wildebeest to a standstill, then taking over completely and actually killing the wildebeest.

In December 1965, at daybreak, in the range of the Scratching Rocks clan in the crater, I noticed two hyenas dash into a herd of wildebeest and then stand watching them scatter. The herd split up into a number of small, tightly bunched running groups. Suddenly one female wildebeest was running on her own. She was immediately set upon by the hyenas, who overtook her after some 300 m when she reached the bank of the Mungi River. One hyena bit her from behind while she charged the other, and the killing would have been a long-drawn-out business if some other hyenas had not turned up within the next few minutes. Four minutes after she was caught there were about twenty-five hyenas pulling the wildebeest down; her tail was bitten off at the root and she was bleeding from wounds in the loins and around the anus. Then suddenly the hyena alarm call sounded, and all but three of the attackers ran off; I looked around and saw two male lions about $\frac{1}{2}$ km away galloping toward the commotion. They arrived at the scene 3 min later, by which time all the hyenas were over 50 m away. One of the lions ran straight to the wildebeest, who was still standing with her back to the tall vegetation along the stream. She lowered her head and charged the lion as he came close, but while she charged, he grabbed her head and neck with his paws. Because of her speed, she dragged the lion for a short distance, while he managed to bite at her throat. By this time the lion was half lying on the ground, and he slowly pulled the wildebeest down beside him, biting, and holding her with one front paw over the shoulder and the other on her neck. One minute after the lion's first attack, the wildebeest collapsed and the lion got up and stood next to her, still firmly holding her throat. Then the other male lion arrived and soon they both started to eat—the hyenas watching from a distance.

At night, it seems to be the noise of hyenas on a kill that attracts lions; this noise is, indeed, audible over a large area. The calls are made mostly by animals squabbling among themselves. It seems that it would be an obvious advantage for the hyenas if they were silent when eating, but apparently the advantage of using calls in the one hyena versus another context is greater than the disadvantage of giving the kill away to lions. That it is often the calls which betray the place of kills to lions is suggested by the fact that lions often turn up at a hyena kill immediately after an outburst of calls, for instance after a clash between clans (p. 251). This was shown experimentally: tape-recorded hyena calls, made near a kill, were played back through a loudspeaker in both the Serengeti and Ngorongoro (for the purpose of attracting hyenas to check up on the proportion of marked animals), and lions were repeatedly attracted to my car containing the loudspeaker. Once, early in the morning in the Serengeti, I saw four male lions run from over 1 km away to a place in the long grass where six male hyenas were making a good deal of noise around a female in heat (p. 232). The squabbling sounded to me like the calls of hyenas on a kill. The lions rushed up to the hyenas, then lay down again.

Invariably, when one or more lions turn up at a kill hyenas scatter and run away, calling out (pl. 11). The big cats then settle on the kill (pl. 12) and begin to eat, although sometimes they chase the hyenas well away from the kill first. Hyenas are sometimes killed by lions when they are near the carcass, but I have never seen this. In my experience the hyenas stood or walked around, or lay surrounding the lions at the kill, at a distance of 10 m to 50 m, occasionally gathering courage and approaching with loud outbursts of calls.

Lions may take a long time to finish a kill, and usually the hyenas stay around (on one occasion when the lions had taken over a hyena-killed eland in the Serengeti, the hyenas waited at least 35 hr before the last lioness finally left). When they do leave the kill all the hyenas immediately throw themselves on the remains; the lion often wheels round and chases the hyenas off again and then remains a short time before walking away. Only twice did I see hyenas and lions eating simultaneously from the same kill (pl. 14)—this was exceptional and would only occur when a lion is particularly sluggish and the hyenas extremely hungry. Sometimes lions do not get away with it so easily; on six occasions I saw hyenas running away and then returning when the lion was on the kill (pl. 13). The hyenas approached the lion from behind in aggressive posture, calling loudly and in close formation. On four occasions this alone was enough to make the lion leave before he was replete, but twice the hyenas actually bit the lion before he left, as the following incident illustrates.

> At dawn in November 1966 I found twenty-one hyenas who had just pulled down a male wildebeest along the upper reaches of the Mbalageti. Shortly after this, three young male and four female lions came running up; the hyenas ran off and the lions settled down to feed. The lions had obviously already eaten and they did not eat much more. After 50 min, although part of the carcass was still uneaten, six of the lions walked off and one female remained behind. Even she was bloated with food and eventually she lay down next to the kill. This brought the hyenas into action—they all stood up and one small group walked, in aggressive postures, lowing and whooping all the time, to within 10 m of the kill. The lioness got up and walked over to the other lions. The hyenas immediately rushed in and started feeding, but this proved too much for one of the young male lions who had been watching from some 100 m away. He galloped toward the kill, scattering the hyenas for up to 50 m and then, grunting and growling, he lay down next to it. The hyenas stuck up their tails and, with a chorus of deep lowing calls and whoops, immediately walked right up to the growling lion. Twice the lion jumped up and lashed out at the hyenas without leaving the carcass. Then one of the hyenas came in from behind the lion, jumped over the carcass, and bit the lion in the rump. The lion jumped around, lashed out a paw at the hyena (and missed), growling loudly all the time with his ears flat back, then ran off at great speed with the whole pack behind him. But with a choice between pursuing the lion and eating from the kill, the hyenas quickly chose the kill and the lion trotted off to join the rest of the pride.

If hyenas are present in large numbers around an animal killed by lions, interactions are similar to situations where hyenas are the killers.

Hyenas and lions: discussion.   Clearly, whenever the two species come into contact with each other, there is a great deal of active competition between them. Most often, the hyenas are chased off by lions, but the reverse does also occur. These data refer mostly to the two species' interest in a kill, and for further useful discussion we will have to consider to what extent their other interests coincide. For instance, How do their diets compare?

Since this question is particularly relevant to the Serengeti, only data obtained in that area will be discussed. The diet of lions in the Serengeti National Park, according to Kruuk and Turner (1967), consisted of 49% wildebeest, 26% zebra, 8% buffalo, and 10% gazelle. Gazelle were underrepresented in that sample, as were other smaller antelopes, but later data collected by Schaller (personal communication) in areas of hyena abundance confirm the conclusion that in comparing these figures with the diet of hyenas (table 11) there is an enormous overlap in the choice of prey species. There are some differences—for instance, the occurrence of really large animals in the diet of the lion and the hyenas' ability to eat large bones. However, the overlap in diet between lions and hyenas is greater than that between any of the other large carnivores, as studied by Kruuk and Turner (1967). There are differences in habitat selection between the two species—for instance, lions are more likely to choose the vicinity of cover (along rivers or in woodland, kopjes, and so on) than hyenas, but there is a large overlap.

From the above it might appear that lions and hyenas occupy almost the same ecological niche—at least in the Serengeti, where the two species have the same selection of prey animals, though this need not necessarily hold true for other areas. It is likely, however, that their food selection is not as similar as it looks—there are clear indications that selection of individuals within the prey species is done differently by the two carnivores—which would allow the two species to live from the same resources. Most important, it is likely that, at least in the Serengeti, the population-limiting factors are different for the two predators. Both hyenas and lions are affected by the migratory movements of the ungulates; the numbers of lions are probably to a large degree determined by what game is left in their territories during the "lean" time of the year (Schaller, personal communication), the hyena numbers probably by the movements of migratory herds and the distances these are from the denning sites (p. 103). Thus, although there is a keen competition for food between the two species, this is unlikely to affect the numbers of either—at least in the Serengeti.

Hyenas and Cheetahs

Cheetahs seem to be very easily frightened, and hyenas have no difficulty in stealing kills from them. On three occasions, I saw one hyena run up to a cheetah on a kill (in one instance, a mother with two cubs); on seeing the hyena running toward it the cheetah took fright and fled. Obviously this is not uncommon; Schaller (1968) found that cheetahs in the Serengeti lost 4% of their kills to hyenas. I have never seen or heard of cheetahs stealing somebody else's kill.

The cheetahs' diet is quite different from that of hyenas, as they specialize in catching small antelopes and the young of medium-sized ones, and they rarely hunt adult medium-sized prey (Graham 1966; Kruuk and Turner 1967; Schaller 1968).

Hyenas and Leopards

One evening in December 1964 I saw a leopard high up in an acacia tree beside the Seronera River in the Serengeti. Some 30 m away from the tree were the half-eaten remains of a Thomson's gazelle, and it seemed fairly certain that the leopard was the rightful owner of this carcass. After I had watched the leopard from a distance for some time, it came down from the tree and began to eat, but in a few minutes two hyenas came running up from downwind, apparently having smelled the food. On their arrival, the leopard ran back to the tree (chased by the hyenas), and one of the marauders carried away the carcass.

On another occasion in the Moru kopjes in October 1967, I found a hyena eating from a carcass near a leopard in a tree. Examination of the carcass, together with the red mouth of the leopard, indicated that the leopard had killed the tommy and that the hyena had been the scavenger. However, S. Downey (personal communication) observed the opposite happen in the Serengeti; a hyena was eating the remains of a tommy carcass (left by a cheetah) and did not notice an approaching leopard until it was only a few meters away. After a very short scuffle, the leopard ran off with the kill, chased by the hyena, and disappeared into a sausage tree. After the leopard had eaten the remains of the kill, it came down from the tree and charged the hyena, who was still waiting at the foot of the tree. Smith (1962) describes an incident in which a leopard approached nine hyenas on a greater kudu kill at a waterhole in the Kruger National Park. One of the hyenas chased the leopard up a tree.

The diet of leopards shows little overlap with that of hyenas; it consists mostly of small animals (including small rodents and birds) and the smaller antelopes like gazelle and reedbuck (Kruuk and Turner 1967).

Hyenas and Wild Dogs

In his study on the social behavior of wild dogs, Kühme (1965) noticed that they were able, very effectively, to keep hyenas several hundred meters away from their den by chasing the hyenas and biting them in their hindquarters; on one occasion, a hyena was bleeding badly after it had been attacked by wild dogs when 5 m from the den. Hyenas would sometimes come and try to steal the kill of wild dogs, but, according to Kühme, the wild dogs operating in a pack had little difficulty in warding off the solitary hyenas. Estes and Goddard (1967) saw many clashes over kills between wild dogs and hyenas and came to essentially the same conclusions as Kühme. In their observations the dogs were invariably the killers and the hyenas came in individually to steal a bite. A hyena was usually set upon by several dogs, who tried to bite his rear end; this caused the hyena to squat and protect its more vulnerable parts, growling loudly all the time. In Estes's and Goddard's observations hyenas often managed to grab at least part of the kills, but this happened almost only when just a few of their pack of twenty-one wild dogs were present, either the first one or two dogs which had caught the prey or the last few dogs to leave when the carcass was almost entirely eaten.

These observations are substantiated by my own. Of sixty-two wild-dog kills that I watched in the Serengeti and Ngorongoro, hyenas were present at forty-six and ate at least part of the kill on thirty-seven of those occasions. But on five occasions, I saw wild dogs chase hyenas off their kill; once this was a zebra the hyenas had found dead and the other times, Thomson's gazelle killed by hyenas. It is clear from my data and those of Estes and Goddard that wild dogs scavenging from hyenas is fairly rare and on the whole, the relation between wild dogs and hyenas is of one-sided benefit for the hyenas.

Hyenas are attracted to wild dogs even when no kill is present and the dogs are merely lying resting for the day. Frequently, when one comes across a pack lying asleep, there are hyenas lying some 100–200 m away, and often much nearer; once I saw a hyena asleep in the middle of a pack of wild dogs and they were actually touching one another. Similar instances have been recorded by others (e.g., Kühme 1965). Usually a hyena approaching a stationary pack of wild dogs will go downwind of them, as they do when approaching a lion; the dogs may watch the hyenas, but usually show no interest beyond this, except when they are lying on their den. Sometimes up to ten hyenas may be asleep near a pack and when, at the end of the day, the pack takes off to hunt, the hyenas follow, after first having inspected the place where the dogs have been lying, and eaten the wild-dog feces they find. Once the dogs begin chasing their quarry, the hyenas follow them closely, sometimes even managing, with an effort, to run in front of some of the dogs. More often, however, hyenas are unable to keep up with the pack and lose it completely. It sometimes happens that after the first one or two dogs have caught a prey the hyenas are there before the other dogs and in this way are easily able to steal the kill from the hunters. In a few cases I saw wild dogs grab the victim, which was then killed and eaten by the hyenas. Twice, on the other hand, hyenas hunting with the wild dogs were able to grab gazelle before the wild dogs could do so, but on both these occasions the wild dogs chased away the hyenas and ate the kill. Alan Root (personal communication) saw a pack of dogs chase a herd of zebra over a long distance and finally grab one; at the same time, some hyenas turned up and grabbed another zebra from the same herd. The dogs were unable to kill their quarry (an adult mare) and let it go after a long bloody struggle. They then ran over to the feeding hyenas and chased them off their zebra carcass.

The usual way for a hyena to obtain food from a wild-dog kill is to approach the feeding dogs slowly, often in a posture indicating fear (pls. 15 and 16). They move in this way for several minutes until they are within a few m of the kill, or a part of it—then, if they are still ignored by the dogs, they may suddenly run in and grab a bit of meat and carry it off (pl. 17). But even at this stage the dogs are often able to dissuade hyenas from taking their meat—several of them bite at the hyena's rear end until it drops the food. Such fights are accompanied by very loud growls from the hyenas and high whimpering calls from the dogs. Hyenas often operate in groups but rarely in unison; wild dogs usually assist each other in attacking a single hyena.

In any fight over a kill between wild dogs and hyenas, the outcome is by no means dependent only on the number of each species present. Once I saw two hyenas keeping a pack of nineteen wild dogs away from a gazelle carcass that the wild dogs had killed but that the hyenas quickly ate. The wild dogs in this case were rather hungry, for immediately afterward they caught another gazelle. On another occasion, I noticed a pack of five wild dogs followed by two hyenas; the five wild dogs came across five hyenas eating from a dead zebra they had just found near Seronera. The wild dogs immediately, and with no difficulty, chased away the hyenas, but were only able to enjoy their easy meal for a very short time because the two hyenas who had been following them ran in snapping at the dogs and chased them away without any trouble. After staying around for a few minutes while the two hyenas were eating, the wild dogs wandered off, and only then did the original five hyenas return.

Sometimes hyenas are able to eat with the dogs from the same carcass with the dogs only occasionally snapping at them. I have seen this four times; for all four observations young hyenas were concerned (between ten and sixteen months old), and they came up uttering their begging call. They responded to the dogs' attacks only by crouching with their ears flat and their mouths half open, and they showed none of the customary fleeing or active defense of the adult. One of these young hyenas, a badly limping ten-month old, was thus able to work his way right into the middle of a pack of twenty-two dogs eating an adult topi and actually disappeared completely inside the carcass. With the submissive posture, then, young hyenas are often able to snatch pieces away from individual dogs without receiving the usual summary punishment.

These instances show that there is not a simple dominance-subdominance relation between wild dogs and hyenas as there is between lions and hyenas; it is more complicated, and their relationship may well depend on the interaction of a number of factors such as the number of each species, hunger state, previous experience, and individual differences. Generally, however, wild dogs are able to dominate hyenas. Although wild dogs sometimes benefit from hyenas by stealing their kills, on the whole, the relationship between wild dogs and hyenas is a typical predator-scavenger one.

In prey selection there is little similarity between the species, and the diet of wild dogs consists largely of wildebeest calves and gazelle (Estes and Goddard 1967; Kruuk and Turner 1967; table 36); There is some overlap in the lists of food items, but on the whole the similarities are few.

Hyenas and Jackals

There are three species of jackals in the Serengeti—the golden, the black-backed, and the side-striped. The last is fairly rare in the Serengeti, and we will not be concerned with it here. Golden jackals are animals of the large open grass plains. The black-backed jackals occur much more often in bush country or near cover and, in the wet season, also on the long-grass plains; there is, though, a fair amount of overlap between the ranges of the two species, and it is not uncommon to see them scavenging together from a kill. They seem to behave very similarly, especially in their interaction with other animals. Estes and Goddard (1967) described differences between golden and black-backed jackals in their reactions to wild dogs, but I could not confirm this in my own observations. In the following, therefore, I will refer to these two species together.

The diet of jackals, both in the Serengeti and in Ngorongoro Crater, consists largely of small mammals, insects, some fruits, food scavenged from kills, and the young of the smaller gazelle. There seem to be large variations depending on the area in which the jackals occur; the Ngor-ongoro jackals seem to subsist almost entirely on bits scavenged from hyena kills, whereas in the Serengeti it was more usual, in particular seasons, to see the jackals themselves catching and killing young gazelle, or eating the fruits of *Balanites* trees. When scavenging, the jackals and hyenas often managed to eat together, and although the jackals were often snapped at and chased short distances by the hyenas, they came back immediately and usually stayed just out of reach of the larger carnivores. Jackals have a better chance than hyenas when a lion takes over a kill, because their fleeing distance from lions is very small in-deed; jackal and lion often feed together from scraps, whereas hyenas are kept at a much greater distance. If there were only hyenas on a kill, there was often no opportunity for the much smaller jackal to grab its share.

There are relatively few jackals compared with hyenas, and they are so much smaller that the benefit they reap is hardly detrimental to the hyenas' food supply. On the other hand, there are instances in which the hyena benefits from the presence of jackals. Whenever the Thomson's gazelle are fawning in an area, jackals are very effective in detecting and catching the young and, not infrequently, hyenas are able to steal a fair proportion of such kills.

> Example: June 1965, 1830, in Ngorongoro. Two golden jackals found a young Thomson's gazelle and caught it after a chase of some 100 m. The fawn bleated loudly when chased, and this probably attracted two hyenas asleep on the den about 500 m away. The hyenas ran up, but were slightly off course; after covering approximately the right distance, they stopped and looked around. They were 100 m to the side of the kill; they began to run about in a slow zigzagging gallop until after a minute one hyena got downwind of the kill and dashed up

to it; the jackals ran off with a sharp bark and left the hyena to it. The other hyena was not allowed to eat.

One one occasion in Ngorongoro Crater, two black-backed jackals came upon a wildebeest mother with her newborn calf. The jackals jumped at the calf and bit it in the loins and legs and, although the mother tried to chase them away, they might have succeeded in killing it had not the commotion attracted two hyenas. They came running up from a distance and soon nothing of the calf was left for the jackals.

Hyenas and jackals do not seem to like each other as food. On several occasions when I saw jackals near the carcass of a hyena, they were obviously not interested in it. Myles Turner (personal communication) once saw a hyena chase a golden jackal a long distance across the short-grass plains in the Serengeti; after overtaking the jackal, the hyena bit it across the back and killed it. Since the hyena was disturbed after making the kill, it was not known whether he had killed for food, but I did see hyenas eat a jackal on another occasion. Then, also, it was obvious that hyenas did not really like the jackal meat; it took four hyenas over half an hour to eat a golden jackal. Otherwise, the two species seem to ignore each other when not on a kill, except for when hyenas venture near a jackal den where there are young cubs. On these occasions, a single jackal or pairs of them will attack the hyena from behind and bite at its hind legs, to which the hyena invariably responds by fleeing slowly, occasionally snapping back at the jackal.

On the whole, the relationship between hyenas and jackals may be characterized as of rather small mutual benefit, especially in Ngorongoro, though jackals profit most.

Hyenas and Man

Hyenas are proverbial scavengers around human settlement; moreover, they are frequently successful in snatching away livestock. These are obviously the major benefits that civilization has for hyenas, but there are others. Many African tribes, for instance the Masai around the Serengeti National Park and in Ngorongoro, still dispose of their dead by putting the body out in the bush for hyenas to eat. Once I found some human hairs in a sample of hyena feces from the southwest boundary of the park.

Hyenas also prey on people; witness, for example, some recent newspaper items:

Under the headline "Hyaenas Attack People," the *Tanzania Standard*

of 22 January 1968 wrote, "Hyaenas have bitten more than 60 people recently at Loliondo, northwest of Arusha, some in their houses, veterinary officials reported. The victims were mostly women and children. Hyaenas were also reported to be terrorising an area just over the border in Kenya."

Or in that same newspaper on 1 February 1967, "Hungry Hyaenas Grab Cyclist": "Three hungry hyaenas chased a schoolmaster, Nyirendas Luggage, as he was cycling to work, flung him from his bicycle and badly mauled him before villagers answered his cries for help." Or on 19 December 1966, "Hyaenas Kill Patient"; "A 70-year old patient in Shinyanga Hospital was killed by hyaenas on Friday night when he was leaving the hospital without permission. . . . The hospital staff rushed to rescue him but they found him already dead."

Balestra (1962) gives an account of the death of twenty-seven persons in the Malanje district in Malawi, where some hyenas apparently specialized in this kind of prey. Attacks take place particularly when people are asleep and are mostly on children; instances of this kind have been reported many times (e.g., Brehm 1877).

Although hyenas may profit considerably from the presence of man, the reverse can hardly be said. I am probably one of the few people who scavenge from hyenas by occasionally stealing their kill for my own consumption. Hyena meat is generally despised, even by tribes who eat many other unusual types of meat. One recognizes the public service hyenas do by clearing up the rubbish and acting as undertakers, but even this role is generally not appreciated here in East Africa.

Only rarely are the scavenging habits of hyenas viewed with gratitude, and the most interesting example I know is the town of Harar in Ethiopia, where they walk in the streets without being molested. Occasionally they are even fed by the inhabitants and they become extremely tame (Kruuk 1968; pl. 18).

Like most other animals in East Africa, hyenas have a large fleeing distance in response to a walking person; this is greater than for any other animal, often over 300 m. At night this distance is much reduced. In the Serengeti, instances have been recorded of a group of hyenas following somebody walking; even in daylight they once came within a few meters, to the distress of the person concerned (A. Sinclair, personal communication). This behavior may well be comparable to the mobbing described in reaction to lions (p. 134).

People's reactions to hyenas are usually fairly aggressive and, wherever possible, hyenas have been persecuted. Even in national parks they have often been shot on sight for no particular reason. Masai herdsmen try to kill hyenas, and Africans poaching in a national park make it a primary duty to rid the area around their camp of hyenas (by snaring and shooting with poisoned arrows), since they often take animals caught in snares. At the same time, people, especially the indigenous Africans, are afraid of hyenas. This is clear from their reactions to a tame hyena. Thus, the human response is ambivalent; this is shown in the fact that laughter is a common reaction to the hyena, even when the mere word "hyena" is mentioned. It is greatly despised (an obviously ambiguous feeling) and ridiculed in many African stories; in some parts of Africa hyenas play an important role in witchcraft (see Huxley 1964).

On the whole, the relationship between human beings and hyenas is of one-sided benefit to the hyenas; to man, hyenas are a fairly unmitigated nuisance, because man may be the victim in the prey-predator relationship and because hyenas are competing carnivores.

Hyenas and Vultures

In both the Serengeti and Ngorongoro Crater, six species of Aegipiinae vultures are common: the white-backed vulture, the Rüppell's griffon, the lappet-faced, the white-headed, the hooded, and the Egyptian vulture. They are the scavengers par excellence, and their feeding habits have been the subject of several publications (Petrides 1959; Attwell 1963; Kruuk 1967). They live almost exclusively off the remains of kills and on carcasses of dead animals, and only rarely will a white-headed or lappet-faced vulture kill, for instance, a small gazelle itself. They are often seen feeding from the same carcasses as hyenas (pl. 19) and, since there are a great many of them, there is competition for food between vultures and hyenas. Other carrion-eating birds may also be seen around kills—for instance, marabou stork, African kite, tawny eagle, steppe eagle, white-necked raven, lammergeyer (very rarely), and once even a fish eagle; they are, on the whole, of little importance compared with the very numerous vultures. The point has been made that the Serengeti vultures, especially the more numerous species (the white-backed, Rüppell's griffon, and lappet-faced), may induce the carnivores to kill more than they would if no vultures were present (Kruuk 1967). Whenever hyenas are on a kill during daylight hours, vultures will almost invariably be there (once, even at 2130 on a moonlight night, I saw vultures with hyenas on a kill). Vultures may be seen circling over hunting hyenas before the prey is brought down, and on three occasions in Ngorongoro when I was playing tape-recorded sounds of hyenas on a kill, vultures turned up—one hooded vulture arrived before any of the hyenas. This indicates the vultures' ability to recognize sounds of hyenas on a kill.

Sometimes hyenas benefit from vultures, for the way a vulture descends onto a kill can indicate the presence of food a long distance away. I have seen hyenas reacting to the whistling sound of air through the feathers of an alighting vulture (suddenly waking up, looking at the vulture, then running to the place where it alighted). The mere sight of the large birds plummeting from the sky is enough to bring hyenas galloping miles to a carcass they could not possibly have seen (because it was behind a rise) or smelled (because the wind was in a different direction). An interesting natural control experiment on this observation was provided several times when, usually in November and December, large flocks of Abdim's and white storks first arrived and hyenas could be seen running up to where they had alighted. When a hyena arrived at such a stork gathering, he would stand there with his head up, alertly looking around, and then slowly walk away again.

Hyenas often snap at vultures on a kill, especially at the larger species. Both hooded and Egyptian vultures often take food from immediately between or around hyenas on a kill, whereas the larger species (especially lappet-faced and white-headed vultures) stay at least several meters away. White-backed and Rüppell's griffon vultures do occasionally feed at the same time as hyenas from one carcass, but they usually keep well out of snapping distance (Kruuk 1967). On a few occasions, I did see hyenas actually grab hold of a vulture, but the bird was released again immediately.

Both the vultures and the hyenas, then, seem able to use each other to obtain food. It is a complicated relationship of mutual benefit and competition.

Hyenas and Other Meat Eaters

Once in October 1967 in the Serengeti, I saw a crocodile cause ten hyenas to leave their prey. The hyenas had chased a wildebeest into the Mareo River (in the west of the park) at 2330 hr and killed it there. This is a fairly regular occurrence (p. 152), but on this occasion the feasting crowd of hyenas suddenly rushed out of the water with a great splashing; a crocodile had appeared, which proceeded to devour the carcass in its customary fashion (Cott 1961). Usually, hyenas keep a safe distance from crocodiles. Once I found a pool in the Grumeti River where crocodiles had killed three zebra, eating only part of each one; over two weeks, hyenas visited the shore, but did not set foot in the water, leaving the carcasses to rot. As soon as I pulled a crocodile-killed zebra from a neighboring pool out of the water, the hyenas devoured it.

Apart from these interactions with a reptilian competitor, I saw few meetings with other carnivorous animals; those I did see were with bat-eared foxes and honey badgers. Bat-eared foxes often have their holes remarkably close to hyena dens; their food consists largely of insects. The hyenas show no interest in the foxes, who avoid them by 5 to 10 m. This has also been recorded by Cullen (1969). But on two occasions, hyenas were found with freshly dead bat-eared foxes which they had almost certainly killed. I once saw two honey badgers (ratels) who were trotting over the Serengeti plains meet a pack of hyenas, who at first ignored them. But when one of the ratels ran up and snapped, the hyenas avoided them and ran away for a short distance, showing no inclination at all to further contact. Cullen (1969) reports an observation of a ratel attacking a striped hyena.

Summarizing the relations between hyenas and carnivorous animals, there is almost always some mutual benefit but the balance is usually tilted one way or the other, in that to one of the parties the presence of the other is more detrimental than beneficial. Hyenas clearly profit from the presence of leopards, cheetahs, wild dogs, and man. Relations with lions, jackals, and vultures are more ambiguous, and hyenas probably more often provide food than take it.

Competition for food between hyenas and other carnivorous animals may take the form of aggressive clashes over kills or of mere utilization of the same prey species as a food resource. Thus we can distinguish four possible categories of competition: hyenas as scavengers, removing kills from predators; hyenas as scavengers, competing with other scavengers; hyenas as hunters, being scavenged from; hyenas as hunters, competing with other predators.

In table 28 I have tried to summarize, in a simplified way, the extent of competition between hyenas and other carnivores. The table shows that hyenas compete more with lions than with any other species; they are obviously ecologically very similar. Hyenas scavenge from all the carnivores mentioned, but only a few of the carnivorous animals scavenge from hyenas, or compete in scavenging from other sources. As hunters, hyenas select prey which are also often chosen by other carnivores but, as I have shown above, there are large differences in diet, though perhaps they are smaller between hyenas and lions.

TABLE 28 *Competition between hyenas and other carnivorous animals*

Predator	Hyenas as scavengers		Hyenas as hunters	
	Taking kills from	Scavenging from the same source as	Scavenged upon by	Hunting the same prey species as
Lion	+	+	+	+
Cheetah	+			•
Leopard	+	•		•
Wild dog	+		•	•
Jackal	+	+	+	•
Vulture	+	+	+	
Man	+			+

NOTE: Indicated as + (considerable), • (unimportant), or virtually absent.

HUNTING BEHAVIOR

It has been shown in the previous section that hunting, even more than scavenging, plays a very important role in the hyenas' life, and I will now go into this method of obtaining food in more detail. Since hyenas hunt their various prey species in different ways, I will discuss separately the hyenas' hunting method for a number of prey species.

Hyenas Hunting Adult Wildebeest

1735 hr on a cold, rainy, misty afternoon in Ngorongoro Crater, November 1966. Six hyenas from the Lakeside clan were walking over the grass flats in the center of the crater. Their activity at this time was probably due to the unusual weather. As they walked past a herd of several hundred wildebeest, two hyenas made a short, not very fast, dash at the wildebeest, causing them to flee for about 100 m. They then stopped and turned around to look at the wildebeest, then walked quietly on. At 1740 one of the hyenas stopped, looked at some wildebeest and ran toward them, with a second hyena following close behind. This time they went on running and were obviously chasing an adult wildebeest bull. The chase became faster and faster, the hyenas running some 20 m to 40 m behind the wildebeest, which was then going away from the herd in a straight line. All the other wildebeest ran a short distance to get out of the way, but let the hyenas pass at very close range. It was evident that the hyenas' activities were not directed at the other wildebeest, who merely sidestepped to avoid them.

The other four hyenas of the party ran only a short distance, then gave up, and soon the two hunting hyenas were out of sight. The quarry ran on at a steady speed of 40 to 50 kmph, and after about a minute one hyena was just behind him and the other about 30 m away. After a run of almost 3 km, the bull reached a shallow stream, some $1\frac{1}{2}$ m wide, which would usually be no obstacle at all to a wildebeest. This time, though, the hunted animal stopped at the stream and turned to face his pursuers. The hyenas tried to bite him in the hindquarters, sides, and especially the testicles, while he in turn struggled to horn his attackers. Often one hyena would stand in front of the wildebeest, eliciting charges, while the other hyena bit him from behind. The wildebeest gave the impression of being exhausted after the long fast chase; even when the hyenas relaxed for a few seconds, he made no attempt to escape. About three min after he stopped two more hyenas arrived on the scene, and all four bit simultaneously at the loins, testicles, and anal region of the wildebeest, paying little attention to his horns. The mobility of the victim was very much impaired by the four pursuers hanging on to his hindquarters. Another two min later, the wildebeest had a large gash in the right loin, the testicles had been bitten off, and he stood as if in a state of shock. Occasionally he made some frantic movements and was able to struggle free from the hyenas, but then some member of the pack would renew the attack. The hyenas kept up their biting of the hindquarters, and eight min after the wildebeest had stopped running he went down and the hyenas stood over him pulling out his insides. Another two min later, the wildebeest died. Gradually more hyenas came up; 10 min after the wildebeest died, the first hyena ran off with a hind leg, and 45 min after the death, only the head and spine remained, with 2 hyenas eating from them. A total of fourteen hyenas had finished the fully grown, 185 kg wildebeest bull.

This observation is one out of many that I have made in the Ngorongoro Crater, and the ones in the Serengeti followed the same pattern. There are a number of clearly definable elements in the wildebeest hunt: the search, the random dash into the herd, the chase, and the kill. During the search hyenas, alone or with one or two others, may just walk past the wildebeest herds. Usually the hyenas' heads are low, their tails hang down, and they occasionally stop to look at the wildebeest but go in no particular direction—they just roam around. In this attitude, they may walk right up to the wildebeest, who will only react (head up) when the hyenas are at a range of 10–20 m.

Suddenly a hyena may start a dash or random chase by running directly toward the herd, or toward a lone wildebeest, and this causes the animals to run away. The hyena gallops or runs, never at full speed, with its head up, ears cocked forward, and tail horizontal or slightly higher. This may develop into a chase of one particular wilde-beest, or the hyena may stop and merely watch the running animals and the wild melee the chase has caused. Other hyenas may stand alongside, watching the running wildebeest. From this watching position the hyena may take up the chase or merely walk to the next group of wildebeest. It is likely that the main function of the random chase is to make the wildebeest run, which enables the hyena to easily spot any physically inferior individuals. It is probably much easier to size up a herd for a potential prey animal this way than to just watch the undis-turbed wildebeest.

> One dawn, in August 1967, I followed one of my marked hyena males whom I called "the butcher," and who was from the Scratching Rocks clan. He walked toward a herd of some 2,000 wildebeest, He began galloping while he was a long way from the herd, running straight into it, then following a zigzag pattern through the wildebeest, which bunched up into tight little groups. These small groups of wildebeest ran just out of the hyena's path, turning and looking as he passed, often within 10 m of them. The hyena ran in different directions but stayed in an area of approximately 200 × 500 m. Usually he just galloped slowly ("bobbing along"), but occasionally he stopped, then sped up and pressed hard upon one particular wildebeest; he was continually shifting his attention to different animals. After some three min another marked male hyena joined him, but they seemed to operate fairly independently. A minute later they both stopped and stared; the wildebeest halted too and stood in a large circle around the hyenas. In the meantime, the commotion had attracted six other hyenas, who stood and watched the herd from the outside, some 100 m away; they lay down when the two in the middle stopped. The quiet did not last long. After 7 min, the two hyenas ran again, though only for half a minute before they lay down once more. All was peaceful for 25 min, with the wildebeest grazing and the hyenas lying down—then "the butcher" began to chase one wildebeest, or wildebeest group, after another within the same area. The wildebeest just avoided him and remained in tightly bunched groups. All the other hyenas got up and stood watching the activity, but this time the commotion died down after a minute. Forty minutes later the same thing happened, for just over 1 min; "the butcher" chased around inside the herd while the others were watching from the outside, some 30–10 m away. Then he too stopped and slowly walked away from the scene to the stream, where he lay down. The other hyenas stayed where they were.

In the great majority of cases the actual chase (after one particular

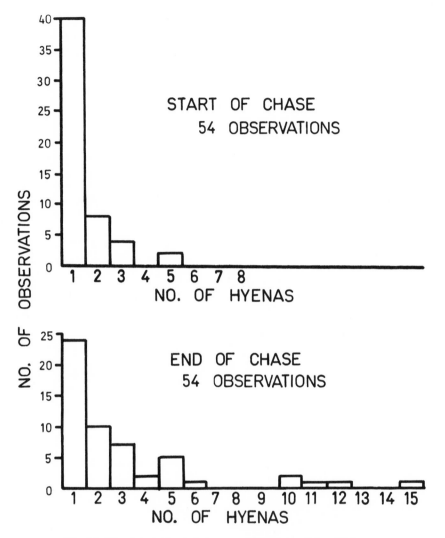

Fig. 35. Numbers of hyenas in groups hunting adult wildebeest.

individual) is initiated by just one hyena (fig. 35); the first case related above is somewhat unusual in that before the chase six hyenas were walking together. However, even there only two actually took up the chase, and the other four did not appear to be very interested. I have seen chases as long as 5 km, but more usually they are less than 2 km and often no more than a few hundred meters (fig. 37). Hyenas can run very fast during these chases, and with the Land Rover I have clocked them at speeds over 60 kmph (Walker 1964, mentions 65 kmph).

However, the average speed is probably closer to 40–50 kmph as they slow down rapidly. Estimating the average speed of chases in thirteen observations, I clocked over 50 kmph in three instances and between 40 and 50 kmph in the other ten. Wildebeest are obviously able to run faster than hyenas, at least over short distances, but I often had the impression that, at least at the beginning of the chase, the victim did not run as fast as it could, but merely kept out of reach of the predator. Although the chase is usually started by one hyena only, more are attracted to it during the chase and when, in the end, the quarry is brought to a halt or the hyenas give up the chase, the average number of hyenas present is often considerably larger (fig. 35).[11]

Often a pursued wildebeest will run into a lake or stream, in which case it is always killed, at least in my experience. The tendency to run into water varied slightly in different clan ranges, probably because of the presence or absence of water; it may well have influenced the hyenas' hunting effectiveness. In the Serengeti, wildebeest hardly ever make for water when chased, simply because there is very little about. But 22% of 108 wildebeest killed by hyenas in Ngorongoro were killed in the lake or in a stream (table 29).

TABLE 29 *Ngorongoro clans killing wildebeest in water*

Clan	Percentage killed in water	Total kill
Mungi	23	30
Scratching Rocks	24	42
Lakeside	23	13
Other clans	17	23

If the victim was grabbed on land, it stopped after being bitten in the hind legs or loins, and a number of hyenas then converged on it. Once the victim was stopped, it was invariably killed even if only one hyena was present. Schaller (personal communication) observed a wildebeest being hamstrung in both hind legs by hyenas in the Serengeti, after it had been run down. I have never seen this, although sometimes some hyenas bit at lower parts of the hind legs of a captured wildebeest while others were tearing at its abdomen.

11. $\chi^2 = 13.11$; $df = 3$; $p < 0.01$.

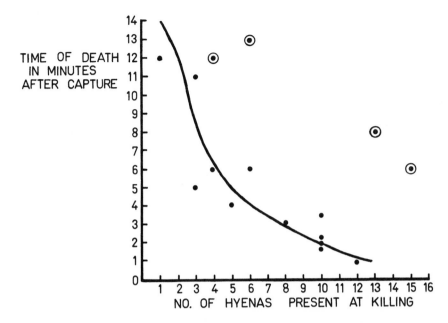

Fig. 36. Relation between number of hyenas present and killing efficiency for adult wildebeest. Curve fitted by hand, excluding ⊙ (observations in which other hyenas interfered).

Hyenas did not use a specific killing bite or killing method as do the cats, viverrids (Leyhausen 1965; Dücker 1965), and mustelids (Eibl-Eibesfelt 1956; Wüstehube 1960); but, like wild dogs (Estes and Goddard 1967; Kruuk and Turner 1967), they killed the victim by eating it. It is rare that the victim puts up any significant active defense; usually a group of hyenas has no difficulty in attacking the hindquarters of an animal, biting its loins and anal region and, if there are many hyenas, also the throat and chest (pls. 20, 21, 22, and 23). They tear chunks away of skin, muscles, and intestines, and this will bring down the victim and kill it in anything from 1 to 13 min (average 6.3 min).

The relation between the number of hyenas present and the time it takes for the victim to die after first being grabbed (fig. 36) is not obvious at first sight. However, there is a clear trend if one considers separately those observations where there was some interference with the killing (by other hyena clans for instance). Generally, with large numbers of hyenas participating, the prey is killed faster.

Selection of a wildebeest.   Merely from watching hyenas while they make dashes into herds or walk through the wildebeest immediately before an actual chase, it seems likely that selection of the animal that is going to be chased is largely, or entirely, by sight. Wind direction does not seem to play any role at all in determining the direction of approach as it does in social encounters (p. 226); this virtually rules out the use of scent in selection. Hearing is important for spotting kills made by other hyenas—as I showed by using tape-recorded sounds to attract hyenas to my car—but almost certainly it plays no role of importance in choosing one wildebeest rather than another.

If a potential victim is selected visually, hyenas could react either to differences in appearance or to differences in behavior. The first of these is probably used infrequently, as it is only rarely that one is able to distinguish differences in condition by external appearance. The manner in which hyenas dash into herds to induce the wildebeest to run also suggests that it is behavior and performance that the hyenas are looking at. Appearance must play some role, however, and it is likely that any abnormalities will be spotted quickly. In 1960 H. F. Lamprey (personal communication) marked a number of adult wildebeest in Ngorongoro by painting their horns white. In the following months, almost all of these marked animals were killed;   this suggested that it was the striking appearance of the wildebeest that caused them to be selected by hyenas. It would be interesting to follow up this idea by experiments.

There are several suggestive observations indicating that hyenas pay a great deal of attention to unusual behavior. For instance, when driving about in my car at night I saw several times that some wildebeest were dazzled by the headlights of the Land Rover; their behavior became slightly disorientated and they ran in an unusual way with small and somewhat uncoordinated steps. Hyenas (and other carnivores) are much less affected by lights and several times chased such a dazzled animal over some 100 m (far outside the beam of the headlights) before giving up. The headlights' effect on the ungulates is a factor that one has to keep in mind when observing the hunting behavior of any nocturnal carnivore—it can seriously bias an observation (e.g., Eloff 1964, describing lions attacking a gemsbok in the headlights of a car).

Once, in the Serengeti, I saw a hyena walking past a herd of several hundred grazing wildebeest. Inside the herd one male wildebeest was lying on the ground, horning and rolling as they often do on their territory (Estes 1969). Its behavior would have been normal in a territorial network, but there in the middle of the grazing herd, it immediately attracted my attention and also that of the hyena. The latter walked downwind straight toward the bull and then chased it for

about 150 m before giving up. It had readily picked on this odd-man-
out, but probably gave up the chase because, after a short run, the
quarry appeared quite normal.

It is extremely difficult to get any idea about the condition of animals
chased by hyenas; it is obvious that hyenas are able to detect differences
in performance between individual wildebeest that I cannot see.

Reactions of wildebeest to hyenas. In the wildebeest, as well as in the
hyenas' other prey species, antipredator mechanisms must be viewed
in the context of social organization. An outline of this social behavior
of wildebeest has been presented by Estes (1969). Briefly, the wildebeest population is divided into three social categories: the territorial
bulls, the bachelor herds (nonterritorial bulls), and the cow-calf herds.
Territorial bulls defend a small area against other bulls, the same area
almost the whole year round in Ngorongoro; in the Serengeti the area
moves with the migrations. The herds of bachelors and of cows and
calves may contain up to several thousand animals (pl. 24); they may be
very scattered during daylight hours, but at night they usually concentrate in very dense masses. As yet there are no indications that the herds
have a clear internal social organization; their composition and numbers change with time. Activities of individuals within the herd are
highly synchronized.

Hyenas often avoid the large dense herds of wildebeest and will walk
around rather than through them—if they do walk through or too close,
groups of wildebeest may chase them.

A hyena can walk past a herd of grazing wildebeest some 20 m from
the nearest animal without the wildebeest's even pausing in their grazing, and it can come as near as 6 m and the wildebeest will merely
look at it. On the other hand, a herd of wildebeest may sometimes panic
and run away from the hyenas when they are as much as 200 m away;
there is a huge variation in reactions, and it is clear that wildebeest
are not merely responding to the presence of hyenas but to minute
details of their behavior. The number of hyenas, the events immediately
preceding the observation, and the "social status" of the wildebeest
(whether territorial or not, females with or without calves, etc.) also
appear to play a role in determining response.

Before going into some details of these variations, I will try to outline
a number of general aspects of wildebeest reactions. The distance from
any hyena at which a wildebeest shows an overt reaction to the predator
is small compared with that of their reaction to many other carnivores.

A wildebeest which is farther than its "reaction distance" from a hyena merely continues to behave as it was before it noticed the hyena. Within the reaction distance, wildebeest may cease their activities and look at the hyena, they may flee from it, they may attack it, or they may move toward the hyena without showing a tendency to attack (a behavior which I provisionally labeled "curiosity"). Fleeing is not accompanied by any special behavior patterns; the animals merely wheel around and run, often swishing their tails and closing up together in tight groups. The attack is much less a communal affair; individual wildebeest may run toward the hyenas, often with their heads held low trying to horn them. Wildebeest exhibiting curiosity will either walk or run toward a hyena or follow it, usually with heads held fairly high and tightly bunched together if in a herd. During curiosity or just before fleeing one particular call, the "snort," is frequently uttered. Immediately after fleeing there is often an increase in the frequency of another call, the "grunt."

If a hyena is moving over open country in its ordinary fairly slow walking gait, without overt hunting intentions, reactions of wildebeest are fairly clear-cut. Territorial male wildebeest will largely ignore it at distances over 8 m, or maybe just stand, head up, watching it; at a closer range the hyena may trigger an attack, with the wildebeest, head low and tail swishing, running after the hyena, but never for more than a few meters. Only occasionally will a bull snort and avoid a hyena. Single female wildebeest or nonterritorial males avoid the hyena at longer range (20–30 m), but when in a herd they react at 10 m to 20 m. Reaction distances of wildebeest in front of a walking hyena are larger than those of animals which are obviously being passed by, and all these observations refer to adults without calves.

Although wildebeest in herds usually merely avoid a single hyena, groups of wildebeest will occasionally follow it, sometimes snorting, and the hyena's typical reaction is then a slow fleeing. This may result in a short chase, during which it is very difficult to distinguish whether the wildebeest shows curiosity or actual aggression.

If several hyenas are walking together the fleeing distance is enlarged, and a wildebeest bull on his territory is less likely to attack and more inclined to flee. On the other hand, the reactions of herds to hyena groups appear to contain more curiosity elements than their reactions to single hyenas.

If one or more hyenas are lying down and a herd of wildebeest is filing past, the wildebeest will often stop and look at the hyenas for some time, sometimes advancing a few steps in their direction and even snorting. Hyenas are never attacked in such encounters, and sometimes wildebeest may graze or even lie down as close as 10 m from a hyena lying down (pl. 25).

Some quite different wildebeest behavior may result when one or more hyenas are hunting. If they come running toward the herd, the reaction distance increases to about 100 m. The wildebeest first stand with heads up, often snorting, then wheel around and flee, bunching up at the same time. If the hyena runs into the center of the herd, he often causes it to split up into a number of small groups with the wildebeest running very close to one another. These small groups may merge, split up, and so on, in one enormous melee. While running, wildebeest are silent, but as soon as the hyena stops and they come to a halt 20–80 m away from him, a very spectacular chorus of grunts is made by the herd, and several wildebeest, standing closest to the hyena, will be snorting. I have never seen the hyena's short dashes unequivocally directed at territorial male wildebeest, but if a male wildebeest finds himself in the path of a running hyena, he will wheel around and flee, often in the striking gait that in horses is called the "extended trot" (fast, with long stiff-legged strides). This will change into a proper run if he is really chased. As soon as the hyenas are after one particular wildebeest, the others just move 20 m to 30 m out of the way and watch the hyenas run past. When the party of hyenas is pursuing a particular quarry and running straight toward another wildebeest, the fleeing distance of this one is much smaller than when a hyena runs toward a wildebeest without a quarry in sight. Thus, once a victim has been selected by the hyenas, wildebeest are able to distinguish this as well as I am, and their reactions to the hyenas change accordingly.

A wildebeest which has been singled out and is being chased will usually run in a fairly straight line, often clearly aiming at concentrations of other wildebeest. The main function of this is probably to confuse the hyenas and, as is shown on p. 159, this does indeed sometimes work. After a short chase I once saw a wildebeest go for about 50 m in a gait called "stotting" (described for gazelle, p. 191); the hyena pursuing him had meanwhile given up and the wildebeest finally came to a halt.

In seven out of forty-nine observed chases, the pursued wildebeest ran into the water, although probably it might have been able to avoid this had it attempted to do so (see also p. 152). All seven incidents ended with the death of the wildebeest, either by drowning or by being killed by hyenas in the usual way, the wildebeest's mobility being very much hampered by the water. One observation was reported to me in which the wildebeest escaped after running into the water, and while the hyenas stopped at the edge of the lake the wildebeest swam on (S. Trevor, personal communication); but since the wildebeest was heading for the middle of the lake it is not known whether it survived. This aquatic habit of the wildebeest does not seem to have any survival value (at least in this situation), and even appears detrimental to the chances of escape. More observations are needed in this and other areas, and also of the interactions with other predators, in order to explain the biological function of the aquatic habit.

After a wildebeest has been brought to a halt by the hyenas, whether on land or in the water, it will hardly defend itself. Only some faint attempts at dealing out blows with the horns and a swaying of the head may be observed; generally speaking the quarry just stands uttering loud moaning calls and is torn apart by the hyenas. It appears to be in a state of shock.

Hyenas' success in hunting adult wildebeest. It is customary to define hunting success as the percentage of hunting "attempts" leading to a kill; however, since it is difficult to state where hunting attempts begin, and even more difficult to compare this for different prey species and predators, the concept of hunting success has to be handled with great care. One might be tempted to classify the dashes of hyenas into a wildebeest herd as hunting attempts, but this would probably be unjustified. It has been argued above that during these dashes, hyenas merely make the herd move, which may assist them in prey selection; this behavior is almost certainly not directed toward a particular individual. I have defined a hunting attempt as an effort by hyenas to catch a selected quarry. For hyenas catching adult wildebeest the only observations considered, to establish hunting success, will be the ones where hyenas have chased a particular wildebeest individual over a distance of at least 50 m (thus excluding attempts to merely get an individual to move). Hyenas were successful in eighteen out of forty-nine observations of hunts. In thirty-nine instances I was able to estimate the distance over which the chase had taken place. There appeared to be a relation between hunting success and the length of the chase (fig. 37): chases of up to 1 km were 15% successful, and chases of 1.5 km and over were 54% successful.[12] These figures can be interpreted in various ways;

12. $\chi^2 = 4.53$; $df = 1$; $p < 0.05$.

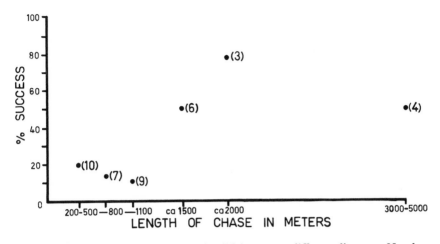

Fig. 37. Success of hyenas hunting adult wildebeest over different distances. Number of observations in parentheses.

it may be that in the short-distance observations, hyenas were merely half-heartedly trying out their quarry, or it could be that the wildebeest's resistance decreased during the chase, for instance, through fatigue, or that the greater the distance a hyena was able to run the more likely it was to catch the quarry. And probably more explanations are possible.

I have shown that whereas a hunt is usually started by only one hyena, at the end there may be several participants. To see whether the latecomers serve a useful purpose, I compared the success of hunts where different numbers of hyenas were present at the finish of the chase (fig. 38). There appears to be no relation between number of hunters and degree of success.[13]

Whenever possible, I recorded the probable reason the hyena failed to catch the wildebeest. In thirty observations of unsuccessful hunts, the wildebeest outran a pursuing hyena (57%); it is of course impossible to estimate the effort put into the chase by the hyenas. In one instance, (3%) the hyena switched to other quarry. In 20% of the observations, however, hyenas just gave up the chase when the quarry disappeared into a herd of wildebeest and, in a number of these instances, it had seemed that the hyena stood a good chance of catching the wildebeest before it disappeared. One cannot say with any certainty that it was the actual merging with the herd that contributed to the hyena's giving up the chase, but certainly the field observations were very suggestive of

13. $\chi^2 = 0.26$; $df = 2$; $p < 0.90$.

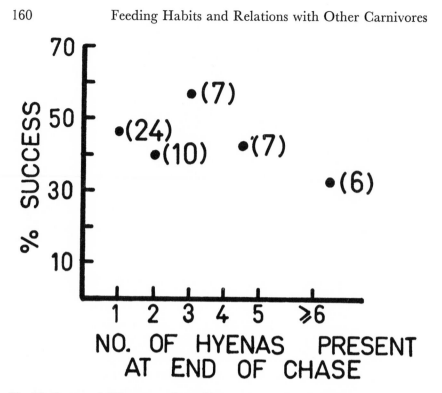

Fig. 38. Success of different numbers of hyenas cooperating in hunting adult wilde-beest. Number of observations in parentheses.

this. The same kind of uncertainty surrounds the observations (20%) in which wildebeest escaped from their pursuers by getting into the range of a neighboring hyena clan; it may well be that in such instances, the hyenas would have given up anyway, but here also the timing of abandonment of the chase (on crossing a clan boundary) was very suggestive at the time of the observations. So there is at least the strong suggestion that some 20% of hunting failures in Ngorongoro are caused by hyena social reasons—that is, the presence of clan boundaries.

Hyenas and adult wildebeest: Summary. Hyenas catch adult wildebeest after a chase of up to 5 km, at speeds of up to 60 kmph. The chase is usually initiated by one hyena, who is later joined by several more. There is little or no active defense by the wildebeest, which sometimes runs into water, where it is then invariably dispatched by the hyenas or drowns. Hyenas probably select a potential victim from a herd by sight; they dash into a herd to make the animals move, sometimes briefly chasing several individuals in succession, and then single out one wilde-beest, which they attempt to run down.

On the whole, wildebeest allow hyenas to come very close without responding to their presence. But the reaction distance varies with (among other factors) the behavior of the hyenas, their numbers, and the social position of the wildebeest. Reaction distance is greatest when the hyenas are definitely hunting. Apart from a loud snort and an occasional "extended trot," the wildebeest shows virtually no behavior patterns that might specifically serve to alarm others.

Forty-four percent of chases after adult wildebeest were successful. Hunting success appears to be related to the distance over which the chase took place, but not to the number of hyenas partaking. If a wildebeest escaped its foes, this was most often by outrunning them, by disappearing into large herds, or by indirect interference from other hyenas.

Hyenas Hunting Wildebeest Calves

One morning in February 1967, on the open plains in Ngorongoro, I saw a hyena slowly walking up to a group of five wildebeest cows, each with a calf. After watching the approaching hyena for a short time, the wildebeest turned around and ran away while the hyena was still over 100 m away; immediately the hyena took up the chase. One cow and her very young calf soon began to fall behind the others and after they had run about 100 m, the hyena caught up with them; the calf was then about 5 m behind the cow. When the hyena was within a few meters of the calf, the cow suddenly turned round and attacked the hyena, hitting it very hard with her horns and completely bowling it over. The calf stopped and stood next to its mother as soon as she had ceased attacking the hyena. The hyena got up and stood at some 20 m distance. Again, the calf wheeled around and began to run away. The mother chased the hyena for another 20 to 30 m; she then ran after the calf at an extended trot and together they ran on, not very fast, while the hyena stood watching them disappear.

Two days later, in the same area, a group of five hyenas was slowly bobbing, heads up, through rather sparse herds of wildebeest; suddenly one hyena accelerated, changed course, and started chasing a newborn wildebeest calf which obviously could not yet run very fast. After a chase of about 200 m the hyena overtook the calf and its mother while the other hyenas were almost 100 m behind. Then the wildebeest cow turned around very suddenly and charged at the hyena, hitting it at full tilt, in the ribs, with her horns. She bowled it over and butted at it again when it was lying on the ground. The calf ran on, however, and the cow followed it; the hyena then jumped and followed behind the cow. A few seconds later, the cow again turned back and attacked the hyena, hitting it and bowling it over. The calf merely ran on; its mother followed and it was obvious that the one hyena had little chance of getting anywhere near the calf. In the meantime, though, the other hyenas had caught up and several of them overtook the cow, who attacked one of them; but as she was doing so, the other hyenas attacked the little calf. One hyena grabbed it in the lower part of the leg and immediately the other hyenas were there as well, one taking it in the loin, and another biting hard in the nape of the neck and slowly shaking it. Almost immediately the calf dropped, and while its mother watched from some 40 m away, more hyenas converged upon the calf until there were eight eating from it.

Hyena predation on wildebeest calves has frequently been observed by students of wildebeest ecology and behavior (Talbot and Talbot 1963, Watson 1967, Estes 1969); it is often seen in daylight. Clearly, wildebeest calves are exceedingly vulnerable to attack by hyenas, but the species shows several ecological and behavioral mechanisms which reduce this kind of mortality. Since the interaction between wildebeest calves and hyenas is relatively easy to observe and very interesting, I will discuss it at some length.

The great majority of calf-hunting observations in both the Serengeti and Ngorongoro were made in the early morning, between first light and about 0900 hr. Figure 39 expresses the general course of events fairly adequately for the daylight hours; it shows a great deal of hunting activity in the early morning hours, a little hunting in the evening, and hardly any at midday. Many calves must also be killed at night, but I have no means of comparing this with daylight observations.

When hyenas are hunting wildebeest calves, they are usually alone, though sometimes there are two or more together (table 30). They may

TABLE 30 *Number of hyenas chasing wildebeest calves*

No. of hyenas	No. of observations	Percentage
1	74	68
2	18	17
3	8	7
4	5	5
5	3	3
6	0	0
	108	100

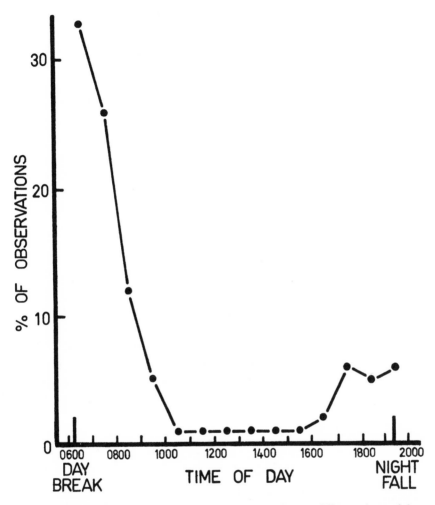

Fig. 39. Observations of hyenas hunting wildebeest calves at different times of day. Night observations have been omitted.

take up the chase when one or more wildebeest mothers with calves come past, but more often the hyenas actively seek calves by approach-ing a herd, or small groups, or single adult wildebeest with calves. Usually the hyena approaches in its ordinary walking posture and gait, coming straight for the wildebeest. During the approach of the hyena, the behavior of the wildebeest changes from grazing, or whatever it was doing before, to an alert posture in which it watches the hyenas approach before wheeling around and running. Very often, the hyena and the wildebeest start running at about the same time, and it is usually difficult to decide which of the two began running first. Sometimes hyenas may walk along the edge of a herd of wildebeest, though not directly toward any individual, and in this way they are often able to come much closer to their possible quarry. As in hunting an adult wildebeest, a hyena may dash into a herd, then after a very short run, stop and watch the fleeing wildebeest and then select the calf it is going to chase. As in chasing adult wildebeest, wind direction does not seem to play a role, and so calves also are probably selected entirely by sight.

If more than one hyena is involved in the hunt, one will usually begin to run first, and the others may either follow it immediately or wait until engaged in the chase. This may make it difficult to decide whether just one or several hyenas are actually hunting. I have assumed that one hyena was hunting if the others did not follow until it was already clear that the first hyena would either get, or not get, the calf on his own. It may well be that the reluctance of other hyenas to partake in the chase enables them to size up the hunt as likely to hit or miss, which may affect the figures of hunting success of one or more hyenas mentioned in figure 44.

The ensuing chase may take the animals over any distance up to 4 km, the median length of chase being between 300 m and 400 m. There may be virtually no chase when the calves are still very young (born in the past half hour or so), but high speeds are reached when the calves are older, although they are slightly slower than adult wildebeest. The end of the chase is considered to be when the hyena has stopped running, because it has given up, has grabbed the chalf, or is doing battle with the mother. Often the wildebeest cow will actively defend her calf when the hyena has overtaken it, or is about to do so, and hyenas may have great trouble in dodging the horns of the mother (see below). I have never seen calves end a chase by running into water.

When a hyena actually catches a calf, it is often difficult in the commotion to see exactly how it is grabbed. Frequently it is taken from behind, in one of the hind legs or the flank, and sometimes in the neck. If there are several hyenas around, one of them often grabs the calf in the neck at the moment of capture, or immediately afterward. This hyena may then make a few small shaking movements with his head which either stun or kill the calf. However, this neck grip by no means always occurs, and in the majority of cases the calf probably is ripped apart alive. Immediately after a calf has been caught, more hyenas converge and eat with the hunters; on the average, 5.8 hyenas were seen

to feed off a young wildebeest calf in Ngorongoro (seventy-two observations) and 4.9 in the Serengeti (fifty-nine observations).

In the wildebeest calving season of 1967, I spent much time with the
hyenas of the Scratching Rocks clan in the Ngorongoro Crater. A relatively large number of hyenas in this clan were marked, or clearly
recognizable, which allowed me to note that on many occasions, several
hyenas used to kill one calf after another, eating little or nothing themselves but leaving the carcass for other hyenas (often immature ones)
to eat. Once a group of four hyenas (three male and one female) killed
four calves in this way within $1\frac{1}{2}$ hr without eating anything of them,
although they had easy access to the carcasses. This was evidence that
hyenas were hunting and killing without being obviously hungry
themselves. If this were a common occurrence, it would of course lead
to wholesale slaughter. This never seemed to be true, however, and all
calves killed by hyenas during my observations were also eaten largely
by hyenas, except for the few stolen by wild dogs or lions. It is not unlikely that the activity of these "hunter" hyenas is still somehow geared
to the food demands of the clan; it may well be that if a calf is killed
and other hyenas do not come running up immediately to eat it, the
hunters may be less likely to leave the carcass. I do not have evidence
of this.

Calf selection.   It always seemed that the youngest calves were the ones
captured by hyenas, and if there were no newborn calves in a particular
group, hyenas would give up after only a short dash. If a wildebeest
was followed by a calf that was obviously unable to run very fast
(less than an hour old), a hyena seeing this would invariably attack.
The selection of the youngest is especially apparent at the end of the
season of wildebeest calving. Then newborn calves are conspicuous and
are easily picked out by the hyenas.

> One February morning in 1967, I followed a hyena who after some
> time approached a herd of about twenty wildebeest cows with their
> calves. The hyena was walking slowly, but already, at over 100 m
> distance, the wildebeest began to move away from it. One cow, however,
> stayed behind with her calf, which was just staggering to its feet for the
> first time and was still wet. The hyena immediately galloped toward it,
> and so did two others from different directions. The wildebeest mother
> ran around her calf, vigorously attacking the three hyenas with her
> horns, but within a minute one of the hyenas took the calf while the
> cow was attacking another hyena. The calf was grabbed in the neck and

held down on the ground while the hyena shook his head slightly. Then the others began to tear at the calf from behind; the wildebeest attacked the hyenas several more times, but then lost interest and the hyenas had their way.

Protection of wildebeest calves against predation.   I have calculated that hyenas kill approximately three-quarters of the calves every year in Ngorongoro, and probably most of these die in their first week of life (p. 165). The chance of being killed so young is considerably smaller in the Serengeti, but there also the predation pressure is heavy on the young calves. One would expect wildebeest to have developed a considerable number of antipredator devices—but these devices, such as they are, are not very efficient.

There are several ways a prey species could prevent an encounter with a predator. This might be achieved, for instance, by camouflage and accompanying behavior patterns or by habitat selection. Young calves may be protected if members of the species in a small area synchronize their calving activities, thus "swamping" the predators.

Wildebeest appear to make use of some of these preventive mechanisms to protect their calves, but certainly not all. Camouflage, for instance, seems to be lacking in calves as well as adults. The wildebeest is one of the most conspicuous animals on the plains, even at a great distance, and although, at first sight, calves appear to be well camouflaged (they are pale brown with a dark face) they are very conspicuous as soon as they join a herd. Their coloring might be protective if calves were to lie still in the vegetation for at least the first hours of their life, but that does not happen; they struggle to their feet as soon as possible after birth (in 5–10 min; Walther 1965, and my own observations), and if they are disturbed before they can run properly, they will still try to get up and stagger about. Within the herd they would probably be much better protected against detection by predators if they had the same coloring as the adult wildebeest—as it is, they are very conspicuous to us, and probably also to any nearby hyenas. It may be that the pale brown color is some protection against long-range detection, if the calf is walking alone with its mother, but this is fairly difficult to assess. The effect of color at night is as yet uncertain, but to us it seems to be the same as by day.

Camouflage, therefore, seems to be of little consequence in preventing predation on the wildebeest calves; the same cannot be said of the synchronization of calving. According to Watson (1967), about 80% of the calves are born in a three-week period between mid-January and mid-February and, although he has no data to show this, the statement does convey the general impression of synchronization. It means that over a relatively short period, the hyenas find themselves swamped with wildebeest calves as an easy source of food, and it is very likely that the mere number of calves eases the pressure of predation on individual calves. This synchronization of calving can function all the better, of course, if combined with crowding in space. Calves are born in large calving herds, and I have several times seen wildebeest cows with new-born calves actively seeking the company of others in the same situation. This is most striking early in the calving season when the few calves that are found in the huge herds are mostly grouped together (table 31).

TABLE 31 *Clustering of wildebeest calves within the large herds during early calving season*

No. in cluster	No. observations	No. of calves	Percentage of calves
1	33 ⎤	33 ⎤	4.9 ⎤
2	22 ⎬	44 ⎬	6.5 ⎬ 31.6
3–10	31 ⎦	136 ⎦	20.2 ⎦
11–20	12	169	25.0
21–30	4	100	14.7
31–40	2	80	11.9
41–50	1	49	7.3
51–60	0	0	0
61–70	1	64	9.5
	106	675	100.0

The most noticeable of the immediate responses of wildebeest with calves to the presence of hyenas, whatever way the hyena may behave, is the greater fleeing distance. This fleeing distance is usually more than twice as far as that of an unaccompanied female wildebeest. The following observation is quite indicative. The first wildebeest calf I saw in 1966 (in early January) was in a herd of about forty adults along the Mungi River in Ngorongoro. The herd walked slowly down a gentle slope to the river, the mother and calf on the outside. They came closer and closer to a hyena sleeping in the open, which I was watching. The hyena looked up now and then, but did not appear to notice the calf. The herd passed the hyena at some 80 m distance and suddenly the mother of the calf noticed the recumbent hyena—she was on the side

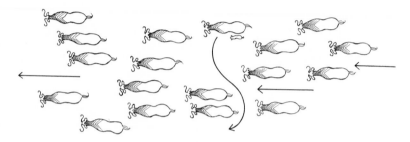

Fig. 40. Herd of wildebeest passing a sleeping hyena. One wildebeest cow has a calf and avoids the hyena, whereas the others ignore it.

nearest him. She stopped, stared a moment, then walked fast with her calf to the other side of the herd. Some of the other wildebeest looked briefly at the hyena, then walked on. The calf and its mother continued their journey on the side of the herd farthest from the hyena, who appeared to be oblivious of what was happening (fig. 40). In the presence of a predator, a calf always sticks close to its mother, running immediately next to her, almost touching her; it will relinquish this position only during a fast chase, when it may run in front of the mother.

I often got the impression that calves passing a stationary predator with their mother tended to keep on her offside, but I have no statistical evidence of this; a great number of other variables also influence the calf's position.

The speed of the fleeing calf in the first few days of its life is somewhat lower than that of an adult wildebeest, but they are very soon able to keep up with the whole running herd. During one observation in which a hyena chased a solitary female wildebeest with her three or four day old calf, the hyena had to give up after a chase of approximately 4 km during which speeds of around 50 kmph had been reached. While being chased, and especially when somewhat separated from their mothers, calves call continuously with fairly short single bleats. It is likely that these calls play an important role in the interaction between cow and calf, especially when the calf is endangered. Several observations suggest that it is largely this calling which brings about defensive action by the cow against predators; it is often striking that once a calf is grabbed by hyenas, the mother will go on attacking as long as the calf is calling, but she stops when it becomes silent.

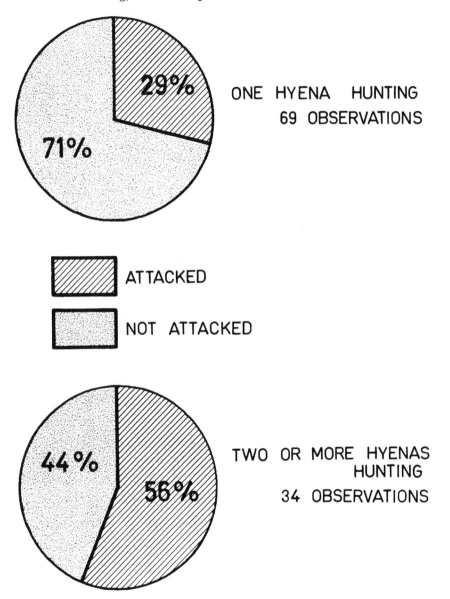

Fig. 41. Likelihood of different numbers of hyenas being attacked by the wildebeest cow when her calf is threatened.

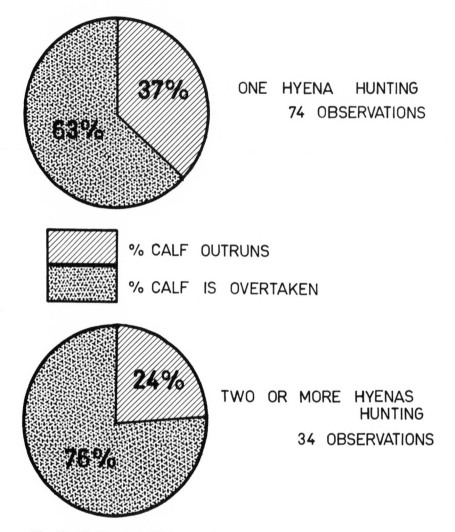

ONE HYENA HUNTING
74 OBSERVATIONS

% CALF OUTRUNS

% CALF IS OVERTAKEN

TWO OR MORE HYENAS
HUNTING
34 OBSERVATIONS

Fig. 42. Likelihood of wildebeest calf outrunning different numbers of hyenas.

Once the hyena overtakes the running calf, or gets near it, the cow may charge the predator with her head low, trying to horn him. Hyenas are often able to dodge these attacks, but they frequently are hit and bowled over. However, I have never seen a hyena seriously injured in this way. But the female wildebeest does not always attack; in fourteen out of thirty-three observations (42%) in which hyenas grabbed the calf and the aggression could be established, the cow did not actively defend her offspring. There is a relation between the likelihood of the

female wildebeest's attacking and the number of hyenas involved;
figure 41 shows that the single hyena chasing a wildebeest calf was
attacked in 29% of the observations, whereas two or more hyenas were
charged by wildebeest in 56% of the observations.[14] This phenomenon
may occur partly because a calf is able to outrun a single hyena more
often than two or more hyenas (fig. 42); hence "confrontation" is
more often seen when several hyenas are chasing a calf; however, the
differences between outrunning one hyena and more hyenas are not
statistically significant.[15] Even if they were they would not be large
enough to relate the different rates of attacks to different numbers of
hyenas. It appears, then, that once the calf has been overtaken, the
wildebeest cow is less likely to attack if there is one hyena than if there
are several. The effect of the attacks on the hyenas will be discussed
below. Sometimes hyenas are attacked while chasing a calf not only by
the mother, but also by bull wildebeest in their territories, or sometimes
even by zebra stallions if the calf has taken refuge near a zebra family.
On the whole, these attacks by outsiders are rare, and the hunting of
wildebeest calves by hyenas is almost exclusively an affair between the
predator, the calf, and its mother.

Female wildebeest attack hyenas only when defending their own
offspring, but the presence of a calf is not essential for releasing this
behavior. Whereas wildebeest cows without calves would not attack a
hyena, one cow I watched just before she gave birth (the front feet of
the calf had already emerged) went quite far out of her way to attack a
hyena which was merely walking past and obviously had not noticed the
condition of the cow. After this, the cow clearly avoided other hyenas
and lay down in a quiet place among other wildebeest to have her calf.
I have several times seen this avoidance of predators just before a cow
gives birth.

Sometimes, though rarely, a wildebeest calf loses its mother in the
large herds, and if it does not find her again it is doomed, as no other
cow will adopt a strange calf. It has been suggested (Watson 1967)
that hyenas specialize in these lost calves, but only one of 108 observations of calf hunts concerned such a lost calf; thus they make up only a
small proportion of the calves that fall prey to hyenas.

Efficiency in hunting wildebeest calves.   On the 108 occasions when I saw
hyenas hunting wildebeest calves, the latter managed to escape in

14. $\chi^2 = 5.90$; $df = 1$; $p < 0.02$.
15. $\chi^2 = 1.55$; $df = 1$; $p < 0.30$.

68% of the observations, whereas in the remaining 32%, hyenas were successful. In any particular attempt, therefore, wildebeest calves stand a fair chance of escaping hyena predation, and how this is achieved is indicated in table 32. This shows that the most common way for calves

TABLE 32 *Likely causes of failure of hyenas to catch wildebeest calves*

Cause	1 hyena hunting	2 or more hyenas hunting	Total		Percentage
Calf outruns	28	8	36	=	49
Calf disappears in confusion of herd	4	2	6	=	8
Calf shakes off hyena after being grabbed	1		1	=	1
Mother of calf attacks	21		21	=	29
Other wildebeest or zebra interfere	5		5	=	7
Other hyenas interfere (direct or indirect)	2		2	=	3
Hyenas not really trying hard	2		2	=	3
	63	10	73	=	100

to escape hyenas is to outrun them; the attack of the mother wildebeest also plays an important role. Calves are able to outrun hyenas over both short (less than 100 m) and long distances (over 4 km); there is no significant difference in their chances of outrunning hyenas over distances shorter or longer than the median (fig. 43).[16]

In figure 44 the hunting success of a single hyena is compared with that of two or more. Cooperation between hyenas appears to be highly rewarding,[17] and it is worth analyzing the figures further to find what makes this cooperation so beneficial. This may be partly because calves are slightly more proficient in outrunning a single hyena than two or more (fig. 42), but these differences are not significant statistically. If this were true, it could be that two or more hyenas overtake a calf more easily because the following hyenas cut the corners made by the calf when trying to escape the first hyena (as do wild dogs; Kruuk and Turner 1967). Or more likely, it might be that the second hyena only

16. $\chi^2 = 0.05$; $df = 1$; $p < 0.90$.
17. $\chi^2 = 30.53$; $df = 1$; $p < 0.001$.

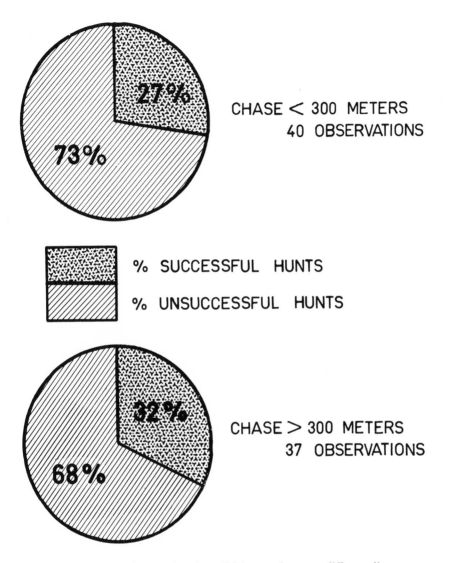

Fig. 43. Success of hyenas hunting wildebeest calves over different distances.

takes part in the hunt when he has sized up the calf as a likely target after watching the first hyena chasing it.

Most of the success resulting from two hyenas' cooperating is due to their being able to avoid the attacks of the mother wildebeest once the calf has been overtaken. The wildebeest cow can take on only one hyena at a time, which enables the other hyena to deal with the calf. In figure

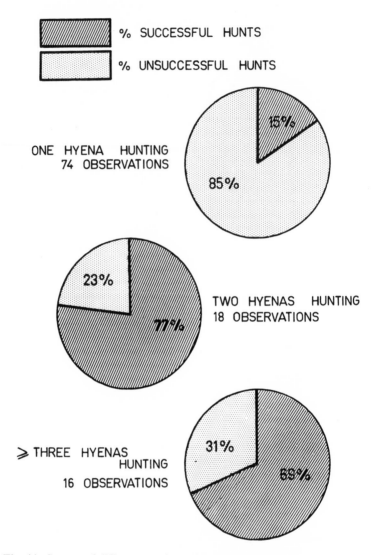

Fig. 44. Success of different numbers of hyenas hunting wildebeest calves.

45 it is shown that if the female wildebeest does not attack, two hyenas are more effective than one at catching a calf, but not significantly so (in this category calves avoid capture largely through outrunning hyenas or disappearing into larger herds).[18] However, if the female wildebeest does attack, the result is that a single hyena is 100% ineffective in catching a calf, whereas two or more hyenas together are 100% suc-

18. $\chi^2 = 0.76$; $df = 1$; $p < 0.50$.

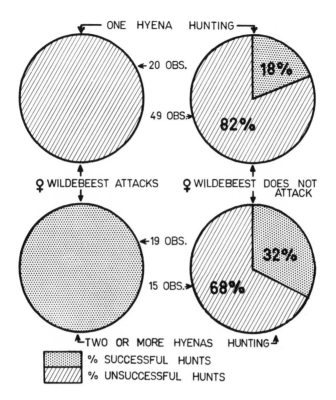

ONE HYENA HUNTING

20 OBS.

18%

49 OBS.

82%

♀ WILDEBEEST ATTACKS   ♀ WILDEBEEST DOES NOT ATTACK

19 OBS.

32%

15 OBS.

68%

TWO OR MORE HYENAS HUNTING

% SUCCESSFUL HUNTS
% UNSUCCESSFUL HUNTS

Fig. 45. The effect of attacks by wildebeest cows on the success of different numbers of hyenas chasing their calves.

cessful in doing so.[19] Sometimes I had the impression that the female wildebeest could be more effective in her attacks against two or more hyenas if only her behavior were better synchronized with that of the calf and vice versa; if, after a chase, a calf would remain with its mother instead of running far away it would probably be more difficult for the hyenas to get near it and at the same time avoid the horns of the cow. Jackals are also much more successful in catching gazelle fawns if they hunt in pairs (67% success) than if they hunt alone (16%). As with wildebeest, the gazelle mother has difficulty in defending her fawn against two or more predators (Wyman 1967, and my own observations).

These figures demonstrate the benefit that carnivores may derive from cooperation between members of the same species; they also expose the inability of a female antelope to defend her offspring against

19. $p < 0.0001$ (Fisher e.p. test).

more than one predator at a time, and show the survival value of active defense against a single predator.

Hyenas and wildebeest calves: Summary. Wildebeest have their calves in a very short period of the year; during that time, hyenas concentrate their prey-catching activities almost entirely on the newborn wildebeest. In this period they often hunt during the daytime, especially in the early morning. Calves are probably selected by sight and are usually caught after a fast chase by one or sometimes more hyenas. At the end of the chase, the wildebeest cow may defend her calf.

Calves probably derive little benefit from concealing coloration; synchronization of calving seems to be one of the most important antipredator mechanisms. The fleeing distance of cows with calves in response to a hyena is much greater than that of cows without.

A chase may be as long as 4 km, but on the average it is between 300 m and 400 m; there is no relation between success on the hyenas' part and the length of the chase—overall hunting success is 32%. Outrunning the hyena is the most successful way for a calf to escape, and defense by the mother is the next most successful. This defense, however, is useless if the calf is pursued by more than one hyena, although a group of hyenas is more likely to release attacks than a single one. Thus two or more hyenas are much more successful as hunters than one on its own.

Hyenas Hunting Zebra

In this section, the hunting of both adult zebra and foals is discussed, because neither the hyenas' hunting methods nor the zebra defense differs much with the age of the victim.

> One evening in December 1965, from 1850 to 1900 hr, hyenas belonging to the Lakeside clan had been gathering in the rapidly approaching darkness on a small area some 300 m from their den. They lay down there or sniffed around a bit, and then, exactly at 1900, eight hyenas began to slowly walk off together toward the nearest group of zebra, a family of twelve, less than a km away in the middle of wildebeest. The hyenas walked slowly up to the zebra, keeping very close together, and without showing any obvious interest in them. Five minutes later, when the hyenas were very close, the zebra stopped grazing and closed up together, their heads up. When the hyenas were about 4 m away, the stallion turned toward them and charged, head low and teeth bared. The hyenas scattered out of his way and the stallion immediately turned back to his family. The zebra bunched up

and began running slowly (at a speed of 20 to 25 kmph) away from the hyenas. The stallion ran just behind his family; several times he charged the hyenas and tried to bite them, and once he kicked out with his hind legs. The eight hyenas galloped just behind the zebra, five of them close around the stallion and the other three just in front of him. Several times some of the zebra barked excitedly. The whole party still moved at the same fairly slow speed over the plains; the zebra stayed closely bunched together and the hyenas ran in a semicircle behind them.

When the stallion was a little farther behind than usual, the rest of the family made a 90° turn, bunched up till they were almost touching each other, and virtually stopped; again the stallion attacked a hyena, chasing him right around the zebra family. The zebras moved on again with the hyenas following. Now and then a hyena managed to get very near to the family or even in between the zebra, biting at their flanks. The speed still did not increase. By 1907 hr seven more hyenas had been attracted by the commotion and there were fifteen hyenas following the zebras, but otherwise the picture was unchanged (fig. 46). Suddenly one hyena managed to grab a young zebra while the stallion was chasing another member of the pack. This young zebra, which was between nine and twelve months old, fell back a little, and within seconds twelve hyenas converged on it; in 30 sec they had pulled it down while the rest of the family ran slowly on. More hyenas arrived,

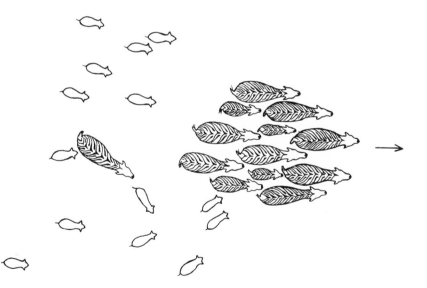

Fig. 46. Zebra hunt. The zebra mares and foals run in a very tight group, followed by the stallion, who also repeatedly charges at the hyenas running behind the zebra family.

and the little zebra was completely covered by them. At 1917, 10 min after the victim had been caught, the last hyena carried off the head and nothing remained on the spot but a dark patch on the grass and some stomach contents. Twenty-five hyenas were involved, and the whole process of dismembering took exactly 7 min.

One evening in September 1967, between 1825 and 1900 hr, I watched three female and two male hyenas arrive on the den of the Mungi clan. Two of the females suckled their cubs and the males walked around, sniffing the others and taking part in meeting ceremonies. Led by a female, four of the five (two females and two males) left the den at 1905 and walked away at a steady pace through the herds of wildebeest surrounding the den. There were no zebra in the neighborhood, and several times the hyenas stopped and looked at the wildebeest around them. The wildebeest bunched up in tight groups at the hyenas' approach; once the leading female came to within 7 m of a group of thirty wildebeest, stood looking at them for a moment, and then walked on again. At 1915 they were joined by another hyena (it was too dark to determine its sex, although the moon had already appeared). They continued in the same direction, and a few minutes later met yet another hyena; the whole group spent a minute sniffing each other, leg lifting, and so on. Immediately after this the last two hyenas to join the group fell back and gradually disappeared in another direction. The others continued and presently began to speed up, running in the same direction for several hundred meters; they all had their tails up and ears cocked. The reason for this run appeared to be another group of five hyenas which were walking on a car track; the two packs met, exhibiting all the usual behavior patterns (p. 226); they then stood looking in the direction of the nearest neighboring territory (that of the Oldonyo Rumbe clan), the boundary of which was about 500 m away. I could not see anything in that direction except some wildebeest, but several hyenas were calling in the distance, well inside the other clan's territory. All the hyenas took off in the direction of the calls, running in a very tight group with their tails up. They stopped on the boundary between the two ranges and spent about 5 min at a latrine area there, scent marking, scratching, and defecating (p. 222), often staring into the neighboring area before they returned by a slightly different route to their own grounds.

The time by now was 1945, and the pack of nine was moving at a steady pace, sometimes rather scattered, but with two females clearly in the lead most of the time. At 2010 hr, just in front of our cabin, they met another group of eleven hyenas from the same clan; meeting ceremonies took place for some 6 min before the whole pack of twenty moved off to the nearest mixed herd of wildebeest and zebra. Before the hyenas were within 40 m of it, this herd was in great turmoil, with the zebra joining up in a tight herd of about one hundred animals and the wildebeest moving off in another direction. The hyenas all ran after the zebra; there were clouds of dust everywhere, and the zebra were barking loudly. The chase went rather fast, about 30 kmph, in a large circle for about 1 km before one of the zebra at the rear was grabbed by first one, then several hyenas. There were no signs of aggression from any of the other zebra. The herd ran on while the pack of hyenas hung on to the captured mare, biting her in the loins, anal region, and neck. Within 30 sec of being grabbed, the mare fell and was immediately covered by hyenas; she died less than 1 min after falling (2025 hr). Thirty-eight hyenas ate from the carcass, and at 2040 hr only the head of the zebra was left; all the rest had been eaten or carried away.

The kill took place near the territorial boundary between the Mungi and the Scratching Rocks clans. Almost everything of the zebra was eaten before hyenas from the Scratching Rocks clan caught up with events. Ten of them were active at a latrine area on the boundary while the Mungi hyenas were still eating. Twelve Mungi hyenas went chasing toward the ten Scratching Rocks hyenas and were chased in return, then the Mungi group chased again, and so on. No physical contact was made between the two clans, and at 2115 all was quiet again, the hyenas having disappeared in various directions over their own ranges.

One of the most important aspects of the hyenas' hunting of zebra is that they operate in packs. The hyenas, when they set out on a zebra hunt, almost invariably walk together in a group (fig. 47, pl. 26); the mean group size is 10.8 hyenas. The group forms long before the hyenas

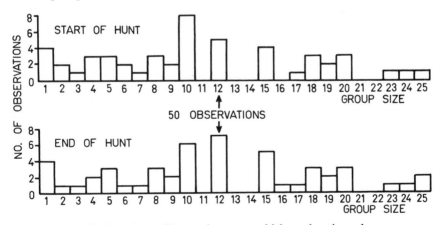

Fig. 47. Numbers of hyenas in groups which are hunting zebra.

get near the zebra, and while there may be other kinds of prey present. A point of great importance is that these zebra-hunting hyena packs can be recognized as such by the observer long before they have selected a quarry—they are setting out to hunt zebra rather than any other prey.

Before a pack of hyenas becomes involved in the hunt, they often indulge in other activities such as visiting the latrine areas and scent marking in various ways. Such activities may well have a synchronizing function for activities of the individuals belonging to the pack (see p. 242). Hyenas come together from all over the range after lying up singly or in small groups. They may join up anywhere in the clan range, but often a special place is used as a gathering point for weeks or months at a time, the "club." Packs contain more males than females and are led by one of the older females (p. 234). Zebra hunting occurs in bouts, and hyenas of a clan may sometimes hunt zebra exclusively for several days before again switching their attention to other prey.

When one or more hyenas get close to the zebra, a short dash (as described for hyenas hunting wildebeest) may occasionally be seen; the hyenas walk after the zebra (pl. 27) and even run for a short distance before giving up, but this is a rare occurrence. Most often the pack approaches slowly to within 4 or 5 m of the zebra. The zebra stallion sometimes attacks the hyenas (pl. 28), and this may cause them to turn around and walk away again. If the hyenas stay, after a period of up to a minute the zebra may very slowly, and close together, walk away from the hyenas without their following. I have not included these observations in the figures concerned with success of hyenas hunting zebra; they are not always easy to identify as hunting incidents, and I have taken into account only those observations where a chase of at least 100 m occurred, or where hyenas made a definite attempt to bite a zebra.

After the first approach a chase may ensue which is initiated either by the zebra's fleeing or by one or more of the hyenas' dashing at the zebra and the zebra's responding by fleeing. Almost invariably the hyenas chase a group of zebra, rarely a single individual. During the chase, the group of zebra walk or run in a tight bunch, and the hyenas usually follow in a crescent formation behind them. Almost always, if a family of zebra is chased, the stallion keeps between his family of mares and foals and the hyenas. The chase is usually relatively slow, with a median estimated speed of between 15 and 30 kmph (46% of twenty-four observations; in 21% the speed was below this, in 33% between 30 and 50 kmph). Sometimes the zebra did not move faster than 10 to

12 kmph and occasionally even stopped completely and stood very
close together before moving on again after a few seconds. Although it
is generally not very long, the total distance covered in a chase may be
considerable, sometimes over 3 km (fig. 48); on the whole, the faster a
chase goes, the greater the total distance covered. Very few other hyenas
join in once the chase has started (fig. 47); the pack size increases from
10.8 to 11.5 on the average, an insignificant increase.[20]

Although hyena packs are usually led by a female before the hyenas
have made contact with the zebra, this order seems to disappear
during the chase and each hyena acts independently; some hyenas
always seem to hang back a little more than others. The hyenas attempt
to bite the zebra stallion, his family, or any zebra of the herd that they
may be chasing. At the same time they have to dodge the attacks of the
stallion running behind the group. If one zebra falls only a little out of
the formation, because it is in less good condition than the others or
because one or more of the hyenas has managed to get a grip on it, all
the other hyenas will immediately concentrate on this individual (pl.
29). The zebra is grabbed and pulled down in the same way as the
wildebeest (pl. 30) and usually does not make any attempt at defending
itself once it is stopped. More hyenas join in the feast if no other carnivores interfere. In Ngorongoro a mean number of twenty-two hyenas
(13.4 in the Serengeti) will eat from the carcass and finish it completely
(pl. 31).

Responses of zebra to hyenas.   The social structure of the zebra population
has been described by Klingel (1965, 1967, 1969a), and is of obvious
relevance to the relation between zebra and hyenas. Two social categories exist. There is the family consisting of one stallion, one to six
mares, and a number of foals—all together up to sixteen zebra per
family (on the average 7.7) in Ngorongoro and up to eleven (on the
average 5.1) in the Serengeti. Then there are the bachelor groups consisting of up to fifteen stallions. These small units may aggregate in
fairly large herds, especially at night, but the units themselves remain
stable—they do not defend a territory. Generally the whole zebra
population is much more dispersed than the wildebeest population,
especially in the Serengeti. Within the family units there is a clear
social order; one of the mares always leads the family while the others
follow. The stallion usually walks behind, defends his family against

20. $\chi^2 = 0.64$; $df = 5$; $p < 0.80$.

other stallions, and often keeps his family together by herding straying members.

Perhaps because zebra live in less concentrated groups than do wildebeest, the zebra's reproduction is much less synchronized than the wildebeest's. Zebra foaling also shows a peak in January and February (Klingel 1965, 1969b), but only 61% of the foals were born during the three months of the main foaling season. Hence zebra do not swamp predators with young foals during a short period and in a small area, as do wildebeest.

It may well be that the typical stripe pattern of zebra has a survival value as a concealing coloration. The stripes may act as camouflage; in suboptimal light conditions, zebra seem to us to blend into the landscape and the predators may experience the same optical illusion. But it is likely that there is something more to the stripe pattern; it may well have a confusing effect on a predator at close range, particularly when the predator is confronted with many zebra at the same time. Or, as Professor Hardy suggested (personal communication), the varying widths of stripes may create an optical illusion about the direction in which the animal is moving, thus misleading the predator. But these are all necessarily speculations; there is nothing in my observations to suggest any likely function of the zebra stripes with regard to hyena predation.

On the whole, a single hyena just walking about is virtually ignored by zebra; in fact, hyenas often avoid the zebra rather than the other way around. Hyenas are able to walk within 5 m to 10 m of a family or herd of zebra, and the zebra will merely look at the hyenas without moving away. This reaction is seen even to hyenas which are about to hunt zebra, and a hyena pack may be able to walk quietly up to a herd of zebra (which is aware of their presence) and start a chase from very close proximity. But sometimes when a pack of hyenas in their alert posture, obviously hunting, approaches a group of zebra, the latter may flee from a distance of over 100 m, especially when there has been some chasing immediately before. On rare occasions, zebra may be heard to snort at the approach of the hyenas. When zebra are walking past hyenas who are either standing or lying down, they may stop and look for several seconds at the hyenas, in the head-up posture, sometimes going several steps in their direction. Occasionally zebra approach or follow walking hyenas, but never for more than a few meters. Generally, zebra show very little curiosity about hyenas and have only a short reaction distance. A mare with a young foal has a much longer reaction distance than one without, and when she moves away from a hyena, the rest of her family will follow. Before fleeing from hyenas, members of a zebra family show a clear tendency to bunch up and members of different families may cluster into dense groups. Foals run immediately alongside their mothers, tending, like wildebeest calves, to stay on the side farthest from the predator. When zebra are fleeing from hyenas, they usually run slowly, and often it is obvious that they could run much faster. During the run, and especially immediately after, they bark excitedly, and the chorus coming from a large herd is very impressive.

I have never seen zebra take to water when chased, as wildebeest do. Child (1968) also noticed the reluctance of zebra to enter water when they were chased on islands during rescue operations in Lake Kariba, Rhodesia.

Aggression toward hyenas is shown by zebra almost exclusively in two contexts—first, when the stallion defends his family, and second, when the mare defends her foal. Only one individual from a zebra family group attacks the hyenas as they approach; the others remain completely nonaggressive. On a number of occasions I was able to identify this individual as the family stallion, but in the dark identification was, in most instances, impossible. In these cases, I extrapolated from my daytime observations and assumed that the one attacking individual was indeed the stallion. I never saw a stallion defend a zebra that did not obviously belong to the same family. The mare shows aggressive behavior only when defending her foal if she finds herself cut off from the rest of the group, or if the foal is grabbed or nearly grabbed in an attack on the whole family. The zebra stallion almost inevitably attacks when his family is threatened by hyenas, though the intensity of the attack varies.

A zebra attacks a hyena by trying to bite and to kick it with the forelegs, and only rarely attempts to kick with the hind legs. The stallion can run fast after one individual, sometimes chasing it over distances of up to 100 m with his head rather near the ground, teeth bared, and ears flat. I have never seen hyenas caught this way, but they are certainly put to great trouble to dodge such attacks. Cullen (1969) reported a female zebra's killing a hyena with her forefeet when defending her foal, and on another occasion a stallion grabbed one hyena of a pack of five by biting it in the back and then casting it aside.

One one occasion, I saw a zebra move aggressively toward an approaching hyena; the hyena lay down flat as the zebra came within a few feet. Immediately the zebra stopped, looked for several seconds at the hyena, and then turned back to his family. It seemed that here the stimulus for the zebra to attack was removed when the hyena lay flat. Aggression from the stallion occurs especially at the beginning of a hyena hunt, and often during the course of a hunt he is more inclined to flee with his family than to attack the pursuers. When this happens the zebras speed up considerably, and it is not unlikely that their very low speeds at the beginning of a hyena hunt are related to the stallion's active defense when he has to stay behind. Several times, I saw a zebra family stop completely when the stallion had stayed a long way behind and then move on again when he rejoined them. I have not been able to record the attack frequency of the zebra stallion, nor do I have an indication of its intensity. Since some form of zebra aggression was almost always present in a hyena attack, I am unable to draw any conclusions about the effect of the zebra attack upon the hyenas. Members of a bachelor group will also occasionally attack hyenas, but these attacks generally appear less intense than those of a stallion defending his family.

Although hyenas try to bite the stallion as well as his family, it is clear that they usually concentrate on the family and dodge the attacks of the stallion: his attacks seem to have at least some immediate effect. It is interesting, therefore, that in the hyena kill record for both the Serengeti and Ngorongoro, female zebra figure more prominently than males: for every one hundred mares, only forty-five stallions are killed (p. 91). It seems that the stallions are better able to protect themselves than their families.

Hyenas' success in hunting zebra.   Once a chase had started, hyenas were 34% successful in pulling down a member of the group (forty-seven observations). In 31% of these successful hunts, the victim was a foal of less than one year old. I cannot say why zebra manage to escape hyenas in some cases and not in others. I found it very difficult to classify the variations of zebra behavior. It sometimes appeared that a very determined attack from the zebra stallion right at the start of the hunt was enough to deter the hyenas, but I have no systematic evidence of this. The number of hyenas taking part in any hunt has no statistically significant effect on the outcome of their efforts.[21] It may be that hyenas are better able to catch their quarry after a long chase than after a short one (fig. 48), but this effect is also nonsignificant.[22] It is not possible

21. $\chi^2 = 0.38$; $df = 1$; $p < 0.70$.
22. $\chi^2 = 3.32$; $df = 1$; $p < 0.10$.

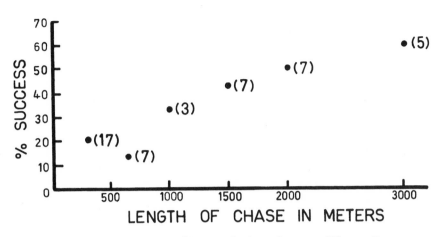

Fig. 48. The hunting success of hyenas chasing zebra over different distances.

to say at present which factors in the zebra's or hyenas' behavior contribute to the zebra's chance of escape.

Hyenas and zebra: Summary.   Hyenas set out to hunt zebra in packs of ten to twenty-five animals which they form shortly before the hunt, often before making any contact with the quarry. They catch zebra after a chase of up to 3 km, usually at low speeds.

A striking feature of the hunt is the active defense of zebra families by the stallion; the other members of the family do not attack hyenas, except for a female zebra which defends her small foal. Mares with young foals stay farther away from hyenas than do the other zebra; on the whole, hyenas are able to walk within a few meters of zebra without the zebra's making any effort to avoid them. If hyenas are not hunting, they themselves avoid zebra. Apart from a loud snort, zebra have no behavior patterns that may serve to act as an alarm.

Thirty-four percent of the zebra hunts observed were successful. Hunting success may be related to the number of hyenas taking part and the distance covered by the hunt, but these effects are not statistically significant. It is not known which factors contribute to the zebra's escape.

Hyenas Hunting Thomson's Gazelle

One early morning in June 1966, I followed an old female hyena who was walking alone over the open Serengeti plains, about 10 km south of Seronera. There were many Thomson's gazelle scattered about but few other antelopes; the hyena slowly zigzagged her way through the tommies with her head held low to the ground, occasionally looking around and scanning her surroundings. Suddenly a small tommy fawn jumped up from the short grass about 10 m in front of the hyena and sped away from it, stotting at first but then running at full speed bleating continually. The hyena immediately took up the chase, but as the distance between the two increased from 10m to 20m, it looked as if the fawn was going to outrun the hyena. Both seemed to be running at full speed, and the hyena's tail was streaming out behind her. Almost as soon as the young gazelle began to run, an adult female tommy, presumably the mother, ran toward it and then followed, keeping between the hyena and the young tommy, often zigzagging slightly and running just in front of the hyena's nose. Soon, though, the hyena began to gain on the young tommy, apparently paying no attention to the mother. When the hyena was within $1\frac{1}{2}$ m of the fawn, the fawn suddenly turned sharply and gained a little on the hyena. But the hyena soon managed to reduce the distance again, and when she drew close a second time, with the female tommy running almost next to her, the fawn stumbled. The hyena shot past it, only to turn back in her tracks almost immediately and grab the fawn over the back before it could get up. At the same time, three more hyenas arrived from various directions, perhaps alerted by the bleating of the fawn. The female ran off with the fawn dangling limply from her mouth; the hunt had taken about 2 min and the distance covered must have been almost $1\frac{1}{2}$ km. The recently arrived hyenas soon caught up with the one carrying the fawn; there was a short scuffle in which they each managed to obtain a little bit, and in a matter of seconds the fawn had vanished.

In October 1965, also on the northern Serengeti short-grass plains, around 0700, a hyena had just come to a halt after chasing a young tommy and was watching it disappear into the distance. The hyena had stopped about 10 m from an adult male Thomson's gazelle who was standing in his territory; the arrival of the hyena made him move away in the typical stotting gait. The hyena, after watching the tommy fawn, took one short look at the male and then began to run after him. The tommy kept up his high stotting gait until the hyena was only 10 m behind and gaining rapidly. Then he gradually changed his gait to ordinary fast running, but nevertheless the hyena was able to keep up with him. They both ran, seemingly as fast as they could, for about 4 min, by which time the hyena had almost caught up with the tommy. Then the tommy turned a very sharp corner which the hyena was slow to follow; it took him some time to change course and catch up with his quarry again. When almost within touching distance, the tommy again turned sharply to one side and gained a lead of 3 m or

4 m. This process was repeated eight times; then the hyena began to slow down and gave up the chase, having gone at full speed for 8 min. In the first 4 min of the chase, the two animals must have reached speeds of between 50 and 60 kmph.

At certain times of the year in the Serengeti, Thomson's gazelle can be an important item in the diet of hyenas, even at times when there are few, if any, young tommy fawns around. I have, however, been able to collect few observations of hyenas catching adult Thomson's gazelle. This may be partly because adult Thomson's gazelle are one of the few animals in the hyenas' diet which are more often scavenged than killed. Furthermore, the hunt of a Thomson's gazelle is very fast and extremely difficult to follow at night. Also, quite a few adult tommies were caught by hyenas in long grass, where observations are difficult at any time of day.

Generally, a hyena chasing Thomson's gazelle, adult or fawn, is alone and is only rarely joined by another hyena during the chase (fig. 49).[23] Especially at those times of year when there are many tommy fawns around, single hyenas can be seen walking through the vast herds of gazelle, or slowly wandering around nearby. Young tommies are usually born in short grass and spend the first two weeks of their lives lying in concealment, often surrounded by some slightly higher grass (pl. 33). Their mothers move far away and visit them occasionally for feeding (see below). Hyenas looking for tommy fawns inspect the patches of high grass where the little fawns are often crouched. This searching appears to be largely visual and only occasionally is by smell; wind direction seems to be unimportant during searching. The detection area around the hyena is relatively small; tommy fawns are well camouflaged when they press themselves against the ground, and on several occasions I saw hyenas pass within 2 m of a fawn without seeing it. On the average, the detection distance seems to be about 1 to 3 m. That is, of course, if the fawn does not move; if it jumps up, as in the example above, the detection distance may be increased to over 100 m. If a hyena comes across a tommy less than a day old he usually has no need to run for his meal, as he can just pick up the fawn and eat it.

Sometimes, after a tommy fawn has been grabbed, hyenas shake it (totschütteln) as dogs and foxes do (e.g., Tembrock 1957a, b, c), but this by no means always happens. The tommy often is either killed or stunned by the first bite, which is usually somewhere across the back or the

---

23. Number of hyenas at beginning and end of hunt: $\chi^2 = 0.00$; $df = 1$; $p = 1$.

neck; if a young tommy jumps up in front of the hyena, there may be a chase of up to 5 km (table 33)—the length of this probably depends considerably on the age of the fawn. The hyena runs as fast as it can

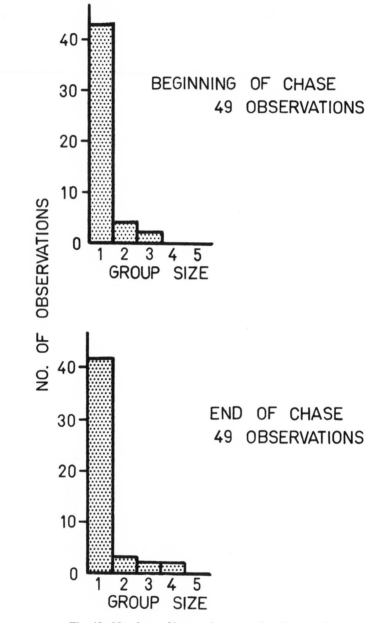

Fig. 49. Numbers of hyenas in groups hunting gazelle.

after the tommy, its mouth slightly open, and tries to grab wherever it can. The chase usually goes not in a straight line but in a circle, which meant that with the car I was unable to estimate the undoubtedly high speeds reached. But by comparing from memory the hyena's effort and speed in this situation with other occasions when I could estimate the speed from the speedometer reading on my Land Rover, the animals must run at some 50 to 60 kmph. At the end of the chase, when the hyena is closing in on its quarry, the fawn will almost invariably make some sharp turns which the hyena is unable to follow immediately; it overshoots before wheeling around after the tommy again.

I have never seen hyenas make dashes into gazelle herds as they do into wildebeest herds. When a hyena walks through tommy herds, however, it is continually watching the surroundings and the animals moving about, and it would be able to select a potential victim in this way. Hyenas occasionally "try out" gazelle by chasing one victim after another through the sparse gazelle herds, and such trials may develop into a proper chase.

TABLE 33 *Distance covered by hyena hunting gazelle*

Distance	Young fawns	Adults
0	6	–
100 m or less	9	–
200– 500 m	10	2
700–1,200 m	1	–
ca. 1,500 m	5	3
ca. 2,000 m	2	1
3,000–5,000 m	2	1
	35	7

The chase of adult Thomson's gazelle appears very similar to the chase of fawns. The distance covered is larger (table 33),[24] and the quarry is less inclined to move in a circle and appears to move faster. On grabbing an adult tommy, a hyena does not make a killing bite, but takes any part of the body, and when the animal falls it tears open the belly.

The defense of the tommy. The social system of Thomson's gazelle has been extensively studied by Walther (in preparation), who found that

24. Fisher e.p. on distances of hunting adults/fawns over $\leqslant 500$ or > 500 m $= 0.04$.

the females live in herds and the males either in bachelor herds or in their own territories, which they defend against other males. Generally, Thomson's gazelle are far more widely scattered than any of the species discussed previously and, probably associated with this, at least to the human eye, they blend into the landscape much better. The young Thomson's fawn does not accompany its mother during its first two weeks of life, but stays crouched in one particular spot. The mother wanders away over fairly large distances, visiting the fawn now and then to feed it. The very young tommy is darker than the adult, and when, in the face of potential danger, it freezes with its head on the ground and ears flat, it is beautifully camouflaged.

Many female gazelle give birth at the same time, during the beginning of the rains, but fawns are also born in other seasons. There is therefore some degree of synchronization of gazelle births, though not to the same extent as in wildebeest; also, many fawns are dropped in the same area. This may well affect hyena predation.

When describing the immediate responses of Thomson's gazelle to hyenas, one is again confronted with great variability. Reactions vary with the number of hyenas present, the direction they are moving with regard to the gazelle, social status of the tommy, behavior of neighboring tommies, and so on. Many of these variations are described by Walther (1969).

When a single hyena walks at a steady, ordinary pace toward a male gazelle standing on his territory, the tommy will stop grazing and look at the hyena when it is between 20 m and 50 m away. He stands with his head up, watching the hyena, until it comes within 10–25 m, then he turns and runs a short distance. Immediately before the gazelle runs, one may sometimes hear a soft snort and he may stamp his front feet. Usually he does not run directly away from the hyena but runs at right angles to the direction the hyena is moving. The tommy stops, turns and watches the hyena again; if the hyena shows no hunting intentions, the tommy returns to his territory once the hyena has passed.

The reaction distance of female gazelle or males in bachelor herds is greater than that of territorial males. When a hyena is walking through the herd of tommy, it is surrounded by a large circle, of 20–50 m radius, in which there are no gazelle; they quietly move out of the way when the hyena approaches and close up again behind it. Only rarely will gazelle follow a single hyena, though they will more frequently follow a group of hyenas. The empty area is not quite circular; it is more like an oval with the long axis in the direction the hyena is walking —gazelle move away earlier when they are in the hyena's path than when they are alongside. If there are two or more hyenas, the empty circle may be over 100 m in radius. It is interesting to see the extent to which the reactions of gazelle are affected by those of their neighbors, and a well-synchronized reaction to the predator is shown in the "false alarms" that one sometimes sees in gazelle herds. These occur especially after sunset, when, for instance, a few gazelle fleeing from a warthog may set off a wave of fleeing behavior that one can follow through the vast herds, well out of sight of the warthog.

Just when they begin to run, gazelle often show a very conspicuous twitching of the flank, which is all the more striking because of the large black stripes on the flank (Brooks 1961; Estes 1967a). This twitching does not always occur and, at least in response to an approaching Land Rover rather than to a predator, females are more likely to show it than males (females in 57%, males in 21% of my observations[25]). Estes (1967a) called the twitch an alarm signal, but Walther (1969) argued against this, since gazelle also show it in intraspecific situations whenever they begin to run, whether to attack or to flee. It seems very likely, though, that this conspicuous behavior associated with the color pattern has some significance as a signal ("I am going to run"). It may well act as an alarm signal when a predator is about and convey another message in a different context. Also, the snort, which is sometimes uttered just before fleeing, as well as on other occasions, can act as an alarm signal, for as soon as they have heard it, neighboring gazelle look up and stare in the same direction as the snorting animal.

If an approaching hyena runs up instead of walking, or if there is more than one hyena, the reaction distances increase considerably, up to 500 m in some cases. When the gazelle turn to flee from running hyenas, they often "stot" (named by Percival [1928]). Stotting is a very striking gait in which the animal moves with large bounds at high speed, taking off from all four legs almost simultaneously. The legs are held stiff and straight and the feet are about half a meter from the ground at the highest point of the jumps. It is a performance not often seen in intraspecific situations (except in play), but is common in all reactions to fast-running predators. If the running hyena does not follow the tommy, but continues on his course, the gazelle will run or stot for only a short distance. However, if the hyena continues to chase the tommy, the gazelle will go on stotting until the hyena is very close on its heels, then finally will break into a fast run. If the hyena then gives up, the tommy

25. $\chi^2 = 25.95$; $df = 1$; $p < 0.001$.

stots again for a short distance before stopping. Stotting occurs, therefore, when there is a high tendency to flee but not when such a tendency
is at its optimum.

   Young fawns particularly are apt to stot not only when fleeing from
hyenas but also when fleeing from a car. Their stotting is more conspicuous because they keep their tails straight up, exposing the white
perineal area in which the hair is erected; adults rarely do this. Fawns
also seem to keep up stotting longer than adults; when one sees a hyena
chasing such a young animal, one cannot help but think that if only the
fawn would merely run fast right from the beginning, the hyena would
have less chance of catching it. But this conspicuous gait must have some
survival value, and when a fawn is being chased, its function is probably
to attract the attention of the mother to what is happening. The female
gazelle strays up to 500 m away from her fawn (Walther, in preparation),
and a conspicuous display is therefore necessary if she is to notice it;
besides stotting, a fawn being chased keeps up a continuous bleating. I
once inadvertently injured a fawn crouching in the grass and its bleating
calls attracted six female gazelle, from distances of over 200 m, who
could not possibly have seen it. This suggested that the function of
the bleating call may be to attract the mother gazelle and that female
gazelle will react to calls of fawns which are not their own. The stotting
of a fawn may have a similar function and effect; in any case, in 39% of
the instances when fawns were chased by hyenas, at least one adult
female gazelle was on the scene and several times more than one. The
mother may, of course, have been present in more than 39% of the
observations, but I could score with certainty only those cases where one
or more adult females were performing "distraction displays" (see
below). A second question is whether the presence of the mother is
useful to a fawn threatened by a predator. This is doubtful when the
predator is a hyena, but the female gazelle may be useful in an attack
by jackals, and the behavior may have evolved in that context rather
than in response to hyena pressure.

   Although this explanation may help us to understand stotting in
young fawns, it does not as yet provide us with a functional explanation
for this behavior in adults. It may give an immediate advantage to the
pursued individual, but this seems unlikely. More probably stotting
acts as an alarm signal; it may well be an advantage to a tommy to
induce other gazelle to flee from the same predator, as this might create
"confusion" in which it is easier to escape. Any behavior which causes
other gazelle to behave similarly would be advantageous when con-

fronted with a predator, as it stops the individual from being "unique" in the eyes of the pursuer.

The female gazelle who comes running up when her fawn is being chased by hyenas goes on to show some behavior which in birds would be called "distraction display." Many ducks, waders, plovers, ostriches, and others respond to the presence of a predator near their nest by "playing the broken wing" and other displays (suggesting a disability) which have the likely function of distracting a predator's attention from the brood and luring the danger away (Simmons 1952, 1955; Brown 1962). The tommy mother runs between the hyena and her fawn, often very close to the hyena, or else she crosses just in front of it or runs immediately alongside, keeping just out of reach the whole time. Usually just one female does this, and I have assumed her to be the fawn's mother, but I have seen up to four female gazelle "distracting" at the same time in aid of the same fawn—all to no avail, as the presence of a distracting adult does not seem to affect the hunting success of a hyena. In twelve observations of female gazelles distracting, the hyena succeeded six times and failed six times. Out of nineteen observations where the female did not use distraction behavior, the hyena succeeded five times and failed fourteen times.[26]

When a hyena closes in on a stotting gazelle, the quarry continues at a run. If the hyena is still able to keep up, the tommy will double back sharply and cause the hyena to overshoot. The end of a successful chase is characterized by a number of these sharp zigzags, which can be quite effective in increasing the distance between pursuer and pursued. Finally though, the hunter usually gets his way if the hunt has reached the zigzag stage (only once did I see a hyena give up after a number of these sharp turns). For a fleeing animal, zigzagging is an obvious last resort; if it were employed when the pursuer was still too far away, he would be able to cut corners, thus abnegating all the possible benefit. Once captured, adults as well as fawns utter a loud, long-drawn-out guttural bleat, sometimes incessantly until they die.

Hyenas' success in hunting tommy. In forty-three observations that I made of hyenas hunting tommy, the hyenas were successful in 33%. In addition to this there were the occasions on which hyenas merely picked up a tommy fawn crouching in the grass, but, as one cannot express the number of misses, I left these out of the total calculations. The 33% successful hunts included hyenas hunting juveniles as well as adults;

26. Fisher exact probability test, $p = 0.14$.

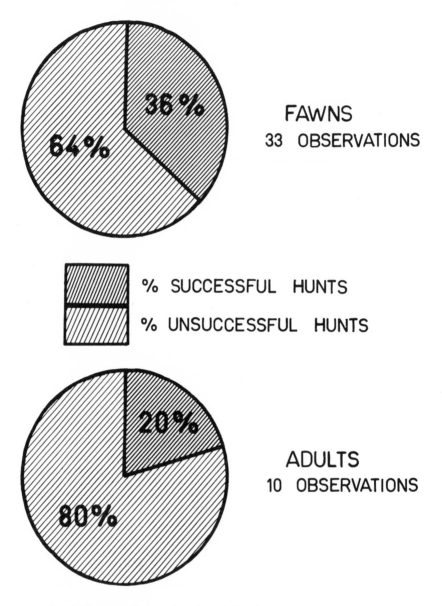

Fig. 50. Success of hyenas hunting adult or juvenile Thomson's gazelle.

figure 50 shows that the hyena's success in hunting juveniles (excluding the "picked up" fawns) is 36% and in hunting adults, 20%.[27] The number of observations in this latter category is very small, however.

27. Difference in hunting success of adult versus young gazelle: $\chi^2 = 0.34$; $df = 1$; $p < 0.70$.

Little is known of the factors contributing to the success of the hyenas. The number of pursuing hyenas is almost always the same, the zigzag performance at the end of a chase seems rather ineffective, and when a juvenile tommy is being chased, it makes little difference whether a female tommy shows distraction behavior (see above). If anything, fawns whose mothers tried to distract were caught slightly more often; if this result were consistent in further observations, it might be explained in terms of the age of the fawn chased. A tommy mother may be more likely to show distraction behavior when a very young fawn is involved than when the fawn is older. The age of the quarry is obviously a very important aspect of the interaction between fawn and hyena, and one that is very difficult, if not impossible, to assess in the field. Hyenas seem, almost exclusively, to chase very young fawns, and their hunting success decreases from probably nearly 100% in the first week of the gazelle's life. Factors contributing to the adult gazelle's chances of escape are still wholly unknown, although one might guess that individual variations in speed and endurance are very important.

Mass killing of Thomson's gazelle by hyenas.   On the morning of 16 November 1966, on the Mukoma Plains about 12 km southwest of Seronera, where many thousands of Thomson's gazelle had gathered during the previous two weeks, I found scattered over an area of about 8 km² 59 dead Thomson's gazelle and 27 badly injured ones; another 23 dead and injured gazelle were found later by Schaller. All together we accounted for 109 animals, and there may have been more which we overlooked. In and around the area were 19 hyenas, all with extremely distended stomachs, but from only 13 of the 59 dead gazelle did I find that anything had been eaten; in most cases, this was only a very small amount. It seemed most likely that the hyenas had eaten several gazelle completely, leaving no traces of them. The night had been very dark (two days after a new moon) with thick cloud cover, very heavy rain, and strong gales. From the evidence in the mud beneath and on top of the gazelle, it appeared that they had died during a shower or between two showers, and tracks around the carcasses left no doubts that hyenas had killed the animals. I collected a number of the victims and studied their injury pattern (table 34), which suggested that the victims had been grabbed randomly at any part of their body and had been finished off by a bite in the head or neck region. A number of gazelle "escaped" with severe injuries. The tracks showed that the hyenas had walked quietly from one animal to another, a number of them operating quite independently of each other; after killing a gazelle they left it and walked on to the next one.

TABLE 34 *Injuries of gazelle killed by hyenas during "massacre"*

Injured part of body	No. injured	Percentage
Head/neck	42	82
Back/flanks	16	31
Loins	20	39
Forelegs	9	18
Hind legs	11	22

NOTE: $N = 51$.

As I have only once come across a situation like this, it is probably very rare, although clearly vultures would be able to wipe out evidence of this kind of event within hours. The observation shows the tommies' vulnerability to predation on a very dark night, and the circumstances of this mass kill are remarkably similar to those observed in a black-headed gull colony, where foxes may kill great numbers of gulls without eating them (Kruuk 1964). There the number of birds killed was correlated with the darkness of the weather.

Apart from providing evidence on the hyenas' killing techniques and showing the importance of environmental circumstances to predation patterns, the phenomenon of mass killing is important in considering numerical relations between predator and prey; some ecological aspects were discussed on page 89. The observation shows what results when the normal antipredator behavior breaks down. A more detailed discussion is given by Kruuk (1972).

Hyenas and Thomson's gazelle: Summary. Hyenas usually hunt gazelle on their own. The quarry is most often a young fawn, merely picked up from its hiding place. Older gazelle are probably selected by sight, and if a chase ensues, whether after adult or young gazelle, this may cover a distance of 5 km at speeds of up to 60 kmph.

Almost invariably, the gazelle move in a kind of springing gait called "stotting" when they are first chased; if the pursuing hyena comes closer, this stotting will change into a flat-out run. If the hyena gives up, the gazelle starts stotting again before finally stopping. But if the hyena catches up with the gazelle, the latter will zigzag before being caught. Besides stotting, gazelle have several other responses to hyenas, with a probable alarm function, including a conspicuous twitch of the flank and a snort. Female tommies do not defend their fawns against hyenas, but they show a behavior which has the likely function of distracting the hyena's attention from the fawn.

Thirty-three percent of the chases ended with the gazelle's being caught. I could not find any effect of the female's distraction behavior on the hyenas' hunting success, nor did the zigzagging appear very effective. Sometimes mass killing occurs, when the antipredator behavior of gazelle breaks down under special circumstances.

Interactions with Some of the Less Common Prey Species

At one time or another, hyenas must have hunted and killed every species of large mammal in this part of Africa, even elephant (Bere 1966) and man (Balestra 1962). In this section, I will discuss some observations of the hunting methods employed with respect to less common animals, and the latter's reactions.

> *Eland.*   One morning at dawn in January 1966, a hyena was following an eland calf of a few weeks old in the Ngorongoro Crater. The calf was walking close behind a large old eland bull, and there was not a single other eland in sight. The calf stuck close to the old bull, who paid no attention either to it or to the hyena. The hyena often came as near as 2 m behind the calf, but was clearly afraid of the bull. Then, from a distance, another hyena came running straight up to the calf and bit it in the middle of the hind leg. The calf jumped high up in the air and struck out with its hind legs, hitting the hyena very hard in the snout before running to shelter again against the bull's shoulder. The hyena that had bitten the calf stopped and stood still for a minute, pawing his mouth now and then, and then turned round and slowly walked off. The first hyena stayed behind the bull and the calf. About 4 min after the calf had kicked its attacker, it walked close up to the head of the old bull, who was grazing, and almost pressed against him. The hyena was by now only 1½ m away from it. The bull had had enough of the calf and butted it hard; again the calf pressed against the bull's shoulder for a few seconds, and then it ran away from him at full speed. In a flash the hyena was after the calf; at first it looked as if it would outrun the hyena, but after a chase of about 300 m it was within 4 m of the calf and gaining ground rapidly. Two more hyenas came running up from a distance, and the calf's chances seemed very slim indeed.
>
> Then the chase went over a little rise, on the other side of which a very scattered herd of thirty-one female, one male, and five other calf eland were grazing. The nearest eland cow, who was about 100 m

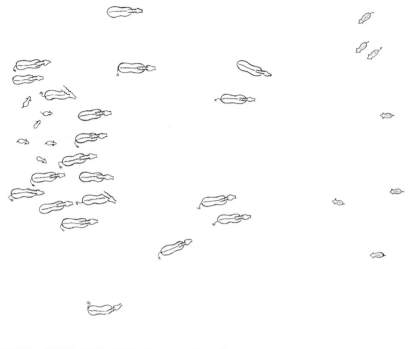

ELAND COWS AND CALVES   ELAND COWS   HYENAS

Fig. 51. Eland threatened by hyenas. The hyenas are approximately 100 m away from the group of cows and calves; opponents face each other.

from the calf, started to run, at great speed, toward the hyenas, immediately making a very agile attack, with her head low, on the one nearest the calf. The calf ran away from the cow toward the other eland; two hyenas immediately went after it, and five more appeared over the rise. Now there were eight hyenas on the scene, but suddenly female eland came running up to the calf from all directions, attacking the hyenas and chasing them in all directions and over long distances. One minute after the first eland cow had attacked, the calf had joined the other five calves and they were standing in a tight bunch surrounded by twelve cows, the whole group gathered together in an area about 20 m across. The eight hyenas were about 100 m away from this cow and calf group, standing well apart from each other and watching; between them and the calf group were another eight eland cows, all facing the hyenas (fig. 51). The rest of the eland cows and the bull were beyond a little rise and not actively involved in what was happening. This situation was maintained for approximately 5 min, then the eland began to slowly wander off, leaving the hyenas on the spot.

I have seen eland reactions to hyenas on another occasion when hyenas were hunting zebra and were vigorously attacked by a few eland cows that were walking with the zebra. So, although I can say little about the hyenas' hunting of eland in general, it seems justified to conclude that eland have an aggressive defense against hyenas and that the cows cooperate in defending their calves; they also do this when defending their offspring against wild dogs (Cullen 1969). Eland are socially organized into discrete units of usually fewer than a hundred individuals—either cow herds accompanied by a bull, or herds of "bachelor males."

Buffalo. Buffalo live in large, well-defined herds of up to one thousand animals, bulls and cows together; there are also old bulls who live solitarily or in small groups.

Interactions between hyenas and buffalo are rarely observed, partly because of the nature of the buffalo's habitat. Hyenas are able to kill fully grown adult bulls; once, in Ngorongoro, I passed a large bull who was by the side of the road, only to find him a few hours later killed by hyenas, with sixty-nine of them eating from him in broad daylight. Sinclair (1970) darted a young bull in the Serengeti in order to mark it; the drug was not fully effective and a hyena began to chase the bull soon after it had been hit. The buffalo was some distance from the herd and soon the hyena was joined by eight others; after a chase of less than 1 km, it stopped next to a large fallen tree and turned to face the hyenas. The bull defended himself with his horns, his back to the tree the whole time—the hyenas made several attempts to get behind him, but after about 10 min, they gave up and slowly drifted away again. I once saw a herd of buffalo walking slowly across an open plain come across two hyenas. The hyenas avoided the buffalo at about 15 m distance, but even so, two cows (one with a calf) charged at them with their heads low.

In the northern half of the Serengeti, hyenas have been seen several times in close proximity to herds of buffalo, especially when there are calves. There is no doubt that if any calves were unable to keep up with the herd, they would be easy prey for hyenas.

Rhinoceroses. On five occasions I saw hyenas bothering rhinos in Ngorongoro. In three of these observations hunger did not seem to be the motivating force behind the hyenas' behavior, but rather they seemed to be "mobbing" the huge animal (see p. 134 for other mobbing behavior). Once a female rhino was accompanied by a small month-old calf with a broken hind leg (pl. 34). There were fifteen hyenas around the pair attempting to bite the calf, trying especially to grab the ears (which were half torn off) and the tail, while the mother and the calf itself made repeated short charges at them. The calf stood smaller than the hyenas at the shoulder and stayed close to its mother. It was limping very badly, and the bone of the broken leg was sticking through its skin. The hyenas would probably have killed it in the end, but it was shot for study purposes by another scientist.

On another occasion six hyenas were closely following a rhino mother with a calf about six months old. The hyenas were obviously interested in the calf and bit it once in the hind leg, whereupon it charged at them; the mother showed no interest in the hyenas. But on other occasions, I have seen rhinos go quite far out of their way to charge at hyenas lying or standing on the plains—the hyenas avoided the rhinos at distances of over 20 m. According to Goddard (1967) young rhinoceroses (up to the age of four months) are vulnerable to hyena predation; he observed three instances when hyenas tried unsuccessfully to catch a young calf, but they were always repulsed by the charges of the mother or of the calf itself.

Hares. I once saw a hyena chasing a half-grown hare in Ngorongoro for about 40 sec, running in fairly small circles, with the hare doubling back every time the hyena came near. The hyena managed to grab it, however, and swallowed it in 15 sec. Another time I found tracks in wet sand near our house in the Serengeti from which I could deduce that a single hyena had surprised a hare, chased it with long jumps over about 20 m, and caught it without the hare's even starting one of its zigzags.

Warthogs. Only once did I see the end of a chase in which a hyena was after a warthog; the mother hog ran behind the hyena, who was on the heels of her four-month-old youngster. The young warthog disappeared into a hole hind legs first (warthog fashion), but the hole was not very deep and the hyena was able to reach down and grab its snout. While the mother stood nearby without showing any aggression, the young warthog was dragged squealing out of the hole and was killed when its abdomen was ripped open. Only then did five more hyenas join in and eat from the carcass.

Warthogs can often be seen very close to hyenas; the two species live in holes near each other and often share mud wallows and lie down within a few meters of each other (also in Deane 1962). Sometimes an adult warthog may make a short dash at hyenas, who take good care to avoid the large warthog tusks. Warthogs live solitarily or in family groups (Frädrich 1965).

Hyena Hunting Methods: Discussion

For the purpose of comparing the interactions between hyenas and the various prey species, I will first discuss some of the differences and similarities in hyenas' responses to different quarry. The most striking comparison is between the reactions to wildebeest and zebra, animals which are hunted by the same hyenas in the same area, sometimes on the same day. Zebra are hunted by packs of up to twenty-five hyenas, whereas wildebeest are chased by solitary hyenas or hyenas in groups of two or three, which are later joined by others (fig. 52). The zebra-hunting packs have some internal structure in that they have a leader, but when the hyenas engage in the actual chase the structure seems to disappear and every hyena hunts on its own (though all members of the pack usually chase the same quarry). Before the hunt, hyenas have different ways of "testing" wildebeest and zebra; wildebeest are often made to run by a hyena's dashing into the herd; the hyena then stands watching the running prey. With zebra, a pack of hyenas usually merely walks close to a group and looks at them from nearby before the zebra start slowly drifting away or the zebra stallion charges the hyenas.

There are some differences between hyena hunting zebra and wildebeest which are clearly due to differences in the antipredator behavior— for instance, the speed of the chase (which is slow after zebra and fast after wildebeest). But the differences in numbers of hyenas setting out are often apparent long before the hyenas have sighted a quarry; when hyenas are seen in a pack, even if there are no herbivores near, one can predict with a fair degree of certainty that they will eventually hunt zebra, even if this involves walking for miles through herds of wildebeest. This means that hyenas set out to hunt a certain kind of prey to the exclusion of others. Hyenas of one clan may be completely taken up with one kind of prey for periods of several days, even if other prey species are more abundant.

It is interesting to speculate about the function of this "preselection," for it indicates that at a particular time, hyenas prefer to hunt one kind of prey rather than another. This is probably only a short-term preference; the annual percentages taken from the prey populations are

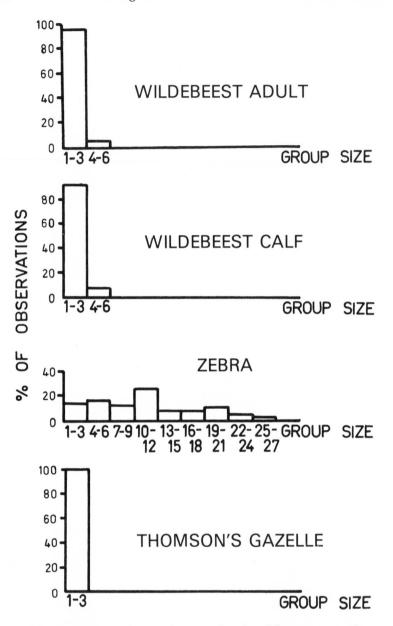

Fig. 52. Numbers of hyenas in groups hunting different prey species.

close to expectations of numbers taken if no particular long-term preference exists; also the hunting success for the two kinds of prey is
rather similar. The short-term hunting preference may be caused by a

tendency to vary the diet or by hunting success in the days immediately before the observations (for instance, if wildebeest were difficult to obtain yesterday, hyenas may hunt zebra today), and there may be other factors involved. With a given prey preference, it may be advantageous for the hyenas to adopt different hunting formations even before the prey is contacted. I will argue later that the hyenas' hunting methods are very well adapted to the requirements of catching different kinds of prey; the antipredator mechanisms of wildebeest and zebra are so unlike each other that they call for very different hunting action. If the hunting formation has to be taken up before meeting the adversary this would have the consequence of causing hyenas to concentrate on one kind of prey only.

Comparing a zebra hunt with a hunt after any of the other species to which I paid most attention (wildebeest adults and calves and Thomson's gazelle), I found that the number of hyenas setting out was significantly larger (fig. 52).[28] Wildebeest calves were chased by more hyenas than were gazelle, but the differences are only just significant. On the average, a pack of hyenas consisted of 10.8 animals when starting a zebra chase, 1.6 when chasing wildebeest calves, 1.4 when chasing wildebeest adults, and 1.2 when chasing Thomson's gazelle. In this sequence, the speed of the prey increases from zebra to gazelle, whereas the amount of aggression encountered by hyenas decreases. It is likely, therefore, that the number of hyenas participating in the hunt is adapted to the behavior of the quarry rather than the size. At the end of the chase there is an increase in the number of hyenas when an adult wildebeest is chased (up to an average of 2.5 hyenas), but not in the chase of other quarry. Finally, there are large differences in the number of hyenas eating from one carcass (p. 120), to some extent adapted to the amount of food available.

Apart from these clear quantitative differences in hunting methods, there are some that are less tangible; for instance, in the stage at which hyenas select their potential victims from a herd. These variations are less easy to summarize, and I will have to refer to the descriptions in the appropriate sections. These differences, as well as the pack size of hyenas, are probably more than immediate responses to variations in

---

28. Number of hyenas hunting: adult wildebeest versus zebra, $\chi^2 = 58.44$; $df = 1$; $p < 0.001$—adult wildebeest versus calves, $\chi^2 = 0.30$; $df = 1$; $p < 0.70$—adult wildebeest versus tommy, $\chi^2 = 2.25$; $df = 1$; $p < 0.20$—zebra versus tommy, $\chi^2 = 54.78$; $df = 1$; $p < 0.001$—wildebeest calf versus tommy, $\chi^2 = 5.59$; $df = 1$; $p < 0.02$—zebra versus wildebeest calf, $\chi^2 = 47.69$; $df = 1$; $p < 0.001$.

the antipredator behavior or social structure of the prey species. But of course there are also a large number of immediate prey reactions to species-specific behavior, and when one follows hyenas on various hunts one is impressed by the range of prey protection patterns that they can cope with. Hyenas deal with the aggressive zebra, with the wildebeest or rhinoceros mother defending her calf, with the fast adult gazelle and its well-camouflaged fawn, with a wildebeest jumping into water and a warthog backing down a hole: they are obviously very versatile. But before I attempt to summarize hyenas' hunting behavior in the face of all this diversity, it is necessary to discuss a few more aspects of their hunting and killing, especially the phenomenon of "surplus killing," and their hunting success with various kinds of prey.

On at least one occasion, hyenas killed more than they could eat. In several observations made at a time when wildebeest calves were in abundance, hyenas were seen to kill and leave the carcass for other hyenas to eat; here I could not be certain that the killing hyenas were not, in fact, also hungry. But once a few hyenas killed more than a hundred gazelle in one small area, mostly without eating them. In this observation, they were able to kill so many because of a breakdown in the antipredator system of the gazelle. Almost certainly, no chasing had been involved; the gazelle were mostly killed by a bite in the head or neck. The observation strongly suggested that the actual killing of prey is independent of a hunger motivation (as in cats; Leyhausen 1965). The question arises why, then, hyenas do not usually continue with hunting after they have eaten. One likely answer to this might be that hunger initiates the first links in the chain of behavior patterns leading to killing—for instance, the searching, the "trying out" or the chasing, or all of these; once a hyena is close to the victim, the killing follows regardless of hunger. A system like this could keep hunting in check (as would be necessary to maintain a proper predator-prey balance), for prey can only rarely be caught without a search and chase. As far as the biological function of "surplus killing" is concerned, it might well be of benefit to a hyena's offspring, clan fellows, or even individuals themselves (if they store the surplus, see p. 119) if they kill those kinds of prey which are easily obtainable, even if at the time of the kill the hyenas do not feel hungry.

The differences in success of hunting various kinds of prey are surprisingly small, especially in view of the diversity of hunting methods. Hunting wildebeest adults was successful in 44% of the observations, calves in 32%, zebra in 34%, and gazelle in 33%.[29] If we remember

29. $\chi^2 = 0.72$; $df = 3$; $p < 0.90$.

that these percentages do not refer to encounters with prey or even to "try outs" but to definite hunting attempts aimed at one particular animal or family (p. 158), the similarity of these figures suggests that they express the hyenas' ability to gauge the chances of securing the quarry.

Finally, I will try to extract a common pattern from the different hyena hunting methods. Hyenas can approach all species of prey very closely; they do not stalk, nor do they ambush or rely in any way on surprise attacks. They watch from close quarters for a potential victim among the ungulates; they often make herds run by charging at them, then stand and look, presumably checking on physically inferior animals. When an individual is selected, a chase begins which is usually fast and covers distances of up to 5 km. If a quarry defends itself or is defended by others of its species, hyenas may combine their efforts in packs of up to twenty-five. In almost all prey species, outrunning is the most important means of escape, which is one of many indications that hyenas select the physically least able. Victims are usually killed by disemboweling, which hyenas also do with dead carcasses. Killing by a bite in the neck or head does occur, but only when the prey is very small (gazelle fawns) or in times of superabundance of moderately small game (mass killing of adult gazelle).

Protection of Ungulates against Hyenas

In a previous study, I argued that the antipredator mechanism of a species can be separated into a direct and an indirect system (Kruuk 1964). The direct antipredator system consists of the immediate responses to a predator's presence and has the function of increasing an individual's chances of survival in an encounter with a predator. The indirect system consists of behavioral and other characteristics which are shown regardless of the presence of a predator, with the function of decreasing the chance that an encounter between predator and individual will take place at all. This last category includes phenomena such as camouflage, synchronized breeding, herd structure, and so on; most of these patterns have a direct bearing on other parts of the species' ecology as well (e.g., food utilization, social behavior). Because of this functional connection with other aspects of the prey species' ecology, the indirect antipredator system is likely to have evolved under selection pressures additional to those from predation; this is of importance in understanding the whole antipredator mechanism, especially when making comparisons between species.

The prey species I am dealing with here can conveniently be divided into four categories with different group size and structure. These are: (1) large amorphous herds (wildebeest, Thomson's gazelle); (2) slightly smaller discrete and structured herds (buffalo, eland); (3) small, very discrete and structured groups (zebra); (4) solitary individuals (warthog, rhinoceros, hare).

I will briefly discuss some aspects of the antipredator mechanism of each of these categories.

1. Wildebeest and Thomson's gazelle, living in large amorphous herds show no active defense (or almost none) against hyenas, except for female wildebeest defending their calves. Running is the major means of escape, and individuals do not assist each other against predators (again except for females and calves, and the use of alarm calls; see below). Wildebeest often cluster together when chased. The defense of a wildebeest calf by its mother can be very effective against one hyena but has virtually no success against more. The female gazelle shows a distraction display to protect her fawn but no actual defense. Wildebeest calving is highly synchronized, a phenomenon which is probably very effective in "swamping" predators with this easy food (Darling 1938; Kruuk 1964; Estes 1969). Gazelle fawns, on the other hand, rely on camouflage and corresponding behavior patterns for protection.

One remarkable thing is the number of different alarm signals that one can see performed by gazelle. Many of these are given by males as well as females and, at least at the time, appear to be to the disadvantage of the signaler but to the benefit of other nonrelated gazelle. In this species, a more elaborate signal may be called for when other individuals are to be alerted, because gazelle are better camouflaged and individuals are more spaced out. One might argue that it could be of advantage to the individual signaling to alert other gazelle so that many may respond to the danger; in this way no individual would make itself conspicuous by being the only one responding.

2. Eland and buffalo live in fairly small to large herds, which are clearly discrete units. I have only very few observations in this category; these indicate that the reactions against hyenas are characterized by aggression and mutual assistance of individuals: the members protect the herd. Calving is to some extent synchronized within the herd (Sinclair, 1971 for buffalo). Their aggressive response to hyenas can be very effective, not only because of the size of these ungulates but especially because of their cooperative reaction.

3. The families and stallion bands of zebra form small and very distinctive units. These may at times aggregate into larger herds having no infrastructure (Klingel 1967). They exhibit an aggressive defense against hyenas (biting and kicking) in which members of the family unit protect each other (stallion defends mares and mares defend their own foals) but no other members of the species. Apart from aggression, zebra also show fleeing behavior, during which members of a family, and several families together, may cluster into tight groups. Foaling is to some extent synchronized in the whole population but less than in the wildebeest.

4. The various solitary prey species show a variety of responses; the rhinoceros shows almost pure aggression to hyenas (if it reacts at all), hares will run, and warthogs go to ground. There is little in common between the antihyena reactions of these species.

Ignoring the last category, which is in fact rather a ragbag, this brief survey suggests that there is a relation between group size and cohesion and the antipredator response. Mutual assistance between individuals occurs in the discrete groups that have a certain permanent composition, and in the species concerned there is a clear factor of aggression in the direct response to hyenas.

If there is indeed such a connection between the direct antipredator responses on the one hand and indirect antipredator mechanisms like group size and structure on the other, and if the indirect antipredator mechanisms are important factors in other aspects of the species' ecology, as discussed before, one must then, when comparing the reactions of different species to one predator, also take into account the whole ecology of these various species. The direct antipredator behavior of *one* prey species may be very well adapted to the ecological importance and behavior of *different* predators (Kruuk 1964, and p. 284), but it is difficult, if not impossible, to make this kind of simple comparison between antipredator behavior of *different* prey species to *one* predator.

In the previous pages, it has been shown that the way each prey species copes with hyena predation is very intricate, especially when one considers the detailed reactions to variations in the behavior of the predator (most of all to indications of readiness to hunt). But there are several aspects of the protection against hyenas which make one wonder whether in fact the ungulates could not do better. For instance, Why allow hyenas to come so close before responding? Why do wildebeest run into water when chased? Why do not all wildebeest females defend their calves or combine in defense? Why do not zebra mares attack hyenas as the stallions do? Why do gazelle stot for so long when being chased before going into a fast run? Many more similar questions could easily by brought up.

Some of these apparent inadequacies may be caused by the fact that antipredator patterns are also tied up with other aspects of the species' ecology, so the animals' behavior is determined by conflicting selection pressures. For instance, although it might be good antipredator policy to avoid any hyena on sight, this would mean many more and longer interruptions of grazing and other behavior, especially since hyenas are common. In the case of some wildebeest females failing to defend their calves, we have to remember that hyenas are dangerous to the adult wildebeest too.

In other instances, it would be a disadvantage for one individual to acquire a certain habit, although it would be advantageous to the population if all members did. For instance, it would be detrimental to one wildebeest's chances of survival to defend his neighbors against hyenas, but if all wildebeest would do so, the species would almost certainly fare better in contests with this predator.

However, it is still hard to see why zebra mares should defend only their own foals whereas eland come to the assistance of calves which are not necessarily their own (but in the same herd), and why wildebeest head for water when chased by hyenas is equally mysterious. Obviously, many more observations are needed to gain insight into these functional aspects of ungulate behavior.

PLATES

1. Serengeti landscape: The edge of the Serengeti plains, with wildebeest and zebra.

2. Removing the dart from an immobilized female hyena.

3. Marked hyena, with others on a kill. The ear-notch code of this individual reads L(eft) $_{13}$: R(ight) $_3$.

4. The teeth of a spotted hyena. Note the carnassial shear and the three conical bone-crushing premolars. Match = 4.5 cm.

5. Hyenas are very social feeders, with relatively little aggression between them at mealtimes. Note marked hyena (L $_2$: R $_2$) and white-backed vulture.

6. A female hyena walking off with the leg of a wildebeest for quiet consumption elsewhere.

7. Hyenas with the carcass of a male wildebeest, killed in the salt lake of Ngorongoro. Note the radio collar on one hyena.

8. Hyenas and six male lions sharing a waterhole on the Serengeti plains. Also in the picture are Egyptian geese.

9. Hyenas mobbing a male lion.

10. Lioness bowling over an old female hyena; Serengeti.

11. Young male lion chasing hyenas off their wildebeest kill in the Serengeti.

12. Same lion on the kill, hyenas in threatening postures around it.

13. Hyenas moving in, lion swatting at a hyena who had bitten him just before the picture was taken; note aggressive postures of approaching hyenas, fleeing posture of hyena being swatted (open mouth, flat ears), hooded vulture (*front right*).

14. Hyenas and young male lion sharing carcass of hyena-killed buffalo, Ngorongoro.

15. Hyena and golden jackal near wild dogs who are killing a Thomson's gazelle. Note hyena posture, and proximity of wildebeest attracted to the scene.

16. Hyena approaching wild dogs on a gazelle kill, creeping nearer with high fleeing tendency apparent from open mouth, folded ears, and posture.

17. Hyenas scavenging from wild dogs'. kill.

18. Hyenas in Harar, Ethiopia, keep the town clean and are tolerated, even fed, by the local inhabitants; © 1968, National Geographic Society.

19. Hyenas on zebra kill in the Serengeti, with white-backed vulture (*left foreground*), lappet-faced vulture (*landing left and taking off second from right*), white-headed vulture (*landing center, taking off right foreground*), and hooded vulture (*center background*).

20. Group of hyenas pulling down a wildebeest bull, Ngorongoro.

21. Group of hyenas attacking a wildebeest bull, after he had been run down by one hyena only. Night photograph.

22. Same bull as above, hyenas attacking hindquarters.

23. Seconds before dying. Note hyena with radio collar in left of picture.

24. Large herd of wildebeest in the Serengeti.

25. Wildebeest bull lying within a few meters of a hyena "club," Ngorongoro.

26. Eleven hyenas before a zebra hunt. Night photograph.

27. Initial stages of a zebra hunt; hyenas walk very close to the edge of a concentration of zebra families. Night photograph.

28. When hyenas approach a group of zebra families, a zebra stallion will often walk out toward them.

29. One zebra is grabbed and falls behind the rest. Night photograph.

30. Zebra pulled down by the pack; one black-backed jackal watching. Night photograph.

31. Hyenas eating zebra victim; scavenging are one black-backed and one golden jackal. Night photograph.

32. Female hyena searching for fawns of Thomson's gazelle, Serengeti.

33. Thomson's gazelle, a few days old, in hiding.

34. Rhinoceros protecting her injured calf (broken hind leg), Ngorongoro.

35. Hyena looking out of a hole in which it spends the day.

36. Hyenas yawning (*foreground*) and calling ("lowing") near a lion who has stolen their kill.

37. "Pasting": depositing secretion of anal glands on grass stalk.

38. Attack of strange hyena after "parallel walk." Note biting directed at shoulder region, protruding rectum of attacker, and fleeing posture of victim.

39. "Parallel walk": threat behavior directed at a third hyena.

40. Posture immediately before attack.

41. "Female baiting": four males attacking a female (*left*). Note difference in postures.

42. Meeting: sniffing each other's heads.

43. Meeting ceremony: simultaneous leg-lifting, with penis or clitoris erection.

44. Unsuccessful attempt at mounting. Note difference between male and female.

45. Unsuccessful mounting attempt; note male's chin on female's shoulder; female is uncooperative.

46. Sexual behavior: male (*left*) scraping in front of uncooperative female.

47. Hyena den with four adults and four cubs; Serengeti.

48. Hyena cub, two months old, "pasting" (ineffectively; note rectum).

49. Hyena cub, about five months old.

50. Hyena cub, about eight months old.

51. Hyena, approximately one and one half years old, licking adult.

52. Adult hyenas playing in river pool.

53. Border clash between Scratching Rocks clan and Mungi clan.

54. "Latrine," with at least twenty-one sets of feces.

55. Wild dog holding down young male Thomson's gazelle by its ear, after running it down, and waiting for the rest of the pack to arrive before dismembering. Note wildebeest approaching in "curiosity." Ngorongoro.

56. Wild dogs pulling down yearling wildebeest in the Serengeti after running it down.

57. Thomson's gazelle attracted to a single wild dog.

58. Wildebeest attracted to a hunting cheetah.

6 Interactions between Hyenas

SOME MORPHOLOGICAL CHARACTERISTICS

Naturalists have marveled at the anatomy of the spotted hyena from the time of Aristotle onward; its social and other behavior began to surprise observers some time later. Wickler (1964, 1965a, b) was the first to have an inkling that the peculiar morphology and social behavior are closely linked.

The first striking aspect of the hyena's morphology is its external shape: the animal has a strong, well-developed neck and forequarters and relatively small hindquarters (although this apparent discrepancy is not anywhere near as large as popular writings make one believe). The slightly sloping back is especially conspicuous when a hyena is running away from man or another enemy with its tail between its legs, but much less so when the tail is carried high as, for instance, in an aggressive posture. One of the functions of the very strong forequarters is apparent to anyone who has seen hyenas feeding in a group when individuals try to secure a large lump of meat (a leg or a head) and carry this off. They are able to run at considerable speed while carrying a wildebeest head weighing some 15 kg, holding it well above the ground. The rump seems rounded rather than angular, which enables a hyena to offer an attacker coming in from behind (other hyenas or wild dogs) a rounded area with little chance of getting a grip on it.

The color and spotting of the hyena's coat varies a great deal and changes with age. Figure 53 clearly indicates the decrease in the number of spots as the animal gets older,[1] and I have often used this criterion in the field to decide a hyena's relative age. The large individual variation in coat color as much as anything else has given rise to systematic confusion, the history of which is given by Matthews (1939c). Up to nineteen subspecies of hyenas had been described, but systematic collection

---

1. $\chi^2 = 57.31$; $df = 6$; $p < 0.001$.

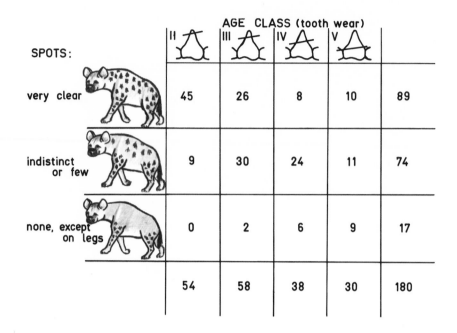

SPOTS:	AGE CLASS (tooth wear)				
	II	III	IV	V	
very clear	45	26	8	10	89
indistinct or few	9	30	24	11	74
none, except on legs	0	2	6	9	17
	54	58	38	30	180

Fig. 53. The relation between spot pattern and age. For toothwear, see figure 7.

from one area by Matthews showed that the described subspecific differences were in fact merely individual variations.

What has surprised observers of hyenas more than anything else is the sexual dimorphy or, rather, the lack of it. Several authors have commented on the anatomy of the hyena's genitals (Gordon 1777; Watson 1877, 1878; Chapman 1888; Grimpe 1916, 1923; Neuville 1935, 1936a, b; Davies and Story 1949; Wickingen 1959), and especially accurate descriptions of the hyena's internal and external reproductive organs have been presented by Matthews (1939a). The male anatomy is not particularly unusual, but the external genitals of the female are striking in that they exactly resemble those of the male. The clitoris resembles a penis and is in the same position, capable of similar erection; two sacs filled with fibrous tissue look very much like the scrotum. This resemblance between male and female anatomy has given rise to the suggestion that hyenas are hermaphrodites, discussed as early as Aristotle (384–322 B.C.) but firmly shown by Matthews (1939a) to be a figment of the imagination. The story still lingers on, however (references in Deane 1962).

In fact, sexually mature males and females are distinguished in the field by the presence or absence of large nipples, size, and the slightly different appearances of the scrotum and "sham scrotum." I still cannot distinguish the sex of immature hyenas without anatomical inspection. Thus, although there are differences between the two sexes, it is the similarities which are most striking.

What is the biological function of this likeness, which occurs only in spotted hyenas and not in related species? Wickler (1964, 1965a, b) suggests that the structure of the female genitals has a signal value that expresses itself in behavior patterns, but does not give any specifications. To me also, the significance of the structure became apparent when observing the hyena meeting ceremony (p. 226), and it is likely that behavior observations can provide us with an explanation for this curious phenomenon.

Another odd morphological aspect of the hyena's biology, already pointed out by Matthews (1939a), is that females are considerably larger than males. Matthews measured head and body length for both sexes and found that the commonest measure for males was about 110 cm and for females about 120 cm. Dr. Sachs and I weighed twenty adults (eight females and twelve males) collected in the Serengeti; here, too, we found a significant difference, females averaging 55.3 ± 4.06 kg and males 48.7 ± 2.32 kg.[2] The females ranged in weight from 44.5 to 63.9 kg and the males were from 40.5 to 55.0 kg. Wilson (1968) found an average of 67.6 kg for males and 69.2 kg for female hyenas in Zambia; the animals there are obviously much heavier than in the Serengeti. Thirteen skulls from Queen Elizabeth National Park, Uganda, which I measured there were on the average 7% longer and wider than skulls from the Serengeti, suggesting that Serengeti hyenas are particularly small. I have no data on these points from Ngorongoro. That females are the larger sex is a curious phenomenon which is rare among mammals; as in the lack of sexual dimorphism, an explanation may be found when studying the animal's social behavior (page 246).

Daily Activity

The behavior of hyenas is literally shrouded in darkness, which is the main difficulty to be overcome when studying these animals. However, there is some activity during daylight and this was very helpful. Also, the moonlight in the few days around full moon is very bright in East Africa, and through a good pair of fieldglasses, I could distinguish hyenas more than 2 km away. I have tried to study hyenas at night

2. $t = 2.974$; $df = 18$; $p < 0.01$.

with infrared light, but the narrow field and short effective distance rendered these devices useless for my purpose.

To get a more exact idea of the diurnal periodicity in the hyena's activity, I collected observations in two ways. First, in three different areas in Ngorongoro and the Serengeti, I spent four periods of 24 hr noting the activity of the hyena population at 3-hr intervals. These observations were made in June and July 1965 during moonlit nights, and the results have been summarized in figure 54. In this method of observation, bias is likely: an active hyena is more likely to be observed than a hyena which is lying down either in the open or in a hole. This bias is largest at night, but at least observations should be comparable between different times of the night. The main conclusions to be drawn from figure 54 are that hyenas are very nocturnal and that the highest activity is in the first half of the night, after which there is a steep decrease followed by a lower peak at dawn. The exact timing of the first, higher activity peak and following drop varied somewhat, but not the time of the "dawn peak." The overall trend is the same in all observations.

In 1967, I followed one female hyena for twelve days in Ngorongoro Crater, keeping the animal under uninterrupted observation. We were aided by a radio transmitter on a collar around her neck, and a receiver

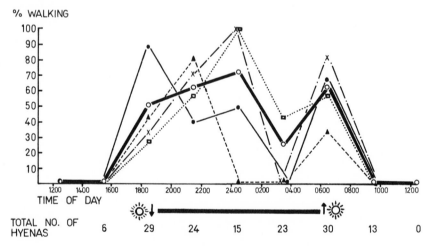

Fig. 54. Percentage of hyenas active in sample areas of Ngorongoro and the Serengeti.
——————— = Serengeti plains, 10 km²
- - - - -⎫
. . . . . .⎭ = Mungi clan range, Ngorongoro, 5 km²
.—.—.—. = Hippo clan range, Ngorongoro, 6 km²
——————— = Average

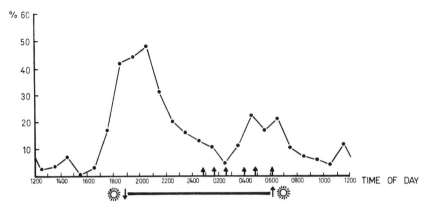

Fig. 55. Activity of one female hyena with radio transmitter, Scratching Rocks clan, Ngorongoro. Observations over twelve days (281 hours). ↑ = time of wildebeest kill.

in the observer's car; we also kept a visual minute-to-minute check. I carried out these observations with the help of Mr. William Holz (we alternated 12-hour periods). The results of these observations on the hyena's activity are shown in figure 55. This series of observations has not suffered from the bias reported for the previous set, and figure 55 gives a more accurate picture of the activity than figure 54. Although data were collected from one individual only, it was noted again and again that the activity of other hyenas with which our individual associated, or which could be observed simultaneously, showed essentially the same activity rhythm during the day and the night.

In the observations on the single hyena with the radio collar, this individual was active 15.8% of the time; in other words, she spent 84.2% of the time lying down. In the first set of observations, an average of 65.4% of hyenas were lying down, but this estimate is almost certainly too low. In both cases, these figures show how little a carnivore like a hyena is active; moreover, only a small part of the species' activity is spent foraging and feeding. The car with the radio-collared animal traveled on average 10.1 km per day; the animal herself must have walked somewhat more.

The double peak of activity during the night is a common phenomenon among nocturnal animals. Aschoff (1966) showed that the second peak is usually the lower; he called the double peak the "bigeminus pattern," which in most species is not environmentally induced but an independent property of the animals' behavior.

Figures 54 and 55 give an outline of the way a hyena's day is divided into active and resting periods. However, the way various behavioral patterns (feeding, social behavior, territorial, sexual) are fitted into the diurnal pattern is susceptible to a large amount of variation, and my observations are too crude to analyze this. It was very striking, for instance, when observing a group of hyenas over a long period, that the time of day in which kills were made seemed to remain the same for many days in sequence, then to change fairly suddenly. I have been unable to trace a relation between the time of day when hyenas were hunting and the time of day when they are most likely to be active. For instance, in figure 55 I have also indicated the times of day when the clan (to which the particular individual we were following belonged) made its kills; in that period, all prey was caught at a time when most hyenas were inactive. This was almost certainly due to the activity of a few individuals, and after the kill was made all the hyenas used to quickly fill themselves, then lie down again. The same clan, some two weeks later, was consistently killing at dawn, and I have more examples of similar shifts of a particular activity from one time of day to another. The majority of my observations on hyenas hunting or feeding were in the evening or early morning; however, this was undoubtedly seriously influenced by my own activity rhythm, and no further conclusions can be drawn from this. However, when I observed a kill during all-night watches it usually occurred in the first half of the night or early morning, and little happened in the darkness between those periods.

This curious phenomenon of groups of hyenas keeping to a certain habit over a period, then changing fairly suddenly was also observed in the timing of the beginning and end of hyenas' daily activities. These changes occurred for no apparent or obvious reasons. For example, a particular clan in Ngorongoro may, for weeks on end, be active in the morning till 0800 hr and then sleep until it is well dark; when observing this same clan a few days later, no hyenas would be seen walking around after 0630 hr and a lot of activity might already be starting at 1700. The same thing often happened in Serengeti. But figures 54 and 55, I believe, represent a good overall cross-section of activity periods.

There is a great deal of variation between individuals, clans, areas, and seasons in where and how hyenas spend their resting periods. Here again individuals may use one particular resting place for weeks on end, then suddenly change for no obvious reason. Sometimes a female, especially one with very small cubs, will spend the whole day on the den, but generally hyenas look for a cool shady place, usually to themselves. If the weather is not very hot, they may sleep out on the open plains, but otherwise they go down an unused hole (usually away from the den), lie on the edge of a lake or stream in the mud or inside a dense shrub, or improvise all kinds of other variations on this theme. In the Ngorongoro Crater, members of the Lerai and Airstrip clans sleep in the shrub high up on the slopes, but in the wet season a number are found on patches of mud out in the open. The Scratching Rocks hyenas more often sleep along the Mungi River, which, in their range, runs as a deep cleft in the plains; the hyenas lie immediately next to the water, usually under overhanging banks, some two meters below the level of the plains. The hyenas from the Mungi clan also tend to sleep along the river, but they use the shade of deep gulleys running down from the rim more than the actual Mungi River bed. Hyenas from the Ol-donyo Rumbe clan are the only ones who often sleep inside the actual den, which is much more extensive and has much larger pipes than any of the other dens I know. The Lakeside clan members go down separate holes or lie on mud flats next to the lakeshore and, for the first two years of my study, some hyenas of that clan regularly swam out in the mornings to the little island in the large lake, slept in the bushes or among the high grass, and then, in the evening, crossed the 200-m stretch of water again.

Hyenas on the Serengeti plains usually sleep in holes (pl. 35) or, if they are near any of the hills with their bushy vegetation, they often look for a shady place high up the slopes. They like to lie inside the granite outcrops, the kopjes, or in any thicket in the woodlands. During the rains, hyenas are more frequently found sleeping out on the open plains or on little mud patches. In both areas, hyenas sleeping at night lie anywhere in the open.

COMMUNICATION

I gradually gained the impression that hyenas could see in daylight about as well as I could. However, their vision at night is clearly superior to ours, and, from their reaction to prey animals and other hyenas, they appear to see far greater detail in unfavorable light than we can. For instance, they could, at night, recognize another hyena (whether he belonged to the same clan or not) even when the other hyena was coming from downwind in complete silence, whereas I could hardly see that there was an animal at all. Hyenas were able to react immediately to a small disturbance in a herd of wildebeest miles away when we could hardly see the herd with the naked eye. Hearing is also better developed in hyenas than in man; a hyena lying down at night might suddenly jump up and run in a particular direction (not necessarily upwind) toward a place where a group of hyenas were engaged in the noisy consumption of a kill—sometimes we ourselves could definitely not hear these sounds from the place where the hyena was lying. The hyena's sense of smell is almost proverbial, and they are able to pick up the scent of a carcass far downwind. This sense is important in social encounters; for instance, a hyena approaching a group of others will often circle at some distance until downwind, then stop and stand before approaching nearer. They elaborately sniff each other on meeting and on other occasions. Finally, the sense of touch appears important in some contexts, especially during a behavior pattern which I called "social sniffing" (p. 241).

The importance of vision and hearing in the social communication of hyenas is reflected in the various postures, which probably have a display function, and in the calls. To what extent information is carried by smell is still difficult to assess. In the following section I will try to describe some behavior elements which are of obvious importance in understanding hyena social structure.

Elementary Social Behavior Patterns

Attitudes and Postures

In the responses of one hyena to the presence of others, a number of elements can be distinguished which appear in almost every posture. These are attitudes of the tail and ears, shape of the mouth, and the overall pose of the body.

The bushy black tail is normally carried hanging straight down. If a high tendency to flee is apparent, it is bent below the belly; during attack it goes straight up, and on occasions when a hyena is very closely associated with others, excited but apparently not motivated by either sexual or aggressive tendencies, the tail goes right forward over the back. They do not wag their tails, but they may sometimes flick them horizontally when the tail is hanging down. This flicking is a brief movement and it occurs either for no apparent reason or, more frequently, when an animal is approaching a dominant one or on other occasions where apparently there is a slight tendency to flee and to stay at the same time. The tail-up position does not always indicate aggression, for it can also be observed in situations where only a social attraction and no hostility is apparent. All intermediate tail positions are used, and the tail attitude

Fig. 56. Some body positions and behavior patterns: *a*, lying down on brisket (typically, legs stretched out behind body); *b*, lying down on side; *c*, rubbing back; *d*, licking genital area; *e*, yawning; *f*, standing on hind legs (rare; e.g., looking out over tall vegetation); *g*, pasting (depositing secretion on grass stalk); *h*, defecating.

gives a fairly good idea of the animal's "mood," if one takes into account the context of the observation (fig. 58).

The ears, when folded flat, indicate a high likelihood of fleeing, whereas when cocked forward they indicate a probable approach; ear-flattening is often combined with baring of teeth and slightly open mouth.

Fig. 57. Some common attitudes: *a*, normal walk; *b*, slightly alert (e.g., when approaching prey); *c*, alert, likely to approach prey or other hyena; *d*, alert, likely to attack other hyena; *e*, approaching, but with high avoidance tendency (e.g., male near den); *f*, high tendency to flee and stay, and bite back if necessary (e.g., subdominant near food); *g*, defensive posture when attacked by other hyenas or wild dogs.

As extremes in the complex of attack/fleeing attitudes, one can see (*a*) the attack posture, just before or during an all-out attack, in which the head is held high, ears cocked, mouth closed, mane erect, hindquarters high, tail vertically up; (*b*) the fleeing posture, in which the ears are flat, mane sleek against the body, and tail curled under the

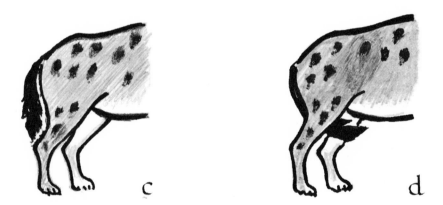

Fig. 58. Tail attitudes: *a*, likely to attack, or during "social attraction"; *b*, high "social attraction"; *c*, normal; *d*, likely to flee.

belly while the animal runs off; (*c*) the defense posture, when one hyena is attacked by several others without running away, in which the ears are flat, mouth open, and teeth bared, hindquarters crouched, forequarters rather low, and tail under the belly.

There is one curious posture, commented upon already by Darwin (1872), in which hyenas sometimes approach a dominant one. In this, they walk on the carpal joints of their forelegs ("knees"), with hind legs bent, ears flat, mouth slightly open, and tail often straight up or bent forward. This is not shown by aggressive animals, as asserted by Darwin, but is a submissive posture. It may be derived from the attitude in which young hyenas walk in the tunnels of their dens; cubs usually flee underground when afraid of something.

So far, sexual behavior has not been mentioned. Apart from actual mating, no postures I have seen are indicative of sexual tendencies. An important display, and a very frequent one, is the erection of the penis or clitoris; however, this is seen in "social" contexts rather than in sexual ones (p. 233), especially during meeting ceremonies. It is shown especially frequently by cubs. The penis/clitoris can be erected until it almost touches the ground, and it is sometimes drawn sharply backward, sometimes stretched forward under the belly. I have been unable to distinguish between circumstances in which the various attitudes of this organ are shown.

Calls

The loud melancholy "who–oop" call of the hyena is one of the most characteristic sounds of Africa, and the maniacal laughter of this species is also very well known. But hyenas produce many other sounds besides; they are very vocal, and during my study I was able to distinguish between a number of different calls: whoop; fast whoop; grunt; groan; low (pl. 36); giggle; yell; growl; soft grunt-laugh; loud grunt-laugh; whine; soft squeal.

I have tried to describe these calls, their accompanying postures, and the most common situations in which they occur in appendix D. 8. Distinguishing between these calls is a fairly subjective procedure, and all kinds of intermediates are frequently heard. Most calls grade into each other and may probably be considered part of a large sound "continuum."

There is little I can say about the underlying motivation for the call complex; I have the impression that usually the very high-pitched calls involve either a strong tendency to flee or have a strong submissive quality (e.g., during begging), whereas the loud, low-pitched calls accompany a high tendency to attack. It seems that the staccato element, whether in the giggle or the grunt-laugh, comes with great excitement, maybe indicating a strong conflict between tendencies to flee and to stay. But there is obviously much more to it than this, and many more systematic observations will have to be collected.

The whole sound continuum shows gradations, especially in quality of pitch, tone (oo–oo–oo sounds), staccato, and vibration. It has been pointed out by Struhsaker (1966) that, for vervet monkeys, a system of grading vocalizations offers a greater scope for vocal communication than a system of discrete sounds; an almost infinite number of combinations are possible. In a species like the spotted hyena (nocturnal, highly social, but also, and often at the same time, solitary), it must be of great advantage to have an elaborate system of calls for communication, the need in this case being greater than, for instance, among wild dogs, which are largely diurnal and much more exclusively gregarious.

Since a call is almost invariably accompanied by other behavior elements, the effect of calls is difficult to evaluate, for it cannot be separated from the effect of the postures. If a hyena approaches another which is lying down and the latter utters a grunt without otherwise moving, the approaching hyena may stop or withdraw. Then it seems fairly certain that it is the grunt which makes the approaching hyena react. The whoop is often uttered by a hyena walking alone, and is probably not directed at any particular individual. It sometimes causes a response from another hyena who answers the call, and in some observations I saw hyenas walk up to the calling animal, although it was out of sight. Sometimes I noticed a hyena approaching a den and uttering a whoop at some distance away, upon which hyenas from the den came up to it (for instance when a female arrived and the cubs ran out to their own mother).

Often, calls have a clear side effect, particularly in hyenas squabbling over food. The giggles, yells, and growls which accompany the little attacks and chases over bits of food around a kill may attract other hyenas from a great distance—as I could ascertain by playing back these calls through a loudspeaker from the Land Rover. The sounds of struggle with another hyena clan or with a lion over a kill are also highly attractive to hyenas (and also to lions, p. 135, and vultures, p. 146). From the context in which these calls occur, I concluded that most of them are directed only at one or two competing individuals and the secondary effect is the attraction of other hyenas to a kill (which increases competition over food). So there is a distinct disadvantage in calling, although this may be outweighed by the advantage to the individual gained through the primary effect of calls. In Ngorongoro, where lions often steal hyena kills, I sometimes found myself watching the hyenas over a kill and wishing for their own sakes that they would be quiet, because their deafening noise attracted lions from miles away!

Scents

Several scent glands are probably employed in social encounters, but I am aware only of the use of anal and interdigital glands. The use of scent glands in encounters between individuals is probably related to their use in scent marking, and I will describe this last phenomenon first.

Both sexes possess two anal glands, which open into the rectum just inside the anal opening (Matthews 1939a). The whitish creamy secretion of these glands is pasted onto grass stalks (or, in captivity, onto a side of the cage; Schneider 1926; Grimpe 1916) in the following way. The animal stands in front of the stalk, which is some 30–80 cm long, and sniffs it for a few seconds about 40–50 cm from the ground, often slightly turning its head. It then walks forward, thus bringing the stalk bending forward between its forelegs; one of the forelegs is usually lifted and bent round the stalk. The hyena slowly walks on, dragging the stalk between the hind legs. The hind legs are slightly bent, the tail is pointing forward over the back, and the penis or clitoris is erected and curved down or backward; the crouched posture allows the stalk to be dragged past the anal opening (pl. 37). Simultaneously with the slight bending of the hind legs, the rectum is pressed out through the anus, producing a bulge some 3 cm long which carries along its sides the openings of the anal glands. The anal bulge touches the grass stalk, and a thin layer of the secretion is left on some 2–5 cm of the stalk. After the animal has passed and the stalk has erected itself, the hyena usually turns around and repeats the procedure on the same stalk, sometimes four or five times. The paste has a strong smell, rather like the smell of cheap soap boiling or burning; even humans can detect it several meters downwind. Pasting may be done by either sex and even very young cubs often go through the motions except for the anal bulging (which means that the whole maneuver is quite ineffective, pl. 48). It is very much stimulated by the presence of secretion from other hyenas; as soon as a hyena smells the paste on a grass stalk, he will walk up to it, sniff it elaborately, and then paste his own on top (or, for cubs, go through the motions). Pasting may be seen on a number of different occasions, by hyenas walking around alone, by hyenas around a kill after they have had a good feed or when lions are present, by males and cubs on or near dens and most frequently, by parties of hyenas, especially on the boundaries of clan territories (p. 259). The striped hyena and the related aardwolf paste in rather similar fashion.

Pasting is very often either followed by, or alternated with, violently scratching the ground with one of the forepaws, looking down all the time. Although this pawing leaves clear scratch marks, probably more important is the scent; fresh scrapes have a distinct smell, which is probably from a secretion of the interdigital glands.

An activity closely connected with pawing and pasting is defecating. The parties of hyenas mentioned above which have been seen pasting grass stalks often also visit "latrine areas" (Matthews 1939b; Hediger 1951; Bigalke 1952; Verschuren 1958), here simply called latrines. These are conspicuous because of many large white hyena feces; they are often over 10 m in diameter and situated in distinct localities (p. 258). When a party of hyenas visits such a latrine, they defecate simultaneously (described also by Bigalke 1953), and immediately afterward paw the ground next to their feces, often scattering some earth over the droppings (but this seems more accidental than functional). They may also deposit pastings on the latrines during the same visit. Defecating is not done exclusively on the latrines: hyenas often defecate wherever they happen to be, frequently after walking a short distance after getting up. When they are on the den they deposit droppings some distance away. Only on latrines is defecating followed by pawing. Urinating, on the other hand, does not occur in any special context or situation; it is performed wherever the animal happens to be, lying, standing, or walking, sometimes with slightly bent hind legs. It is stimulated especially when hyenas are standing in water.

Pasting, especially when carried out by a number of animals simultaneously, can be stimulated by the presence of hostile hyenas (p. 257). One essential element is the pressing out of the rectum (anal bulging), which exposes the openings of the anal glands. This can be observed not only during pasting but also in direct agonistic encounters; hyenas in an attack posture often show fairly fast expulsion and protraction of the last part of the rectum; sometimes one sees several hyenas showing anal bulging when a group is feeding from a carcass and there is much squabbling over food, and sometimes it is also seen in encounters with lions.

It seems, therefore, that at least in some situations, both pasting and its component anal bulging may be partly aggressively motivated. Thus it is possible that anal bulging has the function of a "scent display," indicating likelihood of attack. It will be argued on p. 258 that pasting has the function of marking a territory—but for this conclusion, we must first consider what role territory plays in the hyena social system. However, running ahead of the arguments, it is tempting to speculate here that this kind of territorial marking has evolved from an aggressive display.

As for pawing, this is also stimulated by the presence of hostile hyenas or by a lion on a kill, and in fact it is more often seen in that sort of agonistic situation than is pasting. It also occurs on other occasions, for instance when a male who attempts copulation is frustrated by an uncooperative female (p. 232). An element of aggression is mostly evident, and here too, it is interesting to point out that a behavior which is probably a display in social encounters (and one in which olfactory information plays at least an important role) is used for marking territory.

SOCIAL INTERACTION WITHIN THE CLAN

Aggression

It is common to see some aggression between hyenas within the large groups in which they are organized. But although hyenas are well able to inflict injuries, it is very rare to see blood flow in these tussles; I have witnessed this only in the curious "baiting" (p. 225). Hyenas not only have a very tough skin and are almost impervious to pain (which I noticed when punishing my tame one, and when I had to pull out his rotten tooth), but also serious fighting occurs extremely rarely. Prevention of actual combat is probably the main function of the hyenas' many displays and calls, as it is in so many species (Tinbergen 1951).

An attack on an opponent is usually directed at his neck (pl. 38), but hyenas may, of course, bite anywhere else as well (ears, rump, legs, flanks). The attacker holds its head high and bites slightly downward. If the opponent is not merely fleeing, it also counters that attack with the mouth, either in the head-high attack posture or with head held lower, slightly bending away but still facing, in which case he is more likely to flee immediately afterward. Both contestants usually growl loudly. But a fight of this kind is always very short, a matter of seconds, then one of the two runs away or they both continue with what they were doing before (e.g., feeding). If the opponent flees and the attacker pursues, bites are directed at the fugitive's hind legs, the latter often giggling or yelling or both. But, as stated before, most conflicts are settled with various calls and displays, for only if the two opponents are very close to start with (for instance, eating together or if one is sleeping and the other comes up and sniffs) is there no room or time for threat.

A clash usually involves only two individuals, but one may sometimes see two hyenas threaten a third by approaching in the attack posture, walking shoulder to shoulder while almost touching each other. I have called this the "parallel walk"; it is directed especially at strange hyenas a fairly long distance away, but it is also used against clan members (pls. 39 and 40).

Whenever one sees aggression within the clan, it is usually in one of three contexts: (a) over food; (b) near the den; or (c) while "female baiting."

Food fighting has been described on page 124; one of the important points about it is that it occurs so infrequently, even if there is very little food among many hyenas.

Around a den, hyenas are frequently chased away by others, or snapped at if they get too close. Almost always these are cases of females chasing males, though sometimes females snap at each other, or one of the more closely tolerated males around the den chases one of the other males. Females with small cubs (less than one week old) keep everybody away from them by aggressive postures and sounds, but here also, clashes rarely lead to physical contact. Occasionally one may see a male being snapped at and chased by a female, and immediately afterward, the fugitive turns on another male instead of snapping back at the female.

During the phenomenon I called "baiting," the female sits or lies in a crouched position, ears flat and teeth bared, while between three and nine (on the average five) males stand around her, ears cocked, tails up, manes bristling (pl. 41). The males try to sniff or actually bite a female, especially in the hindquarters and over the back, while lowing, giggling, and fast whooping. The female defends herself, uttering loud growls and yells. In one out of the fifteen observations the female received bites which made her limp and bleed, but on nine occasions she was hardly touched and the males gave the impression of merely trying to sniff her. I once saw the female bite a male in the leg, causing him to limp away bleeding, but sometimes it looked from her behavior immediately after baiting (walking off with the pack of males, tail up and obviously no longer afraid) as if it had been only a game. I do not know the significance of this behavior; it seems unlikely that it has a sexual function, though this may be true. It is a situation in which the usually dominant female is harassed by a group of males, each of whom would on his own be subdominant to the female (p. 234).

From this account it appears that the function of aggression within the hyena communities is mainly the acquisition of food and the protection of offspring; maybe the maintenance of a dominance hierarchy (which in itself may be related to the first two values) is important. I have no clues about the significance of baiting.

Meeting and Appeasement

Since hyenas roam freely on their own throughout the range of the clan, and since they also are frequently attracted to other hyenas, meetings between individuals are an often-recurring phenomenon. These meetings may take place when two animals accidentally come across each other or when a hyena joins a group, approaches the den, and so on, and even between hyenas who have been together for a considerable time already, for instance, sleeping together or after a kill or an unsuccessful hunt. On occasion, two hyenas who are usually companions may go through a whole meeting ceremony immediately after one has snapped at the other for some reason.

If two individuals recognize each other, this recognition takes place from a considerable distance away and well before physical contact is made. One of them will often face away while the other approaches, a behavior pattern that finds exact parallels among many mammals and birds (e.g., in canids, Fox 1969a; and in gulls, Tinbergen 1959; Manley 1960). Either may show some hesitation before moving very close to the other. One may walk in a large circle, perhaps of 5–15 m radius around the other hyena until it gets downwind, then stop and stand, sniffing the air with head held alternatively high and low, before approaching nearer. Either of the two may show indications of fear— for instance, by tail and ear attitude, body posture, and so on. Usually one hyena is dominant over the other in that he shows the fewest signs of fear before, during, and after the actual meeting ceremony and may even become aggressive.

On meeting, hyenas usually briefly sniff the side of each other's mouth, head, and neck, as if in passing, often with the mouth slightly open; often the meeting stops at that (pl. 42). But frequently the two proceed and stand parallel next to each other, heads in opposite directions. Then both animals (sometimes only one) lift the "inside" hind leg well up, usually bent, sometimes stretched backward (pl. 43). The penis or clitoris has become erect during the approach and the two animals then sniff each other's genitals, occasionally even licking them for as long as half a minute, but more frequently for 10–15 sec. They sniff the penis or clitoris over its whole length and especially at the base, as well as the area immediately behind it and in front of the scrotum or pseudoscrotum. Then the animals go back on all four legs and often walk off without so much as a backward glance at each other. Immediately before and during the meeting, hyenas often utter a soft, deep call ("groan"). When one is very excited (e.g., after a long parting), it may roll on the ground, exposing the genitals at the same time.

Meeting ceremonies occur between hyenas of both sexes and of any age, and they seem particularly frequent between cubs and adults. In cubs, the morphological structures associated with the meeting ceremony are very well developed, relatively even more so than in adults; the penis or clitoris of a cub is almost as large in an absolute sense as that of an adult.

In trying to establish the function of the meeting ceremony and the associated morphological features, it is important to find out whether there are any consistent agreements between animals taking the initiative in this ceremony. It is often possible to assess which of the two is "keener" when the hyenas are walking up to each other. A clear and objective measure is which of the two lifts its hind leg first. In the 104 observations in which I noted either the relative age or the sex of partici-

TABLE 35 *Animal taking initiative in meeting ceremonies (leg-lifting)*

Individual	Number	Percentage
Male-female meetings		
Male	16	80
Female	4	20
Undecided	2	—
Total	22	
Cub-adult meetings		
Cub	41	91
Adult	4	9
Undecided	9	—
Total	54	
Male-male or female-female meetings		
Smaller	7	100
Larger	0	0
Undecided	21	—
Total	28	

pants, it turned out that when an adult meets a juvenile it is the juvenile who takes the initiative, and when a male and female meet it is the male (table 35).[3] Signs of fear are frequently apparent in the animal which takes the initiative (ears low, tail between the legs, body posture). Since smaller cubs are always dominated both by larger ones and by adults, and since females are clearly dominant over males (p. 234), it appears that the subdominant animal takes the initiative. In addition, in those cases of male-male and female-female meetings in which there was a noticeable size difference, the smaller of the two animals took the initiative. If one of two meeting hyenas is stationary, the animal arriving will often lift its leg first.

Some field notes:

> January 1967, dawn, Scratching Rocks clan. An old female hyena stands on the plain, obviously about to lie down for the day. From several hundred meters distance, a male comes walking up, without hesitating, straight toward the female. He shows signs of nervousness, tail flicking, teeth slightly bared, and penis erected. The female gazes straight ahead of her, seemingly ignoring the male. When the male reaches the female, he quickly touches the side of her head with his muzzle, then lifts his leg, whereupon the female does the same, both now showing full erection. They spend about 8 sec sniffing each other's genitals, then separate, both walking away in opposite directions.

> July 1967, dawn, central Serengeti. A male hyena walking along comes across two cubs of ten to twelve months old who were lying together watching the male approach. When the male is still some 30 m away, both cubs look in the opposite direction until the male actually arrives. Then one of the cubs gets up, sniffs, and lifts its leg; the male follows suit and they spend several seconds "meeting" before the male walks off again.

> August 1969, dusk, western Serengeti. Four lactating females are lying on their den; only one is suckling her cubs, the other cubs are underground. One cub of one to two weeks old comes out of the den, walks around one of the females, then walks off to a large shrub some 10 m from the den. The mother gets up, picks the cub up by the neck and carries it back to the den. Another female rises and walks to the female carrying the cub and snaps at the other female with a growl. Immediately the other female presents her genitals by turning round

3. Binomial tests: adult/juvenile, $p < 0.001$; male/female, $p = 0.006$;   large adult/small adult, $p = 0.008$.

and lifting her leg; both spend 2–3 sec sniffing each other before returning to the den, where the cub has meanwhile disappeared down a
hole again.

It is worth considering these observations in order to outline some
possible function of it all. The meeting ceremony and its associated
morphological structures offer a number of apparent anomalies. First
of all, here are animals exposing the most vulnerable area of their bodies
to the teeth of potential opponents. Second, it is the subdominant in
most meetings who takes the initiative in this. Third, in the female,
who is the dominant of the two sexes, the peculiar shape of the genitals
has evolved, and Wickler (1964, 1965a, b) is probably right in saying
that it is a mimic on the same structure in males. At present, it is impossible to think of any other purpose for this special female feature
than for use in the meeting ceremony. Fourth, this same structure is also
particularly well developed in cubs, which are obviously subdominant
in any meeting.

It is known that among baboons, the "presenting posture" is used by
females not only in copulatory behavior but also as a general act of
"appeasement" (Zuckermann 1932; Kummer 1957); as such, it is also
used by males and juveniles. In one species, the Hamadryas baboon,
the males too are adorned with the typical red swelling that in other
species is possessed only by females (especially females in estrus).
Wickler (1963, 1965a, b, 1968) argues that we are dealing here with an
example of "intraspecific mimicry," in which the male mimics the
female structure or behavior pattern or both and uses this as an appeasement gesture as do the females. In baboons, the males are the dominant
sex; it may be that this mimicry is a parallel to what has happened in
the spotted hyena female. In baboons also, it is the subdominant of any
two individuals that "presents."

It may well be that the elaborate meeting ceremony of hyenas has
the function of keeping two individuals close together for a short period
with attention diverted from the main "weapons" (the teeth), thus
allowing any possible tensions between them to subside. This would be
advantageous especially in a species like the spotted hyena, which is
very social but often also solitary; the reestablishment of close relations
is often called for. It may also be, then, that an individual with a familiar
but relatively complex and conspicuous structure sniffed at during the
meeting has an advantage over others; the structure would facilitate
this reestablishment of social bonds by keeping partners together often

over a longer meeting period. This could be the selective advantage that has caused the evolution of the females' and cubs' genital structure.

If I have interpreted the function of the meeting ceremony and its attendant structures correctly, this would also accommodate the observation that the subdominant individual takes the initiative—that this would be the one to seek proximity. The animals that most need to socialize with other hyenas are the cubs, and they are particularly well equipped for the meeting ceremony.

Exposing the genital area to other hyenas may indeed be as dangerous as it looks; one male I saw in the Serengeti was healthy except for a badly wounded penis, which seemed to have been bitten, and he may well have sustained this injury during a meeting ceremony.

It will be extremely difficult to ascertain whether the meeting ceremony does, indeed, have an appeasement function, although the observations are suggestive. When Wickler (1964) says that hyenas who did not "present" were often chased away, it is impossible to discover what is cause and what is effect. I also saw clear aggression toward hyenas who did not partake in a meeting ceremony, but the chases were always initiated at such a distance that the meeting ceremony could not have started in any case, and usually it was clear from the behavior of the hyena about to be chased that it did not belong. It is obvious that the decision between aggression and nonaggression is usually taken before the animals get close enough to be able to sniff one another.

Relations between Males and Females

Mating.   Mating has not been described from observations in nature but has been documented in detail from captivity (Schneider 1923, 1926, 1952). Clear sexual behavior is not often seen in wild hyenas, largely because mating is a relatively short affair, usually taking place quietly at night with no other hyenas present; it may also be that the female does not come into heat very often (see below). On the fourteen occasions when I saw clear sexual behavior, this came to a probably successful copulation in only five observations. Some field notes may illustrate the sexual relations between hyenas.

> February 1965, dawn. A male and female were walking together over the Serengeti plain; as usual, the male followed the female, although the female was a young one, probably only two years old and smaller than the male. Suddenly the male galloped slowly up to the female and raised his forequarters, attempting to mount; the female turned and snapped at the male, who immediately jumped back. This happened

five times in 8 min, sometimes the female merely avoided the male at the last moment, but sometimes she actually snapped at him. Then the female stopped with the tail slightly lifted; the male came up behind her and mounted for about a minute, attempting all the time to insert his penis, but repeatedly sliding back from the female onto his haunches (pl. 44). When intromission finally took place, the male rested his whole underside on the female's back with his chin on her shoulder and his hind feet on the ground. Four and one-half minutes after mounting, the male dismounted and walked some 8 m away, and both partners sat down and licked their genitals. Six minutes later, the male walked up to the female again and mounted and copulated. He dismounted 5 min later and walked 10 m away and both licked themselves again. After another 2 min, the female approached the male, who avoided and walked away. The female slowly galloped after the male for half a minute, then they both stopped, rolled in the dust next to each other, and again licked their genitals. They remained apart for 11 min, then the male again approached the female and copulated, dismounting 6 min later. They separated about 6 m apart and washed themselves again. Six minutes after dismounting, the male got up and walked off, the female following. I saw the female slowly gallop up after the male five times, but he always avoided and ran away when she got near. She stopped every now and then to lick herself again. Thirty-four minutes after the last dismounting, the female stopped and lay down, the male following suit some distance away, and they both slept.

During the whole of the above observation, the female was clearly the dominant animal; the male (although larger) invariably showed signs of fear when near the female (ears, tail, body posture). Characteristically, a number of copulations followed each other with short intervals between them. It was also interesting that the female went to follow the male after a few copulations, whereas the male appeared to lose interest; this change was not apparent in other observations. At no time did the female show erection of the clitoris, whereas penile erection was conspicuous in the male.

In another observation (lasting from 0600 till 1100 hr in September 1967), made on the Scratching Rocks clan in Ngorongoro, one female was followed by three males, who always kept to a certain order. The smallest of the three males was closest to the female, trying to mount her continually, but being either ignored or snapped at by the female whenever he got close. There was no sign of aggression between the males except that they kept their distance, and when the female chased and attacked the nearest male, he invariably retaliated by attacking the male nearest to him instead of biting back at the female. The other males were also sexually interested in the female and tried to mount whenever the first male was not looking. The males' attempted mountings consisted of slowly running up behind the walking female but suddenly facing away when touching her and stopping while she walked on, or running away when she snapped back. The female was lactating and when she arrived at her den she suckled a cub of about ten months. At the den, the cub several times chased the smallest male (the one who tried to mount), though the cub was not very persistent. The female first lay down next to the den, where the male made several more unsuccessful mating attempts (pl. 45), but then she went down in a hole with only her face showing and the small male stood just beyond the hole while the other two lay down some distance away. The male nearest the female showed several "displacement activities," lying down, rolling in the sand, and pawing it very viciously (pl. 46)— by this time he had a penis erection. After some 10 min of this, he suddenly walked to the cub, which was lying about 6 m away, mounted it without inserting, and ejaculated. Then he walked back to the female in her hole, looked at her for a few seconds, and then went back to the cub and mounted it again, and so on. The cub struggled in the beginning to escape this rape, then ignored it completely as far as that was possible. This happened eight times; several times the male mounted the cub sideways or the wrong way round and ejaculated with the cub struggling slightly as if in play. After every mounting, the male went and looked at the female, and during the mountings he faced her. Eventually he wandered away from the den as the other two males had done.

The early mounting attempts looked exactly similar to those in other observations; clearly the male was (as usual) afraid of the female, and it seemed to be the lack of cooperation on the female's part that made the copulation fail. It was interesting to see that the female was in heat while still suckling a cub, and another important aspect of the observation was the tolerance between rival males. The rape of the cub was extraordinary, especially as it happened every time after the male looked at the uncooperative female. Schneider (1952) described how male hyenas showed copulation behavior in vacuo when in captivity.

In August 1968 in the Serengeti, I saw a female in heat who was being followed by six males; she mated several times successfully, with only one of the six. The other five males were very excited, watching the copulations, uttering many lowing calls and chasing each other without fighting. The one male that managed to mate often chased one of the other males briefly immediately after dismounting, but this never developed into anything more than a very short chase. The noise made by the party was considerable, enough to attract three male lions, who came galloping up from about 1 km away but lay down again when they found no kill. I, too, had come up expecting a kill! This shows that hyena mating may sometimes develop into fairly noisy parties, but this is the exception. Any aggression between rival males is no more than squabbling. It is interesting that in both this and the previous observation, only one male out of several mated with the female.

Generally, it is true to say that mating consists of a number of relatively short copulations of a female with one male; the partners do not "hang" together as dogs do. Usually no other males are present, but if they are, still only one male mates. This one male is not necessarily the oldest or the strongest, but his presence does keep other males away. However, the "pair bond" can only be a very weak one, as I have not seen a female associating with one particular male for any length of time. During mating, the male tends to show penile erection only immediately before copulation; no clitoris erection is apparent in the female. This suggests that the pattern of erections during the meeting ceremony is not motivated by sexual drives but has probably become divorced from sexual behavior during evolution. During mating behavior, little or no aggression is apparent from the male toward the female; this too suggests that the behavior described as "baiting" (p. 225) is not related to courtship. There may be some (but little) aggression between several attending males; this is sometimes expressed as an attack immediately after the female has shown aggression to the leading male.

Some of these observations are not consistent with those of Schneider (1923, 1926, 1952), who, for instance, described elaborate behavior patterns immediately before actual mating, and actual intromission as taking place only once during a mating sequence. His observations were carried out in close confinement, however, and on hyenas that were introduced to each other immediately before the mating; this must have altered their behavior considerably. But Schneider's observations on morphological details of intromission are important and would be impossible to obtain in the wild.

Other relations between male and female. Although I have elaborated on various morphological differences between males and females, the outstanding phenomena in this comparison are the similarities rather than the differences; the same is true for their behavior. The females hunt, defend the clan territory, and visit and use communal scent-marking places just as the males do, and, except for when females have cubs and during actual mating, there are few behavioral characteristics to distinguish the two sexes. But there are some differences, and while keeping in mind the great similarity, I will discuss some of these in more detail.

First of all, in the majority of interactions between sexes the female is dominant, which ties in with her larger size. In a squabble over a bit of food, it is the female who gets it; if a male is lying in a comfortable one-hyena-size mudhole, he will leave it if a female wants to come in; if a male and a female meet each other, the male gives way, often showing clear signs of fear. Males are tolerated around the den to a limited extent only and usually only a few well-established males are allowed close—even they are chased away every so often. This dominance is not merely a matter of difference in size; I have seen it expressed by females over males larger than themselves and also far from the den. If two or more hyenas walk together and one is a female, she usually takes the lead, and sets off first after a halt, followed by the males. Hyenas often walk in pairs, a male and a female, especially in the Serengeti; almost invariably the male will walk behind the female. One of the exceptions to this female dominance has been mentioned already; it occurs when a number of males "gang up" on one female.

Some field notes:

> July 1966, early morning in Ngorongoro. Two female hyenas were each chewing on a bone some 200 m apart. Almost simultaneously one was approached by two males and the other by four, all the males obviously interested in the bones. Both the females fled, not very fast, with their booty, whereupon each was pursued by males. Then the females joined together and stopped; immediately the two groups of males drew back from the females and most of them showed signs of fear by their postures. The females walked off, still followed by the males, but at a much larger distance, and soon the males gave up.

> November 1966, dawn in the Serengeti. Two males slowly approached a den on which one female was suckling a cub. When the males were about 10 m away, the female arose, looking at them; the males showed a clear tendency to flee, but stood their ground, although they had their tails right under their bellies. Then the female made a short dash in

the direction of the males with her tail straight up; the males ran off fast, giggling, and stood about 40 m away watching the female return to the den.

February 1967, evening in Ngorongoro. A female was lying in the open when a male walked up to her. She snapped at him as he came close; he avoided this with his ears flat and tail between his legs. Then he walked up again and sniffed at the female's mouth while she ignored him. Although the female made no further movement, the male got more and more nervous while he sniffed and even licked the female; finally he slunk off with his tail between his legs and ears flat back.

February 1967, early morning in the Serengeti. Driving over the plains, I came across a female eating from a wildebeest head; the wildebeest must have died several hours before. Six males stood around her, all keenly interested in what was going on but keeping a distance away. When I came close with the car, all the hyenas walked off; one of the males was the first to come back and try to drag off the wildebeest head—thus showing that it was indeed the food that the males were interested in and the female who had kept them away from it.

Although hyenas are not infrequently seen in pairs, there does not seem to be a permanent pair bond, at least in the areas I studied. This may well be different in areas with a permanently very low density of hyenas, but I have no data on this. There is probably no advantage in a permanent pair bond within the sort of groups that hyenas live in here in the Serengeti and Ngorongoro.

Some Other Dominance Patterns

Even in the large, well-settled hyena clans in the Ngorongoro Crater there is no simple linear dominance order. But there are some clear dominance rankings; there is also evidence of a more complicated set of individual relationships. Here I have been unable to do more than scratch the surface of what is obviously an important subject from several points of view.

I have already discussed the dominance of females over males; another dominance rule is that cubs and immature animals usually give way to adults—especially on a kill. Even when there are many hyenas to a carcass, however, an animal not fully grown may still be able to work his way into the pile of eating adults—but more often, the young ones are seen waiting till the end of the struggle when only the more difficult bits are left. At the end of the feast, a common picture is a group of immatures and cubs and a few adults cleaning up the spoils.

If an adult and a young hyena are both after the same bone, the adult usually gets it. When adults and immatures are moving in a group, the young animals most often make up the rear—except when a cub is specifically following its mother, who may be leading the pack. Sometimes a mother will protect her eating cub (even when it is fully grown) against the attentions of other hyenas (p. 125).

If a large adult hyena meets a smaller one, the smaller one usually gives way. This may enforce the rule of females dominating males and adults dominating young ones, but I have also several times seen large males give way to smaller females, so it is likely that the dominance of the female sex is a phenomenon on its own.

There are other occasions on which one individual clearly dominates another, without any of the above "rules" indicating why this should be so. The radio-collared female we followed for twelve days in the crater (see pl. 7) was obviously very low in whatever dominance order there might be—she continually avoided other hyenas and, although even she did not give way to single males, she invariably ran off with her tail between her legs whenever she came near another female; she was very wary near kills and moreover she was more shy of lions than any of the other hyenas we watched simultaneously. She never came near the central den of the Scratching Rocks clan (to which she belonged), and her two cubs of approximately six months old were always suckled away from the den. Similarly, a very old marked male of the same clan would always lag behind the others, and was very easily chased off by any of his fellow clan members. The evidence mentioned on p. 231 also indicates that certain males stand in a special relation to certain females, even if only temporarily; this is known to the others and may create a "pecking order" in a group of males following a female.

These last few observations merely indicate that there is much more to the social organization of hyenas than the simple dominance rules I postulated above could cover. There is a gap in our knowledge here that urgently needs further investigation.

Groups and Group Structure

In both the Serengeti and Ngorongoro, hyenas often walk around in groups of up to twenty-five animals. These groups may be hunting or visiting marking places (see p. 257), or simply moving about without any apparent purpose. But hyenas also very often move about singly or in pairs, and the extent to which this happens may well be a function of the density of the hyena population. Previously the hyena has been called a solitary animal (Stevenson-Hamilton 1947; Verheyen 1951), or it has been said that "there is some degree of gregariousness, but it appears to be little developed beyond random proximity" (Matthews 1939b). It is clear, however, that at least in areas with a sufficient number of hyenas, the animals often associate in packs with an internal structure.

It is difficult to compare two areas with different hyena densities to establish the extent to which hyenas are solitary or social; in an area with a very high density like Ngorongoro, it is much more difficult to distinguish between a solitary hyena and one belonging to a group than in the Serengeti. I have not, therefore, tried to quantify this; the overall impression is that on the whole, the Serengeti hyenas are more likely to walk about on their own than are their Ngorongoro colleagues. I did collect some observations on those groups which could be clearly distinguished as such and compared data from the two areas (fig. 59). Excluded are all those observations in which a number of hyenas were seen eating together from a kill, or lying together in a mud wallow, on a den, and so on. I considered only those groups that were actively walking, so that there was a good likelihood of consistency of group structure immediately before and after the observation.

Figure 59 shows that, of the groups observed, 46% in the Serengeti and 22% in Ngorongoro consisted of groups of only two hyenas.[4] These groups of two usually consisted of a male and a female (72% in the Serengeti, 75% in Ngorongoro). Generally, therefore, it is true to say that in the Serengeti hyenas are more likely to move about singly and, if they do go with others, they are likely to do so in pairs rather than in larger concentrations, unlike the Ngorongoro animals. As far as the true "packs" of three or more hyenas are concerned, these are on the average larger in the crater than in the Serengeti.[5]

On the whole, males are more likely to be pack members than are females; whereas the overall sex ratio is nearly equal (p. 27), the ratio of male to female in packs of three or more hyenas is 1.6:1 in the two areas together. But here there are again differences between the two areas; a pack of hyenas in Ngorongoro usually contains more females than one in the Serengeti. In the Serengeti, the overall percentage of females in the packs is 36%, and in Ngorongoro Crater this is 43%; packs of four hyenas and more contain 26% females in the Serengeti

4. Serengeti/Ngorongoro, groups of two versus larger ones: $\chi^2 = 7.03$; $df = 1$; $p < 0.01$.

5. Overall group size, Serengeti/Ngorongoro: $\chi^2 = 17.80$; $df = 3$; $p < 0.001$.

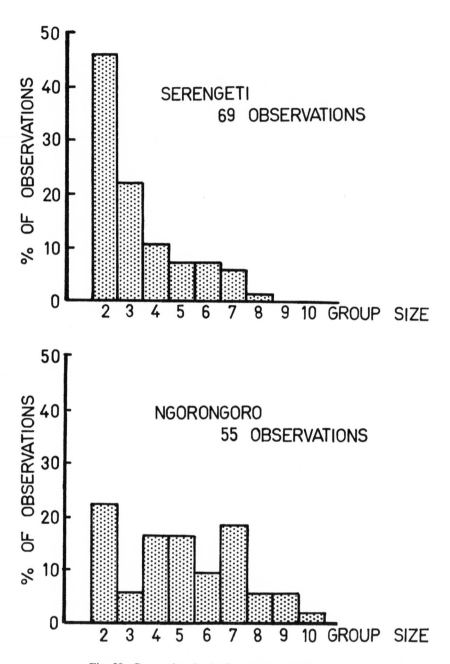

Fig. 59. Group sizes in the Serengeti and Ngorongoro.

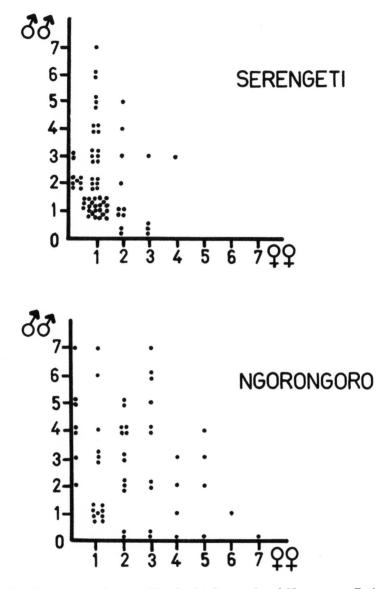

Fig. 60. Group size and composition in the Serengeti and Ngorongoro. Each dot represents the observation of one group of hyenas, consisting of X females and Y males.

and 42% in Ngorongoro. In the Serengeti, the common thing is a pack of one female and several males; in the Ngorongoro mostly more females are involved (fig. 60).[6] This is not just a consequence of the larger group

6. Serengeti/Ngorongoro, packs of 1 female and several males/several females and one or several males: $\chi^2 = 14.29$; $df = 1$; $p < 0.001$.

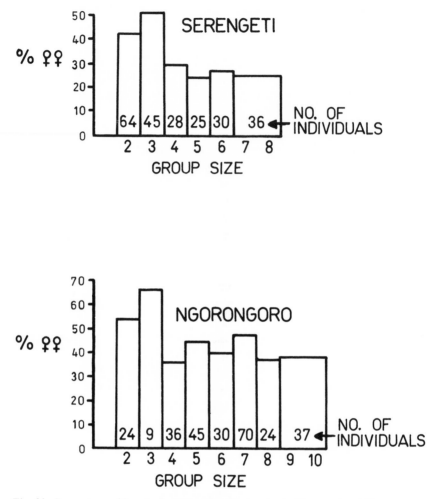

Fig. 61. Percentage of females in different pack sizes in the Serengeti and Ngorongoro.

size in the crater; when comparing groups of equal size in the two areas, the difference persists (fig. 61). In both areas, groups of two or three hyenas contain relatively fewer males than larger groups; the percentage of males in groups of four and over is fairly constant.

It is tempting to speculate about the possible function and mechanism of these divergences, and it might be valuable to compare them with variations in food supply, hunting, and hyena density. For instance, the difference in group size might be related to the fact that, in the Serengeti, the population of hyenas is migratory, whereas that of Ngorongoro is sedentary; in the Serengeti, the constantly changing composition of the hyena population in an area (p. 45) might prevent individual hyenas from getting to know each other well, which is probably a prerequisite for the formation of packs. So, on the whole, hyenas in the Serengeti are more solitary than in the crater, and this ties in with some other aspects of their life. As was stated before, hyena packs are usually either hunting or patrolling territorial boundaries. The only prey species that is commonly hunted in packs is the zebra, and it is hunted more often by Ngorongoro than by Serengeti hyenas (tables 11 and 12). Also "boundary patrols" are seen much more often in the strictly territorial Ngorongoro hyenas (p. 257).

About the difference in participation of females in packs, it should be noted that in both areas females are less likely to join large groups than are males. It may well be that in Ngorongoro, where there is so much more competition over food between hyenas than in the Serengeti (p. 102), there is a high premium on being at the kill from the beginning— and for this females would have to join the hunting packs. In the Serengeti, a female might still get her chunk of meat arriving late; she always has her dominance over males.

Social Attraction

In many behavior patterns a clear attraction is apparent between individuals which seems to exist regardless of sex or family tie. This is most obvious when one watches communal activities like zebra hunting, fighting between clans, pasting, social defecating, and so on. But with some activities, I had the impression that they were performed with the sole function of "doing something together," the best example being "social sniffing." Typically, a group of hyenas would walk together at a brisk pace, fairly close, several with their tails up. Suddenly one would stop, sniffing the ground in a place apparently randomly chosen—immediately all the others came rushing up, all starting to sniff the same place or immediately next to it. While sniffing, they appeared very excited, with their tails up and making many fast head movements. One important aspect of the picture was that the participants touched each other while sniffing, mostly with their necks; often one hyena would lean over the neck of another to sniff the ground or lean sideways against the other. One or two might even lie down on their briskets, tails up, sniffing excitedly. They might wander off after a half minute or so and repeat the performance a dozen times in an hour. Frequently, a party of hyenas thus involved would also visit pasting places or latrines or both, or they might hunt or bait a female (p. 225). The places at which they sniffed seemed to have little or nothing in common. They might do it in a place where another was lying who ran away at the approach of the group, or at a latrine or pasting place—but most often I could not see or smell anything particular about it. The hyenas moved from place to place regardless of the wind direction, suggesting that they were not attracted to these places by smell. I could release this behavior in our tame hyena, if he was in the right mood, by making the same kind of excited movements with my hand on any piece of ground; it seemed most likely to me that they generally did it any place at random, with perhaps a preference for those sites that smelled of other hyenas. Both males and females indulged in social sniffing, but I have not seen young cubs below ten to twelve months to it.

As I watched these hyenas, it looked as if it is not the collection of olfactory information that is the function of social sniffing but rather the performance in company. This may also be an important aspect of some activities related to scent marking, for example, the social pasting and defecating. Although the immediate function of these last behavior patterns appears to be the distribution of glandular products, there would be no need for doing this socially. These activities may, therefore, have social integration as a side effect.

Dens, Cubs, and Adults

Dens. Hyena dens usually have a number of entrances, sometimes a dozen or more. They are, with few exceptions, on flat ground; only rarely do hyenas use holes of an underground-river system or tunnels dug out in soft tuffs in a vertical surface. The tunnels are mostly oval in section, more wide than high, and they narrow down from an entrance width of $\frac{1}{2}$ to 1 m to sometimes less than 25 cm; they are $1\frac{1}{2}$ to 3 m long. Sometimes large tunnels extend considerably farther; they may go on for several meters, usually horizontally, about $\frac{1}{2}$ to 1 m under the surface. Most of them join underground. Percival (1924) mentions that in rocky country in East Africa, hyenas use caves as dens, and the same has been said for national parks in the Congo (Verheyen 1951). Matthews (1939*b*) states that also in the Serengeti, along the Seronera River, hyenas have their dens in kopjes, but I have not been able to confirm this. Hyenas do use kopjes as sleeping places during the daytime. There are large bare patches immediately around the entrances of the dens on which hyenas lie or walk about.

It is clear from the dimensions mentioned above that adult hyenas cannot really use the full extent of the burrow and cannot even have made it themselves; this is, in fact, largely the work of the cubs (who do a lot of underground digging) and of previous smaller owners. The adults go down warthog holes, and so on, to sleep during the day; at the den, they may lie in the entrance but very rarely go completely underground. The only exception I noticed was in a den in the Ngorongoro Crater where the Oldonyo Rumbe clan occupies a den formed by an old underground water system; the tunnels of this den are so large that even a man can go many meters deep into them (to emerge covered with fleas). In this den, the adults of the clan often sleep the whole day down one of the holes, and they sometimes flee into them when frightened—this never happens at an ordinary plains den. (Wickler's [1964] photograph of a hyena mother inside a den entrance is in fact of a young three-quarter-grown cub.) Cubs are efficient diggers, as we also noticed with our tame one. The advantages for them of being able to withdraw into the narrow tunnels are obvious in a community of animals where the parents may be away from the den for days on end, and every strange adult hyena may be a cannibal (see below). Young hyenas keep very still underground; they freeze even when the den is disturbed by digging. They move around in the tunnels by walking on the carpal joints of the forelegs with the feet bent back under the body.

Although large dens are often in use off and on for many years, the smaller ones are mostly temporary, filling in or being taken over by other animals once the hyenas have moved on. I do not know whether hyenas ever start an entirely new den; in every case I watched, there was always some beginning of a hole already there, made by warthogs, springhares, jackals, or others. There are so many of these unoccupied holes in the plains that it is obviously not worth a hyena's while to start a completely new set. They always do some digging themselves, though, and a hyena den is clearly recognizable as such by the shape of the tunnels, and so on. Immediately around the den, one often finds a few bones and quantities of regurgitated hair and hooves from prey animals. Hyenas rarely defecate near the den; they usually go at least 20 m away to deposit their droppings and walk back to the den again. But they urinate wherever they happen to be, inside or outside the den, and this causes the pungent smell which often comes from the holes.

Adults and cubs. A den is used mostly by several females at once (pl. 47), and it is not unusual to see over a dozen cubs around, even up to twenty (each female has only two at a time). In the Serengeti, the number of cubs per den fluctuates with the time of year (see p. 57). All cubs play together and often play with any of the adult males and females, but I have never seen a cub suckling from any hyena other than one which must have been its own mother. Perhaps a female occasionally adopts a cub, but certainly as a rule they allow only their own cubs to suckle. Other cubs often try—at least they may show a great deal of interest in the teats of females who are not their mothers—but after that they either turn away on their own accord or, more usually, the female snaps at them and they avoid.

I was surprised to find that the female does not feed her offspring by regurgitation; obviously cubs would benefit from this, especially when the hyenas are feeding a long way from the den. Adults do regurgitate near the den, but what comes out is almost invariably a large slimy ball of hair and bone slivers with nothing edible about it. The reaction of any hyena (also a cub) to the sight and sound of another one regurgitating is to run up, sniff the results of this action, and then immediately roll in it, shoulder first, then with the whole back, legs bent and head lifted. Often the regurgitating animal joins in.

Hyenas also do not carry any substantial amount of food to their cubs; they may occasionally take a bone or a head along, but this seems comparable to taking it to their lying-up place, where they can chew it in peace. Cubs may chew these bits, but only after the original owner has finished with them. Older cubs are more likely to carry bones to their den than adults; they sometimes take them down their holes, but more usually these are left in front of the den, or in the entrance. Some dens accumulate quite a collection of bones around the entrance, contrary to the belief expressed, for example, by Hughes (1954a, b, 1958, 1961), but this does not often happen; it may be more common among brown hyenas (Pienaar 1969). It is possible that porcupines are in some cases responsible for the bone collection, as asserted by Hughes (1961); however, I have several times actually observed spotted hyenas carrying bones to their holes. This means, therefore, that they could well be responsible for the fossil bone accumulations which are sometimes held to be made by prehistoric man (Dart 1949, 1957; Ardrey 1961). Moreover, bones splintered by hyenas or regurgitated bone slivers have a remarkable semblance to those bone pieces that are considered to be artifacts by these same authors (Thenius 1966b; Sutcliffe 1970).

In areas where hyenas are residents, females with cubs commonly visit the den in the morning and evening; during the day they may also be on the den (especially when the cubs are still small), but more often they sleep away from it. When the evening activity begins, the first move is usually toward the den; after the cubs have suckled or when they have spent some hours there, the females leave again on a foraging expedition. Before bedding down in the morning, they usually return to the den. Some females have their cubs not in the central den but some distance away from it; the female with the radio collar in the Ngorongoro Crater had two cubs (about six months old) which we never saw on the den, as she met them anywhere on the clan range. During the twelve days we followed her, she suckled the cubs only four times. But there were good indications that this was unusual; the cubs looked in bad condition, they were not on a den, and the particular female was low ranking.

When a female arrives at the den, she first goes up to some or all of the hyenas lying on or near the den and sniffs or mouths them, including the cubs. Her own cubs, if they are above ground, will usually start following her straight away, often uttering begging calls and trying to grab at a nipple every time she stops. The female lies down on her side and the cubs lie down next to her to drink. A favorite suckling position with the cubs is on their sides, parallel to the female, with their tails near the female's head; the mother usually puts one of her forelegs over the cub. If more than one cub is drinking simultaneously, one will lie in the above position and the other at right angles to the female or between her hind legs. The female has two teats only (out of 116 captured females, one had four). She will sometimes take up the suckling posture only after prolonged begging from the cubs, but on other occasions, she will do so without any calls from the cubs at all, apparently inviting them to suckle. If the female arrives at the den and her cubs are still underground (which happens especially with very young cubs), she puts her head into the den entrance and sometimes one can hear her calling them with a soft groaning sound (see also Deane 1962). At this the cubs emerge and follow the female until she lies down for them to suckle. They may suckle for a very long time, and I once timed two cubs suckling for just over 4 hr.

Although a mother may stay on the den more or less permanently when her cubs are still very young, only leaving it for a quick feed now and then, this picture gradually changes into one of regular visits—at least in areas where the prey can be found fairly close to home. But when feeding from migratory prey populations, hyenas have to walk vast distances before getting food, and so females have to leave their cubs behind in the den for many days (p. 60). When returning from these foraging trips, a female has very swollen udders, sometimes so much that they are bleeding from chafing against the hind legs. Arriving at the den, she is greeted by incessant whining calls from the young ones and very elaborate meeting ceremonies with the other adults and cubs (at such times, the female herself often utters soft squeals, lying or creeping on the ground while the other hyenas sniff at her).

All the cubs of a large clan may share the same den, play together, and sleep underground together regardless of their family ties. Only when the cubs are very young, just new born, are they usually some distance away from the den, joining the group when they are two to three weeks old. They are probably always born in some hollow or the entrance of a hole near the main den, and are left completely exposed when the mother is disturbed, for example, by man.

The mother barely tolerates other females near her offspring until they are about two weeks old, and males are invariably snapped at and chased. Later the cubs can get into their narrow tunnels on their own accord and probably have less need of the mother's protection. But even large cubs are shielded by the mother when suckling (she snaps at males coming too close) and later the mother stands guard when her cubs are eating from the remains of the carcass in which other hyenas are also interested. This protection against other hyenas is a very necessary behavior pattern for the cubs' survival; hyenas are cannibals. Adult hyenas killed in a clan fight (see p. 256), or by lions or some other means often are eaten by their fellows—although these clearly prefer the meat of the regular prey species to that of their own kind. It may take from several hours to a whole day for a hyena carcass to be eaten by other hyenas, whereas in the same area a wildebeest would disappear in less than an hour. But they do eat fresh hyena meat (contrary to beliefs expressed by Deane 1962; Hughes 1958). And another important observation—when Solomon, our tame hyena, was six months old and walking around the house at 0200 one night, he was grabbed and carried off by the neck by an adult hyena, his jaw being broken and his throat punctured in the process. Hearing the noise, I managed to rescue Solomon some 100 m from the house, and I had no doubts that he would have been eaten had it not been for my interference. The possibility that any strange hyena constitutes a danger to the cubs is of obvious importance in understanding the size difference between male and female and the dominance of the female sex. It may well be that natural selection favored the greater size of the female for defending cubs against males. Since both sexes participate almost equally in territorial defense (unlike many other species of mammals where only the males take up this role), there would be no selection pressure in favor of large males for this purpose, nor for male adornments giving the impression of large size (as, for instance, the lion's mane).

Development. A hyena is born with its eyes open, its body covered with soft, brownish black hair, average weight 1.5 kg (Pournelle 1965), and unable to walk. However, within ten days of its birth it can already move at quite a speed. A diversity of calls becomes apparent during the first week; the cubs can utter a high-pitched whimpering begging call and a series of very high-pitched but clearly recognizable whoops (uttered with the same head movements that adults use). The black color of the cubs gradually changes into the spotted coat of the adults, beginning at one and one-half to two months, with the head turning light gray (pl. 48), the white hairs gradually extending over the neck, which then becomes clearly spotted (two and one-half to three months), and at four months, spots are beginning to appear on the flanks as well (pl. 49). The legs are the last part of the body to maintain the dark color (pl. 50), and animals of as much as a year old often still have dark legs. A hyena is virtually fully grown at one and one-half years old (pl. 51), and males probably become sexually active at two. Females take longer and they are not sexually mature until after they have attained full adult size, probably when about three years old (Matthews 1939a). On one occasion I saw a female that I estimated to be slightly less than two years old mate with an old male.

Very early in life, hyenas show a number of surprisingly adult behavior patterns. For instance, before they are one month old, they perform the leg-lifting ceremony with other cubs or adults, showing complete penis or clitoris erection. These erections are also shown when being sniffed or licked by other hyenas, and the organ involved is very large in relation to the small animal, relatively larger than in adults (see also p. 227). Another interesting performance of the cubs is pasting —we saw this in our tame hyena for the first time at two and one-half months, in wild cubs even at one to one and one-half months (pl. 48). The cub goes through the complete marking performance described on p. 222, but without the anal bulging. At this stage it does not actually excrete anything, and does not do so until it is well over a year old. Nevertheless, this pasting by cubs is a very frequent behavior pattern around the dens. One of the important external stimuli for releasing it is clearly the smell of another hyena's anal gland excretion, and this may be why it appeared so much later in Solomon than it does in the wild, since the tame animal seldom comes across hyena marks. When I first showed him a straw marked by another hyena, he immediately reacted by going through the marking motions himself; later he rolled over the marked straw, which made him smell of soap all over.

In the beginning of their lives, cubs are very afraid of any other large animals, whether dangerous or harmless to them, and if, for instance, an adult wildebeest comes walking up to the den, the cubs run away or go to ground long before any of the adults move. When walking out on the plains with our tame Solomon, he would stay close to me, except if I came too close for his liking to any of the ungulates; a group of zebra more than 200 m away would make him stop and stare, then turn and run back. This changed as he grew older and, at about ten months old, he would go as close to zebra and wildebeest as I would. He was less frightened of any of the animals when taken close in the car; by doing this, I found some interesting things about the relations between young hyenas and really dangerous foes like lions. When I first drove Solomon in the car close to a pride of lions, he looked at them with the same interest as he did at other animals, not showing any signs of fear even at less than 6 m away. We happened to stand upwind of the lions, how-ever, and when driving away from the pride and around it, Solomon caught a whiff of lion when about 20 m downwind. Immediately he was terrified, giggling and struggling to get out. I repeated this experiment and it was obvious that he was reacting to the smell rather than the sight of lions. Solomon was then six months old and almost certainly had never had any experience with lions before. When he was nine months old, a caged leopard was brought into our camp by game scouts to be released in the Ngorongoro Crater, after being captured in a built-up area. The leopard was invisible and made no noise, but one sniff of it made Solomon run away from the camp far out of sight, not to return that day.

When the cubs are a few months old, they begin to follow the mother when she leaves the den after a visit; in the beginning they follow only some 10 m or so, but gradually the distance at which they halt in their tracks, watching the female walk on before hurrying back to their holes, gets longer and longer. The cubs will eat any meat to be had in the immediate vicinity of the den (given the chance by the adults) from the age of five months onward; for instance, I made one observation in Ngorongoro when an adult wildebeest was killed right on the Oldonyo

Rumbe den, and all hyenas present older than five months fed on it. Generally, though, cubs get little meat before they are at least seven to eight months old. Our tame hyena was presented with meat regularly from two weeks old onward and ate his first bit when only eleven weeks old.

Even when cubs have begun to eat meat, the mainstay of their diet is still the mother's milk for a long time to come; they are usually weaned when between twelve and sixteen months old, almost fully grown.

Hyenas are born with erupting milk incisors and canines, and milk-premolars appear in their second month of life. But although they are able to feed on meat when two and one-half months old (at least they do so in captivity), the youngest hyena that I ever saw making an attempt at hunting was about eight months old. Even that was merely a short run after a quarter-grown Thomson's gazelle, which easily outran the clumsy little hyena. Solomon brought in a freshly caught puff adder when he was eight months old (almost certainly killed by himself) and found and killed a newborn hare when ten months old. At the same time, nine and one-half and ten months old, he lost his milk canines and they were replaced by permanent teeth. Hyenas hunting in a pack are rarely accompanied by young ones less than a year old, and these bring up the rear of the group. Thus, they do not start to hunt properly until they are fully grown, first going through a stage in which they follow the hunt but do not participate.

Play. "Play is a general term for activities which seem to the observer to make no immediate contribution to survival" (Hinde 1966). It is an anthropomorphic term, negatively defined; I have merely used it as a label for some activities which in our own species would be named that way. Hyenas play often, especially the cubs, but also adults with cubs and among themselves. As an example of adult play, in the crater four hyenas once walked about 1 km from their den to a small deep pool in the Mungi River in the early morning; when they arrived there, all four took to the water and swam about, pushing each other underwater with their forepaws, biting, and splashing hard (pl. 52). Every so often they chased and ran after each other out of the pool for several hundred meters in a big circle before jumping back into the water again. Apart from an occasional growl, no sounds were uttered. After about 15 min of this they quietly walked together to the hillside, where they spent the day in an erosion gully; they had made a large detour for their swim. Scott (1959) saw a party of ten hyenas in Uganda bathing on a lakeshore, not swimming but wading and chasing each other around. One often sees what appears to be adult play around kills; hyenas who have already eaten most of their fill sometimes seem to invite others to chase them (p. 125).

Perhaps one could also talk about "play" in those observations in which groups of hyenas were seen baiting rhinoceroses, which happened several times while I was watching them in Ngorongoro. Up to eight hyenas walked to within a few meters of a rhino with their tails up and noses low to the ground; if the rhino made the slightest move in their direction, they jumped out of the way, often with a giggle. Usually they tried to get behind the rhino, probably in an attempt to bite his hind legs, but I never saw them actually touch him. It is doubtful whether this behavior can be considered merely as hunting, or merely as play. The rhinos in question were perfectly healthy and vigorous individuals, very improbable prey animals for a few odd hyenas. Almost certainly they were individually known to these hyenas, as they often occupied the same place for a long time. On several occasions, hyenas were seen before and after the baiting, and they showed no interest at all in other potential prey species, but indulged in various activities like social sniffing. A behavior which looks very similar to rhino baiting is sometimes shown to lions, especially solitary lions walking along on their own. But here the play aspect is less striking; I have described it more elaborately on p. 134.

Play of young hyenas and of young and adults together on the den consists of little more than chasing and biting; among the adults it is especially the males who play with the cubs, in the roles of both chaser and chased. Sometimes the chased hyena carries a bone or a stick; the pursuer's object seems to be more to bite his quarry in the hind legs than to get hold of whatever object he is carrying. Adults lying quietly asleep on the den are often pestered by the young ones, which bite their ears or legs, clambering all over them; the adults are remarkably tolerant to these little nuisances. Our tame hyena also had a great urge to bite into whatever object he could find, an urge that fortunately had largely subsided by the time he was nine to eleven months old. People's legs were his favorite chewing objects. Solomon, in common with the wild cubs, also liked to run in large circles around his home, colliding with any object in his way, whether alive or not. Rarely, cubs mount each other, with full erection, but making no attempt to penetrate. The youngest cub I saw do this was six to eight weeks old.

It is interesting to consider the absence of a number of adult behavior patterns from the "play" repertoire. The loin bite is never seen during play; this may be because the pursued hyena does not give his hunter a chance. But I also never saw cubs perform a number of the purely social patterns, for instance social sniffing, social scraping, and communal defecating; and I have never seen among cubs the parallel walk which in adults may precede aggression to a strange individual. It seems that the behavior patterns which entail real cooperation (apart from chasing) do not appear until hyenas are fully grown.

Adult as well as young hyenas will explore any new situation or strange object they come across, which ties in with their catholic taste in food. It is this curiosity that enables them to scavenge efficiently around human settlement.

INTERCLAN RELATIONS

In Ngorongoro

I have shown that the Ngorongoro population of hyenas is divided into a number of groups which I have called "clans." In the Serengeti, the same relations do not pertain, but the situation can be more clearly understood once the social relations in Ngorongoro have been further discussed.

Each of the clans[7] of hyenas occupying the Ngorongoro Crater floor seems to be confined to a limited range (p. 39). The ranges of various clans appear to be very exclusive, so they may be *territories* in the accepted sense of the word, that is, defended areas (Tinbergen 1956). There is, indeed, a good deal of behavioral evidence to support this view. I have classified my relevant observations as follows: (*a*) reactions of hyenas to intruders from another clan and vice versa; (*b*) defense of clan-range boundaries by groups of hyenas; (*c*) marking of boundaries; and (*d*) reactions of hyenas to boundaries of clan ranges.

Reactions to intruders.   A hyena may go undetected for quite some time if he penetrates into the range of another clan. If, for instance, such an intruder joins the resident clan on a kill, the others may not react to his presence until most of them have filled their bellies; then he may be suddenly discovered, viciously attacked (pl. 38), and chased over long distances (up to 3 km) by several members of the resident clan. But on

7. The use of the word "clan" does not imply that animals belonging to these groups are necessarily related to each other, as when the word is used in the anthropological sense.

other occasions, one glimpse of the intruder is enough to start the territory owners off in a slow aggressive approach, often in parallel walk,
which usually results in the flight of the intruder, sometimes with a
chase. Physical contact is usually avoided, but if it does occur, the
intruder may receive some hard bites. In this type of territorial behavior,
in common with all others, females are just as likely as males to take up
the defense.

> June 1966, dusk. One of the marked males from the Lakeside clan
> was walking far inside the range of the Scratching Rocks clan. The
> first hyena he met after I started following him was a young one of ten
> to twelve months old. The intruder immediately flattened back his
> ears and curved his tail under his belly when the other hyena was still
> 30 m away. The young one gave chase and the intruder ran off at full
> speed, not stopping until long after the chase had ended.

> November 1966, dawn. I saw three young male lions running in the
> range of the North clan in Ngorongoro. I followed them for almost
> 1½ km until they came on a party of nine hyenas who had killed a wilde-
> beest; it must have been their noise which attracted the lions. The hy-
> enas scattered when the lions arrived, but stayed around after the
> scavengers had settled on their kill, occasionally uttering whoops and
> lows. Then, about 20 min after the arrival of the lions, a single hyena
> came slowly galloping up from the direction of the neighboring Scratch-
> ing Rocks range. Immediately after he came over the rise within 60 m
> of the kill, the hyenas around the lion jumped up, their manes and tails
> raised, and went after the new arrival. The latter turned and fled but
> was overtaken in a flash and grabbed by a hind leg, bowled over, and
> bitten anywhere the attackers could reach. The intruder kept up a
> loud continuous growling, but the attackers were completely silent.
> Once the victim managed to get on his legs and run off, but it
> was grabbed again and bitten all over, in the hind legs, ears, flanks,
> but then left to limp away on its own. The intruder was bleeding from
> the ears, hind legs, belly, and back. The attacking hyenas walked back
> to the kill, where they lay down again.

Why an intruder is sometimes attacked immediately whereas on
other occasions it is tolerated may well depend to some extent on its
own behavior. Usually an intruder can be recognized as such because
of the fear expressed in its posture; if one follows a hyena from its own
range into a neighboring one, it is clear that its behavior becomes more
cautious and it shows more signs of readiness to flee, especially when
meeting other hyenas. This apprehensive behavior is already conspicuous from a long distance away, and it may well be that the aggression

which such animals elicit is evoked by the attitude of such individuals rather than by individual recognition.

An intruder will eventually become accepted if it persists in returning, hanging around the den and coming in on kills. This may, however, take a long time and complete acceptance may be achieved only after several months. For instance, a marked male who belonged to the Lakeside clan during 1965 and was regularly seen there walked over to the Scratching Rocks range in February 1966. That time he went undetected, but during the following month, I several times saw him being chased very hard. At the end of March, however, he was able to feed unnoticed with the Scratching Rocks clan, although he was still briefly chased after everyone had eaten. Even in June he was still occasionally being chased when not on a kill; in December, he still had to keep out of the way of the others, but was not chased anymore. From February 1967 onward he seemed a perfectly accepted member of the clan, taking part in hunting forays, and in September of that year, I even saw him on the den.

Boundary defense by groups of hyenas.   The most dramatic defense of territory occurs when groups of hyenas of two neighboring clans meet. Two kinds of such meetings can be distinguished; first, clashes over a kill (pl. 53), and, second, meetings of "patrols." The first category is the most frequent, usually in the following form. A pack of hyenas begins to chase one of the larger prey species somewhere in its own range; they will often abandon the quarry when it crosses into the range of another clan (see below), but they may continue and pull it down in the boundary area, or sometimes well inside the neighboring clan range. This, if noticed by the rightful owners of the range, will instantly produce neighborly aggression; a number of hyenas will come running up, either as a pack or in ones and twos, and if the hunting pack has not run off at the first appearance of the owners of the range in the distance, the latter may gather close together near the kill and then attack after a short and noisy interval of displaying and calling.

> December 1967, evening. After a chase of 2 km, a male wildebeest was grabbed by five hyenas from the Lakeside clan, more than $\frac{1}{2}$ km inside the newly expanded range of the Hippo clan. They proceeded to kill, but just as the wildebeest sank to the ground, eight hyenas from the Hippo clan came running up, perhaps attracted by the moans of the wildebeest. The Lakeside hyenas noticed the arrival of the range owners when the latter were still over 30 m away, and immediately abandoned

their quarry, uttering a few soft grunt-laughs (alarm call). They ran
straight back to their own range, leaving the wildebeest bull to be
finished off and eaten by fifteen of the Hippo clan hyenas.

There may be fewer hyenas from the owner clan than from the
hunting pack, but if the kill is well inside the owners' territory, a few
will suffice to drive out the intruders. This is consistent with observations of individual intruders, who were more likely to flee in somebody
else's range.

> June 1966, evening. While I was watching hyenas near the den of
> the Scratching Rocks clan, several of them suddenly got up and began
> to run in the direction of the Lakeside range. They were joined by
> others until there were twelve in all, and after running a considerable
> distance they came near the place where thirty-four hyenas were
> eating from a zebra mare they had just killed. These thirty-four, how-
> ever, did not belong there; although they had killed about 1 km inside
> the Scratching Rocks range, they were from the Lakeside clan. The
> twelve hyenas I was following stopped very briefly about 15 m from the
> kill, standing close together with tails up, manes bristling, and ears
> cocked. The Lakesiders had stopped eating and watched the owners for a
> while—but then the Scratching Rock pack ran forward and mingled
> briefly with the Lakesiders under a fantastic cacophony of sounds (fast
> whoops, lows, giggles, yells, growls, and grunt-laughs), and within sec-
> onds the whole group of Lakesiders ran off, stopping 20–30 m away. The
> Scratching Rocks hyenas hardly pursued the matter, but began to eat
> from the carcass, pulling it away in the opposite direction from the
> Lakesiders. There was little left of the zebra, however; all the internal
> organs and muscles were gone, as were three of the legs and almost all
> the skin. The Scratching Rocks hyenas began to walk back with these
> remains when the Lakesiders attacked again, causing the hyena bearing
> away the head, spine, and rib cage to abandon his trophies. But
> before the Lakesiders had their mouths on it, the owners of the territory
> were back again, this time chasing the Lakesiders with great determina-
> tion. About 200 m from where the zebra was killed, the carcass was
> further dismembered and each Scratching Rocks hyena went his own
> way again. The Lakesiders walked straight back to their own range,
> where most of them lay down. During this clash, several bites were ex-
> changed, but it was difficult to see any details of this because of bad
> light conditions.

But the clash between clans is not always such an easy one; on several
occasions I have seen the hunting clan return to the kill after first having

left it to the owners, and in this way, a kill may change hands many times before the matter is settled—usually in favor of the owners.

> September 1967, dawn. Up in the hills, in the northern part of the crater, the Mungi hyenas had run down a zebra stallion which they killed and proceeded to eat about one-third of the way up the slope. The kill was made in an area where the boundary between the Mungi and the Scratching Rocks clans was not very well defined, and I could not definitely say which range it was inside. Soon the first Scratching Rocks hyenas came running up, and I had a beautiful panoramic view of how the others were following, coming in from all over the Scratching Rocks range. Finally, there were twenty-six of them facing seventeen hyenas from the Mungi range. The Mungi hyenas first continued feeding, but when the tightly packed contenders slowly approached in aggressive attitudes, uttering lowing calls and fast whoops, the Mungi hyenas withdrew to the other side of the carcass. Then the Scratching Rocks hyenas ran forward, some of them chasing Mungi hyenas and some going straight for the carcass. Several of the Mungi clan came back, though, and for a brief while there was a great turmoil of forty-three hyenas chasing each other. Within seconds the Mungi animals fled, and the Scratching Rocks hyenas ate. But their victory was very short-lived; after they had eaten for about $1\frac{1}{2}$ min, the Mungi pack was back again (pl. 52) and the roles were reversed. Again a wild turmoil and chase followed, this time leaving the Mungi hyenas eating. In this way, the carcass changed owners twelve times in 25 min; once the two opposing packs were even pulling at it from opposite ends at the same time. The clash was very noisy, especially when the two packs mixed and bit at each other. But there was surprisingly little physical contact between them, and although I saw several bites hit home, these obviously did not inflict any serious injury. After 25 min, only the head and spine were left of the carcass; the rest had all been eaten or carried off. The Scratching Rocks hyenas began to drift back, fairly dispersed, once more returning for a last threatening stand in front of the Mungi hyenas; then they all dispersed onto their own ranges. Several Mungi hyenas also walked back to where they had come from, but eleven stayed around the carcass, where they were found by three male lions about 15 min later. I had seen the lions come trotting up from the center of the Scratching Rocks range more than 3 km away, obviously attracted by the noise of the two battling hyena packs; when they finally arrived, though, little was left but a few bones and the head of the zebra.

Generally, a clash consists of a great deal of calling and displaying and chasing, and physical contact is rarely made. But if it is, members of either side may be severely mauled or even killed. I have on four occasions found hyenas dead near the site of a kill with clear evidence that they were killed by other hyenas, and on three other occasions I saw animals that were badly mauled, almost certainly by hyenas, judging by their injuries. Several direct observations were made, for instance:

> September 1967, late evening. One hyena from the Mungi clan began to chase a female wildebeest, and with the help of several others managed to pull it down about 200 m inside the range of the Scratching Rocks hyenas, in an area where the boundary was very well defined. More Mungi hyenas joined to share in the kill until all together there were about twenty. But at the same time, the Scratching Rocks hyenas noticed that this was happening and ran up from all directions. There must have been approximately forty of them (it was difficult to count in the dark) advancing to attack the eating Mungi hyenas. The two groups mixed with an uproar of calls, but within seconds the two sides parted again and the Mungi hyenas ran away, briefly pursued by the Scratching Rocks hyenas, who then returned to the carcass. About a dozen of the Scratching Rocks hyenas, though, grabbed one of the Mungi males and bit him wherever they could—especiall/ in the belly, the feet, and the ears. The victim was completely covered by his attackers, who proceeded to maul him for about 10 min while their clan fellows were eating the wildebeest. The Mungi male was literally pulled apart, and when I later studied the injuries more closely, it appeared that his ears were bitten off and so were his feet and testicles, he was paralyzed by a spinal injury, had large gashes in the hind legs and belly, and subcutaneous hemorrhages all over. After 10 min the attackers left the victim and went to feed on the wildebeest carcass. The Mungi hyenas in the meantime had left the area completely; the Scratching Rocks animals also abandoned the site when they had finished with the wildebeest, hardly glancing at the injured hyena, who was lying about 8 m from the wildebeest. I gave the injured animal an injection of succinylcholine chloride to put him out of his misery, but left the corpse on the spot. The next morning I found a hyena eating from the carcass and saw evidence that more had been there; about one-third of the internal organs and muscles had been eaten. Cannibals!

These fights over kills were indeed a frequent phenomenon in Ngorongoro; I saw that in 36 kills out of 109 the hunting hyenas became involved in a clash with their neighbors. This was not really surprising, as almost one in five of wildebeest hunts went over at least 2 km and in several places the clan ranges are less than 2 km across.

The meeting of two "patrols" never led to bloodshed in my observations, but the aggressive motivation of the opposing parties was apparent. I called them "patrols" because one observed a group of hyenas, up to ten, walking in pack formation over the clan range, often along a boundary or sometimes merely as far as the boundary, where they might show various marking activities. These groups gave the impression of taking the course they did for the sole purpose of social sniffing (p. 241), marking, and meeting neighbors; they either showed no interest whatsoever in potential prey animals or first made a large detour in order to reach a territorial boundary before returning to a more central area of their range where they started hunting. Usually these patrols were clearly distinguishable from hunting packs by their different activities while walking along, but one might develop into the other. When the patrols met either a solitary individual or a pack from the neighboring clan, they showed immediate aggression.

> December 1966, dusk. Twelve hyenas from the Scratching Rocks clan walked in close pack formation away from the den area in the direction of the boundary with the Lakeside clan. On the way they social sniffed three times, and when they came near the boundary, they noticed (when still about 800 m off) that seven hyenas from the Lakeside clan were visiting a latrine area just about on the demarcation line. These seven also noticed the twelve Scratching Rocks hyenas and looked at them with their heads up for a few seconds, then slowly moved away, stopping once for a social sniff. The Scratching Rocks animals walked slowly after them until suddenly the Lakeside clan began to run toward a group of twenty wildebeest with one zebra. They chased the zebra for about 50 m then the quarry ran back into the range of the Scratching Rocks. The Scratching Rocks hyenas watched all this, but when the zebra came toward them, they showed no interest in it and began to run at full speed after the Lakeside pack. They chased the latter over about 500 m, well into the Lakeside range, then stopped with tails and manes raised, watching the Lakeside hyenas disappear. The twelve Scratching Rocks hyenas then turned around and walked to the latrine area on the boundary, where they scratched, defecated, and pasted before returning to the center of their area. On their way back, about 1 km inside their range, they met another hyena who obviously did not belong; this one did not wait for the twelve to come close, but ran at full speed as soon as they came into sight. They chased it briefly, performing one more social sniff at the place where I thought the single hyena had been standing, then slowly drifted back. About an hour after they began, they were fairly close

to the den, most of the pack lying down scattered over several hundred meters.

Marking of boundaries. When pasting or pawing or both (p. 222) is done by a group of hyenas, this usually happens on special pasting places which either look no different from the immediate environment or may be slightly conspicuous because of higher grass stalks. Similarly, social defecating and pawing take place on special latrines; these

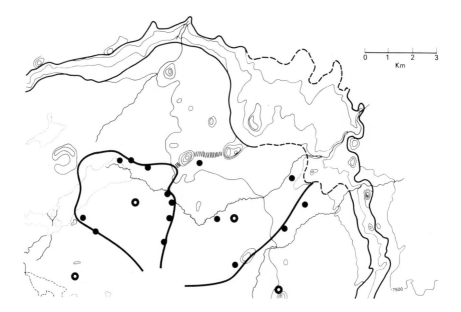

Fig. 62. "Latrines" used by the Scratching Rocks clan and the Mungi clan in Ngorongoro: ● = latrine; ○ = den; solid line = clan range boundary.

usually also carry some pastings (but pasting places are not often used as latrines). It is striking that these two kinds of marking places are usually found on or very near the clan range boundaries (fig. 62). In these areas, they are sometimes used by members of both clans; others, to my knowledge, are used only by one of the clans, and are situated just inside the boundary. It is these latrines and pasting places along the boundary that are visited by the boundary patrols, often after long detours. They are conspicuous also to a human observer; not only do

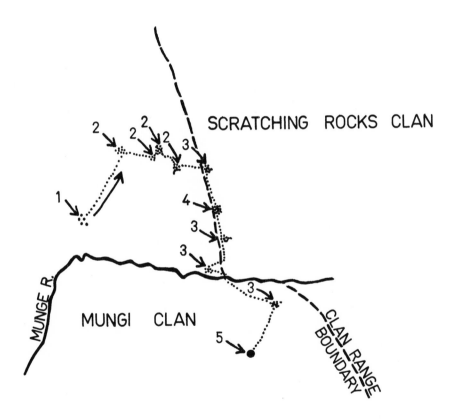

Fig. 63. Course of a pack of Mungi hyenas "pasting" along boundary: *1*, starting place ("club"); *2*, social sniffing; *3*, pasting and pawing; *4*, pasting, pawing, and defecating; *5*, bedding down.

they carry a distinct smell (which to hyenas must be very strong indeed), but the latrines are also plainly visible by the number of large white hyena droppings (pl. 54). Any hyena passing by will be aware of the presence of other hyenas and if, as suggested above (p. 223), in face-to-face encounters these scents are associated with an aggressive motivation of the opponent, it could be that they also have an intimidating effect when used as markers.

> September 1967, late evening. Six hyenas left the place which I called the "club" of the Mungi clan, after sleeping there for several hours, and walking together they went along a car track for about $\frac{1}{2}$ km (fig. 63). Then they stopped and turned off the track, and for several minutes social sniffing went on. They changed their direction after this and headed straight for the boundary with the Scratching Rocks clan. They stopped three more times for a social sniff, but when they reached the boundary of their range, their behavior changed. They went straight toward a patch of slightly taller grass and began pasting and pawing, looking several times in the direction of the Scratching Rocks range. After about 5 min in that particular spot, they again walked off in a different direction, following the boundary. A few hundred meters farther on they stopped in a patch of high grass and went through the whole ceremony of pasting and scratching the ground as before, only this time two of the pack also defecated. Later I noticed that this place was a proper latrine which many hyenas must have visited before. The pasting and pawing was repeated in three more places along the boundary, but there was no more social sniffing. Finally the pack lay down once again, about an hour after they had started out and after covering less than 2 km (see also notes on p. 178).

Reactions of hyenas to boundaries.   Usually hyenas do not cross a clan boundary, and several times I have seen hyenas chasing a wildebeest stop dead in their tracks when their quarry crossed into another clan range (p. 160). In some cases the neighbors then took over the chase.

> December 1966, dawn. Far in the distance, I saw a single hyena come down the hills in the northern half of the Scratching Rocks range, running at full speed behind a wildebeest bull. The hyena was slowly closing in on his quarry; it and the bull crossed the Mungi River and then raced across the open plain. By the time the wildebeest reached the boundary between the Scratching Rocks and the Mungi clan ranges, he must have run at least 3 km but he was still going strong with the hyena on his heels. Exactly on the border, the hyena stopped and watched the wildebeest run off into the Mungi range. The bull had

not covered 100 m beyond the boundary, however, before five hyenas from the Mungi clan jumped up, stood several seconds looking at the running wildebeest and then gave chase to it. Two of the five ran after it for about 300 m, then they also stopped, leaving the wildebeest bull running on for at least another 500 m.

But there are occasions when hyenas do not respect these "political lines on a map." Males have less of a clan attachment than females (p. 41), so sexual attractions on the other side of the boundary may be involved. At the end of 1967, the Scratching Rocks clan found itself with only few wildebeest and zebra in its range; I had never seen so few there. Consequently several hyenas from Scratching Rocks (both males and females) penetrated deep into the large range of the Air-strip clan, where large herds of wildebeest were grazing. These were forays of only a few hours and may have gone undetected by the Air-strip hyenas. It is clear that in cases of serious food emergency, territorial boundaries are not adhered to.

On a number of occasions when watching hyenas, I could hear the sounds of a neighboring clan on a kill, often just on their own side of the boundary. The hyenas I was watching also heard these sounds and were standing in an alert posture, ears cocked in the direction from which the sound was coming. But they did not run up there, nor in fact did they listen for very long; it was clear that they knew it was only their neighbors feeding in their own range, and it would be no good trying to get a bite there.

In the Serengeti

From the resightings of marked hyenas in the Serengeti, it has been shown that they move over large distances (p. 46), and there is a clear association with the migrating wildebeest (p. 55). But marked hyenas also showed a tendency to regularly return to the same areas, and they might stay in one area for several weeks or even months. They tend to stick to certain denning sites for long periods, even when their food species are many miles away. So the overall picture is more complicated than in Ngorongoro, but nevertheless territorial behavior can also be clearly observed in the Serengeti. The basic pattern is that whenever numbers of hyenas stay in a particular place for any length of time, territories are set up; these are of necessity unstable.

Reactions to intruders. In an area where territories, temporary or permanent, have been set up, intruders are treated very much the same as in the crater.

October 1967, dawn. Around Mukoma Hill along the northwestern Serengeti plains, concentrations of wildebeest had been building up for two weeks, and there was a high density of hyenas. Two hyenas came walking up to a mudhole in and around which eight other hyenas were lying. When the two came close, all eight got up and sniffed the new hyenas briefly along their sides and heads; their tails and manes rose as they did so, and suddenly one of the eight snapped at one of the new ones. The latter jumped away with a yell and immediately the two new ones were on the run, pursued by all eight of the others. The pursuers did not catch up with the newcomers, and after a chase of about 1 km they gave up and wandered slowly back to their mudhole.

Once I put three strange hyenas into pens near our house in Seronera; the following night more than ten of the local hyenas were around the pens, loudly whooping, grunting, grunt-laughing, and so on. These local hyenas showed no further interest after the first night.

However, it seems that intruders are generally more easily accepted here than in Ngorongoro, although this is very difficult to quantify, since the definition of an "intruder" is much more vague in the Serengeti. One would in fact expect a greater tolerance to strangers; the difference in site attachment between owner and intruder is probably less than in Ngorongoro, and it is likely that the intruder in the Serengeti behaves less apprehensively. Also, the larger number of vagrants with which range-defending hyenas in the Serengeti have to deal may well cause the aggressive response to strangers to decrease. But in the very fluid territorial situation, it is difficult for an observer to tell where animals belong, and it will not be easy to collect enough data for a direct comparison with Ngorongoro.

Boundary defense by groups of hyenas. Clashes between groups of hyenas over a kill can also be seen in the Serengeti, though much less frequently. These look in every respect the same as in Ngorongoro except that, because of the very temporary arrangement, the position of a boundary is difficult to ascertain, and therefore one cannot be sure of the relations between two agonistic packs in a particular place.

November 1967, dawn. Along the northwestern edge of the Serengeti plains, just north of Lake Magadi, a concentration of wildebeest had moved in, and I found six hyenas immediately after they had killed an old wildebeest bull about halfway between the large den to which the hyenas belonged and the den of their nearest neighbors. They had just started eating when a pack of ten from the neighboring den turned up, running straight up to the kill and chasing off the hunters before any physical contact was made; but the hunters were soon back, mingling briefly with the ten newcomers before the latter left the kill again. In this way, the carcass "changed mouths" three times to the accompaniment of much calling and a few very superficial bites. All the noise attracted more of the neighboring hyenas, though, and when the six hunters were chased away by nineteen of their opponents they ran off completely, spending a long time pasting and scratching about 100 m away while their kill was demolished by the others.

On one occasion in the Serengeti, I witnessed a clash between two groups which took the combatants over a distance of about 3 km.

> November 1968, late evening. Hearing the noise of a clash between hyenas, I searched for and found a group of eighteen hyenas, several of whom I knew belonged to the Seronera "dustbin brigade," involved with a group of at least ten other hyenas. There was no sign of a kill anywhere; the two packs chased each other alternatively without any actual bites reaching home. The situation was further complicated by the presence of about fifteen "onlookers," hyenas who seemed to have no loyalties to either side but who just added to the general turmoil. The pack of ten was chased by the Seronera hyenas over about 3 km in the course of an hour, away from Seronera village. There was a good deal of moving backward and forward and a chorus of calls from both sides. When finally the two groups had separated completely, standing about 200 m apart, both spent a long time social sniffing, scratching, and pasting, and the Seronera hyenas also defecated. During all this, several hyenas of each party kept an eye on the other party. Slowly the group of ten and the various onlookers drifted away, while the Seronera pack walked back a short distance toward the village and then lay down.

This observation confirms the suggestion that the definition of boundaries in the Serengeti is much vaguer than in the crater, where chases never go over such distances. "Patrols" are much less common here than in Ngorongoro.

Marking of boundaries. Here a clear difference from the crater is revealed—the marking places in the Serengeti, especially latrines, are mostly situated along car tracks and hyena paths, the routes along which hyenas move when traveling over longer distances. For example, once when traveling along car tracks in the northern woodlands of the Serengeti I found eight hyena latrines along 70 km of road and none in 230 km of cross-country driving in the same area. From movements of hyenas in relation to these latrines, it seems that they are usually not on territorial boundaries, though they may be when a temporary large hyena concentration has set up territories. I have no evidence on this last point.

Reactions of hyenas to boundaries.   I have never seen hyenas in the Serengeti abandon the chase of a quarry where this could have been caused by a reaction to a boundary. This is probably largely caused by the absence of clear boundaries, but it may also be partly because I have rarely seen hyenas hunting in places where I knew a boundary to be present.

To sum up, there are clear fragments of territorial behavior left in the Serengeti hyenas, but on the whole the strict clan system of Ngorongoro has been abandoned for a more fluid pattern of migrations and population movements. Two factors must be of importance in causing this difference: the movements of the prey population and the difference in hyena density (this, too, is probably related to the prey migrations, see p. 102). These social consequences of differences in a species' food supply will be further discussed in chapter 7.

The Function of Territorial Behavior in Hyenas

A territory can fulfill different functions in various species of mammals and birds, as summarized by Tinbergen (1956). But rarely do we have any real proof of these functions, and in this study I cannot go beyond a mere guess about functional significance. With large groups of hyenas of varying numbers inhabiting each territory, as in Ngorongoro, it seems unlikely that the number of territories in itself would put a limit to the number of hyenas in the whole area. Moreover, even in the crater, the territorial boundaries are not that inflexible (p. 42). However, the territorial system does ensure a spacing out between hyena concentrations.

From direct observations it is clear that boundary defense is often tied up with competition over food, and when hyenas hunt it is usually in their own territory. There are no suggestions that territory is somehow tied up with sexual behavior or protection of offspring. It seems most likely then that the function of the territorial system is linked with the hyenas' food supply. To stick to a certain home range is of clear advantage to a hyena; it can then know the best hunting areas, easy crossing of streams, and also lying up places and denning sites. The defense of this area against intruders may prevent the formation of too large aggregations—if too many adults share a kill, little or nothing will be left for the animals last to come, the cubs. This can be precluded by a distribution of the cubs over a number of concentrations or, in other words, spacing out of clans. It is likely that there is an optimal clan size for each area, determined partly by availability of and competition over food, and also by the need for cooperation between clan members in hunting (caused by species composition of the prey population).

7 Adaptations in Social Behavior and Feeding Ecology

Adaptive Trends in Hyena Behavior

For the purpose of assessing whether the social organization of hyenas and their behavior patterns are in any way specifically adapted to the species' ecology (or vice versa), I will first enumerate a number of characteristics of the hyenas' feeding.

Hyenas are scavengers as well as hunters. Searching for carrion is a solitary occupation, whereas ungulates are hunted either solitarily or in packs, depending on the species of prey. So hyenas may forage either socially or solitarily and they exploit the resources by changing from solitary to social hunting or vice versa at very short notice. When many hyenas are eating together, they may be very closely packed, shoulder to shoulder or sometimes even one on top of another. There may also be fairly young hyenas among those eating, animals who would not be able to fend for themselves. Last, the hyenas' ability to kill and eat almost everything made of flesh and bone (including members of their own species) should be mentioned.

This characteristic foraging behavior requires a social behavior system in which an individual can quickly change from a solitary to an integrated social state or in which an individual can temporarily exist solitarily next to others who are more socially inclined. Of course, these requirements could not be met within a system of individual territories, which is the most common arrangement in the animal kingdom. In order to meet them, a species could either have no territory at all or it could employ group territories. There are advantages in both; the first would allow predators to follow prey movements over large distances, and the second system enables the territory owners to get to know an area for hunting purposes. Having a group territory prevents neighbors from making use of one's kills (but also prevents one from making use of neighbors' kills), and so has the effect of restricting the number of hyenas per kill. The advantage of a system in which fewer kills each provide a larger amount of food per eating hyena over a system in which many kills would each provide only a small amount of food per eating hyena is that the hyenas lowest in the dominance order around the kill, the juveniles, get a better chance to obtain some food. In this context, it is interesting that in the wild dog, a species which does not have a territory, the young animals (pups) have a right-of-way at the kill and therefore food for these physically less able animals is secure. The group territorial system is accompanied by several auxiliary behavior patterns, such as territorial defense, marking, and so on.

Within hyena clans, individual hyenas must be able to change from a solitary to a social state, and vice versa, in a very brief span of time. To allow for this, and to be territorial at the same time (keeping out strangers), an elaborate behavioral mechanism is necessary for rapid integration into groups. This must be the main function of the very elaborate meeting ceremony and its attendant morphological structures.

Like most other carnivores, hyenas are potentially dangerous killers, even of their own kind; they are probably more to be feared by their own kind than are most other carnivores because of their very catholic tastes. Yet considerable social tolerance is required because of the need for cooperation in hunting groups and because of the necessity of eating in close proximity with other hyenas, especially after social hunting.

Behavioral mechanisms are required which restrict all-out aggression to intergroup encounters. Hyenas do indeed show remarkably little aggression when feeding, and relatively many displays, scents, and calls are employed whose main function is to prevent physical contact. Of course, young hyenas would be far more likely to suffer from the cannibalistic attentions of others than would adults; in this context, it may be significant that females are larger than male hyenas (to keep males away from the young ones).

As another protection against cannibalism, cubs are able to creep out of reach of adults into small holes which they dig themselves; in the large communal dens, females keep their litters in close proximity, which allows one female to protect several litters at once if other mothers are away. In this context it is also interesting that, in the Serengeti, the number of females that simultaneously use a den is largest at the time when they have to stay the longest time away from the den for foraging. It would, of course, be highly advantageous if females suckled each other's cubs and if they were able to regurgitate food for them. At least in the case of the latter theoretical possibility, it is likely that other requirements conflict with it. Hyenas keep meat in their stomachs for only a very short time; it is soon passed through into the intestines, from which it can no longer be regurgitated. It may well be that this quick passage through the stomach is an adaptation to irregular food supplies, for it is then possible to eat again very soon after the last meal.

Hyenas, when feeding, compete with each other by eating very fast rather than by fighting. It is likely that this requirement of eating a large amount as rapidly as possible ties in with the lack of a special killing bite in the hyenas' hunting behavior. The victim is merely hampered in its movements by several hyenas hanging on at the same time and it is eaten simultaneously; thus the hyenas are eating while killing. As soon as the carcass can be dismembered, individual hyenas run off with large pieces of meat, often going a long distance away to eat quietly on their own. This carrying of heavy pieces of food is probably one of the most important functions of the very large neck muscles and the relatively strong forequarters of the hyena.

In the previous paragraphs, I have presented a few indications of how the social system and behavior of hyenas are tied in with the feeding ecology; there are of course many more links. The hyenas' social system allows for a great deal of flexibility, and it is interesting that in the two areas studied (with their different food ecologies, distributions, and densities) the social system of the hyenas also shows differences.

Hyenas in the Serengeti scavenge considerably more than those in Ngorongoro, and when they hunt the population of potential prey animals (containing relatively more Thomson's gazelle than in Ngorongoro) requires a more solitary hunting behavior. Scavenging is also a rather solitary occupation. Hyenas in the Serengeti are indeed more solitary, and if they are seen in groups, these are smaller. The number of females per group is also relatively smaller than in Ngorongoro (it tends to be one), and I have indicated that this may also be adaptive (p. 241).

The herbivore migrations are almost certainly the cause of hyena movements in the Serengeti; the pattern of hyena movements is completely different from Ngorongoro, and the migration system makes permanent establishment of food territories impossible. The way the prey population affects the hyena population composition has been discussed on page 102; of course, this also indirectly affects the hyena social system.

It is striking how the social and foraging behavior are in harmony with each other; continuing this line of thought, it will be useful in the next section to compare some of these hyena behavioral characteristics with those of their carnivorous relatives. The main purpose of this is to gain an idea of the extent to which these behavioral characteristics of hyenas are present in other species of different phylogenetic proximity in comparable ecological niches. Such a comparison not only may allow us to draw conclusions about adaptive radiation and evolutionary convergence, but may also provide a guideline for extrapolating our results from carnivores to other mammals, for example, primates.

ADAPTIVENESS AND PHYLOGENY

Ethologists have often used behavioral characteristics for studying systematic relationships between species. In some cases behavior can provide very useful clues in addition to morphological ones, although great care must be taken with the interpretation (Baerends 1958; Hinde and Tinbergen 1958). In other studies, behavioral characteristics have been used in a way which is in fact the reverse: given systematic relationships, behavior patterns are compared to investigate adaptive radiation and convergence (e.g., Tinbergen 1958; E. Cullen 1957; J. M. Cullen 1960).

With this last approach in mind I would like to compare the behavior of the spotted hyena with that of other carnivores; their systematic relationships are relatively well established on the basis of fossil and karyological evidence. In this comparison, I will endeavor to establish which patterns hyenas have in common with their close relatives and which patterns resemble the behavior of ecologically comparable but systematically distant forms. The main purpose of this comparison is to detect evolutionary convergences in behavior among species that are attempting to meet similar ecological requirements. Here social species deserve special attention, because this kind of comparison may give important clues to the function of communal living.

Systematic Affinities

The hyena looks rather like a dog, and one is slightly surprised to find that it is more closely related to the cats, and especially to the Viverridae (genet cats, mongooses, etc.). This has been established from recent studies of chromosome patterns (Hsu and Arrighi 1966; Wurster and Grey 1967; Ulbrich and Schmitt 1969), and particularly from fossil evidence, as summarized by Thenius (1966a) and various handbooks (e.g., Young 1962). The present hyenas' fossil history has been portrayed in figure 64, which shows the direct descent of Hyaenidae from the Viverridae; these two families, together with the Felidae, constitute

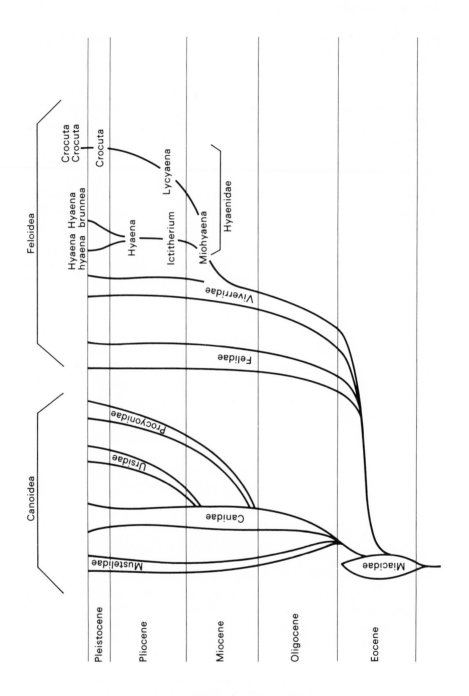

Fig. 64. Phylogenetic affinities of hyenas.

the superfamily of Feloidea. The ancestors of spotted and striped hyenas have existed separately since the Miocene (von Koenigswald 1965; Thenius 1966*a*).

Keeping these phylogenetic relationships in mind, I will now briefly discuss some of the hyenas' behavior patterns which appear to be homologous or analogous with some of the other carnivores' conduct. I am aware that this subject requires a great deal more study, and that a comparison between hyenas and other carnivores will suffer greatly from our present ignorance; nevertheless, I think it is worthwhile.

I have drawn mostly from the following sources for information on other carnivores' behavior: for Viverridae, from Dücker 1962, 1965; Ewer 1963 (especially *Suricata*), Hinton and Dunn 1967, and my own observations (mongooses); for Felidae, from Leyhausen 1956, Schaller 1967 (tiger), 1968 (cheetah), and personal communication (lion), Kiley 1969 (domestic cats), and my own observations (lion); for Canidae, from Fox 1969*a, b*, Tembrock 1954, 1957 (foxes), Schenkel 1948, Murie 1944, Mech 1966 (wolves), Kühme 1965 (wild dogs), Fuller and Dubuis 1962, Kiley 1969 (domestic dogs), and my own observations (foxes, wild dogs, jackals); for Mustelidae, from Wüstehube 1960 (polecats and others), Neal 1949 (badgers), and Lockie 1966 (stoats and weasels).

Comparison with the Behavior of Other Carnivores

Hyenas groom themselves in a way very similar to other carnivores; they stretch and lick, shake, and scratch themselves in an apparently identical manner. However, they do not "wash" their faces as cats and a few viverrids do; they groom themselves often, like cats and viverrids, and have an attitude in which they lick their genitals (sitting on lower back, legs spread, one leg pointing vertically upward) very similar to that of cats.

Hyenas are never arboreal, and in this they resemble dogs again; almost all cats and viverrids climb trees at least occasionally. Also, in their attraction to water and swimming hyenas approximate dogs rather than feloids. Their sleeping attitudes seem fairly universal among carnivores; like some of the Viverridae, hyenas often lie with their hind legs stretched out behind them.

In defecating and urinating the usual carnivore postures are adopted. But hyenas never lift their leg as male canids and even a few viverrids (meerkat) do; urinating has no marking significance in hyenas and almost all viverrids. Thus, the jet of urine directed backward as is known from the male Felidae will be not observed from a hyena. Social defecating is known for hyenas as well as for several viverrids and mustelids; it does not seem to occur among cats or dogs. Scratching the ground after defecating is common in all the families considered here.

Scent marking is performed by pasting a secretion from anal glands onto stalks of grass. Striped hyenas do it in exactly the same way as spotted ones, and aardwolves also paste onto grass stalks, with a slightly different movement (personal observation). The use of anal glands for this is found also among the Viverridae and Mustelidae, usually depositing on a solid substrate; it does not occur among either Felidae or Canidae. Hyenas use interdigital glands for leaving scent marks; this has not been observed in other carnivores as far as I know, but may have been overlooked. Several viverrids and mustelids are well known for the use of anal glands during agonistic encounters, but mostly in defense, rather than accompanying aggression, as in the spotted hyena.

Among the behavior patterns which probably have a visual signal function, tail postures take an important place in many carnivores, especially Felidae and Canidae. This is true also for the hyenas, but not for their close relatives the Viverridae: the latter rarely seem to make use of their tails for signaling, and this is also true for the Mustelidae. The same tail position occurs in different contexts in hyenas, cats, and dogs, and very likely usually has a different motivation and function. There are exceptions, of course, for instance the tail-between-the-legs posture which in both hyenas and dogs indicates fear, and is probably functional in protecting vital areas and keeping the tail out of reach of a pursuer. On the whole, hyenas employ tail positions rather than movements in social encounters; cats and dogs have many more tail movements that are obviously important. It is probable, therefore, that the "tail language" in the three families has evolved quite separately. Facial expressions (positions of ears and mouth especially) are commonly used throughout the Feloidea and Canoidea, and expressions that are similar in appearance are often used with apparently identical function and in identical circumstances. But here a great deal more study is needed, in hyenas as well as in other carnivores.

The hyena's system of vocalizations is very extensive indeed, especially because we are dealing with a continuous sound spectrum rather than with a number of discrete calls. Nothing comparable is known from any of the Viverridae, and the striped hyena is known to be very silent. Some of the Canidae have a vast repertoire of calls, solitary as well as social species (foxes, wolves). But a species like the wild dog utters surprisingly few different sounds, a phenomenon that may be related to the fact that they are diurnal, and almost always in very close proximity to each other. In the family of Felidae, the lions have a varied repertoire, in which different calls grade into each other as they do in the hyena. Most of the solitary cats are much less articulate.

When hyenas fight, they use only their teeth as weapons, not their claws. This is the same in most viverrids, although in some (e.g., *Genetta*) the claws have developed into important weapons, as they have in the cats. Dogs are similar to hyenas when fighting, and both are likely to chase each other over considerable distances (a feature not shown by any of the other groups).

Mating between hyenas consists of a number of rather short copulations with brief intervals. In this they resemble the cats; the Viverridae show a large variety of mating patterns. Unlike hyenas and the cats, the Canidae mate with a single, long-lasting copulation which typically involves "hanging."

Summarizing some important aspects of the hyenas' parental behavior, they do not regurgitate food for their cubs, nor do they carry food to their dens; the male does not assist in feeding the offspring. Viverridae and Felidae also do not regurgitate, but in Felidae and some of the Viverridae food is often brought to the young. Among Canidae, both regurgitation and carrying of food to the young are common, and the male plays an important role in this. The hyenas' burrowing habits are not shared by most of the Viverridae, nor by the Felidae; but among Canidae the digging of holes is common.

Finally, some aspects of the various feeding behaviors should be discussed. Hyenas catch their prey by running it down, a habit commonly employed by Canidae, but not by cats or Viverridae. The latter two families often stalk or ambush their quarry, then make a rush at it; this method is also employed by some dogs, but never by hyenas. Once the prey is caught, Viverridae and Felidae kill it by biting in the throat, neck, or around the mouth, sometimes shaking it; hyenas rarely do this, whereas most dogs do show this behavior (not the wild dog). Both Canidae and Hyaenidae are fast feeders and are able to gulp down large quantities of food in a short time. This is in contrast with the Feloidea, which take things more slowly. Some carnivores will store food for later consumption if it cannot all be eaten at once. This habit is common among the Canidae, and is also shown by the spotted hyena, but it does not occur in the Viverridae and is seen in only one of the Felidae (leopard).

Summarizing these behavioral comparisons, hyenas appear in several aspects to resemble the Canidae more than the phylogenetically closer Viverridae and Felidae. Neither dogs nor hyenas are arboreal; they are running hunters which catch their prey with their teeth rather than their claws. They eat their food fast, and may store it. Their callous feet with large, blunt nails are adapted to running and fast turning; in fact, their whole bodies are shaped for running rather than stalking. The absence of sharp, retractable nails in hyenas and dogs is reflected in their way of intraspecific fighting, which is with teeth only, and in their burrowing habits; they also do not use their paws for grooming. Thus, the resemblance between hyenas and dogs lies especially in their hunting and feeding, and in some other aspects of behavior in which the claws are used. But in most other behavior patterns mentioned the hyenas' phylogenetic affinities are expressed, such as in their grooming, scent marking, defecating habits, mating, parental behavior, and so on. It is in the foraging of Canidae and Hyaenidae that we find a clear indication of evolutionary convergence.

There are a number of behavioral phenomena that hyenas have in common with carnivore species from different families which may have evolved in conjunction with the organization in large social groups. In order to look at this more closely, I will first briefly discuss a few behavioral and ecological differences between some other social carnivores and their close, nonsocial relatives.

The Function of Social Hunting

Crook (1964, 1965) showed in his studies of weaverbirds that a close relation may exist between a species' food resource and the way it is exploited and its social behavior. When using this approach on carnivores and comparing the prey selection of social carnivores with that of their solitary close relatives, the hypothesis presents itself that the function of social hunting is the ability to overcome prey much larger or faster than the predators themselves. Bourlière (1963) suggested that, on the whole, carnivores select prey of about their own size or smaller. This may be true in general, but the social carnivores form a distinct exception. Thus, I am informed by East African residents that the diet of the solitary striped hyena contains many small creatures, even dung beetles, apart from what is scavenged from kills; this contrasts sharply with that of the spotted hyena, who regularly kills prey much larger than himself. Similar trends are known for the cats; the food of the leopard (Turnbull-Kemp 1967; Kruuk and Turner 1967), cheetah (Kruuk and Turner

1967; Schaller 1968), serval cat, and wildcat consists almost invariably of prey considerably smaller than the hunter itself. The lion's preferred prey, however, are ungulates heavier than an individual lion; the solitary tiger usually preys on animals its own size or smaller, though it is able to overcome ungulates several times its own size.

The prey of Canidae is also usually much smaller than the killer; this has been ascertained for foxes (*Vulpes vulpes*, Southern and Watson 1941; Southern 1964; Kruuk 1964; *Vulpes fulva*, Scott 1943, 1955; Scott and Klimstra 1955), Arctic foxes (Braestrup 1941), coyotes (Murie 1935, 1945; Sperry 1941; Fichter, Schildman, and Sather 1955), and jackals (van der Merwe 1959; own observations), to mention only a few examples. In contrast, the prey of wolves may exceed the predators in weight many times (Murie 1944; Young and Goldman 1944; Cowan 1947; Stenlund 1955; Crisler 1956; Burkholder 1959; Mech 1966). The usual prey of African wild dogs is about their own size or slightly larger and occasionally very much larger (van der Merwe 1959; Hirst 1967; Mitchell, Shenton, and Uys 1965; Estes and Goddard 1967; Kruuk and Turner 1967).

There are exceptions to this, of course; for instance, among Viverridae the food of the two social species that occur in the Serengeti (the banded and the pygmy mongoose) consists of invertebrates and vegetable matter, and the same is true for social mustelids, for instance the badger (Neal 1949). In these cases the group organization may have a function related to the distribution of food, or to antipredator behavior, as in the banded mongooses, who react with a spectacular "crowding response" to the threat of an aerial or ground predator.

There are some aspects of the social behavior of spotted hyenas, wolves, wild dogs, and lions which support the hypothesis that it is the social behavior, and nothing else, that enables these species to exploit the food resources they do. For hyenas, I have shown that different group sizes are employed in hunting different prey species—group sizes well adapted to the amount of resistance they are likely to meet. Furthermore, when hyenas are hunting wildebeest calves, they are able to overcome the aggression of the calf's mother only if two or more are hunting together. In lions, hunting success of the much smaller, but swift, Thomson's gazelle is greater when two or more lions cooperate than when they try alone. The much larger prey species like buffalo, which would be almost impossible for a single lion to kill, are, as far as we know, attacked only by several lions at once. Comparing data from several authors on the hunting method of wolves, it is striking that in this species as well the number of animals in a hunting pack is related to the kind of prey that is being chased. In A. Murie's description (1944) of wolves hunting Dall sheep and caribou, almost invariably only one or two wolves were involved, and the same is true for Banfield's (1951*a*, *b*, *c*), Crisler's (1956) and Burkholder's (1959) observations on caribou hunts. When the wolves are chasing moose, however, their packs often number over ten participants (Burkholder 1959; Mech 1966). In wild dogs, no relation was found between the number of animals in the pack and the species of prey hunted (Kruuk and Turner 1967). But I did once observe how one wild dog caught a gazelle far away from, and unnoticed by, the rest of the pack; it was unable to kill its prey and just stood there holding it by an ear for 2 min (pl. 55) until a second dog appeared and the tommy was dismembered and killed. Apart from the killing technique, which is adapted to the presence of several dogs, wild dogs are also dependent on the presence of others in their hunting behavior. Almost invariably, at the end of a chase, gazelle perform a series of sharp zigzags which are very effective in increasing the distance between the quarry and the lead dog, but which often enable the second or third dogs in the hunting sequence to cut across corners and catch up with the prey.

It seems reasonable to conclude that in spotted hyenas, lions, wolves, and wild dogs, the acquisition of large or fast prey is an important function of their social grouping. To stress the various parallel developments and differences among these four species, I will briefly review some of our knowledge of the last three for comparison with hyenas.

Hunting and Social Behavior of Wolves

From the references quoted above and from Pimlott (1967), wolves are known to be occasional scavengers, also eating mice and hares, but usually confining their diet to large mammals, mostly deer. So within the range of available kinds of food, wolves select in a very catholic way, even more so than hyenas. Their hunting behavior has been elaborately described and in many details seems to be similar to that of spotted hyenas. When searching for prey in woodlands, wolves apparently use their noses more often than I have observed hyenas doing, and they are inclined to follow tracks of a potential quarry. Wolves are also more likely to travel in a single line when searching or even when following prey, especially through snow (Mech 1966). But their attack of the prey is very similar indeed, and the way wolves "try out" herds or single individuals of Dall sheep, caribou, or moose is very reminiscent of what I observed in hyenas. Killing methods are also basically the same. Even large packs of wolves are relatively peaceful when eating at a kill, and they may play after feeding, one chasing another with a bone (Mech 1966), just like hyenas. Few details are known about actual prey selection from several different prey species; it is interesting that a group of wolves followed by Burkholder (1959) killed in sequence six moose, twelve caribou, four moose, and two caribou; a similar phenomenon was found in hyenas selecting between wildebeest and zebra.

Mech's assessment of wolves' hunting efficiency cannot be compared with that of hyenas; he expressed hunting efficiency as the percentage of moose killed out of the number "tested," whereas in hyenas only prey that was actually hunted could be taken into account.

It is still not known whether wolves have family territories or group territories, or perhaps both at different times of the year. They stick to certain home ranges, and enmity between packs and other individuals may even lead to a single wolf's death (Cowan 1947), or to chases over long distances (Mech 1966). Wolves also leave scent marks in the familiar manner of domestic dogs. The reported numbers in wolf packs vary widely from frequent observations of solitary individuals, to packs of over thirty members within which there is a strict social hierarchy (Schenkel 1948; Mech 1966).

The family life of wolves is less social than that of hyenas; litters from several females are not, or only rarely, found in the same den. Most likely, therefore, wolves are fairly solitary or family animals during the reproductive season; it may be that during that time, nonreproducing animals are more inclined to form packs.

It is likely, therefore, that wolves often face the difficulty of transition between a solitary and a social existence, as hyenas do. Accordingly, they have a large number of displays (tail postures, body postures, facial expressions, and a large number of calls; Schenkel 1948; Fox 1969a). Tembrock (1954) stressed that the number of communication patterns in the wolf is 32%–36% greater than in the solitary red fox.

Hunting and Social Behavior of Wild Dogs

In table 36, I have summarized observations on wild-dog kills in the Serengeti, made in the same period during which I studied hyenas. It is interesting to compare their diet with that of hyenas in the same area (table 11), and we can also do this for the diets of these two carnivores in the Ngorongoro Crater (Estes and Goddard 1967, table 1; this volume, table 12). Generalizing, this comparison shows that on the whole the wild dogs select smaller prey than do hyenas from the same populations. Wild dogs scavenge very little, and also they have hunting techniques which are much more uniform than those of hyenas: they exploit the vast populations of gazelle and others by hunting down their quarry at great speed, usually over shorter distances than hyenas, in a rather stereotyped hunting formation that enables the second, third, and following dogs to cut through corners made by the gazelle in response to the first dog. This hunting technique has been described in detail by Lang (1963), Estes and Goddard (1967), and Kruuk and Turner

TABLE 36 *Prey of wild dogs in the Serengeti, 1964–68*

Prey species	No. of kills observed		Percentage	
Wildebeest adult	7	} 27	6	} 23
Wildebeest calf	20		17	
Zebra adult	1	1	1	1
Thomson's gazelle adult	50	} 66	43	} 57
Thomson's gazelle fawn	16		14	
Grant's gazelle adult	9	} 11	8	} 10
Grant's gazelle fawn	2		2	
Warthog adult	2	} 4	2	} 4
Warthog juvenile	2		2	
Topi adult	1	} 2	1	} 2
Topi calf	1		1	
Ostrich chick	4	4	3	3
	115		100	

(1967). The hunting success of the dogs is high, but it is almost impossible to assess accurately because of the turmoil caused by a pack of dogs hunting as they switch from one quarry to another, often pursuing several at a time. They kill in the same way as hyenas (pl. 56), and when eating from the carcass there is less aggression among them than among any of the other carnivores—they are indeed remarkably peaceful. An interesting aspect of their group life is that young wild dogs have the right-of-way at a kill before they are fully grown; as soon as they arrive at a carcass killed by the adults, the adults withdraw, often after slight signs of aggression from the young ones. The adult dogs do not return to the carcass until the young ones have finished (Kühme 1965; personal observation).

Wild dogs operate virtually only in packs, which range in size from two to forty dogs (average 11.3 in 46 observations). Only three times did I see a dog on his own. There is some interchange between packs, but not very much; sometimes packs may split up (maybe during hunts). On the whole, however, wild dogs always stay extremely close together —whether sleeping or hunting, on the move or stationary in one area. Only when one or more females of a pack have pups does the mother (or any one of the other dogs) stay behind when the others hunt— this separation never lasts more than a few hours. All members of a pack feed the puppies (Kühme 1965), and all feed each other when not all members of the pack have been present at the kill (for instance, when adults stay behind at the den with pups, when part of the hunting pack gets lost, or when an individual in bad condition is unable to keep up with the chase). Thus, wild dogs are probably the most social feeding community of all carnivores. They are very dependent on each other for both hunting and killing (see page 276). There are very few observations of interaction between packs; what there is suggests that they merely avoid each other when they accidentally get close. They do not have a territory or a home range, but there again, they have never been observed in high densities (in the Serengeti, I estimated fewer than 0.01 per km^2). Within groups there is little evidence of a social hierarchy, but sometimes during a chase a certain order is maintained (Kruuk and Turner 1967).

Unlike wolves and hyenas, wild dogs are permanently social. Separation is almost invariably short and is usually associated with hunting; when the dogs meet again, they perform an elaborate behavior sequence. It is interesting to note that this meeting ceremony has probably evolved from the puppies' begging (Kühme 1965), and if one of the meeting dogs has fed, he will regurgitate. On the whole, the wild dogs' repertoire of communication is very simple indeed; there are very few (discrete) calls, and tail postures are little used. It is likely that in this species the extreme socialization has allowed a reduction in communicative behavior to take place—there may be less need for displays with animals who are closely packed together the whole time and in which any aggressive drive is extremely reduced.

These behavioral differences must be viewed against a background of the wild dog's exploitation of a narrow band of the food spectrum, which they can almost only do socially. They are very efficient at this, but obviously they would be less able to switch to other kinds of food in case of need, as, for instance, hyenas and wolves probably can (e.g., to scavenging). Evolution has made the wild dog into a social specialist par excellence.

Hunting and Social Behavior of Lions

Most of our knowledge of this social cat has been collected by Schaller in the Serengeti (personal communication), and a good summary of previous knowledge is presented by Guggisberg (1962). In the Serengeti, the species composition of the lion diet is very similar to that of the hyena, with the important exception that it includes very large ungulates (buffalo, giraffe). Furthermore, lions also scavenge a great deal. Lions select from each prey species in a way different from what we have seen so far; whereas hyenas and wolves catch the hindmost animal (and probably wild dogs do the same), lions appear to select according to criteria which are little known—often, it seems, randomly from a herd. Their hunting technique is vastly different from that of hyenas or canids, consisting of a short rush after a long stalk or from an ambush. Although they are often solitary hunters, lions frequently cooperate; this gives them access to their largest prey species (especially buffalo) and increases the hunting success for smaller prey like Thomson's gazelle. After a prey is caught with the claws, it is usually killed by suffocation or strangulation through a bite in the throat or around the muzzle. When more than one are eating from a kill, lions are very aggressive to each other over their food and often there is a great deal of growling and fighting. In lions, therefore, competition between pride members over food expresses itself in aggression rather than in fast eating, as occurs in wild dogs, wolves, or hyenas. Although lionesses do most of the killing, the male lions are often dominant at the kill and chase away the others if they get a chance; when there is competition over food between members of the pride, the cubs are usually the ones that suffer.

Lions live in prides of up to fifteen adults and often many cubs; they stay within a limited home range. Some individuals are nomadic, however, and unattached to a pride; in the Serengeti these make up about one-fifth of the lion population. The prides defend territories which have a large overlap between neighbors (Schenkel 1966). This overlap might well be smaller in areas of higher lion density than the Serengeti, where one has the impression of large overlapping home ranges with the occupants defending a small area immediately around wherever they happen to be. The territorial defense is largely left to the males, and it may well be that their spectacular sexual dimorphy is related to this.

Several females keep their litters together within one pride, and they may even suckle each other's offspring like the wild dogs. So, in contrast to their behavior over kills, in this aspect lions have gone further than hyenas and wolves in socializing.

Within the large pride territories, lions can be either solitary or in groups. They possess a vast repertoire of sounds with many calls grading into each other (sound continuum) and many different tail positions and facial expressions; but further evaluation is needed for comparison with solitary cats and other social carnivores.

Discussion

In this very brief comparison between some social carnivores, several interesting parallels have come up, and I think that many others would arise with further study. Three of the species (hyena, wolf, and lion) are not purely social, for they can lead a solitary existence as well, switching from one to the other. These species have very well-developed social signal systems, both visual and vocal; they are dependent on each other for hunting certain kinds of prey, but they can manage without help. The wild dog stands alone in that it is exclusively social with few social signals, less flexible in its foraging methods, and highly successful in its hunting, but very dependent on intraspecific cooperation. Wild dogs regurgitate food for other members of the pack, and pups have the right-of-way on a kill—contrary to what happens in the other species. This may be related to the absence of a territory in the wild dog; in the same vein, it is tempting to speculate that in wolves, lions, and hyenas, it is the juxtaposition of social and solitary tendencies in a hunting species that in evolution gave rise to some highly developed social communication patterns.

It is even more tempting to speculate at this point on the significance of such evolutionary trends for understanding the behavior of other hunting animals, especially man. I will not pretend that I can make here a direct contribution to the understanding of human behavior, but I think that the present study does indicate that a further analysis of carnivore behavior might be of great value for understanding the motivation and function of our own. It has been customary to compare human behavior with that of phylogenetically close species, the other primates. However important this comparison may be, it is also true that the organization of social hunting communities of different species may show great similarities independent of their systematic relationships, owing to convergent evolution. Primitive man is generally considered to have been a social, largely carnivorous species, and our present social behavior and organization has probably been derived from that of our primitive hunting ancestors. If we want to understand the biological basis and function of our own social organization, it may well be much more relevant to compare at least some of our behavior patterns with those of social carnivores like hyenas, wolves, or lions than with those of apes. This may be true for behavioral phenomena as different as meeting cremonies, appeasement, social hierarchy, dominance of one sex, defense of territory, flexibility of group structures, and so on. This point has been made earlier by Washburn and Avis (1958), Kortlandt (1965), and Schaller and Lowther (1969).

It will not be popular to compare human society with that of hyenas or wolves, but this is precisely a study that should be greatly worthwhile. Despite several recent attempts at elucidation (Lorenz 1966; Morris 1967), we still know little about the original biological function of the human territory and about factors which control territorial behavior. It would be worthwhile to try to obtain ideas from a species like the spotted hyena, in which the territorial behavior shows some remarkable parallels with that of man; it might even be possible to analyze several aspects of territory in this species experimentally. One could experiment, for instance, on the relation between territorial aggression and food supply, and on the effects on the hyena community of preventing interclan warfare. Similarly, our understanding of human meeting ceremonies might be increased by comparing them with the meeting ceremonies of social carnivores, not only with those of nonhuman primates. As there are obvious parallels between the human street "gangs" (Block and Niederhoffer 1958; Davis 1962) and some groupings of hyenas within the clans, further knowledge of the latter might lead to an understanding of the biological function of the former. The number of examples could be multiplied many times.

Of course this approach will be profitable only if carried beyond mere comparison. It is not difficult to list a number of analogies between hyenas' behavior and some aspects of human society: the organization in large groups, within which individuals may behave solitarily or very socially; the defense of a group territory with special "boundary" patrols marking the boundary; the hunting groups specializing in large or difficult prey and the individuals on their solitary foraging expeditions; sharing of food among the group; food storing; the aggregation of females and juveniles in a center within the territory, in which each female looks after her own offspring; the very elaborate greeting ceremonies. This list could, of course, be expanded, but it serves to make my point. It should not be left at this. If we were to understand the biological function and the behavioral mechanisms of these phenomena in hyenas, we might obtain some very useful clues in our quest for understanding the behavior of man.

8 The Antipredator Behavior of Gazelle, Wildebeest, and Zebra against Different Carnivores

I have argued that it may not be valid to compare the antipredator systems of several prey species against one predator if we do not also take into account many other aspects of the prey species' biology. We can, however, compare the reactions of one prey species to different predators, as I did previously for the responses of the black-headed gull to its various enemies (Kruuk 1964). In that case, I could show that where the responses to the bird's enemies are different, these differences are adapted to the ecological importance of the predators for the black-headed gull. In this section, I will present evidence to show that among ungulates, the antipredator system is similarly adaptive.

Of African ungulates, the reaction to predators is best known for the Thomson's gazelle, after the work of Walther (1969) and observations by several others. The Thomson's gazelle is preyed upon by more species of predator than any other ungulate I know here—I have seen tommy kills from lion, leopard, cheetah, hyena, wild dog, black-backed and golden jackal, baboon, martial eagle, lappet-faced vulture, and white-headed vulture. Of these, the baboon, martial eagle, and vultures only take an occasional young fawn (for vultures, see Kruuk 1967); but for all the carnivores, Thomson's gazelle constitutes a fairly important part of the diet in the Serengeti. Jackals take almost only fawns, hyenas take fawns and adults, and others mostly take adult gazelle (references to carnivore diet from Schaller 1968 and personal communication; Wyman 1967; Kruuk and Turner 1967). Cheetah and wild dogs are highly efficient and specialized gazelle catchers, whereas for lion gazelle is much less important, as it is for hyena.

Walther (1969) studied the fleeing response of Thomson's gazelle to jackals, hyenas, lions, cheetahs, and wild dogs, and found an increase in the fleeing distance in that sequence. If we relate this to the importance of adult gazelle in the diet of each of these carnivores and its hunting methods, this fleeing distance makes functional sense; the more dangerous a predator is, the larger the fleeing distance. Walther also found an increase in the fleeing distance of gazelle if more than one carnivore (hyena) were walking together. Also this is understandable from a functional point of view, with what we now know of the increase in hunting efficiency of several collaborating hyenas.

There are many indications that there is a large increase in fleeing distance of gazelle when the behavior of the predator to which they are responding indicates that hunting is likely; for wild dogs, for instance, gazelle flee at distances of up to 2 km when the dogs are hunting, but I have seen gazelle stay as close as 50 m when a pack in the middle of the day was merely walking and when even to me it was clear that they were not hunting and were showing no interest in any of the game around them. This same sort of observation has been made with regard to hyenas. This kind of phenomenon, of course, makes it very difficult to generalize and compare the reactions to predators, as Walther (1969) has done. When a lion is walking over the plain in full view of the gazelle, it is almost certain that he is not hunting, whereas wild dogs usually are on the lookout for prey when they walk like that. Thomson's gazelle react to very small differences in the predators' behavior, and this must be of vital importance for their survival. This, among other things, makes it impossible to experiment with gazelle and predator models, as I did with gulls.

The gazelle's reactions to predators are not confined to mere fleeing. Jackals are often viciously attacked by females defending their fawns; this behavior can be very effective when only one jackal is present, but if more than one cooperate, they usually get the better of the mother (confirmed by Wyman 1967). Seeing this behavior, it is strange that the female tommy should have virtually lost the use of her horns—they are only rudimentary or absent. One would think that the horns could be very useful for attacking jackals, and in the females of other Gazellinae, they are well developed (as they were in the tommy's ancestors; Gentry 1966). When hyenas chase tommy fawns, the mother does not show any overt aggression but displays only distraction behavior (p. 193). It may well be, as in birds (Simmons 1955; Brown 1962), that this distraction behavior is partly aggressively motivated but also shows underlying tendencies to flee. This would be a functionally well-adjusted response to hyenas, which often prey on adults as well as fawns, and against which overt aggression would most likely result in the death of the adult gazelle. No signs of aggression are apparent in the reaction of gazelle to any of the other carnivores.

Here I also want to mention that strange attraction of Thomson's gazelle to predators, apparently similar to what I called "exploration" in black-headed gulls, which Walther (1969) named "behavior of fascination." If a cheetah is walking over the plains, gazelle may come running up from several hundred meters away and stop and stare from 50–80 m away when the cheetah is walking slowly, and slightly farther away when it is going fast. Behind the walking predator, the tommies may follow for distances of 100 m and more; all the gazelle have their ears cocked and heads up and are looking at the cheetah, occasionally uttering an alarm snort. Often many gazelle walk very close together— apparently one of the effects of the presence of a cheetah is the expression of this social tendency. It is clear from this behavior that a potential prey species can be very strongly attracted to a predator. In gazelle one sees this behavior most clearly in response to cheetahs and leopards and to a single wild dog (though very rarely to a pack, pl. 57); it is less striking in reaction to lions, and one hardly ever sees it in response to hyenas or jackals. With the exception of the pack-hunting wild dog, the predators evoking most exploration are also the ones that cause the greatest fleeing distance and which are the most dangerous to the gazelle. It is interesting to note that in the white rat exploratory behavior is probably motivated by fear, but is suppressed when the amount of fear evoked is very great (summary in Halliday 1966). If this is also true for this behavior in gazelle, it may explain the lack of exploration in responses to hyena, the very high attraction to a cheetah, and its absence in reaction to a pack of wild dogs. With modifications for the different kinds of carnivores, the same exploratory behavior can be observed in almost all other ungulates in the Serengeti.

What can be the function of this striking phenomenon? On one occasion, I saw a cheetah make a rush toward a "curious crowd" of gazelle and take one of the females from the back of the herd—in fact the individual that first started running when the cheetah slightly changed its gait (a similar observation was made by Walther 1969). Once a cheetah grabbed a wildebeest calf under similar circumstances. These are only very few observations, but they do show that there is danger in this exploration; they would make one expect that these disadvantages are outweighed by some important selective advantage. I can think of only two possible functions: the prey keeps an eye on the danger (for as long as it can be seen, the chances of a stalking predator are slim), or the gazelle are somehow learning and gaining experience of the appearance and behavior of their foes. The second possibility is rather remote, but it has been shown that learning can play an important role in the antipredator behavior of birds (Kramer and von St. Paul 1951). Possibly both functions are important; the first may well be the more prominent.

Summarizing these few aspects of the Thomson's gazelle antipredator behavior, there appear to be clear variations in the species' responses to different predators, probably related to their importance to the gazelle and, apparently, well adapted to the needs.

When a lion or cheetah walks through a herd of wildebeest, the empty circle around the predator is far larger than when a hyena does so. The wildebeest also show many more indications of curiosity about these cats: they may follow them for 100 m or more with their heads up, occasionally snorting. Thus, both the avoidance distance and the curiosity are greater than with hyenas. There are differences between the reactions to the cats: for lions, wildebeest flee at a considerably larger distance than for cheetahs (the median radius of the "empty circle" around a lion is 40 to 50 m, around a cheetah 20 to 30 m, pl. 58). This is different for wildebeest with small calves, who flee at much larger distances for both predators. At this point we should recall that adult wildebeest occur only sporadically in the cheetah diet (but calves frequently), whereas they are the most important single item in the diet of lions.

Wild dogs do not often attack adult wildebeest, and if they do, they are obviously very ill-equipped for handling such large prey (their teeth and jaws are probably not strong enough to easily cut through the skin). Adult wildebeest are largely outside the wild dogs' normal range of prey species. If a pack walks in a quiet trot through wildebeest herds, the ungulates will keep some 20–30 m away from them. Wildebeest bulls on their territory, however, often let wild dogs come as close as 3 m and may even occasionally charge them. But if wild dogs have been hunting adult wildebeest in the area, as they occasionally do, one may observe an enormous increase in the fleeing distance, up to 200 m. Wild dogs, as well as the large cats, release a great deal of "curiosity" (pls. 55 and 58), and they may be followed for more than 100 m by the wildebeest, who keep closely bunched up.

One very rarely sees any aggressive behavior of wildebeest in self-defense against any of the predators; only occasionally a bull on his territory may briefly chase a hyena or wild dog. Once a pack of wild dogs cornered a small herd of wildebeest against a small deep arm of a watercourse; the wildebeest then turned and faced the dogs, and several ran out a few meters to charge them. Immediately afterward, the wilde-beest turned and fled through the water. Also, once a wildebeest cow, who had been caught by hyenas, charged a male lion who had chased off the hyenas to take over their prey; she did not hit the lion, however, and he killed her almost immediately. Only when cows defend their calves against hyenas can we regularly see aggression (p. 170), but this re-sponse is much less frequent to wild dogs that are chasing calves. This may be partly related to the way wild dogs hunt wildebeest calves; they chase a densely bunched wildebeest herd and take any calf that lags behind. The mother may not even notice that it is killed, and if she does the greater tendency of wildebeest to flee from a pack of wild dogs than from a single hyena would probably prevent actual attack. This is probably adaptive too, for attacks would have very little affect on a large pack of wild dogs; I once saw a wildebeest cow defend her calf against a pack of twenty-one wild dogs, and she was killed in the process. A similar observation was reported by Cullen (1969).

Thus, although on the whole the responses of wildebeest to lions, cheetahs, and wild dogs seem well adapted to the ecological significance of the predators, there are a few apparent anomalies that warrant further discussion. The first is the lack of aggression of adult wildebeest in self-defense; to a human observer it is pathetic that an animal lets itself be torn apart without making any active attempt to do anything. Although these same carnivores under other circumstances may sometimes be objects of aggression, nothing is done about them when they are actually attacking a victim, although an adult wildebeest could be a formidable opponent. The explanation could be that the animal is in a state of physiological shock; however, species like buffalo are known to put up a very good fight when confronted by a pride of lions, as do moose when harassed by wolves (Mech 1966). I cannot think of a functional explana-tion; it seems strange that the subtle adaptiveness of a species' behavior would break down just when it is most needed. Another apparent anomaly of wildebeest antipredator behavior is the strikingly small reaction distance to hyenas. Whereas with the other three carnivores discussed this reaction distance is well adapted to the importance of wildebeest in their diets, it seems that this should not be so with hyenas; although adult wildebeest are the most important single item in their diet, wildebeest go only a few meters out of the way for them. This phenomenon has in fact encouraged the public view of the hyena as a scavenger: the argument is that because the wildebeest have so little fear of the hyenas, hyenas cannot be dangerous to them. I think that an explanation must be sought in the hunting methods of hyenas and their local abundance. They are the most common of all carnivores, and they often walk about without any hunting intentions; if wildebeest avoided every hyena at a large distance, this might seriously infringe on their grazing time. Moreover, it is usually evident from the hyena's behavior whether they are hunting or not (posture, speed of movements, grouping); if they are, they are not likely to throw themselves on the nearest wildebeest, as do some of the other carnivores, but they select, often after a great deal of running through herds. It is clear that the hyena hunting methods and the responses of the wildebeest are finely adjusted to one another; in other words, hyenas would have to hunt quite differently if wildebeest responded to them as they do to the other carnivores, and for best survival wildebeest would have to respond differently to hyenas if the latter's behavior were substantially different.

Zebra come high on the list of preferred prey species of lions, but are very rarely taken by cheetahs (Mitchell, Shenton and Uys 1965; Graham 1966; Schaller 1968; Pienaar 1969). Also, wild dogs usually have no interest in zebra, although in 1967 one pack in the Serengeti hunted zebra consistently for several weeks (Schaller, personal communication), and Cullen (1969) also mentions wild dogs killing zebra. On the whole, zebra are unimportant in the diet of wild dogs.

Against this background, it is interesting to see that when a predator is walking quietly over the plain, the zebra keep on the average about 50 m away from a lion, about 20–30 m from a cheetah, and about the same distance from wild dogs; single hyenas can come within 10 m. These distances appear very similar to those I found for wildebeest, and this impression is confirmed when observing mixed herds of wildebeest and zebra with a predator walking through them. But although wildebeest and zebra on the whole keep the same distance, wildebeest give an impression of greater nervousness: they seem to be more curiously attracted than zebra but also more afraid, and often a great deal of darting backward and forward goes on among the wildebeest, whereas the zebra may merely stand and stare at the passing carnivore, maybe moving forward just a few steps. Lions and cheetahs as well as wild dogs release some curiosity from zebra, but I have not been able to compare the differences in this response to the different carnivores.

When wild dogs are actually harassing zebra, they may meet with some aggression—very similar to that in zebra reactions to hyenas—

but it is less common during wild-dog attacks. Once a zebra is grabbed by any predator it shows little aggression.

Zebra also show a strikingly low fleeing distance for hyenas compared with that in reaction to other carnivores; the functional aspects of this have already been discussed for the hyena relations to wildebeest.

Generally, when one compares the reactions of a prey species to several of its predators, it is clear that these responses are well adapted, although a few aspects are not yet understood. The observations suggest that in order to understand the function of the various components of the behavior of a species in response to its predators, this behavior must be related not only to the diet and prey selection of the predator, but also to the hunting methods employed. If one does this, the reactions of gazelle, wildebeest, and zebra to hyenas are not as strange as they might appear at first.

Although interspecies comparisons of only the immediate antipredator responses are not justified, as I argued on p. 207, it is interesting that at least some differences between prey species in their reactions to the same predator are obviously adaptive. For instance, it is striking to see how much greater is the fleeing distance of gazelle in response to wild dogs than that of wildebeest and zebra for the same predator; this coincides with the dogs' preference for gazelle.

Many reactions to African carnivores which I observed have also been recorded from ungulates in response to predators in temperate climates. Wildebeest often seek refuge in water when pursued by hyenas, and so do impala when chased by wild dogs (Stevenson-Hamilton 1947; Cullen 1969). Moose and elk do the same in response to wolves (Cowan 1947). In the Ngorongoro Crater I noticed that wild dogs are able to approach much closer to Thomson's and Grant's gazelle when the gazelle are on a slope and the predators are approaching from below (in full view of the prey) than when they meet on an open plain, or when the carnivores are above on a slope; Murie (1944) noticed the same in the reactions of Dall sheep to wolves. The aerial pictures of the reactions of a herd of caribou to hunting wolves published by Banfield (1951c) show a striking similarity to what I have often observed with wildebeest in response to hyenas. Mech (1966) notes his impression that moose do not flee as fast as they possibly could when pursued by wolves; I made the same observation again and again when watching hyenas chase wildebeest and zebra or gazelle. There must be many more such behavioral analogies in other predator-prey interactions.

The herbivores (wildebeest, zebra, and gazelle) and birds (gulls) that I studied have many basic "elements" in common in their antipredator behavior. These are elements such as fleeing, aggression, exploration, intraspecific attraction, and probably others which are combined in a species-specific way into predator-specific responses. But as shown above, the similarities in species' reactions to their enemies may go even further, even as far as small details in orientation. Further studies of such analogous or homologous details, and of differences between reactions, would give a deeper insight into predators' selection pressures in general, and the limitations of the prey species' response to this.

9 Predators and Management

Here in Africa, as almost everywhere else in the world, carnivores have been immensely unpopular and until recently were all considered vermin, to be exterminated wherever possible (see, e.g., Stevenson-Hamilton 1947; Pienaar 1969). To some extent this aggressive attitude toward carnivores must find its biological origin in the fact that man and carnivores are competitors for the same food supply; also, in other species of animals there are indications that interspecific aggression is greater in species with a large overlap in food selection (e.g., in vultures; Kruuk 1967). However, whatever the cause of our aversion to the wild cats, dogs, and others, in the last decades a change has set in, and a conservationist feeling is being superimposed on the kill-the-wolf instinct. In East Africa, especially the cheetah, leopard, and lion have benefited from this new protection; the cheetah is now completely protected even against licensed shooting, and many measures are being taken to stop the illicit killing of leopards. All three cats are considered prize possessions of any national park.

The large cats, of course, have always had a special appeal to man, as evidenced, for instance, in heraldry. But other species, like various dogs and hyenas, did not even have this aura of "strength" and "courage" to offset the revulsion of man against them, and these are the species which even now are persecuted in many areas. As late as 1958, *Oryx*, the journal of the Fauna Preservation Society, published a note about the shooting of wild dogs to protect ungulates in a game-reserve (Attwell 1958), and both wild dogs and hyenas are even now shot on sight in several game-controlled areas in East Africa. Although these species are now protected at least in national parks, hyenas had been shot in the Serengeti and other national parks until just before my arrival there, and current sentiments among park wardens are still running against them. Of course, this phenomenon is not confined to Africa; the wolf in northern latitudes is probably loathed just as much as the hyena here (e.g., Callison 1948), and serious attempts are still being made to "control" (that is exterminate) it in Russia by shooting large numbers from airplanes (Makridin 1962).

In chapter 1, I indicated the aims of management in the areas in which I studied hyenas. Both in the Serengeti National Park and the Ngorongoro Crater, carnivores are important for management from two points of view. First, most tourists visiting these areas are more interested in the big cats, especially lions, than in other species. The thrill of meeting a pride of lions or seeing a cheetah hunt is for the average visitor the main reason for coming to the Serengeti; this in itself is ample justification for park management to ensure that healthy populations of these species are maintained.

The second aspect of the interest of management in carnivores is the interaction between carnivores and populations of ungulates. As far as hyenas are concerned, I have argued that in the Serengeti hyenas have only a small effect on the ungulate population, whereas their own numbers are probably determined by their (ungulate) food supply at a critical time of the year. The numbers of ungulates are limited by something else; not by hyenas nor probably by any other carnivore; most likely, the food supply in the dry season plays an important role. Thus, if numbers of hyenas were to be artificially reduced in the Serengeti, this would have little appreciable affect on the ungulate populations. Conversely, if ecological or political considerations were to make a reduction of ungulate numbers necessary, even down to as few as, say, one-quarter of their present level, indications are that this would have little effect on the number of hyenas. The study also suggests (in the comparison between the Serengeti and Ngorongoro) that even if we artificially increased the hyena population in the Serengeti, for instance by feeding during the critical time of the year, as much as a tenfold increase in hyena numbers would still have little effect on the wildebeest and zebra numbers, although it would affect their population structure. If, in the Serengeti, the migratory movements of wildebeest and zebra have indeed the suggested effect of suppressing the hyena population size by causing an irregular food supply, it follows that any management action in this area which creates resident ungulate populations (for instance, putting in dams) would have the indirect consequence of increasing the Serengeti hyena population up to a level dependent on the numbers of resident ungulates.

In Ngorongoro, predator-prey relations are entirely different—there we are dealing with resident animals, and ungulate and predator populations mutually affect each other at the level that is probably determined by the ungulates' food supply (i.e., range conditions). Most likely, the effect of a sizable reduction in the hyena population in the Ngorongoro Crater would be an immediate increase in the number of wildebeest and zebra until another source of mortality would take over (most likely related to deterioration of range). If this were starvation or disease, the result of removing hyenas would probably be much greater fluctuation in ungulate numbers instead of the fairly stable situation that we have now. It is likely that this is what occurred in several areas of North America when large carnivores were shot and great fluctuations in deer populations were observed (Longhurst, Leopold, and Dasmann 1952). Mech (1966) suggested that on Isle Royale, in Lake Superior, the numbers of wolves and moose struck a balance determined by the food supply of the moose, a situation very similar to what I think exists in the Ngorongoro Crater. Removal of predators does not need to have the effect of large fluctuations of ungulate populations, if predation is taken over by man, as in the exploitation of saiga antelope in Kazakhstan (Bannikov 1961). An artificial reduction in the number of ungulates which are at present grazing in the Ngorongoro Crater would most likely be followed by a fairly rapid adjustment of the number of hyenas, possibly after some fluctuation depending on the size of the reduction. This adjustment of the number of carnivores might be expedited by carefully controlled human interference.

Both the Serengeti National Park and the Ngorongoro Crater have a vested interest in lions, and the feeding interactions between lions and hyenas as I described them make it possible that lions would be affected if hyenas were artificially controlled. In the Serengeti, the immediate contact between the two species is fairly limited, and the effect of management of one species upon the other would accordingly be small. In Ngorongoro Crater, lions obtained most of their food from hyenas and would have to hunt for themselves to a greater extent if hyenas were cropped. It is possible that if lions found it less easy than at present to obtain their prey, this would ultimately be expressed in their numbers. My observations on interactions between hyenas and cheetahs, leopards, and wild dogs make it clear that the food supply of none of these tourist attractions is seriously affected by the presence or absence of hyenas, and vice versa (chapter 5). Hyenas may occasionally kill a small cub or pup, but there is no evidence to suggest that this would affect the numbers of any of these other carnivores.

One of the important aspects of hyena predation is the way it interacts with other sources of mortality; if hyenas can eat animals that have died from other causes they prefer to do so, but if no such mortality factors are present, hyenas kill for themselves. If they kill for themselves, they take the weakest first. This phenomenon is bound to have a damping affect on any fluctuations that might occur in ungulate populations owing to other causes of mortality, and it is another way hyenas contribute to stabilizing the interaction between ungulates and their environment.

As far as the ecological importance of predators other than lions and hyenas in the Serengeti and Ngorongoro is concerned, we are still largely left in the dark. It is clear that the leopard, cheetah, and wild dog occur only in small numbers, which at least superficially appear rather stable; I have no suggestion about what keeps them at such a low density in the face of large numbers of prey, apparently the whole year around. It is unlikely that they have a sizable effect on the populations of common ungulates, but it has been suggested that less common prey is more appreciably affected (e.g., reedbuck by leopard; Kruuk and Turner 1967). Lions are much more abundant, but their effect on the migratory prey populations, although in the Serengeti greater than that of hyenas, is probably small (Schaller, personal communication). At least in some areas of the Serengeti, lion numbers may well be controlled by food supply during a critical time of the year.

A number of generalizations can be made for the purpose of management in other areas, based on the conclusions reached in this study. First of all, and most important, it is clear that predator-prey relations can be vastly different in different areas. It follows that wherever a management policy with regard to predators is laid down, a study should be made on the spot—extrapolation of results from one region to another is possible only with the greatest caution. If numerical relations between predators and prey species are such that the former are likely to have a substantial effect on the latter, they will probably stabilize the balance between herbivores and range. And at the same time, numbers of carnivores may well be affected by numbers of herbivores, as indicated in Ngorongoro. This kind of relationship is most likely to occur in nonmigratory game populations; in truly migratory ones (as in the Serengeti) carnivores probably have only a minimal effect on herbivores, at least on the common species among them.

It seems clear that for most wildlife areas in East Africa—whether game-controlled area, national park, or otherwise—a policy of non-interference with the population of hyenas and other carnivores is ecologically sound. I hope, however, that this book has also contributed by showing that the hyena is worthy of protection on its own merits. Not only is the species useful as a stabilizing factor in the management of communities of herbivores and other species of carnivores such as the big cats, but the hyena itself is a fascinating animal. Further study may teach us a great deal more about the evolution of behavior of carnivores and of ourselves, and about the selection pressures exerted by hyenas on the ungulates. Last, apart from being of scientific interest, hyenas are fun to watch; it is as exciting to see them hunt as it is to watch any other carnivore, and it is delightful to see the cubs playing on their den. I, for one, have no doubt that hyenas are assets rather than liabilities.

APPENDIXES

A. Capturing Procedure

For various purposes, a total of 265 hyenas were captured during the present study, 53 in the Ngorongoro Crater and the remainder in the Serengeti. Each hyena was administered a dose of 22–24 mg succinylcholine chloride powder dissolved in water. A dart with a barbed needle containing the drug was fired from a Palmer Cap-chur gun (a CO_2-powered rifle); on impact with the animal, a plunger inside the dart, pushed forward by an explosive charge, caused the drug to be injected (Klingel 1968). I used the gun from the Land Rover while standing still, if the animal allowed me to come close enough, or I fired the dart while driving alongside the running animals at speeds of up to 50 kmph. The first method was always preferable, and all the hyenas in Ngorongoro were treated this way; in the Serengeti the animals were much more apprehensive and the second method usually had to be employed.

After a hyena was hit it usually ran away, then tried to bite at the dart and dislodge it. This biting almost invariably destroyed the dart, or the hyena dropped it in flight so it could not be found again. Since these darts are expensive, I tried to prevent this biting by either placing the dart in the upper neck or by keeping the animal on the move after it had been hit. After 3 to 6 min, the hyena would collapse and could be handled, though a small number of animals did not go down at all. Some individuals, usually heavier, were still well able to move and bite after going down and had to be forcibly restrained. They were then able to run off almost immediately after being marked, aged, and so on, whereas others might be unable to move for periods of over an hour, although usually it was 15–30 min.

After having darted some 255 hyenas without any fatalities in 1965 and 1966, it came as a most unpleasant surprise in April 1967 when three hyenas died of an overdose and one could barely be rescued by artificial respiration. These hyenas were darted during the height of the rains, whereas the others had been captured during fairly dry weather; after checking on all the causes I could think of for these sudden failures (procedural mistakes, drug action, and so on), it seemed most likely that the different season caused a lowering of the resistance against succinylcholine chloride. It was found that at that time a dose of 15 mg had the same effect as 22–24 mg during the dry season.

B. Number of Hyenas in Ngorongoro

During the study period, I spent sixteen observation periods of up to four weeks in Ngorongoro. For nine of these periods, I obtained a figure for the hyena population in each of the clan ranges (described on p. 39) by establishing the proportion of marked hyenas in every area as observed over the whole of that observation period

299

and comparing this with the number of marked hyenas I assumed to be present there at the time. The proportion of marked hyenas was assessed by noting every hyena I came across and whether it was marked or not. The figures total observations of marked hyenas/total observations of marked + unmarked for each period included a number of repeat observations of the same marked animals, but it was assumed that the proportion of repeat observations of marked animals would be the same as the proportion of repeat observations for unmarked ones. These figures are presented in appendix D. 1. It was also assumed that marked and unmarked hyenas mixed randomly within the clan areas (and there are many observations to suggest that this is indeed so), and finally, that there was little or no immigration or emigration (see p. 32).

Usually a marked hyena stayed within the same clan range (p. 39), but changes did sometimes occur. To establish whether a hyena that was not seen during an observation period had, in fact, been present there, it was assumed that if it had been seen in the same area during any previous and following observation periods it had also been there during the period concerned. If it had been seen in area *a* during the previous period, nowhere during the period concerned, and in area *b* during the next one, it was assumed to have changed areas halfway between the two observations if the shift was permanent or semipermanent. But if the animal's presence in area *b* appeared to be merely a short visit, it was assumed to have resided in area *a*, and so on. If a marked hyena was not seen for five or more consecutive observation periods, it was assumed to be dead (see p. 31); in that case, death was supposed to have occurred immediately after the last observation period, and it was removed from the list of contributors to the Lincoln index for the following periods.

Because of the small number of marked animals involved, the estimates of numbers of hyenas present in a clan range during a certain period fluctuate widely; this may have obscured any long-term trend. But the figures do not show any considerable increase or decrease of hyena numbers over the study period, and for the purpose of overall assessment, numbers were assumed to be stable.

In this way, estimates could be made of the population of six groups in the crater, which were always present in their areas in sufficient numbers. The uncertainty is relatively high, however, and it may be good to consider these figures together with direct observations on numbers which may provide another estimate (appendix D. 1). Generally speaking, the maximum number of hyenas observed at any one time (always on a kill) will provide a good indication of the number of hyenas in the clan range if this is a relatively small area, and a minimum figure if this range is large. Thus, on the small range of the Scratching Rocks clan, the calculated number present is only slightly higher than the largest number seen together, whereas in the comparatively vast Airstrip clan range, the difference is much greater. Taking this into account, we may arrive at a final estimate of 350 hyenas in the "fixed clans"; the very temporary "Northern clan" obviously consisted of hyenas drawn from other clans (see p. 42), and the "Hippo clan," which developed during the study from a small group into a full-sized clan, must have included approximately 35 members. In this way, we concluded that about 385 adult hyenas inhabit the crater floor.

If, during every observation period, the proportion of marked to unmarked hyenas is established regardless of the places of marking and resighting (ignoring the clan system), estimates of the total population are arrived at which do not differ much from the more elaborate method described above (appendix D. 1, bottom). Thus, although the conditions for the application of the Lincoln index are presumably not really met in this way, the results confirm the previous figures.

The number of young and immature animals will have to be added here; this is considerable but is extremely difficult to assess. Cubs of different ages spend much time underground—when very young, they may be in the den for days at a time, although adults never do this. Also, the likelihood of their being seen at a kill, for instance, varies with age and is obviously very different from the probability of an adult's being present. All this makes it difficult to assess the ratio of young to adult hyenas, whereas at the same time it is also difficult to count the absolute number of young present in a range at any one time. Hence the figures in appendix D. 2 offer no more than maximum numbers observed in various clans with an estimate of the approximate numbers of immatures present during the whole study. For further calculations, it is assumed that half the number of immatures take part in kills, as they start eating meat regularly when they are eight to ten months old, approximately halfway through their youth.

C. NUMBER OF HYENAS IN THE SERENGETI

Hyenas in the Serengeti do not remain permanently in one small area, as in Ngorongoro, but roam over vast distances. They have a strong tendency to return to the same areas, however (p. 52), and there is by no means "random mixing" as is required for the use of the Lincoln index. I was myself more likely to visit certain areas than others, and if proportionally more hyenas had been marked there, this would affect my calculations if I used the simple Lincoln index method. To overcome these difficulties, I have split the whole area arbitrarily into a number of smaller regions (fig. 11); on the advice of Dr. J. M. Cullen of Oxford I then used the following formula:

$$P_a = m_a \times O_a/r_a$$

in which

$$O_a = (H_{aa}/s_a) L_a + (H_{ab}/s_b) L_b + (H_{ac}/s_c) L_c + \cdots$$

P_a = population of area a at time of marking
m_a = number of hyenas marked in area a
r_a = total number of resightings in the Serengeti of hyenas marked in area a
H_{ab} = number of resightings in area b of hyenas marked in area a
s_a = total number of all marked hyenas seen in area a
L_a = total number of hyenas seen in area a

The population of the Serengeti is the sum of the populations in the smaller regions; a large part of the area is covered by the movements of the marked hyenas and can therefore be included in the population calculations. But in other areas, I never saw any of the marked ones; for those, numbers will have to be assessed differently.

All together, hyenas were marked in ten different "regions," and resighted in nineteen. To obtain different estimates of the same population, I divided up the resightings into wet-season and dry-season observations (because the hyenas' distribution during these two seasons is so very different, p. 45). In appendix D. 3, I have presented the calculated populations of the various marking regions based on resightings in wet and dry seasons, and the average of these two estimates. The total population has been estimated in this way as 1,917 adult hyenas. It is interesting to note that if, instead of the above formula, the simple Lincoln index were used for dry- and wet-season observations, the estimates would have been 1,999 hyenas based on dry-season resightings and 2,117 hyenas based on wet-season resightings (average 2,058). If the resightings are not separated for different seasons, the estimate is 2,016; the differences are obviously small.

Whereas in Ngorongoro it was possible to account for mortality among marked hyenas, and movements in and out of the crater can justifiably be ignored in calculating the total population, this was not possible in the Serengeti. There I was unable to keep track of individuals, and the only check I had was on a change in marked percentages. This was small (5.3% and 5.0% between seasons, table 1), and for the present purpose I have ignored it, especially because the estimates for other areas in the Serengeti which are to be added to the one for the "Lincoln index area" are so much more crude. The estimated 2,058 hyenas are distributed in the wet season over an area of approximately 12,000 km² (the wildebeest wet-season range; Watson 1967), an average density of 0.17 adult hyenas per km².

The area covered by the marked hyena population is approximately one-third of the Serengeti ecosystem (the area covered by the migrating herbivores). There is no doubt, however, that the number of hyenas there is far greater than one-third of the total number of hyenas in the ecosystem, especially during the rains. Then there are, of course, hyenas all over the area, but in the woodlands they are very sparse (p. 21). Apart from the Serengeti plains proper, it is only on the larger plains in the west of the national park that they can be met in any numbers. They are extremely difficult to estimate, however, and it is only with a knowledge of hyena density in the Serengeti plains that one might hazard a guess about densities elsewhere. In this way, I came to the conclusion that the hyena density in the rest of the Serengeti must be far less than one-quarter of the hyena density during the rainy season in the area covered by the marked animals. Taking this into account, and the approximate 10% for meat-eating young ones (as in Ngorongoro), it seems likely that 3,000 is an overestimate of the meat-eating hyena population in the whole ecosystem. For further calculations (p. 80), I have maintained this estimate, because for the comparison of predation in Ngorongoro and the Serengeti, an overestimate is a conservative one.

D. SUPPLEMENTARY TABLES

D. 1

Estimated numbers of adult hyenas in Ngorongoro clans

Observation period / Clan	March–April 1965	June 1965	August–September 1965	December–January 1965–66	February 1966
Scratching Rocks	53.0 (53; 15)	58.0 (95; 11)	52.8 (66; 12)	43.6 (69; 12)	85.3 (105; 13)
Mungi	29.6 (37; 4)	88.0 (88; 4)	50.0 (25: 4)	76.0 (38; 4)	74.6 (56; 4)
Lakeside	51.2 (103; 3)	48.5 (109; 4)	27.1 (61; 4)	49.7 (87; 4)	37.0 (37; 3)
Oldonyo Rumbe	45.6 (58; 11)	66.9 (117; 12)	36.0 (32; 9)	44.0 (44; 9)	164.0 (36; 9)
Hippo	— (14; 0)	— (23; 0)	— (0; 0)	— (0; 0)	— (23; 0)
Lerai	25.2 (21; 6)	24.3 (34; 5)	33.2 (73; 5)	34.4 (43; 4)	22.0 (11; 4)
Airstrip	85.4 (64; 8)	122.9 (86; 10)	75.0 (60; 10)	60.8 (79; 10)	72.0 (64; 9)
North	— (0; 0)	— (0; 0)	— (0; 0)	— (0; 0)	— (13; 0)
Total	322.3 (350; 47)	384.7 (552; 46)	263.1 (317; 44)	281.5 (360; 43)	426.1 (345; 42)

NOTE: Total number of hyenas observed and the number of marked animals supposed to be present are given in parentheses.

D. 2

Numbers of young hyenas in the Ngorongoro Crater

Clan	Maximum no. observed	Estimated mean no. present in study period	Ratio adult/ juvenile
Scratching Rocks	14	15	4.1/1
Mungi	9	10	5.9/1
Lakeside	11	12	4.2/1
Oldonyo Rumbe	16	16	4.1/1
Hippo	6	8	4.4/1
Lerai	6	8	4.4/1
Airstrip	20	15	5.3/1
Total	82	84	4.6/1

D. 1 (*continued*)

March– April 1966	January– February 1967	September 1967	November– December 1967	Mean	Maximum number observed together	Corrected estimate
78.6 (103; 13)	65.0 (65; 13)	51.7 (219; 13)	64.2 (89; 13)	61.4	52	61.4
58.5 (117; 5)	— (6; 2)	44.4 (177; 2)	16.8 (42; 2)	58.6	45	58.6
57.8 (77; 3)	60.0 (40; 3)	45.3 (182; 2)	43.6 (109; 2)	47.0	50	50.0
53.4 (60; 8)	34.3 (40; 6)	61.9 (99; 5)	— (20; 5)	64.7	44	64.7
— (0; 0)	— (0; 1)	— (5; 3)	66.7 (89; 3)	—	35	35.0
22.5 (15; 3)	— (0; 3)	36.0 (60; 3)	— (6; 3)	25.9	35	35.0
56.2 (16; 7)	72.5 (29; 5)	98.1 (147; 6)	— (0; 6)	80.4	37	80.4
— (24; 0)	— (0; 1)	— (0; 1)	— (0; 1)	—	(23)	—
				338.0		385.1
365.0 (412; 39)	255.1 (180; 34)	334.6 (889; 35)	388.4 (355; 35)	335.7		

D. 3

Number of resightings of marked hyenas in the Serengeti

Marking area	3		4		5		8		10		13	
No. of hyenas marked (total 200)	19		12		32		16		18		14	
Recovery season:	Dry	Wet	Dry	Wet	Dry	Wet	Dry	Wet	Dry	Wet	Dry	Wet
Recovery area												
1	6	1	2		9	12	10	1	4	12		
2									1			
3	4	5					1		1	5		
4	1	3		5	1	13						1
5		1			2	3		1				
6		4							1			
7		1				2		2				
8				1				1		5		1
9		1				2		1	1	5		
10	1				2	2	8	5	16	13		
11												
12		1										2
13		1				6		1	1	4	5	15
14						2		7		2		
15						1				3		
16		1				2				5		
17												
18	2								3			
19									3			
20–21–22												
Total resightings	14	19	2	6	14	45	19	19	31	54	5	19
Population estimate:												
Dry season	209.5		136.5		311.1		132.6		173.4		56.0	
Wet season	233.4		91.0		285.0		163.0		180.0		145.7	

NOTE: For area references see figure 11.

| 14/16 | | 15 | | 17 | | 18 | | Total resightings | | | Total no. of hyenas observed | | |
| 14 | | 21 | | 26 | | 28 | | | | | | | |
Dry	Wet	Dry	Wet	Dry	Wet	Dry	Wet	Dry	Wet	Dry+Wet	Dry	Wet	Dry+Wet
	2		1	2		12	7	45	46	91	517	399	916
								1	—	1	30	13	43
1							1	7	11	18	103	302	405
								2	22	24	22	171	193
						1		3	5	8	22	52	74
					2		5	1	11	12	13	70	83
							1	—	6	6	—	66	66
							1	—	10	10	—	67	67
	2						5	1	16	17	8	103	111
	3			1	2	6	5	34	30	64	119	173	292
	1				1			—	2	2	126	114	240
							1	—	4	4	—	99	99
1	5				1		5	7	38	45	28	339	367
	1				1		3	—	16	16	—	232	232
			43		3		1	—	52	52	6	470	476
	3		2				5	—	19	19	—	251	251
			1		4			—	5	5	2	84	86
		4	1			36	4	45	5	50	280	43	323
								3	—	3	108	—	108
								—	—	—	105	107	212
2	17	4	48	3	14	55	44	149	298	447	1,489	3,155	4,644

131.1		130.8		247.6		205.8		1,734.4 Total dry season					
167.3		196.5		369.6		267.9		2,099.4 Total wet season					

D. 4

*Estimated month of birth of cubs less than ten months old,
in the Serengeti and the Ngorongoro Crater*

Month	Ngorongoro (No. of cubs)	Serengeti (No. of cubs)	Total
January	6	15	21
February	11	15	26
March	8	20	28
April	11	15	26
May	10	19	29
June	7	13	20
July	6	17	23
August	8	17	25
September	1	17	18
October	6	13	19
November	6	9	15
December	0	12	12
	80	182	262

D. 5

Age-class distribution of hyenas, alive and dead

	Ngorongoro				
Age-class	Population composition		Marked animals died		% dead/% alive
	Number	Percentage	Number	Percentage	
II	14	29	5	33	1.16
III	16	33	5	33	1.04
IV	16	33	4	27	0.81
V	3	6	1	7	1.09
Total	49	101%	15	100%	

	Serengeti				
Age-class	Population composition		Skulls collected		% dead/% alive
	Number	Percentage	Number	Percentage	
II	30	16	16	26	1.64
III	45	24	8	13	0.54
IV	82	44	27	44	1.01
V	30	16	10	16	1.02
Total	187	100%	61	99%	

D. 6

*Presence/absence of hyenas and ungulates in sample areas on the short-grass
Serengeti plains, wet season*

		Wildebeest		Zebra		Gazelle		Total
		+	−	+	−	+	−	
Hyena	+	54	13	42	25	61	6	67
	−	19	62	46	35	77	4	81
Wildebeest	+			56	18	68	6	74
	−			32	42	70	4	74
Zebra	+					84	3	87
	−					54	7	61
		73	75	88	60	138	10	444

NOTE: See also table 9.

D. 7

Description of age-class characteristics of prey species
(dental characteristics of lower jaw)

Age-class	Wildebeest	Thomson's gazelle
Pre-I	Up to 12 months, characterized by size and horns. (Watson 1967)	New born. Up to eruption of M_1.
I	12–36 months old; characterized by size and horns. From eruption of M_2 up to presence of all permanent teeth.	M_1 present, eruption of M_2 and M_3. Deciduous PM_4 still present.
II	Inf. of PM_3 and PM_4 open. Table surface of inc. 2 × (or more) as long as wide.	Only permanent teeth present. Posterior inf. of PM_3 large, open or closed. Anterior inf. of M_1 present or just worn off, posterior inf. of M_1 present.
III	Inf. of PM_4 closed, anterior inf. of M_1 is U-shaped. Table surface of inc. 2 × (or more) as long as wide.	Posterior inf. of PM_3 small and circular, or gone. Both inf. of M_1 absent, anterior inf. of M_2 present, or absent on one side.
IV	Posterior inf. of PM_4 absent. Table surface of inc. less than 2 × as long as wide.	All inf. of M_1 and M_2 absent; inf. of M_3 present or absent.
V	Anterior inf. of M_1 small, round/oval, or lacking on one side. Posterior inf. of M_1 is U-shaped. Inc. often not touching each other.	
VI	Anterior inf. of M_1 absent, posterior inf. may be absent on one side. Incisors with round or round/oval table surfaces, not touching each other, often some missing.	
VII	No inf. on M_1, sometimes also not on M_2. Inc. often worn down to gums.	

NOTE: PM = premolar; M = molar; inc. = incisor; inf. = infundibulum.

D. 8
Calls of Hyenas

Name	Description of sound	Posture	Situation
1. *Whoop*	Series of up to 15 (usually 6–9) calls, each lasting 2–3 sec, spaced 2–10 sec. apart; –oo– tone, each call beginning low ending high, though calls in beginning of series may be low-high-low. Last calls of series shorter, reduced to only the low-pitched part. Very loud, may be heard more than 5 km away.	Usually walking, rarely standing or lying. For each call in series mouth opened slightly, bent down to the ground.	Both sexes use it, usually when walking alone, sometimes in company. Rarely "answer" each other's calls; usually call appears to be spontaneous, without external cause.
2. *Fast whoop*	As above, higher pitched, calls and intervals shorter, not "petering out."	Tail horizontal or high, ears cocked; often running; mouth as above bent down.	With many other hyenas present, often in confrontation over kill with lion or other clan; often just before a group of hyenas attacks together.
3. *Grunt*	Soft, very low pitched growling sound, several seconds.	Mouth closed, aggressive posture (p. 216).	On approach of another hyena (e.g., by female with cubs when approached by male, or by either sex when approached by member of another clan) often followed by chasing.
4. *Groan*	As above, more –ooo– sounding, pitch higher but variable, lasting intermittently for up to 15 sec.	See p. 226	Just before and during meeting ceremony.
5. *Low*	–ooo– sound with pitch varying during call, usually low, several seconds.	Mouth slightly open, head rather low but usually horizontal (pl. 36)	As (2), less likely to lead to immediate attack.
6. *Giggle*	Loud, very high-pitched and rapid series of hee-hee-hee, total usually shorter than 5 sec. reminding one of human "mad laughter."	Running away in fleeing posture (p. 218). Mouth slightly open.	When attacked or chased, often over a kill.

7. *Yell*	Loud, with varying but very high pitch, up to several seconds, like a human yell.	As (6)	As (6), usually when actually being bitten; stronger tendency to flee than (6).
8. *Growl*	Loud, with varying but low pitch, up to several seconds, with –aa– and –oh– tones, often with a rattling quality in it.	Defense posture, p. 219	When attacked and bitten, often when about to bite back, loudest when actually returning a bite.
9.a) *Soft grunt– laugh*	Rapid succession of low-pitched, soft staccato grunts, series lasting several seconds.	Mouth closed or slightly open (a) in fleeing posture p. 218 (b) tail horizontal or high, ears cocked.	(a) When surprised by and fleeing from lion or man when on the den or on a kill; (b) When attacking a large prey (infrequent).
b) *Loud grunt– laugh*	Louder than 9 (a) but still not a very loud call. Series often lasting more than 5 sec.	Mouth as 9 (a), tail high, ears cocked.	In encounters between clans or between hyenas and lions over kills, especially during mass approach or mass withdrawal.
10. *Whine*	Loud, high-pitched, long-drawn-out squeals of –eeee– sounds, often with a staccato element (–ee–ee–ee–ee–), very rapid. May continue for minutes with short breaks.	Mouth slightly open, tail hanging down, head rather low.	By cubs when following a female before suckling, or when thwarted in attempts to get food from kill.
11. *Soft squeal*	As (10), but soft, no staccato, several seconds.	Mouth slightly open, ears flat, head often tilted slightly, teeth bared, often rolling over on side.	By cubs, but also adults; when meeting a well-known individual after long separation.

E. SCIENTIFIC NAMES OF SERENGETI SPECIES MENTIONED IN TEXT

English name	Scientific name
Mammals (Ellerman, Morrison-Scott, and Hayman 1953; Allen 1939)	
Aardwolf	*Proteles cristatus* (Sparrman)
Baboon	*Papio anubis* (Fischer)
Badger, honey (Ratel)	*Mellivora capensis* (Schreber)
Buffalo	*Syncerus caffer* (Sparrman)
Cheetah	*Acinonyx jubatus* (Schreber)
Civet	*Civettictis civetta* (Schreber)
Dog, wild	*Lycaon pictus* (Temminck)
Eland	*Taurotragus oryx* (Pallas)
Elephant	*Loxodonta africana* (Blumenbach)
Fox, bat-eared	*Otocyon megalotis* (Desmarest)
Gazelle, Grant's	*Gazella granti* Brooke
Gazelle, Thomson's	*Gazella thomsonii* Günther
Giraffe	*Giraffa camelopardalis* (Linnaeus)
Hare	{ *Lepus crawshayi* De Winton { *Lepus victoriae* Thomas
Hippopotamus	*Hippopotamus amphibius* Linnaeus
Hyena, brown	*Hyaena brunnea* Thunberg
Hyena, spotted	*Crocuta crocuta* (Erxleben)
Hyena, striped	*Hyaena vulgaris* Desmarest
Impala	*Aepyceros melampus* (Lichtenstein)
Jackal, black-backed	*Canis mesomelas* Schreber
Jackal, golden	*Canis aureus* Linnaeus
Jackal, side-striped	*Canis adustus* Sundevall
Kongoni	*Alcelaphus buselaphus* (Pallas)
Leopard	*Panthera pardus* (Linnaeus)
Lion	*Panthera leo* (Linnaeus)
Mongoose, banded	*Mungos mungo* (Gmelin)
Mongoose, pygmy	*Helogale parvula* (Sundevall)
Porcupine	*Hystrix africaeaustralis* Peters
Reedbuck	*Redunca redunca* (Pallas)
Rhinoceros	*Diceros bicornis* (Linnaeus)
Springhare	*Pedetes capensis* (Forster)
Topi	*Damaliscus korrigum jimela* (Ogilby)
Warthog	*Phacochoerus aethiopicus* (Pallas)
Waterbuck	*Kobus defassa* (Rüppell)
Wildebeest	*Connochaetes taurinus* (Burchell)
Zebra	*Equus burchelli* Gray
Birds (Mackworth-Praed and Grant 1952)	
Eagle, fish	*Cuncuma vocifer* (Daudin)
Eagle, martial	*Polemaëtus bellicosus* (Daudin)
Eagle, steppe	*Aquila nipalensis* Hodgson
Eagle, tawny	*Aquila rapax* (Temminck)
Kite, African	*Milvus migrans* (Boddaert)
Lammergeyer	*Gypaëtus barbatus* (Linnaeus)

English name	Scientific name
Ostrich	*Struthio camelus* Linnaeus
Raven, white-naped	*Corvultur albicollis* (Latham)
Stork, Abdim's	*Sphenorynchus abdimii* (Lichtenstein)
Stork, Marabou	*Leptoptilos crumeniferus* (Lesson)
Stork, white	*Ciconia ciconia* (Linnaeus)
Vulture, Egyptian	*Neophron percnopterus* (Linnaeus)
Vulture, hooded	*Necrosyrtes monachus* (Temminck)
Vulture, lappet-faced	*Torgos tracheliotus* (Forster)
Vulture, Rüppell's Griffon	*Gyps rüppellii* (Brehm)
Vulture, white-backed	*Pseudogyps africanus* (Salvadori)
Vulture, white-headed	*Trigonoceps occipitalis* (Burchell)
Reptiles (Loveridge 1957)	
Crocodile	*Crocodylus niloticus* Laurenti
Puff adder	*Bitis arietans arietans* (Merrem)
Python	*Python sebae* (Gmelin)
Insects (Glover 1967)	
Tsetse flies	*Glossina pallidipes* Austen
	G. morsitans Westwood
	G. swynnertoni Austen

References

Allen, G. M. 1939. A checklist of African mammals. *Bull. Mus. Comp. Zool. Harvard* 83:1–763.

Anderson, G. D., and Talbot, L. M. 1965. Soil factors affecting the distribution of the grassland types and their utilisation by wild animals on the Serengeti plains, Tanganyika. *J. Ecol.* 53:33–56.

Andrew, R. J. 1961. The motivational organisation controlling the mobbing calls of the blackbird, *Turdus merula. Behaviour* 17:1–23, 288–321; 18:25–43, 161–76.

Ansell, W. F. H. 1969. A multiple kill by lions, and a stolen kill. *Puku* 5:214–15.

Ardrey, R. 1961. *African genesis*. New York: Atheneum.

———. 1966. *The territorial imperative*. New York: Atheneum.

Aschoff, J. 1966. Circadian activity pattern with two peaks. *Ecology* 47:657–702.

Attwell, R. I. G. 1958. The African hunting dog: A wildlife management incident. *Oryx* 4:326–28.

———. 1963. Some observations on feeding habits, behaviour and interrelationships of Northern Rhodesian vultures. *Ostrich* 34:235–47.

Baerends, G. P. 1958. Comparative methods and the concept of homology in the study of behaviour. *Arch. Néerl. Zool.*, suppl. 13:401–17.

Baker, J. R. 1968. Trypanosomes of wild mammals in the neighbourhood of of the Serengeti National Park. *Symp. Zool. Soc. Lond.* 24:147–58.

Balestra, F. A. 1962. The man-eating hyenas of Mlanje. *Afr. Wildl.* 16:25–27.

Banfield, A. W. F. 1951a. Populations and movements of the Saskatchewan timber wolf (*Canis lupus knightii*) in Prince Albert National Park, Saskatchewan, 1947 to 1951. *Can. Dept. Resources and Development, Wildl. Mgmt. Bull.* 1(4):1–21.

———. 1951b. The Barren-ground caribou. Can. Dept. Resources and Development. Mimeographed.

———. 1951c. Notes on the mammals of the Mackenzie district, N. W. Territories. *Arctic* 4:113–21.

Bannikov, A. G., ed. 1961. *Biology of the saiga*. Jerusalem: Translated 1967 by Israel Program for Scientific Translations.

Bere, R. 1966. *The African elephant*. New York: Golden Press.

Bigalke, R. 1953. A note on the behaviour of a group of five spotted hyaenas. *Fauna and Flora* 3:1–4.

Block, H. A., and Niederhoffer, A. 1958. *The gang*. New York: Philosophical Library.

Bourlière, F. 1963. Specific feeding habits of African carnivores. *Afr. Wildl.* 17:21–27.

Bourlière, F., and Verschuren, J. 1960. *Introduction à l'écologie des ongulés du Parc National Albert*. Bruxelles: Institut des Parcs Nationaux du Congo Belge.

Braestrup, F. W. 1941. A study of the Arctic fox in Greenland. *Medd. Grønl.*, vol. 131, no. 4.

Brehm, A. E. 1877. *Brehms Tierleben*. Vol. II, Die Säugetiere. Leipzig.

Brooks, A. C. 1961. *A study of the Thomson's gazelle* (Gazella thomsonii *Günther*). Tanganyika Colonial Research Publ., no. 25, London.

Brown, L. H. 1969. Observations on the status, habitat and behaviour of the mountain nyala *Tragelaphus buxtoni* in Ethiopia. *Mammalia* 33:545–97.

Brown, R. G. B. 1962. The aggressive and distraction behaviour of the Western sandpiper *Ereunetes mauri*. *Ibis* 104:1–12.

Bruce, J. 1790. *Selected specimens of natural history, collected in travels to discover the source of the Nile, in Egypt, Arabia, Abyssinia and Nubia*. vol. 6. Dublin.

Burkholder, B. L. 1959. Movements and behaviour of a wolf pack in Alaska. *J. Wildl. Mgmt.* 23:1–11.

Callison, I. P. 1948 *Wolf predation in the North Country*. Seattle: Callison.

Chapman, H. C. 1888. Observations on the female generative apparatus of *Hyaena crocuta*. *Proc. Acad. Nat. Sci. Phila.*, pp. 189–91, pls. 9–11.

Child, G. 1968. *Behaviour of large mammals during the formation of Lake Kariba*. Trustees of the National Museums of Rhodesia.

Cott, H. B. 1961. Scientific results of an inquiry into the ecology and economic status of the Nile crocodile (*Crocodilus niloticus*) in Uganda and Northern Rhodesia. *Trans. Zool. Soc. Lond.* 29:211–356.

Cowan, I. McT. 1947. The timber wolf in the Rocky Mountains National Park of Canada. *Can. J. Res.* 25(D):139–74.

Crandall, L. S. 1964. *The management of wild mammals in captivity*. Chicago: Univ. of Chicago Press.

Crisler, L. 1956. Observations of wolves hunting caribou. *J. Mammal.* 37:337–46.

Crook, J. H. 1964. The evolution of social organisation and visual communication in weaverbirds (Ploceinae). *Behaviour*, suppl. 10:1–178.

———. 1965. The adaptive significance of avian social organisations. *Symp. Zool. Soc. Lond.* 14: 181–218.

Cullen, A. 1969. Window onto wilderness. Nairobi: East African Publishing House.

Cullen, E. 1957. Adaptations in the kittiwake to cliff-nesting. *Ibis* 99:275–302.

Cullen, J. M. 1960. Some adaptations in the nesting behaviour of terns. *Proc. Int. Ornithol. Congr.* 12:153–57.

Curio, E. 1961. Rassenspezifisches Verhalten gegen einen Raubfeind. *Experientia* 17:188–89.

———. 1963. Probleme des Feinderkennens bei Vögeln. *Proc. Int. Ornithol. Congr.* 13:206–39.

Darling, F. F. 1938. *Bird flocks and the breeding cycle*. Cambridge: Cambridge Univ. Press.

Dart, R. A. 1949. Predatory implemental technique of the Australopithecines. *Amer. J. Phys. Anthropol.* 7:1–38.

———. 1957. The osteodontokeratic culture of *Australopithecus prometheus*. Memoir Transvaal Museum.

Darwin, C. 1872. *Expressions of the emotions in man and animals*. London.

Davies, D. D., and Story, H. E. 1949. The female external genitalia of the spotted Hyaena. *Fieldiana Zool.* 31:277–83.

Davis, D. E. 1962. The phylogeny of gangs. In *Roots of behaviour*, ed. E. L. Bliss. New York: Harper & Row.

Deane, N. N. 1960. Hyena predation. *Lammergeyer* 1:36

———. 1962. The spotted hyaena, *Crocuta c. crocuta*. *Lammergeyer* 2:26–44.

Dinnik, J. A., and Sachs, R. 1969. Zystizerkose der Kreuzbeinwirbel bei Antilopen und *Taenia olngojinei* sp. nov. der Tüpfelhyäne. *Z. Parasitenk.* 31:326–39.

Dirschl, H. J. 1966. *Management and development plan for the Ngorongoro Conservation Area*. Dar es Salaam: Min. of Agriculture.

Dücker, G. 1962. Brutpflegeverhalten und Ontogenese des Verhaltens bei Surikaten (*Suricata suricatta* Schreb. Viverridae). *Behaviour* 19:305–40.

———. 1965. Das Verhalten der Viverriden. *Handb. Zool. Berlin* 8(38): 1–48.

Eibl-Eibesfelt, I. 1956. Zur Biologie des Iltis. *Verh. Deutsch. Zool. Ges. Erlangen* 1955:304–14.

Ellerman, J. R.; Morrison-Scott, T. C. S.; and Hayman, R. W. 1953. *Southern African mammals 1758 to 1951: A reclassification*. London: Trustees of the British Museum.

Eloff, F. C. 1964. On the predatory habits of lions and hyaenas. *Koedoe* 7:105–12.

Errington, P. L. 1943. An analysis of mink predation upon muskrats in North-central United States. *Agric. Exp. St. Iowa State Coll. Res. Bull.* 320:797–924.

———. 1946. Predation and vertebrate populations. *Quart. Rev. Biol.* 21:144–77, 221–45.

Estes, R. D. 1967a. The comparative behaviour of Grant's and Thomson's gazelles. *J. Mammal.* 48:189–209.

———. 1967b. Predators and scavengers. *Nat. Hist.* 76(2):20–29; (3):38–47.

———. 1969. Territorial behaviour of the Wildebeest (*Connochaetes taurinus* Burchell 1823). *Z. Tierpsychol.* 26:284–370.

Estes, R. D., and Goddard, J. 1967. Prey selection and hunting behaviour of of the African wild dog. *J. Wildl. Mgmt.* 31:52–70.

Ewer, R. F. 1954. Some adaptive features in the dentition of hyaenas. *Ann. Mag. Nat. Hist.* 7:188–94.

———. 1963. The behaviour of the meerkat, *Suricata suricatta* (Schreber). *Z. Tierpsychol.* 20:570–607.

Fichter, E.; Schildman, G.; and Sather, J. H. 1955. Some feeding patterns of coyotes in Nebraska. *Ecol. Monogr.* 25:1–37.

Flower, S. S. 1931. Contribution to our knowledge of the duration of life in vertebrate animals. *Proc. Zool. Soc.* 1931:145–234.

Fosbrooke, H. 1963. The *Stomoxys* plague in Ngorongoro, 1962. *E. Afr. Wildl. J.* 1:124–26.

Foster, J. B., and Coe, M. J. 1968. The biomass of game animals in Nairobi National Park, 1960–1966. *J. Zool. Lond.* 155:413–25.

Fox, M. W. 1969a. The anatomy of aggression and its ritualization in Canidae: A developmental and comparative study. *Behaviour* 35:242–58.

———. 1969b. The ontogeny of prey-killing behaviour in Canidae. *Behaviour* 35:259–72.

Frädrich, H. 1965. Zur Biologie und Ethologie des Warzenschweines (*Phacochoerus aethiopicus* Pallas) unter Berücksichtigung des Verhaltens anderer Suiden. *Z. Tierpsychol.* 22:328–93.

Fuller, J. L., and Dubuis, E. M. 1962. The behaviour of dogs. In *The behaviour of domestic animals*, ed. E. S. E. Hafez, pp. 415–52. London: Baillière, Tindall & Cox.

Gentry, A. W. 1966. Fossil antilopini of East Africa. *Bull. Brit. Mus. Nat. Hist. (Geol.)* 12:43–106.

Glover, P. E. 1964. A review of recent knowledge of vertebrate host–tsetse fly relationships. *First Int. Congr. Parasitol. Rome* 2:987–1030.

———. 1967. The importance of ecological studies in the control of tsetse flies. *Bull. World Health Org.* 37:581–614.

Goddard, J. 1967. Home range, behaviour and recruitment rates of two black rhinoceros populations. *E. Afr. Wildl. J.* 5:133–50.

Gordon, R. J. 1777. Unpublished drawings with comments. In *Rijksprentenkabinet*. Amsterdam: Rijksmuseum.

Graham, A. 1966. East African Wild Life Society cheetah survey: Extracts from the report by Wildlife Services. *E. Afr. Wildl. J.* 4:50–55.

Grimpe, G. 1916. Hyänologische Studien. *Zool. Anz.* 48:49–61.

———. 1923. Neues über die Geschlechtsverhältnisse der Gefleckten hyäne (*Crocotta crocuta* Erxl.). *Verh. Deutsch. Zool. Ges.* 1923:77–78.

Grzimek, M., and Grzimek, B. 1959. *Serengeti darf nicht sterben.* Berlin: Ullstein.

———. 1960a. Census of plains animals in the Serengeti National Park, Tanganyika. *J. Wildl. Mgmt.* 24:27–37.

———. 1960b. A study of the game of the Serengeti plains. *Z. Säugetierk.*, suppl., 25:1–61.

Guggisberg, C. A. W. 1962. *Simba, the life of the lion.* London: Bailey Bros. & Swinfen.

Halliday, M. S. 1966. Exploration and fear in the rat. In *Play, exploration and territory in mammals*, ed. P. A. Jewell and C. Loizos. London: Academic Press.

Hartley, P. H. T. 1950. An experimental analysis of interspecific recognition. *Symp. Soc. Exp. Biol.* 4:313–336.

Hatter, J. 1945. A preliminary predator-prey study with respect to the coyote (*Canis latrans*) in Jasper National Park. Ottawa. Mimeographed.

Hediger, H. 1951. *Observations sur la psychologie animale dans les Parcs Nationaux du Congo Belge.* Bruxelles: Institut des Parcs Nationaux du Congo Belge.

Hinde, R. A. 1966. *Animal behaviour.* New York: McGraw-Hill.

Hinde, R. A., and Tinbergen, N. 1958. The comparative study of species-specific behavior. In *Behavior and evolution,* ed. A. Rose and G. S. Simpson. New Haven, Conn.: Yale Univ. Press.

Hinton, H. E., and Dunn, A. M. S. 1967. *Mongooses.* Edinburgh and London: Oliver & Boyd.

Hirst, S. M. 1969. Predation as a regulating factor of wild ungulate populations in a Transvaal Lowveld nature reserve. *Zoologica Africana* 4:199–230.

Hsu, T. C., and Arrighi, F. E. 1966. Karyotypes of thirteen carnivores. *Mamm. Chromosomes Newsletter* 21: 155.

Hughes, A. R. 1954*a.* Hyaenas versus Australopithecines as agents of bone accumulation. *Amer. J. Phys. Anthropol.* 12:467–86.

———. 1954*b.* Habits of hyaenas. *S. Afr. J. Sci.* 51:156–58

———. 1958. Some ancient and recent observations on Hyaenas. *Koedoe* 1:105–14.

———. 1961. Further notes on the habits of hyaenas and bone gathering by porcupines. *Zool. Soc. South Afr. Bull.,* vol 3, no. 1.

Huxley, E. 1964. *Forks and hope.* London: Chatto and Windus.

Jackson, C. H. N. 1933. On the true density of tsetse flies. *J. Anim. Ecol.* 2:204–209.

Jaeger, F. 1911. *Das Hochland der Riesenkrater und die umliegende Hochländer Deutsch Ostafrikas.* Berlin: Mittler & Sohn.

Jenkins, D.; Watson, A.; and Miller, G. R. 1964. Predation and red grouse populations. *J. Appl. Ecol.* 1:183–95.

———. 1967. Population fluctuations in the red grouse (*Lagopus lagopus scoticus*). *J. Anim. Ecol.* 36:97–122.

Johnston, H. H. 1884. *The river Congo from its mouth to Bolobo.* London.

Kiley, M. 1969. A comparative study of some displays in ungulates, canids and felids with particular reference to their causation. Ph.D. thesis, Univ. of Sussex.

Klingel, H. 1965. Notes on the biology of the plains zebra *Equus quagga boehmi* Matschie. *E. Afr. Wildl. J.* 3:86–88.

———. 1966. Tooth development and age determination in the plains zebra (*Equus quagga boehmi* Matschie). *Zool. Garten* 33:34–54.

———. 1967. Soziale Organisation und Verhalten freilebender Steppenzebras. *Z. Tierpsychol.* 24:580–624.

———. 1968. Die Immobilisation von Steppenzebras (*Equus quagga böhmi*). *Zool. Garten* 35:54–66.

———. 1969*a.* The social organisation and population ecology of the plains zebra (*Equus quagga*). *Zoologica Africana* 4:249–63.

———. 1969*b.* Reproduction in the plains zebra, *Equus burchelli boehmi:* Behaviour and ecological factors. *J. Reprod. Fert.,* suppl. 6:339–45.

Koenigswald, G. H. von 1965. Das Leichenfeld als Biotop. *Zool. Jb. Syst.* 92:73–82.

Kortlandt, A. 1965. On the essential morphological basis for human culture: Discussion. *Curr. Anthropol.* 6:320–26.

Kramer, G., and St. Paul, U. von 1951. Über angeborenes und erworbenes Feinderkennen beim Gimpel (*Pyrrhula pyrrhula*). *Behaviour* 3:243–55.

Kruuk, H. 1964. Predators and anti-predator behaviour of the black-headed gull (*Larus ridibundus* L.). *Behaviour*, suppl. 11:1–130.

———. 1966a. Clan-system and feeding habits of spotted hyaenas (*Crocuta crocuta* Erxleben). *Nature* 209:1257–58.

———. 1966b. A new view of the hyaena. *New Scientist* 30:849–51.

———. 1967. Competition for food between vultures in East Africa. *Ardea* 55:171–93.

———. 1968. Hyaenas, the hunters nobody knows. *Nat. Geog. Mag.* 134:44–57.

———. 1970. Interactions between populations of spotted hyaenas (*Crocuta crocuta* Erxleben) and their prey species. In *Animal populations in relation to their food resources*, ed. A. Watson. Oxford: Blackwell.

Kruuk, H., 1972. Surplus killing by carnivores. *J. Zool.* 166 (2).

Kruuk, H., and Turner, M. 1967. Comparative notes on predation by lion, leopard, cheetah and wild dog in the Serengeti area, East Africa. *Mammalia* 31:1–27.

Kühme, W. 1965. Freilandstudien zur Soziologie des Hyänenhundes (*Lycaon pictus lupinus* Thomas 1902). *Z. Tierpsychol.* 22:495–541.

Kummer, H. 1957. Soziales Verhalten einer Mantelpavian-Gruppe. *Z. Psychol. Anwendung*, suppl. 33, 1–91.

Lack, D. 1954. *The natural regulation of animal numbers*. Oxford: Oxford Univ. Press.

———. 1966. *Population studies of birds*. Oxford: Clarendon Press.

Lamprey, H. F. 1964. Estimation of the large mammal densities, biomass and energy exchange in the Tarangire Game Reserve and the Masai Steppe in Tanganyika. *E. Afr. Wildl. J.* 2:1–46.

Lang, E. M. 1963. Wie jagt der Hyänenhund (*Lycaon pictus*)? *Z. Säugetierk.* 28:314–15.

Laws, R. M. 1952. A new method of age determination for mammals. *Nature* 169:972–73.

Leyhausen, P. 1956. Verhaltensstudien an Katzen. *Z. Tierpsychol.*, suppl. 2:1–120.

———. 1965. Über die Funktion der relativen Stimmungshierarchie (Dargestellt am Beispiel der phylogenetischen und ontogenetischen Entwicklung des Beutefangs von Raubtieren). *Z. Tierpsychol.* 22:412–94.

Lockie, J. D. 1959. The estimation of the food of foxes. *J. Wildl. Mgmt.* 23:224–27.

———. 1966. Territory in small carnivores. In *Play, exploration and territory in mammals*, ed. P. A. Jewell and C. Loizos London: Academic Press.

Longhurst, W.; Leopold, S.; and Dasmann, R. 1952. A survey of California deer herds, their ranges and management problems. Calif. Dept. Nat. Resources, Div. Fish and Game, Bull. 6.

Lorenz, K. 1966. *On Aggression*. London: Methuen.

Loveridge, A. 1957. Checklist of the reptiles and amphibians of East Africa

(Uganda; Kenya; Tanganyika; Zanzibar). *Bull. Mus. Comp. Zool. Harvard* 117: 153–362.

Lydekker, R. 1926. *The game animals of Africa*. London: Rowland Ward.

Mackworth-Praed, C. W., and Grant, C. H. B. 1952. *Birds of Eastern and North Eastern Africa*, vols. 1 and 2. London: Longmans, Green & Co.

Makridin, V. P. 1962. The wolf in the Yamal north. *Zoolog. Zhurn.* 41:1413–17.

Manley, G. H. 1960. The agonistic behaviour of the Black-headed Gull, *Larus ridibundus*. Ph.D. thesis, Oxford University.

Matthews, L. H. 1939a. Reproduction in the spotted hyaena, *Crocuta crocuta (Erxleben)*. *Phil. Trans. Ser. B.* 230:1–78.

———. 1939b. The bionomics of the spotted hyaena, *Crocuta crocuta*. *Proc. Zool. Soc. London. Ser. A.* 109:43–56.

———. 1939c. The sub-species and variation of the spotted hyaena, *Crocuta crocuta* Erxl. *Proc. Zool. Soc. London, Ser. B.* 109:237–60.

Mech, L. D. 1966. The wolves of Isle Royale. Fauna of the National Parks of the U.S. Series, no. 7.

Merwe, N. J. van der. 1958. The jackal, fauna and flora. *Z. Tierpsychol.* 15:121–23.

———. 1959. Die Wildehond (*Lycaon pictus*). *Koedoe* 2:87–93.

Miller, L. 1952. Auditory recognition of predators. *Condor* 54:89–92.

Mitchell, B. L.; Shenton, J. B.; and Uys, J. C. 1965. Predation on large mammals in the Kafue National Park, Zambia. *Zoologica Africana* 1:297–318.

Morris, D. 1967. *The Naked Ape*. London: Jonathan Cape.

Murie, A. 1936. Following fox trails. *Univ. Mich. Mus. Zool. Misc. Publ.* 32:1–45.

———. 1940. Ecology of the coyote in the Yellowstone. Fauna of the National Parks of the U.S. Series, no. 4.

———. 1944. The wolves of Mount McKinley. Fauna of the National Parks of the U.S. Series, no. 5.

Murie, O. J. 1935. Food habits of the coyote in Jackson Hole, Wyoming. U. S. Dept. Agric. Circular, no. 362.

———. 1945. Notes on coyote food-habits in Montana and British Columbia. *J. Mammal.* 26:33–40.

Neal, E. G. 1949. *The Badger*. London: Collins.

Neuville, H. 1935. De l'organe femelle de l'hyène tachétée (*Hyaena crocuta* Erxl.). *Arch. Mus. Hist. Paris* 12:225–29.

———. 1936a. Remarques complémentaires sur l'organe femelle de l'*Hyaena crocuta*. *Bull. Mus. Hist. Nat. Paris* 8:54–60.

———. 1936b. Sur le mimétisme sexuel de l'*Hyaena crocuta*. *Mammalia* 1:49–58.

Nice, M. M., and Pelkwyk, J. J. ter. 1941. Enemy recognition by the song sparrow. *Auk* 58:195–214.

Nicholson, A. J. 1947. Fluctuations of animal populations. *Aust. N.Z. Ass. Advmt. Sci.*, pp. 1–14.

Orr, D. J., and Moore-Gilbert, S. M. 1964. Field immobilization of young wildebeest with succinylcholine chloride. *E. Afr. Wildl. J.* 2:60–66.

Pearsall, W. H. 1957. Report on an ecological survey of the Serengeti Park, Tanganyika. *Fauna Pres. Soc.*, pp. 1–64.

Percival, A. B. 1924. *A game ranger's note book.* London: Nisbet & Co.

———. 1928. *A game ranger on safari.* London: Nisbet & Co.

Petrides, G. A. 1959. Competition for food between five species of East African vultures. *Auk* 76:104–6.

Pienaar, U. de V. 1963. The large mammals of the Kruger National Park, their distribution and present day status. *Koedoe* 6:1–37.

———. 1969. Predator-prey relationships amongst the larger mammals of the Kruger National Park. *Koedoe* 12:108–76.

Pimlott, D. H. 1967. Wolf predation and ungulate populations. *Amer. Zoologist* 7:267–78.

Pournelle, G. H. 1965. Observations on birth and early development of the spotted hyaena. *J. Mammal.* 46:503.

Sachs, R. 1966. Note on cysticercosis in game animals of the Serengeti. *E. Afr. Wildl. J.* 4:152–53.

———. 1967. Liveweights and body measurements of Serengeti game animals. *E. Afr. Wildl. J.* 5:24–36.

Sachs, R., and Staak, C. 1966. Evidence of brucellosis in antelopes of the Serengeti. *Vet. Rec.* 79:857–58.

Sachs, R., and Taylor, A. S. 1966. Trichinosis in a spotted hyaena (*Crocuta crocuta*) of the Serengeti. *Vet. Rec.* 78, no. 20.

Schaller, G. B. 1967. *The deer and the tiger: A study of wildlife in India.* Chicago: Univ. of Chicago Press.

———. 1968. Hunting behaviour of the cheetah in the Serengeti National Park, Tanzania. *E. Afr. Wildl. J.* 6:95–100.

Schaller, G. B., and Lowther, G. R. 1969. The relevance of carnivore behavior to the study of early hominids. *Southwest J. Anthropol.* 25:307–41.

Schenkel, R. 1948. Ausdrucksstudien an Wölfen. *Behaviour* 1:81–129.

———. 1966. Zum Problem der Territorialität und des Markierens bei Säugern am Beispiel des Schwarzen Nashorns und des Löwens. *Z. Tierpsychol.* 23:593–626.

Schneider, K. M. 1923. Beobachtungen aus dem Leipziger Zoologischen Garten über das Geschlechtsleben der Fleckenhyäne. *Verh. Deutsch. Zool. Ges.* 1923:78–79.

———. 1926. Über Hyänenzucht. *Die Pelztierzucht* 2:(8) 1–4, (9) 9–11, (10) 12–14.

———. 1952. Einige Bilder zur Paarung der Fleckenhyäne, *Crocotta crocuta* Erxl. *Zoolog. Garten* n.f. 19:135–49.

Scott, K. 1959. Bathing by spotted hyaenas in Uganda. *J. Mammal.* 40:615.

Scott, T. G. 1943. Some food coactions of the northern plains red fox. *Ecol. Monogr.* 13:427–79.

———. 1955. An evaluation of the red fox. *Biological Notes*, no. 35, pp. 1–16.

Scott, T. G., and Klimstra, W. D. 1955. Red foxes and a declining prey population. *Illinois Univ. Monogr. Series* 1:1–123.

Shortridge, G. C. 1934. *The mammals of South-west Africa.* London: Heinemann.

Simmons, K. E. L. 1952. The nature of the predator reactions of breeding birds. *Behaviour* 4:161–71.

——. 1955. The nature of the predator reactions of waders towards humans: With special reference to the role of the aggressive-, escape- and brooding-drives. *Behaviour* 8:130–73.

Sinclair, A. R. E. 1970. Studies of the ecology of the East African buffalo. Ph.D. thesis, Oxford University.

Smith, R. 1962. Hyena versus leopard. *African Wildlife* 16: 282–86.

Smith, N. G. 1969. Provoked release of mobbing: A hunting technique of Micrastur-falcons. *Ibis* 111:241–42.

Southern, H. N., ed. 1964. *The handbook of British mammals.* Oxford: Blackwell.

Southern, H. N., and Watson, J. S. 1941. Summer food of the Red Fox (*Vulpes vulpes*) in Great Britain: A preliminary report. *J. Anim. Ecol.* 10:1–11.

Southwood, T. R. E. 1966. *Ecological methods with particular reference to the study of insect populations.* London: Methuen.

Sperry, C. C. 1941. Food habits of the coyote. U.S. Dept. Interior Wildlife Research Bull. 4:1–70.

Stenlund, M. H. 1955. A field study of the timber wolf (*Canis lupus*) in the Superior National Forest, Minnesota. *Minn. Dept. Cons., Tech. Bull.* 4:1–55.

Stevenson-Hamilton, J. 1947. *Wildlife in South Africa.* London: Cassell & Co.

Stewart, D. R. M., and Talbot, L. M. 1962. Census of wildlife on the Serengeti, Mara and Loita Plains. *E. Afr. Agric. For. J.* 28:58–60.

Struhsaker, T. T. 1966. Auditory communication among vervet monkeys (*Cercopithecus aethiops*). In *Social communication among primates*, ed. S. Altmann. Chicago: Univ. of Chicago Press.

Sutcliffe, A. 1969. Adaptations of spotted hyaenas to living in the British Isles. *Mamm. Soc. Bull.* 31.

——. 1970. Spotted hyaena; Collector, crusher, gnawer and digester of bones. *Nature* 227:1110–13.

Swynnerton, G. H. 1958. Fauna of the Serengeti National Park. *Mammalia* 22:435–50.

Talbot, L. M. 1961. Preliminary observations on the population dynamics of the wildebeest in Narok District, Kenya. *E. Afr. Agric. For. J.* 28:108–16.

Talbot, L. M., and Talbot, M. H. 1963. The wildebeest in Western Masailand, East Africa. *Wildl. Monogr.*, no. 12.

Tembrock, G. 1954. Rotfuchs und Wolf, ein Verhaltensvergleich. *Z. Säugetierk.* 19:152–59.

——. 1957a. Zur Ethologie des Rotfuchses (*V. vulpes* L.) unter besonderer Berücksichtigung der Fortpflanzung. *Zoolog. Garten* n.f. 23:289–532.

——. 1957b. Das Verhalten des Rotfuchses. In *Handbuch der Zoologie*, ed. W. Kükenthal, vol. 10, no. 15, pp. 1–20. Berlin: W. de Gruyter & Co.

——. 1957c. Das Verhalten des Rotfuchses. In *Handbuch der Zoologie*, ed. W. Kükenthal, vol. 8, no. 5, pp. 1–20. Berlin: W. de Gruyter & Co.

Thenius, E. 1966a, Zur Stammesgeschichte der Hyänen (Carnivora, Mammalia). *Z. Säugetierk.* 31:293–300.

————. 1966*b*. Ergebnisse und Probleme der Wirbeltierpaläontologie. *Naturwiss.* 53:261–68.

Tinbergen, N. 1951. *The study of instinct.* Oxford: Clarendon.

————. 1956. The functions of territory. *Bird Study* 4:14–27.

————. 1958. Bauplan-ethologische Beobachtungen an Möwen. *Arch. Néerl. Zool.*, suppl. 13:369–82.

————. 1959. Comparative studies of the behaviour of gulls (Laridae): A progress report. *Behaviour* 15:1–70.

————. 1965. Von den Vorratskammern des Rotfuchses (*Vulpes vulpes* L.). *Z. Tierpsychol.* 22:119–49.

Turnbull-Kemp, P. 1967. *The leopard.* Cape Town: Howard Timmins.

Turner, M., and Watson, M. 1964. A census of game in Ngorongoro Crater. *E. Afr. Wildl. J.* 2:165–68.

Ulbrich, F., and Schmitt, J. 1969. Die Chromosomen des Ardwolfs, *Proteles cristatus* (Sparrmann 1783). *Z. Säugetierk.* 34:61–62.

Verheyen, R. 1951. *Contribution à l'étude éthologique des mammifères du Parc National de l'Upemba.* Bruxelles: Institut des Parcs Nationaux du Congo Belge.

Verschuren, J. 1958. *Ecologie et biologie des grands mammifères: Exploration du Parc National de la Garamba.* Bruxelles: Institut des Parcs Nationaux du Congo Belge.

Vos, A. de, and Hvidberg-Hansen, H. 1967. Thomson's gazelle population structure. Progress report, Serengeti Research Institute. Mimeographed.

Walker, E. P. 1964. *Mammals of the world.* Vol. 2. Baltimore: The Johns Hopkins Press.

Walther, F. R. 1965. Verhaltensstudien an der Grantgazelle (*Gazella granti* Brooke 1872) im Ngorongoro-Krater. *Z. Tierpsychol.* 22:167–208.

————. 1969. Flight behaviour and avoidance of predators in Thomson's gazelle (*Gazella thomsonii* Guenther 1884). *Behaviour* 34:184–221.

Ward, P. 1963. Contributions to the ecology of the weaver-bird *Quelea quelea* Linnaeus, in Nigeria. Thesis, University College, Ibadan.

————. 1965. Feeding ecology of the Black-faced Dioch, *Quelea quelea*, in Nigeria. *Ibis* 107:173–214.

Washburn, S. L., and Avis, V. 1958. Evolution of human behavior. In *Behavior and evolution*, ed. A. Roe and G. S. Simpson. New Haven, Conn.: Yale Univ. Press.

Watson, A. 1967. Population control by territorial behaviour in red grouse. *Nature* 215:1274–75.

Watson, M. 1877. On the female generative organs of *Hyaena crocuta*. *Proc. Zool. Soc. Lond.* 1877:369–79.

————. 1878. On the male generative organs of *Hyaena crocuta*. *Proc. Zool. Soc. Lond.* 1878:416–28.

Watson, R. M. 1967. The population ecology of the wildebeest (*Connochaetes taurinus albojubatus* Thomas). Ph.D. thesis, Cambridge University.

Wickingen, H. 1959. Über die Geschlechtsbestimmung bei Tüpfelhyänen, *Crocotta crocotta* (Erxleben). *Säugetierk. Mitt.* 4:129–30.

Wickler, W. 1963. Zum Problem der Signalbildung, am Beispiel der Verhaltens-Mimikry zwischen Aspidontus und Labroides (*Pisces, Acanthopterygii*). *Z. Tierpsychol.* 20:657–79.

———. 1964. Vom Gruppenleben einiger Säugetiere Afrikas. *Mitt. Max-Planck-Ges.* 5/6:296–309.

———. 1965*a*. Die äusseren Genitalien als soziale Signale bei einigen Primaten. *Naturwiss.* 52:268–70.

———. 1965*b*. Die Evolution von Mustern der Zeichnung und des Verhaltens. *Naturwiss.* 52:335–41.

———. 1968. *Mimicry in plants and animals*. London: Weidenfeld & Nicholson.

Wildon, V. J. 1968. Weights of some mammals from Eastern Zambia. *Arnoldia* 3:1–20.

Wright, B. S. 1960. Predation on big game in East Africa. *J. Wildl. Mgmt.* 24:1–15.

Wurster, D. H., and Grey, C. 1967. The chromosomes of the spotted hyaena, *Crocuta crocuta*. *Mamm. Chromosomes Newsletter* 8:197.

Wüstehube, C. 1960. Beiträge zur Kenntnis besonders des Spiel- und Beuteverhaltens einheimischer Musteliden. *Z. Tierpsychol.* 17:579–613.

Wyman, J. 1967. The jackals of the Serengeti. *Animals* 1967:79–83.

Young, J. Z. 1962. *The life of vertebrates*. Oxford: Clarendon Press.

Young, S. P., and Goldman, E. A. 1944. *The wolves of North America*. Vols. 1 and 2. Washington: Am. Wildl. Inst.

Zuckermann, S. 1932. *The social life of monkeys and apes*. London: Kegan Paul.

Index

NOTE: Entries refer to the spotted hyena if not indicated otherwise. Gazelle = Thomson's gazelle.